Edited by
Laurence B. Siegel

Foreword by
Rodney N. Sullivan, CFA

Insights into the Global Financial Crisis

RESEARCH FOUNDATION
OF CFA INSTITUTE

Statement of Purpose

The Research Foundation of CFA Institute is a not-for-profit organization established to promote the development and dissemination of relevant research for investment practitioners worldwide.

ISBN 978-1-934667-27-9

16 December 2009

Contents

Governance and Behavior

Economic Theory and Philosophy

CFA Institute
CE Qualified Activity

This publication qualifies for 5 CE credits under the guidelines of the CFA Institute Continuing Education Program.

Foreword

At a recent meeting of the Research Foundation of CFA Institute Board of Trustees, one trustee insightfully commented that a successful Research Foundation book should explore the outer edges of ideas, contributing unique knowledge and perspectives while also being relevant to investment practitioners.[1] This book, a collection of wisdom from today's deepest thinkers on markets and the economy, does just that. The authors deliberately push the boundaries of investment ideas in a way that will cause readers to think differently, yet more constructively, about the world around them.

Although the imminent collapse of financial markets has passed for now, the many consequences of the crisis lie in its wake. Whether the crisis presents a mere flesh wound or something much more severe remains to be seen. At its core, the massive debt owed by developed nations portends weakness in economic growth. An extraordinary moral hazard also remains for financial markets and looms large over the macro economy. These and other pressing economic issues provide the impetus for this book and are confronted with a wide-eyed and clear-headed approach.

We humans possess an unwavering desire for progress, mostly built on innovative tools, ideas, and techniques. Consider how we continually adopt innovations and ideas. My PDA (personal digital assistant) once gave me a competitive edge, but such devices rapidly became ubiquitous and are no longer a nicety but a necessity. This compulsion to adapt, or otherwise fall behind the curve, is firmly entrenched in our human condition. It cannot, and indeed should not, be dispensed with. Further to this point, the wide adoption of ideas and technology mostly produces highly desirable and beneficial societal outcomes. But alas, there is always an exception. In the realm of financial markets, the massive penetration of an idea and/or technology can and has led to dire outcomes. Here, as we are all keenly aware, herding ends badly.

Markets unambiguously work best when we all form our own, independent views. But in forming views, investors, like all people, instinctively fall back on what others are doing around them. This is so because, in grappling with an uncertain future, we figure our view is no better than our neighbors'. Keynes once argued that in the realm of investments, calculating the future is futile, saying that uncertainty in investments has "no scientific basis on which to form any calculable probability whatever" (p. 214).[2] But progress, indeed human survival, has long relied on anticipating the future. The notion of better solutions found by groupthink actually works

---

[1] Thanks to Frank Reilly, CFA, for this succinct insight.
[2] J.M. Keynes, "The General Theory of Employment," *Quarterly Journal of Economics*, vol. 51, no. 2 (February 1937):209–223.

well for some applications (for example, when a young farmer sees the more-seasoned farmers planting their crops in the spring and follows suit in the hope for a bountiful summer harvest) but fails miserably when applied to uncertain financial markets.

In the pursuit of progress, we are thus seemingly hardwired for both groupthink and innovation. Unfortunately, the interaction of these two—innovation and collective delusion—in the realm of financial markets all too frequently feeds a wave that builds until it can do so no longer, inexorably crashing upon the shore with systemic impact.

Contrary to groupthink, this book presents a collection of solidly independent viewpoints expressed through many years of practical, relevant experience. We, and our authors, would have it no other way. The articles presented in this book deal head on with the crucial issues confronting our global economy—those of today and those on the horizon. We hope you will find a careful read as rewarding and fun as it has been for us to put the book together.

Finally, we offer our sincere appreciation to the many distinguished authors presented in this book; all have been so very gracious and generous in contributing their time and talent. We are honored by their commitment to the profession. We also thank the CFA Institute Centre for Financial Market Integrity for its partnership in this important endeavor. We are pleased to present these diverse voices of wisdom speaking on the most critical financial matters of our time. With clarity comes progress.

Rodney N. Sullivan, CFA
Head, Publications
CFA Institute

A Riskless Society Is "Unattainable and Infinitely Expensive"

Laurence B. Siegel
Research Director
The Research Foundation of CFA Institute

> A democracy can only exist until the voters discover that they can vote themselves money.
>
> —Popular saying, origin unknown[1]

Private vices will always thrive. Greed, envy, lust, pride, and my favorite, sloth (I can't help thinking of the two-toed, upside-down mammal) will continue to drive human action as they always have.

Some argue that greed is good. They have a point. Greed certainly makes the engine of the economy hum. Like Adam Smith, I would rather get my dinner from a merchant acting in his own interest than from one pretending to act in mine. Through the processes described by Smith, private vices are channeled in such a way as to produce public benefits.[2] This transformation is well known to students of economics and is seeping through to the general public.[3] But it does not work perfectly all the time.

Private vices are restrained by what Smith called "enlightened self-interest." If you are too greedy, you stand a chance of losing money. Regarding lust, as Danny O'Keefe sang in "Goodtime Charlie's Got the Blues": "you play around, you lose your wife; you play too long, you lose your life."

But private vices with no corresponding public benefits are encouraged when individuals are protected—or think they are protected—from any negative consequences that might arise while getting to keep the rewards. This chain of cause and

---

[1]The origin of this quote (sometimes wrongly attributed to Benjamin Franklin and often worded ". . . vote themselves largess from the public treasury") is hotly debated. It is usually attributed to the Scottish history professor Alexander Fraser Tytler (1747–1813), known as Lord Woodhouselee, but Daniel Oliver, a political writer who chaired the Federal Trade Commission during the Reagan administration, argues that Tytler never said it (see http://spectator.org/archives/2009/03/09/accuracy-is-desirable, accessed on 6 October 2009).

[2]The equation of private vices with public benefits, *under the right conditions,* is usually associated with Adam Smith's (1723–1790) masterpiece *The Wealth of Nations* (1776), but the English philosopher Bernard Mandeville (1670–1733) made the connection—and used the phrase—considerably earlier.

[3]Or it is being re-learned—now that market economics is fashionable once more in the academy, after a half century (roughly 1930–1980) when it was not. We will see if this fashion survives the current financial crisis, which has been blamed by many commentators—almost certainly wrongly—on an excess of freedom in markets.

effect is what economists call "moral hazard," a phrase that has been growing in familiarity since global capital markets began to collapse in 2007 and as the collapse intensified in 2008 and the early part of 2009. The decline in market values, amounting to 57 percent from peak to trough as measured by the daily closing value of the S&P 500 Index of U.S. equity prices, revealed that once-proud financial institutions and other corporations had experienced losses on a mammoth scale.[4] These losses were so large, and the institutions so interconnected through complex contracts and financial instruments, that the whole global financial system was at the point of collapse. Parts of the system actually stopped functioning: For a few weeks in September and October 2008, many healthy businesses could not obtain short-term credit at any price. Although financial conditions have improved dramatically since then, substantial long-term economic challenges remain.

What caused the losses? The chief source was about as unlikely as could be imagined: leveraged speculation on home mortgages. The details of the mortgage bubble and its bursting are explained in many other articles in this book, so I will not repeat them here. But what caused financial institutions, including investment banks, commercial banks, hedge funds, mutual funds, and other organizations supposedly run by well-informed profit seekers, to speculate so recklessly on home mortgages?

There has been broad agreement among observers that moral hazard caused the speculation and hence the crash. As with any moral hazard, the source of the hazard is guarantees or insurance, but explicit government guarantees of particular securities or companies is not what I am primarily concerned with. Instead, I believe that a larger problem exists: Governments around the world, and in particular the U.S. government (the one I am most familiar with), have tried to use macroeconomic policy to achieve a riskless society.[5] These governments are doing nothing Machiavellian or sinister; they are just trying to please the voters who chose them so as to avoid being turned out of office.[6]

But as the physicist Edwin Goldwasser said at a recent memorial service for his childhood friend, the great investment thinker Peter Bernstein, a riskless society is "unattainable and infinitely expensive."[7] We are now paying that expense. The

---

[4]This essay focuses on the United States and refers to data (such as returns on the S&P 500) that are U.S.-centric. However, much of what is discussed here applies likewise to non-U.S. economies.

[5]Although most of the articles in this book distinguish between the central government and the central bank (which are operationally separate in the United States), for brevity, I refer to both institutions combined as "government."

[6]Investors are not blameless; at times they appear capable of believing almost anything, and of pricing assets accordingly. But other authors in this book focus on aspects of investor behavior in fostering the bubble and crash; my focus is the role of government.

[7]Edwin L. (Ned) Goldwasser was one of the founders of the National Accelerator Laboratory (Fermilab), Batavia, Illinois, and was its deputy director from 1967 to 1978. The quote is from his speech at a celebratory memorial for Peter L. Bernstein (1919–2009) in New York City on 15 September 2009.

mystery is how ordinary people—the electoral constituencies of democracies around the world—came to believe that their governments could protect them from all macroeconomic risk.

The Great Moderation—Or Was It?

One clue in solving the mystery is the perception, correct or otherwise, that increasingly wise management of either the monetary or the fiscal aspect of government (or both) has dampened the business cycle. The so-called Great Moderation is a sharp decrease in the amplitude, as measured, of the business cycle between the pre–World War II era in the United States (say, 1787–1941) and the postwar period (1942–2009). This discontinuity is easily visible in Figure 1 of Ray Dalio's article later in this book, and its existence as a real phenomenon is an article of faith among many economists.

But the distinguished economist Christina Romer, who now serves the Obama administration as chair of the Council of Economic Advisers, has argued that the Great Moderation is a data error (see Romer 1986). Specifically, she points out that prewar macroeconomic data (including GNP, industrial production, and unemployment—all key indicators of the business cycle) were collected and analyzed using an outdated methodology that we would not and do not use today. The postwar data, in contrast, were collected using a more modern and accurate method. Most economists would have stopped here and said that the two periods could not be fairly compared, but the fiendishly clever Romer, realizing that she could not go back and collect the old data again using modern methods, re-examined the new, postwar data using the old method! The result, which you have probably guessed by now, is that if one uses the same method to study both periods, the Great Moderation disappears. The amplitude of the business cycle, Romer finds, is the same as it always has been.

The Great Depression

The role of government in the economy, moreover, has grown and grown over time, mostly through the application of monetary and fiscal policy. In the Great Depression era, monetary policy received short shrift (with some arguing that the Depression was worsened by the Federal Reserve pursuing a policy of cripplingly tight money in the face of collapsing real economic activity);[8] instead, fiscal policy, specifically deficit spending, was aggressively used by policymakers, acting under the influence of John Maynard Keynes, to stimulate the economy. Because government intervention in the economy is not a controlled experiment (with one patient receiving a placebo while the other gets the real medicine), we will never know whether the Depression was relieved or prolonged by the Keynesian policies of the

---

[8]See Friedman and Schwartz (1963).

Hoover and then the Roosevelt administrations. Although economists are still fighting over this question three-quarters of a century after the fact, a consensus is emerging among economic historians (but not policymakers) that World War II, not the New Deal, brought us out of the Depression and that many New Deal policies worsened the Depression instead of hastening its end. I happen to believe that the relief programs were justified—that providing relief is what a government is for—but that most of the other programs were not.

What we do know is that the Great Depression did end, after an excruciatingly painful decade, and the economy grew to new heights of prosperity, never again to sink to Depression-era levels of unproductivity. Many people, and apparently most policymakers, believe that the government's role in ending the Great Depression was net positive. At any rate, the prudential principle suggests that if another depression is threatened, one had better take action similar to what may (or may not) have ended the previous one. The analogy to medication is close: If the doctor does not know whether the medication cured the disease last time but does know that the patient got better, the doctor had better administer the medication the next time the disease strikes. There is, of course, a downside: The medication might be hurting the patient (but not so much as to kill him or even keep him from fully recovering). But absent a controlled experiment, one has no way of knowing the potential harmful consequences.[9]

If the government could drag the economy out of the Great Depression, then it can fix almost any economic problem—or so many people believe. But what happens when the economic crisis that threatens has almost nothing in common with the Great Depression? Let's look at the next major dislocation faced by the United States and other advanced economies, the Great Inflation of the 1970s.

The Great Inflation

Government always has an incentive to inflate because inflation enables the government to pay back debts in dollars (or whatever the relevant currency is) that are cheaper, in terms of goods and services, than the dollars that were borrowed.

Some private actors also benefit from inflation. In particular, private (nongovernment) debtors benefit from unexpected inflation. Like the government, these debtors can borrow in rich dollars and pay back with cheap ones. That the inflation is unexpected causes the inflation not to be impounded in interest rates. One can typically pull this switcheroo only once in a lifetime because lenders remember that

---

[9] Economists use *counterfactuals* in an attempt to imitate the controlled experiments used by laboratory scientists. That is, they model a past situation and then vary one historical fact to see what the model says the result would have been. An extensive body of literature describes, supports, and criticizes this method. It suffices to say that counterfactuals are not really the methodological equivalents of controlled laboratory experiments in the physical sciences, and we do not really know what would have happened during the Great Depression if different policies had been pursued.

they were paid back in cheapened dollars and demand an inflation risk premium for the next round of lending; the unexpected inflation becomes expected inflation and is impounded in interest rates. But private debtors may be seen as exerting pressure on the government to cause inflation.

Also, some companies and observers report that low levels of inflation act as a lubricant for real economic growth, as long as the volatility of inflation rates is also low. This claim is hard to evaluate. The investment manager and consultant Charles Gave has said that the history of capitalism is the history of falling real prices; declines in real prices are what economic growth *is*.[10] If Gave is right, we do not need a low level of inflation to lubricate the machinery of commerce. But it suffices to say that there are numerous vocal constituencies for inflation, and they seem to prevail, on average, when a fiat-money standard is used.[11]

The government also has a disincentive to inflate: Savers, faced with the prospect of ruin, especially if their savings are invested in nominal bonds, stand ready to throw the government out on its ear if there is too much inflation. In addition, the bond market makes it expensive for inflation-prone governments to borrow, providing another disincentive.

As I briefly suggested earlier, the inflationary bias exists only if there is a fiat-money standard rather than a commodity-money (say, gold) standard. When the gold standard prevailed, wartime inflation was typically followed by peacetime *deflation*. The United States slowly converted from a gold standard to a fiat-money standard between 1913, when the Federal Reserve was established, and 1971, when President Nixon "closed the gold window" (removing the obligation of the U.S. government to sell gold to foreign buyers at the statutory, but much below-market, price of $35 per ounce). In my view, the key moment in this long, gradual process of conversion from commodity to fiat money was President Roosevelt's devaluation of the dollar from one-sixteenth to one-thirty-fifth of an ounce of gold, combined with his near-simultaneous prohibition of the individual ownership of gold by U.S. citizens.[12]

When the gold window was closed in 1971, I was still in high school, but I remember having a sense of the ship of state having slipped a mooring. I did not know what would go wrong, but I would soon find out.

The pro- and anti-inflation forces described earlier had been roughly in balance, with only a slight inflationary bias, since the early 1950s, when the postwar inflation was abating. From 1950 to 1971, the compound annual rate of growth of the U.S. Consumer Price Index (CPI) was a relatively sedate 2.5 percent.[13]

---

[10] Personal communication with the author.

[11] Note that fiat money (government-issued currency not backed by or exchangeable for any commodity) appears to have been invented by John Law (1671–1729), the promoter of one of the first asset bubbles, that of the Mississippi Company (1716–1720).

[12] Fractions are approximate.

[13] This is the Consumer Price Index for All Urban Consumers, not seasonally adjusted, from Ibbotson Associates (*Stocks, Bonds, Bills, and Inflation* 2009).

After that, spurred upward by an oil embargo designed by the Organization of Arab Petroleum Exporting Countries to punish the United States for its support of Israel and also to make money, inflation rates went crazy.[14] If the rate of growth of the money supply had been kept under control, the huge increase in the price of oil would have merely been a change in *relative* prices, similar to what occurs when there is a wheat shortage or other natural shock to the economy; the overall price level would not have risen much, if at all. But oil was so large an input to the U.S. economy that a large increase in its price would have almost certainly caused a recession.[15] To avoid a recession, the Fed expanded the money supply at rates that were unprecedented in peacetime. The resulting general inflation rate peaked at 13.3 percent on a year-end to year-end basis (much higher rates were recorded over shorter periods). The inflation of the 1970s was reflected in a rise in the price of gold from \$35 to \$800 per ounce, a massive increase in real estate prices, a doubling of the general consumer price level over the decade, and a sharp depreciation of the dollar against harder currencies.

Argentina, postwar Hungary, or Weimar Germany might have regarded such inflation rates as merely pesky, but for the leading economy in the world, this was hyperinflation. No one knew how high inflation or interest rates would go. The U.S. Treasury was forced to pay 15.375 percent compound annual interest on one of its bond issues (resulting, we would later find out, in a windfall for everyone who bought them—but it was not obvious at the time that long-term interest rates would go just that high and no higher). The second Keynesian experiment—the first being the New Deal—had failed.

The Great Inflation came to an end, conceptually if not in the data, on 6 August 1979, when President Carter appointed Paul Volcker, a very strong monetarist and an implacable opponent of inflation, to the chairmanship of the Federal Reserve. It may have been Carter's finest moment. The Long Boom had begun.[16]

But it did not begin auspiciously. Volcker used very high (sometimes exceeding 20 percent) federal funds rates to drive the economy into two sharp recessions, one in 1979 and one in 1981–1982. The recessions were deeply unpopular, and the first one probably caused Carter to lose the 1980 presidential election to Ronald Reagan.

But inflation rates responded exactly as monetary theory predicted. As quickly as by 1982, inflation had fallen to a 3.9 percent annual rate, well within the standard of reasonableness established by the experience of 1950–1971. Inflation rates would

---

[14]A number of other factors were at work in tipping the United States into high-speed inflation. These include union contracts that tied wages to consumer prices and a naive acceptance of the Phillips curve theory, now widely regarded as a fallacy, by policymakers. The oil embargo was, however, the precipitate cause.

[15]Oil is a much smaller proportion of total U.S. expenditure now than it was in the 1970s.

[16]So named by Schwartz and Leyden (1997).

fall further, but they did not need to: The aggressive intervention by the Fed had fixed a disastrous situation. Once again, macroeconomic policy—this time informed by the monetarist and neoclassical views of Milton Friedman rather than by the Keynesian views of the New Dealers—came to the rescue and removed from the scene a critical element of macroeconomic risk, namely the threat of ever-escalating inflation rates tipping into hyperinflation. Americans could save and invest again with confidence. Moral hazard was building: The government once again appeared to get us out of a messy situation.

The story of the taming of the Great Inflation does not quite end here. Sane monetary policy, resulting in moderate and stable rates of inflation, was a necessary but not a sufficient condition for the Long Boom, which really did not get started until 1982 (and which ran until 2000 or 2007, depending on how one thinks about the 2003–07 period[17]). The other condition that needed to be fulfilled was the Reagan administration's dramatic lowering of tax rates, both on personal incomes and on capital gains.[18] Although high marginal rates of individual income taxation destroy initiative and are unfair to the most productive members of society, the biggest tax-related constraint on economic growth at the end of the 1970s came from the "inflation tax" on capital, which was reduced as part of the Reagan tax cuts.

The inflation tax requires some explanation. During an inflation, taxing nominal capital gains as if they are real can produce effective tax rates on real gains well in excess of 100 percent. Suppose that a saver held a hypothetical asset earning the rate of CPI inflation purchased on 31 December 1969 for $100 and thus worth $203.63 on 31 December 1979. If sold, this asset would have produced a $103.63 "capital gain," representing no gain at all in purchasing power but subject to capital gains tax at the going marginal rate of 39.875 percent (for a top-bracket saver in 1979). In this example, the effective tax rate on real gains is infinite, or more precisely, cannot be calculated because there is no real gain.

Under such confiscatory conditions, capital goes on strike. And that is what it did in the early 1980s.[19] Because capital as well as labor is needed to produce goods and services, the freeing up of capital caused by the tax cuts of the 1980s must be regarded as a key precondition of the economic growth that followed.

---

[17] I prefer the longer definition because real GDP *per capita* is the best indicator of prosperity and was higher in 2007 than in 2000.

[18] Details are at www.taxpolicycenter.org/publications/url.cfm?ID=1000588.

[19] One can tell that capital is on strike when long-term interest rates exceed 15 percent and the price/earnings ratio of the stock market hovers between 6 and 8; no one provides any capital to any enterprise, or to a government, except in exchange for the promise of extremely lavish rewards.

The Greenspan Era

Paul Volcker was followed as Fed chairman by Alan Greenspan, also a strong monetarist by training and habit. But during Greenspan's long tenure as Fed chair, 1987 to 2006, a gradual shift took place in public attitudes toward macroeconomic risk and toward the proper role of government in managing this risk.

The sharp 1979 and 1981–82 recessions, which occurred under Volcker's watch, were tolerated (just barely) by a public that recognized sky-high inflation rates as a true national emergency. What surprised many was how quickly inflation rates fell when Volcker's tight-money policy began to be applied, and how stable they remained (at low levels) even as the vigor of the Long Boom might have been expected to put increasing upward pressure on prices. With the inflation problem apparently solved, the Fed could look for other dragons to slay.

Greenspan began to shift from a restrictive to a more-accommodative monetary framework in the wake of the crash of 19 October 1987. The crash, culminating in an unprecedented one-day 22 percent decline in U.S. stock prices,[20] showed that the financial system could be endangered by endogenous events, in this case the widespread use of portfolio insurance combined with a generally overpriced stock market. The Fed's response—to flood the financial system with liquidity, with a subsequent strong recovery in the stock market and no hint of a recession, much less a depression—set the stage for the perception that the public sector, acting mostly through the Fed, owned a "put" option on the stock market and the economy and could exercise it through easy-money policies when warranted so that recessions, credit crunches, and depressions could be avoided or stopped very early.

Moral hazard keeps building: The government got us out of an endogenous panic in the financial system, quite a different problem from that of the Great Depression or the Great Inflation but a potentially very damaging situation nonetheless.

The idea of a Greenspan or Fed "put" was solidified by events in 1994 and 1998 and reinforced by the V-shaped recovery starting in 2003, after the dot-com bubble and bust. It appeared that government had managed most of the risk out of the economy, leading many people to believe that the Great Moderation, which Romer chalks up to measurement error as discussed earlier, was real. Business cycles seemed more muted than ever before as a result of the beneficent effect of "sound" monetary policy—tight money when the economy is in a boom and easy money when it turns down but with an accommodative bias, on average, over time.

---

[20]Declines in other countries' stock markets on that day are discussed in the article in this book by Kaplan et al.

Real economic growth is hard to come by and is very important. As I wrote in 1997:

> There is an asymmetry to history. Life usually proceeds undisturbed, and the economy grows from more to more, but "usually" is not good enough. Progress is common, but it proceeds slowly, and the effect of one good year is small. Catastrophes are rare, but each one undoes many years—even centuries—of progress. (Siegel 1997a, p. 30)

In other words, when the Four Horsemen of the Apocalypse come riding, one cannot have too high a starting point! Real growth in a "usual" year, therefore, is so important that long booms should be encouraged, even if they are accompanied by some inflation and by some accumulation of systemic risk, with occasional asset bubbles and busts. They are almost certainly a net positive for society.[21] At the level of the human race, we are vastly richer than we were in 1979 (or 1946). Of course, some of this "richness" has to do with the end of Communism, the widespread acceptance of free trade, and technological innovation that would proceed at more or less its own pace irrespective of what the monetary authorities were doing. But some of the gain in real wealth has to do with allowing bubbles to bubble so that innovative technologies and processes can be funded, with most new ventures failing but with some succeeding beyond anyone's wildest expectations and—most importantly, as Peter Bernstein has pointed out—with *society getting to keep the technology.*

Thus, unlike some observers, I do not really fault Greenspan for sowing the seeds of the global financial crisis of 2007–2009. I know, "scientifically" speaking, that the bubble is the disease (because it misallocates resources, in the most recent example drawing too many people and dollars into the construction trades and the real estate brokerage and mortgage origination businesses). The crash is the cure (pushing these people and dollars back into more-productive uses). But humanity progresses by jumps. Without high expectations for the payoff to innovation, we might not have the railroad, the telephone, the automobile, the airplane, the electrical grid, the computer, the internet, or any of the other tools of modern life. But to get these gains, we *must* be able to tolerate risk because most attempts at innovation will not work out, stock market fortunes will be lost as well as won, and people will lose jobs.

Applying this principle (not exactly rocket science—we must be willing to tolerate risk if we want reward) to the events of the Greenspan era, I doubt that people would have tolerated the many recessions, periods of slow growth, and lack of innovation that would have resulted if Greenspan had managed away the Long Boom by quashing each asset bubble as it began to take shape.[22] The Greenspan era did not

---

[21] See Bernstein (2001).

[22] Or by quashing each asset bubble as best he could, given the bluntness of monetary policy as an instrument.

produce a Great Moderation (instead, systemic risk accumulated), but a tremendous amount of real wealth that we take for granted was created. With apologies to Shakespeare, if we do not like the consequences—if we are unwilling to pay the "risk price" that must be paid—the fault lies not in Alan Greenspan but in ourselves.

What's the Catch?

As I hope I have shown in the preceding sections of this article, there have been four chief "learning experiences" between the people and their government regarding macroeconomic policy over the last century:

1. The government can get us out of a Great Depression through fiscal stimulus.
2. The government can get us out of a Great Inflation through restrictive monetary policy.
3. The government can foster a Long Boom or Great Moderation, a period of good times, whatever you want to call it, through artful manipulation of the money supply.
4. The government can reverse an endogenous collapse of an asset market by flooding that market with liquidity.

As you have probably figured out, I would argue that the government fixed the problem only once, when it caused the problem. Because, as Friedman and Schwartz (1963) have written, "inflation is always and everywhere a monetary phenomenon," only bad monetary policy could cause the Great Inflation and only a monetary remedy could end it. The Great Depression would probably have ended sooner if serious policy mistakes had not been made during the strong recovery of 1935 and 1936; and the Great Moderation did not take place. The Long Boom, however, was a real phenomenon and was caused by changes in technology; Greenspan and the executive and legislative branches of the government got out of the way and did no harm.

The lesson that appears to have been learned by the voters, however, is that monetary and fiscal policy solutions can be brought to bear on almost any economic problem and the problem will have a successful resolution. Thus, a more or less riskless society, fostered by government, is seen as not only desirable but also possible.[23]

Where is the catch? Well, either government intervention in the economy helps to mitigate risk or it does not. I have argued that it mostly does not help, so the price of a riskless society really is infinite, as Goldwasser suggested; no matter how much of other people's money one spends, risk does not go away. It just moves elsewhere, where it cannot be seen as clearly.

---

[23] Interestingly, although some sort of financial crisis, banking panic, or depression occurred about every 10 years (with wide variation in this frequency) from the founding of the Republic to about 1945, and then again starting about 1971, no such crisis emerged between 1945 and 1971. Future researchers may want to ask what was special about this "calm" period of growth in the United States.

In certain circumstances, however, government intervention really does help. The unfreezing of the short-term credit markets in September and October 2008, discussed later, is a case in point. But no government program or benefit, once delivered, is easy to take away—even if the program or benefit is an explicitly temporary response to a perceived emergency.

Thus, in each emergency, the government grows in size *and stays larger than it was before* because of the basic fact of human nature referred to in the epigraph: "People will vote themselves other people's money if they can."

But what are the economic consequences of this observation? What happens when we try, using other people's money, to purchase something (a riskless society) that is, according to the preceding logic, not for sale at any price? If pursuing a riskless society is a fruitless effort, what should we do instead?

The Ratchet Cycle of Increasing Government Size

Some insights into these mysteries are provided by the Boeckhs, father and son, the elder of whom (Tony) is highly respected for what used to be his industry periodical, the *Bank Credit Analyst*. In a widely circulated series of articles called "The Great Reflation Experiment," Boeckh and Boeckh (2009) refer (correctly as monetarists) to any systematic and extended increase in the money supply as *inflation*.[24]

Because the money supply is a price (it is the amount of money needed to represent all the goods and services that are being transacted), it cannot be increased without some other price in the economy changing. One usually thinks of consumer price increases in connection with inflation, but as the Boeckhs point out, asset price increases can also represent inflation—the increased money supply going to buy long-term assets rather than consumer goods, which have recently been subject to restraints on nominal price increases because of competition from newly industrializing, low-wage countries. The long-term assets, or investments, that have gone into bubble status include internet stocks, financial services stocks, oil, real estate of all kinds and in all places, real estate–backed securities, corporate bonds, and one might now argue, Treasury bonds and gold. When the price of any asset gets to be much higher than its fundamental value, the result is either an orderly bear market in that asset or a crash.[25] And as of mid- or late 2007, we had experienced a lot of money supply growth for a very long time "with virtually no consequence to date (other than periodic asset price bubbles and shakeouts)" (Boeckh and Boeckh 2009, p. 2). The illusion of a nearly riskless society was intact.

---

[24]See also Tempelman (2009).

[25]The fundamental value of gold is its "value in use"—that is, its industrial or decorative (as opposed to monetary) value.

What happened next?

This whole book is about that question, but a quick way of saying "what happened" in September and October 2008 is to observe that the traditional grantors of private credit—banks and other financial institutions—saw the highly leveraged asset sides of their balance sheets deteriorate to the point where they were insolvent or almost insolvent, so they stopped granting credit. Without short-term credit, the economy simply cannot function: Employers cannot meet their payrolls, groceries cannot stock their shelves, farmers cannot farm. As Greenspan said in a speech at the Paulson & Co. investors' meeting in New York City on 17 November 2008, when the private sector fails to provide short-term credit, the public sector *must* step in and provide it (temporarily until the private sector starts again). I know of no economist, not even the most wild-eyed libertarian, who disagrees with this statement or policy.

And the policy was successful: Short-term credit markets started to unfreeze by November 2008. And even as the economy slid deeper into recession in the first quarter of 2009, and as the stock market reached lows not seen since the mid-1990s, credit markets provided evidence of the "green shoots of recovery" of which journalists and politicians spoke so hopefully. As this article is being written, the green shoots are becoming little stems and leaves. Financial conditions as measured by credit spreads and stock prices have improved about as rapidly as they ever have in the early stages of a recovery.

The rest of "what happened" is covered in other articles in this book, so I will not provide the detail here. What matters to my argument is that two distinct types of massive government intervention were brought to bear on the problem: (1) an unprecedented increase in the size of the Fed's balance sheet and (2) a more conventional (but very expensive) multiyear fiscal stimulus package. The effect of these interventions is to send the public debt as a percentage of GDP skyrocketing to levels never before seen in peacetime and close to (and if current trends continue, exceeding) the highs reached during World War II, when the United States was fighting for its existence.

Why do these interventions constitute a great reflation experiment? Both the stimulus package and the purchase of assets by the Fed involve government expenditure in current time, in excess of the amount supportable by current tax collections. In other words, the government, broadly construed to include the Fed, is running a large deficit. The principle known as Ricardian equivalence—as enunciated by Robert Barro (1974), drawing on David Ricardo (1820)—says that, at least as a first-order effect, a government expenditure has the same impact on the economy whether the expenditure is financed through current taxation or deferred taxation (debt). Moreover, any debt incurred by the government can be paid off either through future direct taxation or through inflation (that is, by decreasing the real value of the currency in which the debt is to be repaid). Inflation is thus a form of indirect—but very real—taxation.

If one takes this analysis at face value, the increase in government expenditure associated with the economic crisis of 2007–2009 could be paid for with a tax increase, avoiding any need for the government to issue new debt and then, later, possibly reduce the real value of that debt through an inflationary policy. But the required tax increase would be so large that any hoped-for economic recovery would be choked off immediately, and the voters, moreover, would not and should not stand for it.

A second possibility, to borrow now and pay off the debt later with increased direct taxation, is only feasible if future economic growth is extremely robust, making the needed increase in tax rates much less than it would otherwise be. For example, during the Long Boom, real economic growth caused the government to receive increased *revenues* at historically low tax *rates*, fulfilling the famously controversial prediction of the Laffer curve, although at a much longer time lag than Arthur Laffer originally hoped.[26]

The final and most likely possibility is that the greatly enlarged debt of the U.S. government will be partially inflated away ("reflated" referring to the *return* of inflation, once thought to be defeated). Having borrowed with relatively expensive dollars, the government can pay its debts back with cheaper dollars, and the safety—in nominal terms—of U.S. Treasury obligations is thereby preserved.[27] Private borrowers who have contracted to repay their debts in nominal terms will be helped by inflation, whereas their counterparties—lenders and bondholders—will be hurt. Borrowers and lenders who have contracted in real terms will be largely unaffected. Equities, being essentially real assets—in that they are claims to plant and equipment, patents, labor contracts, and so forth rather than to *money*—should have reasonably favorable prospects, and leveraged inflation-hedging assets should do extremely well.[28]

To sum up, the ratchet cycle of increasing government size works as follows:

- Some sort of crisis occurs.
- The government and/or central bank, expressing or purporting to express the will of the voters, intervene. Such intervention is inevitably inflationary because it involves spending—the injection of real resources—into a situation where there was previously no such injection.
- The crisis resolves. It appears as if the cause of the resolution is the government intervention, although we have no way of knowing whether the same or a better result would have been obtained without the intervention.

---

[26]For an excellent discussion that places the Laffer curve in historical context, see Laffer (2004).

[27]This scenario is complicated slightly by the fact that about 20 percent of U.S. government debt consists of Treasury Inflation-Protected Securities, or real return bonds, the value of which cannot be inflated away; but much higher rates of inflation are still the most likely scenario.

[28]Some of the author's earlier views on the risks of inflation and on the impact of inflation on asset returns are in Siegel (1997b, 1998).

- After the crisis passes, strong real economic growth tends to cause the size of government (relative to the size of the private sector) to recede. We experience tax cuts and a "conservative" period.
- Good times, fueled by easy money, enable the excesses (of prices or debt or whatever) to accumulate, which causes the next crisis.
- When the next crisis occurs, the prudential principle dictates that the same or greater policy response be applied because one cannot disprove that the last crisis would have resolved without it.
- Government thus grows larger over time, although not without periods when it recedes in relative size.

But is there a limit to this cycle? Of course there is. The government cannot deploy more resources than it can obtain, somehow, from the people. (This is what Ricardian equivalence really means.) At any given size of government, the response to a crisis, whether productive or not (let us assume that it is productive), is almost guaranteed to increase that size. Unless a substantial retrenchment in the size of government takes place between crises—which sometimes happens because of increased economic prosperity and thus increased tax revenues during booms—the government has less room to maneuver (by once again increasing its own size) to fight the next crisis. It is certainly imaginable that, having grown to a size where the people are just barely willing to pay the taxes needed to support the government, a crisis can occur that is so severe that the government is simply out of ammunition. I do not think we have reached that point, but someday we may—and we are headed in that direction. A riskless society cannot exist.

Private Credit

The Boeckhs also attack, as economically unsound, the tremendous growth in *private* debt since 1982. I am more sanguine about this issue. They argue that the Long Boom was funded by an expansion of private-sector credit that

> . . . maintained a stable trend relative to GDP from 1964 to 1982. After that, the ratio of debt to GDP rose rapidly for the 25 years leading up to the crash and is continuing to rise. The current reading has debt close to 180 percent of GDP, about double the level of the early 1980s. The magnitude and length of this rise is probably unprecedented in the history of the world. Even the credit inflation that was the prelude to the 1929 crash and the Great Depression only lasted five or six years. (Boeckh and Boeckh 2009, p. 1)

But the Boeckhs do not say what is on the other side of the balance sheet! I would encourage them to look there. Not all of the private credit that was created during the Long Boom went into spending beyond one's means, or into buying toxic assets, or into bidding the prices of existing good assets (such as equities and real estate) into the stratosphere. Some of the newly created private credit went to create new capital—buildings, factories, trucks, computers, and the less obvious asset category of intellectual property: patents, copyrights, and for that matter, college and graduate educations. This new capital is critical to the real economic growth that I argued earlier is so important that we should be willing to pay some sort of risk price to achieve it.

These assets will pay "dividends," mostly intangible, for a long time to come. And in deciding whether the creation of all this private credit was a good idea, the income from the asset side of the balance sheet needs to be netted against the debt service.[29] But the debt service must be paid in cash—not in the present value of future benefits that may or may not eventually be derived from holding the assets—hence the debt squeeze that occurs when current cash income turns down, as it does in the recessionary part of any business cycle. The only things that are different this time are the amount of debt that must be serviced and the interconnectedness of the institutions that hold the debt—with the latter factor posing a degree of systemic risk that we are unaccustomed to. If we want the benefits of private credit creation, we had better get accustomed to systemic risk and devise ways of managing it.

Aftermath of the Crash of 2007–2009

The worst nightmares of the great financial crisis of 2007–2009 have been averted. Capital markets are functioning once again, the real economy is starting to grow, market volatility is approaching historical averages, and stock prices have risen more than 60 percent from their abysmal 9 March 2009 lows. A few corporations and banks have gone under, never to recover. But that is what recessions are for, to drive uncompetitive firms out of business *and remove capacity from the system* (not just rearrange the firms' ownership structures) so that more efficient and innovative firms have room to flourish.[30]

I expect this flourishing to be surprisingly robust and productive—*but* . . . . . Through governmental action, as well as through the natural healing abilities of market forces, we have pushed risk far enough away from our faces that it looks manageable; a few more years and it may look positively benign. But the risk has not gone away. Because of the ratchet effect of ever-increasing government size—and what I really mean is spending, of which debt is only a symptom—more risk is in the system than ever before. The risk, simply stated, is that the *next* massive expansion of government needed (or perceived to be needed) to combat the *next* global financial crisis may not be numerically possible.

---

[29]I am confident that some, not all, of the credit creation in excess of historical trends will, using this analysis, turn out to have been a good idea. Whether it was a good idea or not depends on the productivity of the capital investment that was made with the borrowed funds, but the healthy increase in real *per capita* GDP over the period suggests that much of it was productive.

[30]Joseph A. Schumpeter (1883–1950) had much to say about this process. See Schumpeter (1942).

It has been said that the problem with socialism is that you eventually run out of other people's money. But as the anonymous quote that introduced this article suggests, any democracy is subject to the fault that voters can spend other people's money for their own benefit. In other words, democracies tend toward socialism over time if other forces are not brought to bear in the opposite direction. Peggy Noonan, a political and social commentator who first gained distinction as President Reagan's principal speechwriter, has written:

> [A] big part of opposition to the [introduction of new government programs] is a sense of historical context. People actually have a sense of the history they're living in and the history their country has recently lived through. They understand the moment we're in.
>
> In the days of the New Deal, in the 1930s, government growth was virgin territory. It was like pushing west through a continent that seemed new and empty. There was plenty of room to move. The federal government was still small and relatively lean, the income tax was still new. America pushed on, creating what it created: federal programs, departments and initiatives, Social Security. In the mid-1960s, with the Great Society, more or less the same thing. Government hadn't claimed new territory in a generation, and it pushed on—creating Medicare, Medicaid, new domestic programs of all kinds, the expansion of welfare and the safety net.
>
> Now the national terrain is thick with federal programs, and with state, county, city and town entities and programs, from coast to coast. It's not virgin territory anymore, it's crowded. We are a nation fully settled by government. . . We know its weight, heft, and demands, know its costs both in terms of money and autonomy, even as we know it has made many of our lives more secure, and helped many to feel encouragement.
>
> But we know the price now. This is the historical context. [Those who would expand government still further] often seem…disappointed that the big center, the voters in the middle of the spectrum, aren't all that excited about following them on their bold new journey. But it's a world America has been to. It isn't new to us. And we don't have too many illusions about it. (Noonan 2009)[31]

A Way Forward

If the perception is widespread that nothing really bad will be allowed to happen no matter what one's individual actions are, then people will take many more self-serving risks than they would otherwise. They may also take more "helpful" risks, those that have an upside in terms of innovation or efficiency.

---

[31] Noonan was actually referring to health insurance as the expansion of government that was being resisted by the "big center," but the principles that she relies on are so universal that I have adapted it (if the reader will forgive me) to the question of fiscal stimulus and of government guarantees of financial institutions and securities.

Recalling my Smithian comment at the outset—that private vices are capable of serving as public virtues under the right conditions—it is important to recognize that many risks that appear to be taken merely to benefit the risk taker actually benefit many other people. A great many financial innovations are cases in point: Think of the money market fund; the equity mutual fund; the life, health, or property insurance policy; the life annuity; the home mortgage and reverse mortgage; the concept of the subprime mortgage sensibly and prudently applied—all of these products were developed primarily to earn a profit, not to better mankind. Yet they have produced wonderful benefits to others (consumer surpluses). So, we do not want to discourage risk taking, only the kind of risk taking that depends on a backstop supplied by an unwilling guarantor. In other words, we want to discourage moral hazard.

The unethical behavior of many financial market participants in the recent crisis has been a subject of much discussion. I do not find this to be a surprise. People are imperfect, and good and evil impulses struggle with one another in everybody. Jobs in which large sums of other people's money are handled tend to attract people for whom this struggle is particularly difficult. So, we need relatively rigid rules and a complex private system of checks and balances involving mandatory review of behavior and practices by other people acting in their own self-interest. This private system, operating alongside and in cooperation with the public system of laws and regulations, needs to be reinforced, and it is more important to do so in finance than in fields in which the opportunities for cheating are either infrequent or unrewarding. This view does not mean that we should not study ethics or that we should not exhort people to behave ethically—only that, beyond telling people not to steal money, it is notoriously difficult to prevent ethical violations in finance through moral suasion.

To avoid engaging in practices that create moral hazard, we need to be more tolerant of ups and downs in the economy and in life. Most of us need to save more—not for the good of the country but for the good of ourselves. Equity is the great buffer between certain liabilities and uncertain means of meeting them. As individuals, we have the responsibility to stay ahead of changing trends, to preserve and enhance the value of one's human capital. (If you want to be a steelworker these days, it helps to be born in a newly industrializing country. Keep your skills up-to-date.)

Let government shrink in relative size during easy times.

The tendency of nature and mankind to always and everywhere economize—that is, to do more with less—bodes well for a wonderful future. Economists refer to this tendency as an improvement in technology, and by "technology," they do not mean computers and spacecraft. They simply mean the accumulated body of knowledge and stock of machinery that enables people to exchange effort for output at the rate that they do so. Environmental concerns loom large in the minds of many, but world population (not population growth rates, but *population*) will, incredibly, reach its all-time high within the lifetimes of our children and then decline, which will make it easier for our grandchildren to apply technological solutions to environmental challenges than it is for us.[32] But this wonderful future will be discernibly harder to achieve if we hold on to the belief that everyone can live at the expense of everybody else. It is a costly view to have, as we have seen from the fact that the ratchet cycle of increasing government size has created a massive moral hazard problem. Although voluntary—and some involuntary, or governmental—sharing of resources is a critical element of civilization, we cannot all live at each others' expense. We are, each of us, responsible for our own well-being.

REFERENCES

Barro, Robert J. 1974. "Are Government Bonds Net Wealth?" *Journal of Political Economy*, vol. 82, no. 6 (November-December):1095–1117.

Bernstein, Peter L. 2001. "From the Ashes of Crashes." *Economics and Portfolio Strategy* (15 February).

Boeckh, Tony, and Rob Boeckh. 2009. "The Great Reflation Experiment: Implications for Investors." *Boeckh Investment Letter*, vol. 1.8 (23 July).

Friedman, Milton, and Anna J. Schwartz. 1963. *A Monetary History of the United States, 1867-1960.* Princeton, NJ: Princeton University Press.

Laffer, Arthur B. 2004. "The Laffer Curve: Past, Present, and Future." Heritage Foundation, Backgrounder #1765 (1 June): http://edgeweb.heritage.org/Research/Taxes/upload/64214_1.pdf accessed on 25 November 2009.

Noonan, Peggy. 2009. "There Is No New Frontier." *Wall Street Journal* (17 October):A13 (http://online.wsj.com/article/SB10001424052748704322004574475551644400192.html accessed on 21 October).

Ricardo, David. 1820. "Essay on the Funding System."

Romer, Christina D. 1986. "Is the Stabilization of the Postwar Economy a Figment of the Data?" *American Economic Review*, vol. 76, no. 3 (June):314–334.

Schumpeter, Joseph A. 1942. *Capitalism, Socialism, and Democracy.* New York, London: Harper & Brothers.

Schwartz, Peter, and Peter Leyden. 1997. "The Long Boom: A History of the Future, 1980–2020." *Wired*, issue 5.07 (July).

Siegel, Laurence B. 1997a. "Are Stocks Risky? Two Lessons." *Journal of Portfolio Management*, vol. 23, no. 3 (Spring):29–34.

---

[32] See Wattenberg (2004).

————. 1997b. "Inflation and Investing: An Overview." *Investment Policy* (July/August):15–30.

————. 1998. "Inflation Hedging in a Low-Inflation World: The Plan Sponsor's Rationale." In *Handbook of Inflation-Indexed Bonds*. Edited by John B. Brynjolfsson and Frank J. Fabozzi. New Hope, PA: Frank J. Fabozzi Associates.

Tempelman, Jerry H. 2009. "Will the Federal Reserve Monetize U.S. Government Debt?" *Financial Analysts Journal*, vol. 65, no. 6 (November/December):24–27.

Wattenberg, Ben J. 2004. *Fewer: How the New Demography of Depopulation Will Shape Our Future.* Chicago, IL: Ivan R. Dee.

The Dynamics of a Financial Dislocation: The Panic of 1907 and the Subprime Crisis

Robert F. Bruner
*Dean and Charles C. Abbott Professor of
  Business Administration
Darden Graduate School of Business Administration,
  University of Virginia
Charlottesville, Virginia*

Financial crises recur frequently and respect no borders.[1] The International Monetary Fund has identified 119 country years of banking crises in 31 countries from 1990 to 2005.[2] In its early history, the United States saw 11 banking panics from 1820 to 1914. **Figure 1** projects these panics onto a graph of annual economic growth. Generally, the panics followed periods of robust growth and occurred in the context of a recession, but not every recession featured a panic. Founding the U.S. Federal Reserve System in 1913 has ameliorated but has not prevented financial crises thereafter: The United States has witnessed three major episodes of financial crisis in the last century—1930–1934, the savings and loan (S&L) crisis[3] of 1985–1989, and the current period, 2007–2009 (so far), which I refer to as the "subprime crisis"—and numerous smaller episodes, such as the near collapse of the commercial paper market in 1970, the seizure of Continental Illinois National Bank and Trust Company in 1984, the collapse of Long-Term Capital Management in 1998, and Enron Corporation in 2001. They were all associated with a decline in asset values, constriction of credit, and turbulence in the financial system.

---

[1] A *financial crisis* is an episode of severe threat to the stability, safety, and soundness of the financial system in the economy. A *crash*, or sharp decline in security prices, often precedes or coincides with a financial crisis, although many crashes have occurred without the corresponding financial crisis. A financial crisis typically includes a *panic*, in which depositors and lenders frantically seek to withdraw their money from institutions and markets, threatening a bank with *illiquidity* (an insufficiency of cash) or *insolvency* (an insufficiency of assets with which to meet liabilities). A panic may be only one episode of the longer period of instability. A financial crisis usually triggers or aggravates an *economic recession*, although many recessions have not featured financial crises. A financial crisis commences with some kind of economic shock and ends when financial market conditions return to normal.
[2] Duttagupta and Cashin (2008).
[3] Although not commonly reflected in many lists of U.S. financial crises, the S&L crisis meets virtually all of the attributes of a crisis as described in Footnote 1.

Editor's Note: Robert F. Bruner is the co-author, with Sean D. Carr, of *The Panic of 1907: Lessons Learned from the Market's Perfect Storm*, from which some elements of this article have been adapted.

Figure 1. Banking Panics and Business Cycles as Reflected by Change in Industrial Production, 1820–1915

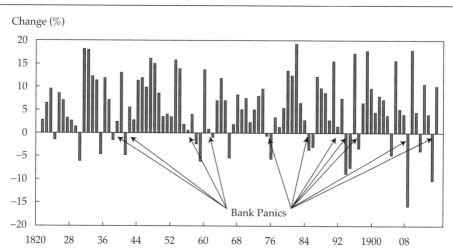

Sources: Bank panics identified in Calomiris (2000, p. 99). Data on industrial production from Davis (2004), the Davis Industrial Production Index, downloaded from the NBER website.

Much of what we understand about financial crises comes from macroscopic research—the study of broad capital market and economic conditions before, during, and after the crisis. These studies tell us, for instance, that crises first appear in financial centers and then spread broadly through interest rate shocks and slumping asset and commodity prices.[4] Crises follow periods of high international capital mobility, but no significant differences exist in frequency or volume of financial crises between developed and emerging countries: "Banking crises are an equal opportunity menace," in the words of Reinhart and Rogoff (2008b, p. 18). The aftermath of financial crises is protracted and typically severe: Housing and equity prices decline sharply; unemployment rises materially and lingers at a higher level for four years, on average; and government debt surges an average of 86 percent because of dwindling tax revenues, not because of bailouts.[5]

Macro insights are useful in setting public policy and in anticipating the behavior of policymakers. Yet, so much of what interests investors and company executives concerns the *dynamics* of the crisis: how a crisis unfolds, what influences its duration and virulence, and where human intervention helps or hurts. In other words, we hanker for more detail about the internal mechanics of crises.

[4]Reinhart and Rogoff (2008a).
[5]Reinhart and Rogoff (2009).

My aim in this article is to provide more granularity to our understanding of the dynamics of a crisis by means of *micro history*. Following is what I think the micro histories reveal: The dynamics of a financial crisis resemble a pernicious accelerating cycle, much like the vortex in a bathtub when the stopper is pulled. What makes the vortex possible is a systemic interdependence among financial institutions, growing instability, a shock, and intervention that is either absent or inadequate.

Banks and near-banks link to form a *system* by virtue of interbank loans and deposits, which means that trouble in one institution, city, or region can travel to other parts. And because financial systems are highly complex, it is difficult to know what might be going wrong.

Buoyant growth stimulates financial innovation in securities and institutions and creates rising demand for capital and liquidity. But growth in the economy makes the financial system more fragile—in part because of the demand for capital and in part because of the tendency of some institutions to take more risk than is prudent in the later stages of an economic boom. (In the late stages of an economic expansion, borrowers and creditors overreach in their use of debt, lowering the margin of safety in the financial system.) Leaders in government and in the financial sector then implement policies that advertently or inadvertently elevate the exposure to risk of crisis.

An economic shock hits the financial system. By definition, a shock must be surprising, material, costly, and unambiguous. Then, the system recoils. The news of the shock triggers a *regime shift*—a dramatic change in outlook among investors, depositors, consumers, and managers. The mood of the market swings from optimism to pessimism, creating a self-reinforcing downward spiral. Each piece of bad news motivates behavior that generates more bad news. Nevertheless, collective action by leaders can arrest the spiral; the speed and effectiveness with which they act will determine the length and severity of the crisis.

Complicating our understanding of the vortex-like dynamics of a crisis is the fact that these factors (system structure, instability, shock, and response) can *interact* in unexpected ways to affect the speed, breadth, and severity of the crisis. The histories of crises illustrate the existence and interplay of these factors.

This article reviews two crises: the Panic of 1907 and the recent subprime crisis. The Panic of 1907 is worth careful consideration in the 21st century because it was the last major crisis before the founding of the U.S. Federal Reserve System; indeed, it was the straw that broke the back of congressional opposition to the concept of a central bank in the United States. By seeing how markets, institutions, and individuals responded before the establishment of the regulatory superstructure and social safety nets in the United States, we can observe how the private market provides remedies to a financial crisis. The Panic of 1907 poses a useful comparison with the subprime crisis that began in late 2006 and continues to the date of this writing (mid-2009).

The Panic of 1907

The San Francisco earthquake of 18 April 1906 triggered a massive call on global gold reserves and a liquidity crunch in the United States. A recession commenced in June 1907. Security prices declined. In September, New York City narrowly averted a failure to refinance outstanding bonds. Then, on 16 October, a "bear squeeze" speculation failed and rendered two brokerage firms insolvent. The next day, depositors began a run on Knickerbocker Trust Company, which was known to be associated with the speculators. Runs spread to other trust companies and banks in New York City. And the panic rippled across the United States. Country banks had learned from past experience that during a panic, withdrawing deposits from reserve city banks could be difficult.[6] Thus, at the first news of bank runs in New York City, country banks rushed to withdraw deposits, which caused some reserve city banks to fall below the minimum reserve requirement set in the national or state banking charters. Banks in many cities suspended the withdrawal of deposits.

Bank clearinghouses issued clearinghouse loan certificates that could substitute for cash. This near-money traded hands at a discount to true cash, reflecting fears about the solvency of the clearinghouses and their banks. At the height of the national panic, about $250 million in these certificates circulated, equal to about 14 percent of all the currency in the hands of the public.[7] Across the country, firms and banks resorted to a variety of substitutes for cash. Streetcar companies in Omaha and St. Louis paid their employees in nickels from the fare boxes or in five-cent fare tickets.[8] Some companies issued certified checks, scrip, or IOUs. Bank checks were useful as cash only locally because in an environment where banks discriminated among payees, being a distant correspondent was a disadvantage.

By 2 November, at least partial suspension of bank withdrawals had spread across the country,[9] a fast contagion given that the first suspension by Knickerbocker occurred on 22 October. The governors of Oregon, Nevada, and California declared legal holidays, which had the effect of closing the banks entirely. South Dakota, Indiana, Iowa, and Oklahoma sanctioned the payment by banks of only small amounts, such as $10. Banks thus discriminated in making payments. There was the perception that banks in reserve cities, such as New York, Chicago, and

---

[6]Andrew (1908a, p. 298).

[7]The estimate of clearinghouse loan certificates issued is from Cannon (1910). The amount this represented as a percentage of all cash in the hands of the public is calculated by the author and draws the denominator, $1.784 billion, from Friedman and Schwartz (1963, p. 706).

[8]Horwitz (1990, p. 643).

[9]Sprague (1908) notes that "the extent to which suspension was carried cannot be accurately determined" (p. 364).

Minneapolis-St. Paul, were slow in remitting deposits back to correspondents in the South and West of the United States. The financial system rocked with the turmoil: 42 trust companies failed as did 6 of 6,412 national banks.[10]

News that some banks had suspended withdrawals triggered a national wave of hoarding currency and gold. As a consequence, rentals of safe deposit boxes "skyrocketed."[11] About $350 million in deposits were withdrawn from the U.S. financial system.[12] Of this amount, the bulk of it was simply socked away—estimates of cash hoarded range from $200 million to $296 million.[13] Arguably, absent the suspension of withdrawals, the amount hoarded would have been considerably greater.

The recession that began in June 1907 worsened considerably. Commodity prices fell by 21 percent, canceling virtually the entire increase from 1904 to 1907.[14] Industrial production fell more than in any U.S. panic up to 1907.[15] In November, United States Steel Corporation's (U.S. Steel's) output was down by 25 percent versus a year earlier; in December, it was down 65 percent. The dollar volume of bankruptcies declared in November spiked by 47 percent over a year earlier; the panic would be associated with the second-worst volume of bankruptcies in U.S. history up to that time.[16] Gross earnings by railroads fell by 6 percent in December.[17] Production fell 11 percent from May 1907 to June 1908; wholesale prices fell 5 percent. Imports shrank 26 percent.[18] Unemployment rose from 2.8 percent to 8 percent[19], a dramatic increase in a short space of time. The *Commercial and Financial Chronicle* wrote, "It is probably no exaggeration to say that the industrial paralysis and the prostration was the very worst ever experienced in the country's history."[20] Milton Friedman and Anna Schwartz concluded that the recession was "among the five or six most severe" (Friedman and Schwartz 1963, p. 156). Other descriptions of the economic contraction in 1907–1908 include "extremely severe,"[21] "extraordinarily violent,"[22] and an "intense depression."[23]

---

[10]Calomiris and Gorton (1991, p. 150).

[11]Andrew (1908a, p. 294).

[12]Sprague (1908, p. 367).

[13]The amount of $200 million is cited in Sprague (1908, p. 367), and $296 million is cited in Noyes (1909, p. 188).

[14]Noyes (1909, p. 207).

[15]Calomiris and Gorton (1991, p. 156).

[16]Calomiris and Gorton (1991, p. 156).

[17]These developments are discussed in detail in Sprague (1908, pp. 368–371).

[18]Noyes (1909, p. 208).

[19]Cahill (1998, p. 296).

[20]Quoted in Cahill (1998, p. 296).

[21]Friedman and Schwartz (1963, p. 156).

[22]See Noyes (1909, p. 211).

[23]*Commercial and Financial Chronicle,* quoted in Cahill (1998, p. 796).

Symptoms of the panic, such as bank suspensions of payment, receded in January 1908.[24] The recession itself ended in June 1908, followed by buoyant economic growth in the United States for the next 18 months. The stock market and industrial production recovered to precrisis levels by late 1909. The economic cycle peaked in January 1910 and then slumped until January 1912. The financial system was stable until the commencement of World War I, when equity trading was interrupted by the closing of the New York Stock Exchange from August through November 1914.

The effects of the panic were not confined to the United States. Some scholars have associated the crash and panic in the United States with financial crises in Egypt (January to May 1907), Hamburg (October), Chile (October), Holland and Genoa (September), and Copenhagen (winter).[25] And the panic had geopolitical repercussions as well. It has been identified as one of the factors provoking the Mexican Revolution of 1910.

Most importantly, the Panic of 1907 was the catalyst for a profound re-examination of the Jefferson–Jackson policy against central banking in the United States. Historian Robert Wiebe wrote:

> The panic of 1907 acted as a catalyst in the [political] ferment. Most obviously, it convinced almost everyone, including the bankers, that financial reform was imperative. . . . The panic released countless little pockets of pressure, turning concerned but comfortable citizens into active reformers and opening many more to the calls for change. (Wiebe 1967, p. 201)

In 1913, Congress passed legislation establishing the Federal Reserve System.

In confronting the panic, the official systems of response failed. The New York Clearing House Association simply refused to clear checks associated with the speculators' institutions. President Theodore Roosevelt, antagonistic toward Wall Street, was drawn late and reluctantly to offer rather bland statements of confidence in the financial system. The U.S. Treasury moved deposits of gold to New York City banks, but the amounts proved inadequate to the scale of the crisis. By mid-November, the Treasury itself held only $5 million in gold, effectively sidelining that institution from further influence over the course of events.[26]

---

[24]Calomiris and Gorton (1991, p. 161) date the end of suspension at 4 January 1908. Friedman and Schwartz (1963, p. 163) note that the U.S. Treasury resumed demanding payments in cash in December but that some banks continued to restrict payments through January.

[25]Both Noyes (1909, pp. 202–206) and Kindleberger (1978) mention that the Panic of 1907 occurred in a context of financial instability in foreign cities. The notion of contagion, or spread, of financial crises has been documented in the financial crises of the late 20th century. But the global contagion in 1907 is not as fully documented. Flows of gold into and out of the United States in 1907 are well discussed in contemporary and recent writings on the Panic. It remains to be shown how these flows (or other mechanisms) actually transmitted the financial crisis globally in 1907.

[26]Tallman and Moen (1990, p. 8).

What is novel about the Panic of 1907 is that the organizer of collective action had no official role or mandate at all. John Pierpont Morgan, then 70 years old and semi-retired, intervened to organize rescues of trust companies, banks, the New York Stock Exchange, New York City, and the brokerage firm of Moore and Schley. His mantle of authority was not a regulatory position but, rather, an extensive and strong network of influence throughout the New York financial community as well as an ability to direct the resources of his own partnership, J.P. Morgan & Company. A few vignettes are instructive in illustrating the instruments of his intervention.

On 19 October 1907, Morgan's partners urgently asked him to return to New York City from Richmond, Virginia, where he had been attending the Triennial Episcopal Convention. Taking a personal express train back to New York City, he arrived on 20 October and immediately convened a meeting of leading bankers in the library of his home at 36th Street and Madison Avenue. This group mobilized teams of auditors to visit the panic-stricken institutions and assess their solvency. On the basis of this firsthand information, Morgan and his circle determined that the Knickerbocker Trust should not be saved but that the next endangered institution, Trust Company of America, was still solvent; at that pivotal moment, Morgan said, "This is the place to stop the trouble then."[27] He organized a rescue pool of funds for Trust Company of America. And every institution that he and his circle determined to save thereafter survived the panic.

Yet, the panic would not recede. Morgan's circle of financiers grew apprehensive that their dwindling uncommitted capital would be sufficient to mount yet more rescues and feared that their failure to do so would trigger a complete collapse of the banking system. Morgan determined that the instability of the trust companies—a new and less-regulated type of financial institution—were at the heart of the panic and that restoring confidence would be assisted by a commitment of mutual assistance among the trust companies, much like the function served by the New York Clearing House that provided mutual support for banks. On the night of 2 November, Morgan convened a meeting of the presidents of the trust companies—some 120 people—at the library of his home. Lacking clarity about the solvency of the various institutions, the presidents were understandably reluctant to have anything to do with each other. The meeting droned on into the early morning. Then one person sought to leave the room and discovered that Morgan had locked the door. Shortly thereafter, Morgan drew out a pen and a draft agreement for mutual assistance and walked from person to person instructing where to sign. As the trust company presidents emerged into the early light of day on 3 November, the trust companies had formed a collective.

---

[27]Strong (1924).

By 3 November, collapsing equity prices had weakened a number of brokerage firms, which depended on the value of securities held as collateral for loans by the brokers to customers. One firm (Moore and Schley) teetered on insolvency owing to a concentration of holdings in the Tennessee Coal, Iron and Railroad Company (TCI), a limping steel company. Fearing that a failure of Moore and Schley would precipitate a new wave of panic, Morgan hastily organized a meeting of the directors of U.S. Steel, of which he was a member. (He had organized the company in 1901.) Explaining the gravity of the situation, he persuaded the very reluctant directors to agree to acquire TCI in a stock-for-bonds exchange. If the deal went through, Moore and Schley's collateral position would be greatly enhanced and the firm would survive the panic. But the directors of U.S. Steel imposed a condition requiring the approval of the U.S. government. President Roosevelt had been busting trusts and other large enterprises. The directors did not want the acquisition of TCI to put U.S. Steel in jeopardy. So, Morgan dispatched the chairman and CEO of U.S. Steel to Washington, DC, to importune President Roosevelt for his approval. With time running out and the prospect of financial collapse at hand, Roosevelt granted the acquisition exemption from prosecution. Moore and Schley was saved.

Dynamics of the Panic of 1907

Embedded in this simple but violent financial crisis is a narrative about crisis dynamics: how they unfold, what influences their duration and virulence, and where human intervention helps or hurts. The narrative begins with the fact that the financial institutions constitute a system; the existence of a system implies a rich range of possible dynamics. The system grows unstable. A shock occurs. Intervention affects the duration and severity of the crisis. Let us consider these four elements.

Financial Institutions Constitute a *System*. A financial system has two vitally important foundations for financial crises. First, the existence of a system means that trouble can travel. The difficulties of one financial intermediary can become the difficulties of others. Second, the complexity of a financial system means that it is impossible for all participants in the financial system to be well informed; this is called an "information asymmetry" and may motivate perverse behavior that can trigger or worsen a financial crisis.

The collection of financial intermediaries in an economy is called a "financial system," reflecting the fact that its parts are linked and interact. The various intermediaries (banks, trust companies, brokerage firms) are lenders and creditors to one another by virtue of the cash transfers that they facilitate. Financial institutions are linked into a system by means of the steady stream of transactions triggered by them and their depositors. The financial system was global, or at least pan-European, as early as the Renaissance in the sense that institutions in different countries were linked through transactions and deposits. Kindleberger (1978) noted that over time, the waves of financial crises have had a strong international dimension to them because of such linkages.

The other relevant aspect of financial systems has to do with opacity of information. Some participants in a market have an information advantage over others. This information asymmetry may lead to the problem of adverse selection, in which the better-informed people might exploit the poorly informed. George Akerlof described this situation as the "lemons" problem, in which the market for used cars features imperfect pricing. Michael Spence extended the insights drawing on the labor market. And Joseph Stiglitz focused on credit markets. Akerlof, Spence, and Stiglitz received the Nobel Prize in economics in 2001 for their groundbreaking work.

In 1983, two economists, Douglas Diamond and Philip Dybvig, suggested that bank panics are simply randomly occurring events.[28] Bank runs occur when depositors fear that some kind of shock will force the bank into costly and time-consuming liquidation. To be last in line to withdraw deposited funds exposes the individual to the risk of loss. Therefore, Diamond and Dybvig hypothesize that a run is caused simply by the fear of random deposit withdrawals and the risk of being last in line.[29]

An alternative theory is that bank runs are explained by asymmetric information: The problem of adverse selection can motivate panic selling or withdrawal of deposits. Calomiris and Gorton (1991), Gorton (1985), and others have suspected that runs could begin when some depositors observe negative information about the value of bank assets and withdraw their deposits. In a world of unequally distributed information, some depositors will find it costly to ascertain the solvency of their banks. Thus, runs might be a rational means of monitoring the performance of banks, a crude means of forcing the banks to reveal to depositors the adequacy of their assets and reserves. Calomiris and Gorton reasoned that if the information asymmetry theory is true, panics are triggered by real asset shocks that cause a decline in collateral values underpinning bank loans. They found that bank panics originated in areas of real shocks and that the cause in these regions was a decline in asset values. In particular, panics tended to follow sharp declines in the stock market and tended to occur in the early and later parts of the year. They also reasoned that the resolution of a bank panic would be created by elimination of an important aspect of the information asymmetry: Gaining clarity as to which banks were solvent and which were insolvent would stop the runs on solvent banks.

---

[28] Diamond and Dybvig (1983).

[29] One researcher, Glenn Donaldson, found some evidence in support of this "random withdrawal" theory: Interest rates during a panic were much higher than in nonpanic times. See Donaldson (1992, pp. 278, 298).

Empirical research gives some support to the asymmetric information theory over the random withdrawal theory, but the findings are not uniformly supportive.[30] Studies have considered how well information asymmetry explains panics by looking at whether (1) deposit losses predict panics, (2) the yield spreads between low- and high-risk bonds peak at the panic, and (3) real declines in the stock market are greater in panic years than nonpanic years; generally, these findings are affirmed.[31] Mishkin (1991) considered evidence from a range of financial crises in the 19th century and concluded:

> The timing and pattern of the data in the episodes studied here seem to fit an asymmetric information interpretation of financial crises. Rather than starting with bank panics, most of the financial crises begin with a rise in interest rates, a stock market decline and the widening of the interest rate spread. Furthermore, a financial panic frequently is immediately preceded by a major failure of a financial firm, which increases uncertainty in the marketplace. The increase in uncertainty and the rise in interest rates would magnify the adverse selection-lemons problem in the credit markets while the decline in the stock market increases agency as well as adverse selection problems, both of which are reflected in the rise in the spread between interest rates for low and high-quality borrowers. The increase in adverse selection and agency problems would then lead to a decline in investment activity and aggregate economic activity. (p. 27)

The System Grows Unstable. The Panic of 1907 ended a 12-year stretch of rapid economic growth for the United States. Since the panic of 1893, the U.S. economy had grown at an annual average real rate of 7.3 percent, a blistering pace. This growth resulted from such factors as the industrialization of the U.S. economy, technological change (e.g., railroads, telegraphy, electrification), and a high volume of immigration that ensured a workforce sufficient to meet the demands of rapid growth. Financing for this growth flowed from the money centers of Europe to support both debt and equity issuances by corporations. "New era" thinking seemed warranted: Prices were reaching a permanently higher plateau; new and less sophisticated investors were entering the stock market; capital for new ventures was relatively plentiful.

Rapid growth stimulated innovation in business models. Trusts, such as the Standard Oil Trust, were formed to eliminate "ruinous competition." During the great merger wave of 1894–1904, more than 1,800 companies disappeared as they were consolidated into 93 companies with an important, if not dominant, share of market in their respective industries. The epitome of this wave was the formation

---

[30] Carlson (undated, p. 4) tests the asymmetric information theory as the explainer of panics and bank suspensions—as opposed to Diamond and Dybvig's random withdrawal theory. He finds the results to favor the asymmetric information theory when tested using state-level data but indeterminate when using local-level data.

[31] See Gorton (1988); Donaldson (1992); Mishkin (1991); and Carlson (undated).

of U.S. Steel in 1901, the first company capitalized at $1 billion. Among financial institutions, the wave of innovation in financial models appeared in the formation of trust companies, unregulated (until early 1907) bank-like institutions that attracted depositors with higher interest rates.

The Progressive Movement rose to address the social and political ills associated with rapid growth, immigration, and industrialization. Beneath the political surface swirled other movements, such as populism, socialism, communism, and anarchism. Theodore Roosevelt came to the White House following the assassination of President William McKinley by an anarchist in 1901. Roosevelt himself earned the sobriquet "trust-buster" by vigorously enforcing the Sherman Antitrust Act to break up large companies. To build political support, he inveighed against Wall Street with heated rhetoric: "malefactors of great wealth" and "predatory man of wealth." Such sentiments, combined with active aggressive regulatory enforcement, spawned anxiety among investors by early 1907.

In short, the environment preceding the Panic of 1907 was one of growing instability and uncertainty about the sustainability of growth, a growing appetite for risk, and growing complexity.

A particular feature of the late stage of growth eras is a greater tolerance for risk. This tolerance is evident in the more aggressive use of debt financing, the reach for higher returns, an increase in "bet the ranch" behavior, momentum-style investing, more herd-like movements in the markets along with the attendant higher volatility, relaxation of lending standards and risk management practices by financial institutions, and proclamations of a "new era" in business opportunities for which old guidelines have become inadequate. This constellation of factors has the effect of eroding the safety buffers in the economic system. For example, the level of capital with which to withstand economic shocks grows inadequate. The financial system grows more vulnerable to the eventual reckoning. The business cycle is associated with a cycle of credit expansion and contraction that significantly amplifies changes in markets and economic growth. The boom part of the credit cycle erodes the shock absorbers that would otherwise cushion the financial system in the inevitable slump. Some banks, eager to make profits, unwisely expand their lending to less and less creditworthy clients as the boom proceeds.

Then some external shock occurs, and the bank directors awaken to the inadequacy of their capitalization relative to the credit risks they have taken. Consequently, banks reduce or cut off new loans available to their clients, which triggers a liquidity crisis that drives both a stock market crash and depositor panic. Hyman Minsky argued that this behavior on the part of the financial system would create phases of "overtrading," "revulsion," and "discredit."[32] The prime cause of economic slumps, according to Minsky, is the credit cycle, the expansion and contraction of loans for

---

[32]These words are used by Kindleberger (1978, p. 19) to describe the model of Hyman Minsky.

businesses and consumers: Easy credit amplifies the boom, and tight credit amplifies the contraction. In this view, Minsky followed John Maynard Keynes. Minsky argued for government intervention to reduce the amplitude of the cycle—more aggressive lending by the government during contractions and tighter regulation of bank lending standards during the booms. Economic slumps, in this view, are associated with financial crises by means of the loss of discipline: Through the boom, banks overreach and extend loans to riskier clients. The buoyancy of economic booms causes riskier creditors to approach banks for loans, which creates what economists call a problem of adverse selection. Some banks succumb to the temptation to make loans to these creditors, perhaps in the belief that luck or a bank clearinghouse will see them through; this is a problem of moral hazard.[33]

Adverse selection and moral hazard ultimately earn their just reward. A decline in asset values causes a decline in collateral for loans; therefore, banks tighten their lending practices.[34] As the slump worsens, the banks with the riskiest clients turn illiquid and then insolvent. System fragility stems not only from the behavior of some banks; it also grows from the structure of the industry. A system with many small and undiversified banks—such as existed in the United States in the National Banking Era—is more prone to panics.[35] In addition, the absence of systemic shock absorbers, such as bank clearinghouses and cooperative agreements, increase exposure to crises.[36]

A Shock to the System. Research on financial crises acknowledges the role of some triggering event. Financial crises require a spark. The shock that triggers a financial crisis will probably have these attributes:

• *Real, not apparent.* Calomiris and Gorton (1991), Sprague (1910), and Friedman and Schwartz (1963) argue that "real disturbances" cause erosion of trust in the banking system and are the precursors to panics. A "real" event is one that affects economic fundamentals: an unexpectedly large agricultural harvest, the introduction of new technology or some other disruptive innovation, a massive industrywide labor strike, the opening of new markets, deregulation or re-regulation, an earthquake.

---

[33]The problems of adverse selection and moral hazard are discussed in Mishkin (1990, p. 2).

[34]See Mishkin (1991, p. 4).

[35]Gorton and Huang (2002) argue that banks are not individually unstable. Rather, the source of instability is in the structure of the industry. A banking industry populated with many small and undiversified banks will be more prone to panic than will an industry with a few large and well-diversified banks. Gorton and Huang (2002, pp. 3, 6) point out that states that permit branch banking have experienced many fewer bank failures than those states with unit-banking laws (laws that prohibit branching). Also, Calomiris and Gorton (1991, p. 118) argue that branch banking systems tend to be less prone to the effects of panics.

[36]See Donaldson (1993, p. 5), Calomiris and Gorton (1991, p. 119), and Calomiris (2000, p. 110).

- *Large.* The trigger of a major financial crisis must be meaningful enough to shake the system. It must cause a regime shift in outlook among most investors.
- *Unambiguous and difficult to repeat.* A shock is a signal to investors. For it to cause a major shift in expectations among investors, the event must stand apart from the noise in the marketplace. Moreover, the signal must be authentic and must be impossible for a casual participant to send.
- *Surprising.* For an event to qualify as a "shock," it must be unanticipated by definition. Indeed, it is the surprise that causes the sudden shift in expectations that triggers the crisis. Predicting shocks is an impossibility. Sornette (2003) attempted to identify telltale inflection points in security prices that might predict market crashes, but he concluded, "Predictions of trend-reversals, changes of regime, or 'ruptures' is extraordinarily difficult and unreliable in essentially all real-life domains of applications, such as economics, finance, weather, and climate" (p. 321).

The San Francisco earthquake of April 1906 meets these criteria. Research by Odell and Weidenmier (2002) identifies the earthquake as the trigger for the Panic of 1907.

Reaction and Intervention. The shock, in the context of an unstable system, produces a remarkable mood swing—from overconfidence to fear and pessimism. In *The Psychology of the Stock Market*, originally published in 1912, G.C. Selden wrote:

> Both the panic and the boom are eminently psychological phenomena. This is not saying that the fundamental conditions do not warrant sharp declines in prices and at other times equally sharp advances. But the panic, properly so-called, represents a decline greater than is warranted by conditions usually because of an excited state of the public mind accompanied by exhaustion of resources; while the term "boom" is used to mean an excessive and largely speculative advance. . . . It is really astonishing what a hold the fear of a possible panic has on the minds of many investors. The memory of the events of 1907 undoubtedly operated greatly to lessen the volume of speculative trade from that time to the present. (2005, p. 69)

This passage echoes the perspective of a range of writers whose very titles argue the case: *Irrational Exuberance* (Shiller 2000), *Memoirs of Extraordinary Popular Delusions and the Madness of Crowds* (Mackay 1841), *The Crowd: A Study of the Popular Mind* (Le Bon 1895), *Manias, Panics, and Crashes* (Kindleberger 1978). In his classic text for investors, *Reminiscences of a Stock Operator* (originally published in 1923), which is believed to be based on the career of the speculator Jesse

Livermore, Lefevre (1994) wrote, "A speculator's deadly enemies are ignorance, greed, fear, and hope" (p. 286). In his analytic exploration *Why Markets Crash*, Sornette (2003) wrote:

> A recurring theme . . . is that bubbles and crashes result from speculation. The objects of speculation differ from boom to boom . . . including metallic coins, tulips, selected companies, import commodities, country banks, foreign mines, building sites, agricultural and public lands, railroad shares, copper, silver, gold, real estate, derivatives, hedge-funds and new industries. The *euphoria* derived from the *infatuation* with new industries, especially the market bubble preceding the great crash of October 1929. . . . As the euphoria of a boom gives way to the *pessimism* of a bust, one ought to wonder what really happens to the buying plans and business projects of overextended consumers and businesspeople. (p. 268) [italics added]

Sornette argued that the root of aberrant market trends is one of the best-documented findings: People tend to be overconfident. His analysis of crashes suggests that herding and imitative behavior by investors lead to self-reinforcing market trends that are ultimately sharply reversed.

Optimism or pessimism is defined *relative* to those prices consistent with underlying fundamentals.[37] The extent to which market prices depart from those dictated by economic fundamentals remains a topic of keen debate at the frontier of economics. The concept of an emotional market "panic" challenges fundamental economic assumptions about the rationality of economic decision makers. Rationality assumes that prices today reasonably reflect an expectation of prices tomorrow and that markets are efficient in impounding news into asset prices. On balance, large markets in standard assets appear to be rational on average and over time. But crashes and panics are the exceptions to such "average" assumptions. To suspend the assumption of rationality admits the possibility of a great deal of bizarre behavior.[38]

In the rapidly changing mood of the market, leadership becomes vital. Friedman and Schwartz (1964) emphasized the importance of leadership in managing financial system liquidity during a crisis:

> The detailed story of every banking crisis in our history shows how much depends on the presence of one or more outstanding individuals willing to assume responsibility and leadership. It was a defect of the financial system that it was susceptible to crises resolvable only with such leadership. . . . In the absence of vigorous

---

[37] See Harris (2003, p. 556).

[38] The theory of rational choice (or "rationality" for short) presumes that individuals are self-interested, prefer more wealth to less, and that their preferences are transitive (if you like A better than B and B better than C, you will like A better than C). Rationality is an attractive foundation in the social sciences for two reasons. First, it simplifies the world greatly. And second, it opens up a number of important and intuitively appealing economic insights. Nevertheless, other researchers in behavioral finance point to disorderly patterns in markets that are not consistent with rationality: herding and excessive volatility, market anomalies, the winner's curse, and loss aversion. See, for example, Shiller (1995, 1989); Capen, Clapp, and Campbell (1971); and Kahneman and Tversky (1984).

intellectual leadership by the [Federal Reserve] Board or of a consensus on the correct policy in the community at large or of Reserve Bank governors willing and able to assume responsibility for an independent course, the tendencies of drift and indecision had full scope. Moreover, as time went on, their force cumulated. Each failure to act made another such failure more likely. (p. 418)

The events of 1907 illustrate how collective action might address a bank panic. Most vividly, we see Morgan and his circle of influential New York bankers asserting "the trouble stops here" with their support for Trust Company of America. Morgan also forced the presidents of the New York trust companies to form their own association to support each other. Ultimately, the legacy of the crash and panic was to nationalize collective action by means of founding the Federal Reserve System. Several scholars have highlighted the important role of collective action as a brake on the severity of financial crises.[39]

Leadership is the decisive resource in collective action. What is the nature of such leadership? Conferred power and authority may be useful, but they are insufficient. Treasury Secretary George Cortelyou had both, but he was distant from the work of organizing the collective effort. Morgan had earned his authority by virtue of his years in the business and his leadership of earlier collective efforts, such as in responding to the financial crisis of 1893. He displayed other qualities of leadership as well: the ability to recognize problems and opportunities; to shape a vision and strategy for responding and to engage others in the vision and strategy; to persuade others; and to organize action. Morgan wielded the instruments of intervention and leadership: superior information, influence, the ability to marshal financial resources, and even coercion.

The Panic of 2007–2009: The Subprime Crisis

What I call the subprime crisis—a name focusing on the origins of the panic of 2007–2009, although it eventually spread far beyond subprime loans and mortgages—had its roots in the collapse of a debt-fueled boom in residential real estate.[40] As house prices began to fall in late 2006, speculators and risky borrowers started defaulting in rising numbers as the opportunity to sell houses at a profit began to fade. The impact of those defaults became apparent in November 2006, triggering failures and losses in the first half of 2007. A liquidity crunch in subprime mortgages began: Investment demand for them dwindled, as did their market values. Mortgage loan originators lost money and/or went bankrupt.

---

[39] See, particularly, Wicker (2000) and Tallman and Moen (1995, p. 1).

[40] A very detailed documentation of events of the subprime crisis may be found at "Credit Crisis Timeline," University of Iowa Center for International Finance and Development, at www.uiowa.edu/ifdebook/timeline/timeline1.shtml. An important supplement is "The Financial Crisis: A Timeline of Events and Policy Actions," published by the Federal Reserve Bank of St. Louis, at http://stlouisfed.org/timeline/default.cfm.

Rating agencies sharply downgraded the credit rating of mortgage-backed securities. Hedge funds that had specialized in those securities reported large losses and began to close. Although the immediate fallout of the liquidity crunch was swift and severe, the destruction of value did not stop there.

In mid-2007, fears rose about the stability of banks. These fears were realized when, in late 2007, banks reported large loan write-offs, closed special investment vehicles that specialized in subprime loans, and cashiered their CEOs. Late 2007 also witnessed the first prominent bank run, Northern Rock in the United Kingdom. Subsequently, the National Bureau of Economic Research declared that a recession had begun in the United States in December 2007. Credit market conditions continued to deteriorate.

To stem the decline, Congress passed a stimulus act in January 2008 that would give taxpayers a $150 billion income tax rebate. These funds arrived in consumers' hands starting in early 2008, where they helped to reduce consumer indebtedness. In late February, a group of banks rescued AMBAC, a mortgage insurer without whose survival it was feared the entire mortgage market would collapse. In March, a run by institutional investors caused Bear Stearns, a leading investment bank, to fail to refinance its trading operations. Over the weekend of 14–15 March, JPMorgan Chase agreed to acquire Bear Stearns with support against loan losses from the U.S. Federal Reserve. The following month, three large institutions (Citigroup, Wachovia Corporation, and Washington Mutual) started efforts to raise capital from private investors—another clear indication of distress among the world's most prominent and, presumably, most solid financial institutions.

Through mid-2008, rising mortgage defaults and deteriorating mortgage values put more pressure on financial institutions. Rating agencies downgraded the credit rating of the mortgage insurers MBIA and AMBAC. The U.S. Treasury and Securities and Exchange Commission (SEC) took action to relieve pressures on Fannie Mae and Freddie Mac, the government-sponsored mortgage investors, who were the focus of intense rumors of instability. The Federal Deposit Insurance Corporation seized IndyMac, a large California-based financial institution.

In early August, the Federal Open Market Committee, a unit of the Fed, indicated its alarm when it declared that "the downside risks to growth have increased appreciably."[41] The credit crisis was not limited strictly to mortgages. Banks simply exited from the intercorporate loan market and waited to see which counterparties were solvent and would survive the crisis. Measures of lender anxiety, such as risk premiums and the premium for credit default swaps, skyrocketed. In Mufson (2008), Mohamed A. El-Erian, a prominent investment manager, asserted that the money market among corporations—the commercial paper market—had "essentially shut down."

---

[41]Quoted from a press release of the Federal Open Market Committee, Federal Reserve Board (17 August 2008).

In September 2008, the crisis intensified: Investor confidence plummeted, credit market liquidity evaporated, and institutions crumbled. The U.S. government assumed direct control (called "conservatorship") of Fannie Mae and Freddie Mac, in effect nationalizing $5 trillion of mortgage loans.[42] On 15 September, Lehman Brothers, one of the largest investment banks, declared bankruptcy, having failed to find an investor, a buyer, or government guarantees. The failure of Lehman and the government's determination not to rescue the firm sharply raised investor fears. In response, the stock market plummeted, reaching levels of volatility not seen since the 1930s, with the exception of the single day 19 October 1987.

Also, on 15 September, Merrill Lynch, by some measures the largest investment bank, agreed to be acquired by Bank of America. On 16 September, the government extended an emergency loan to American International Group (AIG), a large insurance and financial services company; in October, more loans were extended to AIG; in November, the government announced it would buy stock in the company, effectively nationalizing it. On 19 September, Wells Fargo Bank announced that it would acquire Wachovia, a bank with sizable exposure to mortgage loans, creating the second-largest bank in the United States by deposits.[43] And on that same day, the Fed and Treasury announced measures to support money market mutual funds, some of which were invested in the commercial paper of Lehman Brothers rather than the top-quality commercial paper and Treasury bills that had traditionally been held by these supposedly ultra-safe funds. On 22 September, Goldman Sachs and Morgan Stanley, the two remaining large independent investment banks, announced that they were applying to become bank holding companies—a declaration that marked the end of the large integrated investment banks in the United States. Finally, on 25 September, regulators closed Washington Mutual Bank and sold its operations to JPMorgan Chase. Within a few short weeks, the entire financial services industry in the United States was radically transformed—probably forever.

Politicians and policymakers struggled to find a response that would restore confidence and calm. On 3 October, Congress enacted a $700 billion Troubled Asset Relief Program (TARP) for the purpose of buying "troubled assets" (such as subprime mortgages) and investing in financial institutions. A storm of criticism ensued. Six weeks later, the Treasury announced that it would not buy troubled assets after all and instead would only invest to rescue tottering institutions.

---

[42]The estimate of mortgage loans nationalized is from CNNMoney.com, accessed at http://money.cnn.com/2008/09/07/news/companies/fannie_freddie/index.htm?postversion=2008090711 on 7 September 2008.

[43]Data on ranking of bank size by deposits drawn from *Infoplease*, at www.infoplease.com/ipa/A0763206.html.

Meanwhile, the subprime crisis continued to spread globally. The United Kingdom nationalized Bradford and Bingeley Bank, a large retail institution. Iceland seized its largest banks and then obtained an emergency loan from the International Monetary Fund to prop up the króna. Pakistan and Turkey obtained emergency loans. European regulators nationalized Fortis; Germany rescued Hypobank; and the Dutch rescued Aegon; in Japan, Yamato Life Insurance Company filed for bankruptcy—all were large financial institutions. The Russian stock exchange was closed for several days to stem panic selling, and many countries announced programs of government spending to stimulate their economies.

November and December 2008 revealed more restructuring of the U.S. financial sector. Citigroup was rescued by joint action of several government agencies with a package of guarantees, liquidity access, and capital. CIT Group, a consumer finance concern, applied to become a bank holding company, as did General Motors Acceptance Corporation. The big three U.S. automakers appealed to Congress for emergency financing and were denied, but the Treasury agreed to extend emergency loans under the TARP.

By the end of 2008, the financial crisis had affected markets, industries, and the assets of millions of investors and depositors. Damage inflicted by the subprime crisis was enormous. The Conference Board's index of consumer confidence had plummeted from a peak of 112.6 (on 31 July 2007) to just 38 at the end of 2008.[44] The contraction was spreading deep into the real economy. The ISM Business Activity Index had fallen to a 26-year low of 32.4[45] from a peak of 60.7 in June 2007.[46] Unemployment had risen from 4.5 percent in June 2007 to 6.7 percent at November 2008.[47] Financial commitments made by the U.S. government to fight the crisis stood at $8.2 trillion; of these, the government had actually disbursed $3.9 trillion.[48] Financial support by the government extended farther into the private sector than at any time since the Great Depression. The Treasury had purchased a total of $229 billion in the preferred stock of 209 financial institutions[49] and had

---

[44]Consumer confidence data are from www.conference-board.org/economics/Consumer Confidence.cfm.

[45]ISM Business Activity Index data are for December 2008 and are drawn from ISM Report on Business, at Wall Street Journal, http://online.wsj.com/article/SB123090812392149093.html.

[46]ISM Business Activity Index from *ISM Report on Business* June 2007, at www.ism.ws/files/ISMReport/ROB072007.pdf.

[47]Unemployment data from the Bureau of Labor Statistics, at www.bls.gov/.

[48]Data for U.S. government commitments in fighting the crisis drawn from "Parsing the Bailout," *Washington Post* (26 November 2008):A10.

[49]Data from the U.S. Federal Reserve, "The Financial Crisis: A Timeline of Events and Policy Actions" (31 December 2008).

invested $151 billion in nonbank corporations,[50] yielding a total of $375 billion invested under the TARP. Corporate bankruptcies rose significantly. By April, bankruptcies were up more than 40 percent from the previous year.[51] Seizures of financial institutions by federal regulators had risen to 25 in 2008 from 3 in 2007.[52] The stock market in 2008 fell 38.5 percent for the year. Globally, equity investors lost $30 trillion in value.[53]

The events of the Panic of 1907 highlighted four aspects of the dynamics of crises: (1) Financial institutions form a system; (2) the system grows unstable; (3) a shock occurs; (4) response proves to be inadequate. Consider how these elements map onto the events of the subprime crisis.

Financial Institutions Form a Complex System. By late 2006, the global financial system had grown extraordinarily complex in terms of the interdependencies that created the system.[54] This complexity made it hard for decision makers of all kinds, from CEOs to individual investors, to know what was going on and to make intelligent choices. Growing complexity bred information asymmetries at all levels of the financial system.

   ▪ *Individual securities.* Innovations in the design of individual mortgages amplified complexity. For example, a "subprime loan" was a loan extended to a risky borrower, one who has had some payment delinquencies, a bankruptcy judgment, a high debt-to-income ratio, or a low credit score. After 2001, the volume of new subprime mortgages increased and shifted away from the simple fixed-rate structure and materially toward adjustable-rate mortgages (ARMs). Although historically ARMs were just mortgages with a variable interest rate that fluctuated with short-term Treasury yields, the type of ARM that became popular prior to the subprime crisis begins with a low initial interest rate that is adjusted, over time, toward a rate that truly reflects the high credit risk of the borrower. Sometimes called "teaser loans," these ARMs give the appearance of affordability to the borrower who does not look beyond the initial-period cash flow requirements to reflect on the actual

---

[50]The figure of $151 billion is derived from the estimate of $375 billion committed by the end of November, less the sum of investments in bank preferred stock announced by the Treasury, $229 billion. The estimate of $375 billion was published in "Parsing the Bailout," Footnote 48.

[51]Corporate bankruptcies data from www.bankruptcy-statistics.com/index.php?option= com_content&view=article&id=185:corporate-bankruptcies-increase-as-more-near-financial-disaster&catid=84:commercial&Itemid=201.

[52]Data on bank failures from the Federal Deposit Insurance Corporation, at www.fdic.gov/bank/individual/failed/banklist.html.

[53]Equity market performance drawn from "After the Collapse, Guarded Hope for 2009," *Wall Street Journal* (2 January 2009):R1 and from Bloomberg.com, at www.bloomberg.com/apps/news?pid=newsarchive&sid=aYwo1tZqGFgA.

[54]A very detailed discussion of complexity in the subprime crisis may be found in Gorton (2008).

total cost of the mortgage over time. In fact, many ARMs are bets that the value of the house will rise such that the borrower can refinance on more attractive terms than the imminent reset rate embedded in the original ARM.

In effect, the ARM is a string of refinancings, a stream of options to default or refinance, where the strike price is the value of the house. The borrower stays in the loan as long as the value of the house always rises. If the subprime borrower cannot make the higher payment required as of the reset date, he or she will be compelled to refinance or default. The lender, not the borrower, has the choice to fulfill the borrower's request to refinance: If the credit standing of the borrower or the collateral value of the house has fallen, the lender will choose to decline the request. The borrower has the choice to extract equity if the value of the house has risen materially.

These embedded options are very hard to value. Complexity and opacity were amplified by the bundling of subprime mortgages into residential mortgage-backed securities (RMBS). Particularly difficult to evaluate are the RMBS that are further decomposed into securities called "collateralized mortgage obligations" (CMOs), in which various senior and junior debt "tranches," or slices, as well as an equity tranche, are created from the same underlying mortgage cash flows. Like subprime loans, RMBS and CMOs are hard to value and are very sensitive to variation in the value of house prices.

■ *Trading positions.* Financial innovations made it possible for investors to buy or sell risk depending on their appetites. The primary vehicles for such trading were credit derivatives, of which the credit default swap (CDS) was the simplest structure. In a CDS, one party agrees to pay the other in case of default on a specific bond: One party sheds default risk, and the other party assumes the risk. Synthetic collateralized debt obligations (CDOs) are a related kind of default risk insurance that bundle CDS. Insurance of all kinds is based on this type of exchange.

What makes such an exchange rational for either party is the price or premium of this protection and a rigorous assessment of the risk involved. CDS and CDOs, like ARMs and RMBS, are challenging to value. Credit rating agencies, such as Moody's Investors Service, Standard & Poor's, and Fitch Ratings, used computer models that would simulate the probability of default on these instruments; on that basis, they would issue a credit rating. The models apparently were based on optimistic assumptions that produced low probabilities of default; in the words of one critic, this was a problem of "garbage in, garbage out."[55]

In short, the risk of default was mispriced in the credit derivative market between 2004 and 2007.[56] Warren Buffett, CEO of the insurance holding company Berkshire Hathaway, had earlier criticized credit derivatives as "weapons of mass

---

[55] See Partnoy (2006, p. 77).

[56] The President's Working Group on Financial Markets, in a report dated March 2008, stated that underwriting standards had declined. See Gorton (2008, p. 73).

destruction,"[57] a characterization that was to resurface repeatedly during the sub-prime crisis. The various forms of credit default insurance combined with the underlying securities to form extremely complex trading positions.

■ *Institutions.* Complexity grew within established institutions as they founded proprietary trading desks and in-house hedge funds that sought to profit from trading in mortgage-backed securities and in specialized investment vehicles (SIVs)—off-balance-sheet entities that warehoused mortgage securities. Monitoring the risk position of the entire institution proved daunting, and the task of doing so was often assigned to a specialist in risk management. One such manager, Richard Bookstaber (2007), wrote, "My great concern was that the sheer complexity of Citigroup would add so much structural uncertainty that it would become nearly impossible to react to events that were not already on the radar screen" (p. 126).

Complementing the formal financial system of banks and other well-known institutions was a "shadow financial system," consisting of new and unregulated institutions—hedge funds—that arose to speculate on the expansion, with between $2.5 trillion and $4.0 trillion of capital under management.[58] Similarly, mortgage loan originators competed to write new residential home loans. Securitization of residential mortgages enabled mortgage originators to move the assets off their books and into the hands of institutional investors. The resulting mortgage-backed securities (MBS) and CDOs swelled in volume. The separation of origination and distribution (or securitization) distorted the incentives, created agency problems, and amplified complexity and opacity.

A related novelty within financial institutions was *mark-to-market accounting*, which increased transparency somewhat but also amplified liquidity risk within institutions: As the markets in credit securities froze, it became impossible to tell *what* the securities were worth. Ultimately, mark-to-market accounting would worsen opacity during the panic rather than improve transparency.

■ *Markets.* The placement of U.S. residential mortgage-backed securities spread worldwide. RMBS came to rest in pension funds, the portfolios of a village in Norway, and banks in Germany, France, Switzerland, and Australia. Like a game of Old Maid on a massive scale, it became impossible to tell who held the fatal cards. The global financial system in the 21st century grew vastly larger and more complicated owing to economic development, globalization, trade liberalization, technological innovation, proliferation of products and services, entry of new players (such as hedge funds and institutions from emerging countries), cross-listing of securities among global markets, arbitrage among markets, and other factors.

---

[57]See Management Letter to Shareholders of Berkshire Hathaway (21 February 2003):15, at www.berkshirehathaway.com/letters/2002pdf.pdf.

[58]See *AIMA's Roadmap to Hedge Funds*, November 2008, at www.aima.org.

The System Grew Unstable. Globally, the economy grew rapidly in the years immediately following the recession of 2001–2002. The growth of the world's real GDP averaged 4.5 percent annually from 2003 to 2006—compared with about 3 percent for the previous quarter-century[59]—driven partly by explosive growth in emerging countries, such as China, India, Brazil, and Russia. In the United States, GDP grew more sedately at 3 percent, although investment in U.S. real estate took off, running at about 4 percent per year, much faster than the average annual growth rate during the preceding 25 years (0.5 percent).[60]

The buoyant growth in the United States was partly stimulated by policies of the U.S. Federal Reserve Board, which had held interest rates low to stimulate recovery from the 2001–02 recession. The Fed had lowered the targeted federal funds rate from 6.5 percent at the end of 2000 to 1 percent in June 2003—even though by then the U.S. economy had already emerged from the recession.[61] Annual inflation in consumer prices ran at 2.3 percent, 2.7 percent, and 3.4 percent in 2003, 2004, and 2005, respectively,[62] but it was not until August 2005 that the federal funds rate exceeded the rate of inflation. During this time, then, the real interest rate was negative; the Fed was essentially giving money away to stimulate the economy. Critics charged that the Fed had kept interest rates too low for too long, but Federal Reserve chairmen Alan Greenspan and Ben Bernanke responded that it was not *their* fault: The U.S. capital markets were flooded with investments from foreign countries—a "savings glut"—that had depressed interest rates.[63]

A speculative boom in housing ensued. The volume of all mortgage loans skyrocketed in the mid-2000s, and subprime lending took off in 2003. As housing prices rose, homeowners borrowed against the equity in their homes to finance increased consumption. Indebtedness of the U.S. populace reached record levels: All debt (the sum of household, business, and government debt) as a percentage of U.S. GDP reached 350 percent by 2006, having doubled since 1984. Much of the increased consumer spending that was financed by rising debt levels was for goods

---

[59]World GDP statistics drawn from IMF *Factbook*, reported at www.econstats.com.

[60]U.S. GDP growth statistics drawn from the Bureau of Economic Analysis, at www.bea.gov/national/nipaweb/TableView.asp?SelectedTable=1&ViewSeries=NO&Java=no&Request3Place=N&3Place=N&FromView=YES&Freq=Qtr&FirstYear=1947&LastYear=2008&3Place=N&AllYearsChk=YES&Update=Update&JavaBox=no#.

[61]The historical record of federal funds rate targets was obtained from the New York Federal Reserve Bank, at www.newyorkfed.org/markets/statistics/dlyrates/fedrate.html.

[62]Data on inflation in consumer prices in the United States were obtained from the World Economic Outlook Database of the International Monetary Fund, at www.imf.org/external/pubs/ft/weo/2008/01/weodata/weorept.aspx?sy=1980&ey=2013&scsm=1&ssd=1&sort=country&ds=.&br=1&c=111&s=NGDP_Rpercent2CNGDP_Dpercent2CPCPIpercent2CFLIBOR6percent2CGGB percent2CBCBCA&grp=0&a=&pr.x=78&pr.y=4.

[63]See Greenspan (2007, p. 13) and Bernanke's speech on the savings glut, at www.federalreserve.gov/boarddocs/speeches/2005/200503102/.

and services produced outside the United States. The United States had run current account and fiscal deficits for 22 of the 25 previous years; trade and fiscal deficits were financed by the sale of debt securities to non-U.S. investors.[64] The expansive use of "leverage" or debt to finance various economic activities is a common feature of booms that precede crises.[65]

Of course, the boom had other long-term drivers as well: innovation (both technological and financial), deregulation (in finance and other industries), globalization, trade liberalization, and demographic changes. Like the mechanics of the "perfect storm" of a financial crisis, these drivers also reinforced each other, producing an era of dramatic change and buoyancy. Consistent with the boom were sharp increases in the prices of oil, gold, and other commodities in the quarters leading up to the crisis. This boom had all the earmarks of a "bubble."

Rising leverage in the 2003–06 boom had eroded the "shock absorbers" that had existed among individuals, households, corporations, financial institutions, and governments. Equity is the principal shock absorber, enabling small or even medium-sized losses to occur without affecting an individual's or organization's consumption patterns or ability to service debt; income or cash flow is another shock absorber in that equity lost in one period is refreshed by the part of income that can be saved in the next. The inflexibility, or inability to tolerate losses, that so greatly contributed to the panic in 2008 was a consequence of the increase in debt-financed consumption by consumers and households in the United States. It also reflected the increased use of leverage by financial institutions, especially among investment banks and hedge funds. In 2004, the SEC suspended the "net capital rule" for five large investment banks that had limited their debt-to-equity ratio to 12:1.[66] By early 2007, the major investment banks had dramatically increased their leverage. When Lehman Brothers collapsed, it was capitalized at 30 parts debt to 1 part equity—compared with 13:1 at JPMorgan Chase. The roughly 15,000 hedge funds followed various financing strategies and could lever their equity capital 4 to 10 times, yielding total assets of $10 trillion to $40 trillion.[67] Many of these funds were conservatively managed; others used aggressive investing strategies. The erosion of safety buffers meant that trouble could travel quickly through the financial system.

---

[64]Trade and fiscal data from World Economic Outlook Database of the International Monetary Fund, at www.imf.org/external/pubs/ft/weo/2008/01/weodata/weorept.aspx?sy=1980&ey=2013&scsm=1&ssd=1&sort=country&ds=.&br=1&c=111&s=NGDP_Rpercent2CNGSD_NGDPpercent2CGGB percent2CBCA&grp=0&a=&pr.x=63&pr.y=10.

[65]The research by Reinhart and Rogoff and the task force chaired by Gerald Corrigan (CRPMG III, August 2008, at www.crmpolicygroup.org/docs/CRMPG-III.pdf) point to the heavy use of leverage as a precursor of financial crises.

[66]For more on the consequences of the suspension of the net capital rule, see Satow (2008).

[67]Count of hedge funds is from PerTrac Financial Solutions as reported in *The Trade News* (5 March 2007), at www.thetradenews.com/hedge-funds/prime-brokerage/613.

During the period leading up to the crisis, leaders in government and business had taken actions that elevated the risk exposure of the financial system. Numerous bank CEOs oversaw the debt-financed economic boom. Alan Greenspan admitted in testimony to Congress that he was "partially" wrong, giving too much credence to an ideology based on the self-correcting nature of markets and not anticipating the extraordinary risks embedded in the mortgage lending boom.[68] Under the guidance of boards of directors and a Congress that was cheerleading for an expansion of mortgage lending, the CEOs of Fannie Mae and Freddie Mac overexpanded the funding of subprime mortgage loans. Some mortgage loan originators practiced fraud and/or predatory lending in the recruitment of borrowers to take out "liar loans" and to agree to the terms of financing for housing they could not afford. The SEC relaxed capital adequacy rules for large broker/dealers that would allow them to increase financial leverage dramatically; by late 2008, three of the five firms that were granted this greater freedom had collapsed into bankruptcy or the arms of a rescuing acquirer (Bear Stearns, Lehman Brothers, and Merrill Lynch) and the other two had converted to commercial bank holding companies to gain access to the Fed's discount window (Goldman Sachs and Merrill Lynch). Leaders of counties and municipalities (such as Flint, Michigan, and Hattfjelldal, Norway) approved the investment of community funds into securities they did not understand. Christina Kirchner, President of Argentina, nationalized pensions in that country in a move that many fear amounted to a looting of wealth from the middle class. In December 2008, Bernard Madoff, a prominent participant in New York City's financial circles, confessed to operating a Ponzi scheme with total exposure estimated at $50 billion; the financial crisis accelerated the collapse of Madoff's scheme.

Real Economic Shock. The fundamental trigger of the crisis was the decline in housing prices starting in September 2006, as shown in **Figure 2**. Because the current crop of subprime loans was predicated on always-rising housing prices, this turn in the market spelled doom for both debtors and creditors. But the opacity of subprime mortgage securities also meant that the full import of the housing decline would not be known until it showed up in the decline of the security prices themselves, and such news was conveyed in November 2006 by the Markit ABX.HE indices, which measure the risk of default on mortgage-backed securities. First published in early 2006, these indices do not directly measure the value of subprime securities (most of which do not trade frequently and thus cannot offer the prices needed for a conventional market index), but they do measure the premium or price on credit default swaps on those securities that *do* offer frequent prices. Already by February 2007, the ABX.HE index for subprime loans had lost 30 percent of its value. The ABX.HE index was the messenger; the decline in housing prices and rising default rate on subprime loans were the message. The shock set in motion a domino-like reaction among investors and financial institutions.

---

[68] See Andrews (2008).

Figure 2. Index of House Prices, 1991–2008

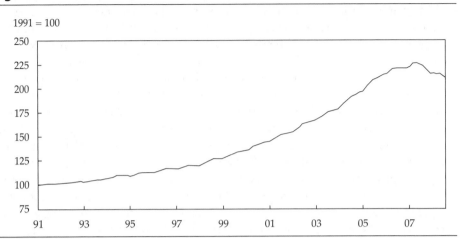

Source: Based on data from "Monthly House Price Indexes for Census Divisions and U.S." data series, Office of Federal Housing Enterprise Oversight (OFHEO).[69]

Response. In reaction to the adverse news, market sentiment changed from optimism to pessimism—at first slowly and then with greater speed and severity. For example, **Figure 3** gives the "TED Spread," the risk premium between LIBOR (the London Interbank Offered Rate, a key benchmark rate of private interbank lending) and the yield on U.S. Treasury securities.[70] This risk premium rose far beyond past peaks and spiked at points of major tension, especially around the sale of the investment bank Bear Stearns and the bankruptcy of Lehman Brothers in March and September 2008, respectively. Other measures of investor mood were reflected in the premium for default insurance, represented by the price for credit default swaps and the volatility of the U.S. stock market. Both increased dramatically over the crisis and especially in the fall of 2008.

Government leaders addressed the unfolding crisis in varying ways. The classic counsel of Walter Bagehot in 1873 was that in stemming a panic, the central bank should lend liberally on good collateral and at penalty rates of interest—in essence, a policy of flooding the market with liquidity. Today, the systemic dynamics of a crisis suggest that more liquidity should be supplemented by improving transparency and restoring confidence. The events of 2007–2009 showed numerous actions taken in these directions.

---

[69] For OFHEO data, see www.ofheo.gov.
[70] TED stands for Treasury–eurodollar, the eurodollar being a term for dollars traded in European or other non-U.S.-domiciled markets.

Figure 3. Percentage Spreads between LIBOR and U.S. Treasury Yields, 8 August 2005 through 1 November 2008

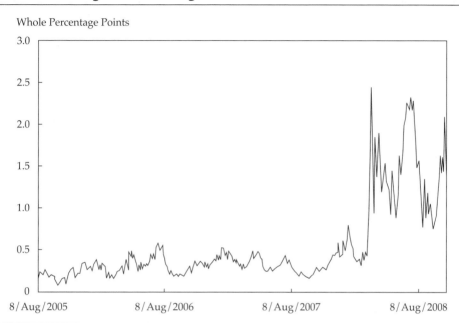

Source: Based on U.S. Federal Reserve data.[71]

The Fed lowered the federal funds rate, lent liberally to banks through the discount window, arranged liberal swap funding agreements with the central banks of other countries, raised the rate of interest paid to banks on their reserves held by the Fed, and as in the case of JPMorgan Chase's acquisition of Bear Stearns, provided guarantees against potential losses in the acquisition of failing banks. The U.S. Treasury aggressively invested in the preferred stock of financial institutions with funds afforded by the TARP and in 2009 dramatically restructured General Motors and Chrysler Group. Federal and state agencies intervened to assist homeowners facing foreclosure. The U.S. Congress passed an economic stimulus bill in early 2008 and enacted another in 2009. The Federal Deposit Insurance Corporation seized insolvent banks.

As it became clear that the contagion of crisis was spreading to foreign countries, the central banks and finance ministries increasingly coordinated rescue operations globally. By mid-November 2008, leaders of 20 leading developed and emerging countries (the G–20) agreed to commence a series of summit meetings, informally dubbed "Bretton Woods II," that would aim to bolster the infrastructure

[71]For U.S. Federal Reserve data, see www.federalreserve.gov/releases/h15/data.htm.

of global financial regulations and crisis management. In April 2009, the G–20 met again and agreed to muster a $1.1 trillion fund to stimulate global economic growth and repair the financial system. Nevertheless, issues regarding regulations, stimulus programs, and system governance sharply divided emerging from developed countries and Anglo-American from Continental countries.

Conclusion

In the subprime crisis, as with the Panic of 1907, the four factors of system structure, growing instability, shock, and response capture a range of interesting dynamics. Rapid growth leads to optimism that for a time may stimulate more growth. Insufficient information fuels optimism and delays collective action. Imperfect information and optimism promote a tendency to discount the effect of real shocks to the system when they occur. Real shocks, an absence of shock absorbers, and a lack of collective action may amplify the conditions of instability. Several conclusions arise from observing how these dynamics played out during the Panic of 1907 and the subprime crisis of 2007.

Financial crises are a recurring feature of market economies. Hyman Minsky, an economist who analyzed financial crises, concluded that financial fragility is a normal way of life.[72] According to Minsky, government regulation may be able to mitigate the severity and duration of crises but cannot eliminate them. Investors, bankers, corporate chieftains, government leaders, and the average citizen should manage affairs to be able to withstand the inevitable future crises. With hindsight, it appears that this lesson was widely ignored. The century following the Panic of 1907 witnessed 19 recessions and 15 major stock market crashes.[73] The largest of all crises occurred in the 20th century: the crash of 1929 and ensuing Great Depression of 1930–1934. From 1934 to 2007, almost 3,600 financial institutions were seized by regulators; only two years witnessed no bank failures.[74] Even in the most recent 25 years, we have seen serious financial market instability in equities (1987, 2002), currencies and financial institutions (Mexico in 1994, much of Asia in 1997), and government debt (Russia in 1998). Since 1945, the world has witnessed 18 major bank-centered financial crises.[75] These are only the major events and ignore a larger number of brief and/or localized events; yet, they all resulted in major declines in asset values, constrictions of credit, and damage to financial institutions. Generally,

---

[72]"There is nothing that can be done to eliminate the inevitability of financial fragility as Minsky defined it" (Kregel 2008, p. 6).

[73]For the data on recessions as declared by the National Bureau of Economic Research (NBER), see www.nber.org/cycles.html. The 15 major stock market crashes of the 20th century are discussed in Mishkin and White (2003, p. 55).

[74]Data on bank failures are drawn from Federal Deposit Insurance Corporation data, at www2.fdic.gov/hsob/SelectRpt.asp?EntryTyp=30.

[75]For discussion of the 18 bank-centered financial crises since 1945, see Reinhart and Rogoff (2008c).

these episodes were followed by contrition and rising government regulation, and unfortunately, such responses proved inadequate to preventing the next episodes. One of the most dangerous statements in the markets is, "This time it is different."

Large institutional rescues seem to mark the start of recovery. The nadir of a panic is marked by the failure, involuntary sale, or seizure of financial institutions, especially those formerly thought to be rock solid. Critics of capitalism have asserted repeatedly that institutional failures in financial crises mark the collapse of the capitalist system, and these voices have been heard especially loudly during the current crisis. Yet, the collective action formed to rescue institutions is like an antibody that fights the virus of panic; in this sense, institutional rescues may mark a strengthening of business and government leadership. In 1907, Morgan asserted, "This is where the trouble stops," and he spent the next three weeks rescuing salvageable institutions. In 2008, the United States and other governments began to intervene massively after the bankruptcy of Lehman Brothers proved to be disastrous, and they helped alleviate the distress of the other large integrated investment banks. Vigorous collective action helps to restore confidence and stability.

Individuals, enterprises, and whole markets prove to be more dynamic and ingenious than those who want to constrain the excesses of the system. Now in the early 21st century, financial markets are protected by regulatory systems vastly stronger than the weak form of oversight that existed in 1907. The regulators and the rules they have now put in place justify a higher degree of confidence in the financial system than was appropriate in the days of Morgan and his contemporaries. Government agencies regulate the entry, exit, and combination of financial institutions; they oversee the transparency of financial reporting and securities underwriting; they influence credit and capital policies of lenders; they manage the money supply, thereby influencing interest rates and inflation expectations; and they provide the electronic system through which vast quantities of cash are transferred. Some central banks are charged with both maintaining full employment and stimulating economic growth. With this much government intervention, it is hard to call the global financial services industry "free-market capitalism," yet this intervention supports a greater degree of freedom to innovate and to direct capital to its highest uses than would be possible without it. Government is involved cheek-by-jowl in the functioning of financial markets. Indeed, government intervention may also play a destabilizing role by creating moral hazard, a tendency on the part of players to be more aggressive in the belief that the government will bail them out.

We should not seek government regulation carelessly. Regulators can become captive to the very industries they regulate. The private sector tends to squirm away from regulators. Make a rule, and executives and their lawyers will find exceptions or a way to skirt it entirely. Private markets innovate relentlessly. This means that, like the general who always prepares to fight the last war, regulators tend to manage the private sector the way it used to be. Like the barking dog that chases, but never catches, the bus, regulators may never catch the wave of new developments in industry. And finally, it is all too easy to saddle taxpayers with the costs of saving firms, jobs, and industries. Are we willing to pay for an absolutely risk-free society? If we are willing to pay the cost, can we get one? Or is a risk-free society beyond our reach because of the inherently risky nature of human endeavor? And finally, would we want one?

There is no "silver bullet," single explanation, for financial crises. The thoughtful person must embrace a variety of factors explaining crises—of which this article offers four that are broadly consistent with research assessments of financial crises[76]—that encompass a wide range of other explanations.

One's perspective on the cause (or causes) of financial crises will have big implications for the actions necessary to fight them. Financial crises are self-reinforcing vicious cycles: Conditions degenerate, impairing confidence and causing investors to withdraw from the markets; their withdrawal causes market conditions to degenerate further. The way to halt a vicious cycle is to intervene, somehow, in the reinforcement process, to flood the system with liquidity and shed some very bright daylight on the value of assets in the institutions' portfolios. Leadership is the vital commodity needed to achieve all this, as Morgan and people like him showed so instructively more than a century ago.

BIBLIOGRAPHY

Andrew, A. Piatt. 1908a. "Hoarding in the Panic of 1907." *Quarterly Journal of Economics*, vol. 22, no. 4:290–299.

———. 1908b. "Substitutes for Cash in the Panic of 1907." *Quarterly Journal of Economics*, vol. 22, no. 2:488–498.

Andrews, Edmund L. 2008. "Greenspan Concedes Error on Regulation." *New York Times* (23 October 2008): www.nytimes.com/2008/10/24/business/economy/24panel.html?hp.

Bookstaber, Richard. 2007. *A Demon of Our Own Design: Markets, Hedge Funds, and the Perils of Financial Innovation*. Hoboken, NJ: John Wiley & Sons Inc.

Bulmer, Martin, Kevin Bales, and Kathryn Kish Sklar, eds. 1991. *The Social Survey in Historical Perspective: 1880–1940*. Cambridge, UK: Cambridge University Press.

Cahill, Kevin J. 1998. "The U.S. Bank Panic of 1907 and the Mexican Depression of 1908–1909." *Historian*, vol. 60:795–811.

---

[76]Mishkin (1990, pp. 26–27) noted that financial panics were always associated with recessions, that interest rates rose and risk premiums widened before the onset of a panic, that the failure of an institution typically triggered the onset of a panic, and that severe crises are associated with severe economic contractions.

Calomiris, Charles W., and Gary Gorton. 1991. "The Origins of Banking Panics: Models, Facts, and Bank Regulation." In *Financial Markets and Financial Crises*. Edited by R. Glenn Hubbard. Chicago: The University of Chicago Press.

Calomiris, Charles W. 2000. *U.S. Bank Deregulation in Historical Perspective.* Cambridge, UK: Cambridge University Press.

Cannon, James G. 1910. "Clearing House Loan Certificates and Substitutes for Money Used During the Panic of 1907." Speech delivered before the Finance Forum, Harvard Business School, New York City (30 March).

Capen, E.C., R.V. Clapp, and W.M. Campbell. 1971. "Competitive Bidding in High-Risk Situations." *Journal of Petroleum Technology*, vol. 23 (June):641–653.

Carlson, Mark. undated. "Causes of Bank Suspensions in the Panic of 1893." Working paper. Washington, DC: U.S. Federal Reserve Board.

Davis, Joseph H. 2004. "A Quantity-Based Annual Index of U.S. Industrial Production, 1790-1915." *Quarterly Journal of Economics*, vol. 119:1177–1215.

Diamond, Douglas W., and Philip H. Dybvig. 1983. "Bank Runs, Deposit Insurance, and Liquidity." *Journal of Political Economy*, vol. 91, no. 3 (June):401–419.

Donaldson, R. Glenn. 1992. "Sources of Panics: Evidence from the Weekly Data." *Journal of Monetary Economics*, vol. 30, no. 2 (November):277–305.

———. 1993. "Financing Banking Crises: Lessons from the Panic of 1907." *Journal of Monetary Economics*, vol. 31, no. 1 (February):69–95.

Duttagupta, Rupa, and Paul Cashin. 2008. "The Anatomy of Banking Crises," IMF Working Paper WP/08/93 (April).

Friedman, Milton, and Anna Schwartz. 1963. *A Monetary History of the United States, 1867–1960.* Princeton, NJ: Princeton University Press.

Friedman, Milton, and Anna Jacobson Schwartz. 1964. *A Monetary History of the United States, 1857–1960.* Cambridge, MA: National Bureau of Economic Research.

Gorton, Gary. 1985. "Clearing Houses and the Origins of Central Banking in the U.S." *Journal of Economic History*, vol. 45, no. 2 (June):277–284.

———. 1988. "Banking Panics and Business Cycles." *Oxford Economic Papers*, vol. 40, no. 4 (December):751–781.

———. 2008. "The Subprime Panic." Yale ICF Working Paper No. 08-25 (http://ssrn.com/abstract=1276047).

Gorton, Gary, and Lixim Huang. 2002. "Banking Panics and the Origin of Central Banking." Working Paper 9137. Cambridge, MA: National Bureau of Economic Research.

Greenspan, Alan. 2007. *The Age of Turbulence: Adventures in a New World.* New York: Penguin.

Harris, Larry. 2003. *Trading & Exchanges: Market Microstructure for Practitioners.* Oxford, UK: Oxford University Press.

Horwitz, Steven. 1990. "Competitive Currencies, Legal Restrictions, and the Origins of the Fed: Some Evidence from the Panic of 1907." *Southern Economic Journal*, vol. 56, no. 4:639–649.

Kahneman, D., and A. Tversky. 1984. "Choices, Values and Frames." *The American Psychologist*, vol. 39, no. 4 (April):341–350.

Keynes, John Maynard. 1936. *The General Theory of Employment, Interest, and Money*. New York: Harcourt, Brace and World.

Kindleberger, Charles. 1978. *Manias, Panics, and Crashes: A History of Financial Crises*. New York: Basic Books.

Kregel, Jan. 2008. "Minsky's Cushions of Safety." The Levy Economics Institute of Bard College Public Policy Brief No. 93A.

Lefevre, Edwin. 1994. *Reminiscences of a Stock Operator*. New York: John Wiley & Sons. Originally published in 1923.

Le Bon, Gustave. 1895. *The Crowd: A Study of the Popular Mind*.

Mackay, Charles. 1841. *Memoirs of Extraordinary Popular Delusions and the Madness of Crowds*. London, New York: G. Routledge and Sons.

Mishkin, Frederic S. 1990. "Asymmetric Information and Financial Crises: A Historical Perspective." Cambridge, MA: National Bureau of Economic Research Working Paper 3400. And in *Financial Markets and Financial Crises*. Edited by R. Glenn Hubbard. Chicago: The University of Chicago Press (1991).

———. 1991. "Anatomy of a Financial Crisis." Working Paper 3934. Cambridge, MA: National Bureau of Economic Research.

Mishkin, Frederic S., and Eugene N. White. 2003. "U.S. Stock Market Crashes and Their Aftermath: Implications for Monetary Policy." In *Asset Price Bubbles*. Edited by William C. Hunter, George G. Kaufman, and Michael Pomerleano. Cambridge, MA: MIT Press.

Moen, Jon, and Ellis W. Tallman. 1992. "The Bank Panic of 1907: The Role of Trust Companies." *Journal of Economic History*, vol. 52, no. 3 (September):611–630.

Mufson, Steven. 2008. "Rescue Package May Not Fully Thaw Credit Markets." *Washington Post* (3 October):A14.

Noyes, Alexander D. 1909. "A Year after the Panic of 1907." *Quarterly Journal of Economics*, vol. 23, no. 2 (February):185–212.

Odell, Kerry A., and Marc D. Weidenmier. 2002. "Real Stock, Monetary Aftershock: The San Francisco Earthquake and the Panic of 1907." NBER Working Paper No. 9176.

Partnoy, Frank. 2006. "How and Why Credit Rating Agencies Are Not Like Other Gatekeepers." In *Financial Gatekeepers: Can They Protect Investors?* Edited by Yasuyuki Fuchita and Robert E. Litan. San Diego Legal Studies Paper No. 07-46, Brookings Institution Press and the Nomura Institute of Capital Markets Research (http://ssrn.com/abstract=900257).

Reinhart, Carmen, and Kenneth Rogoff. 2008a. "This Time Is Different: A Panoramic View of Eight Centuries of Financial Crises," working paper (16 April).

———. 2008b. "Banking Crises: An Equal Opportunity Menace." Working paper (17 December).

———. 2008c. "Is the 2007 U.S. Sub-Prime Financial Crisis So Different? An International Historical Comparison," NBER Working Paper No. 13761 (January).

————. 2009. "The Aftermath of Financial Crises." Paper prepared for presentation at the American Economic Association (3 January).

Satow, Julie. 2008. "Ex-SEC Official Blames Agency for Blow-Up of Broker-Dealers." *New York Sun* (18 September 2008): www.nysun.com/business/ex-sec-official-blames-agency-for-blow-up/86130/.

Selden, G.C. 2005. *The Psychology of the Stock Market.* New York: Cosimo Inc. Originally published in 1912.

Shiller, Robert J. 1989. *Market Volatility.* Cambridge, MA: MIT Press.

————. 1995. "Conversation, Information, and Herd Behavior." *AEA Papers and Proceedings* (May):181–185.

————. 2000. *Irrational Exuberance.* Princeton, NJ: Princeton University Press.

Sornette, Didier. 2003. *Why Stock Markets Crash: Critical Events in Complex Financial Systems.* Princeton, NJ: Princeton University Press.

Sprague, O.M.W. 1908. "The American Crisis of 1907." *Economic Journal,* vol. 18 (September): 353–372.

————. 1910. *A History of Crises under the National Banking System.* National Monetary Commission. Washington, DC: U.S. Government Printing Office.

Strong, Benjamin. 1924. "Letter to Thomas W. Lamont." Benjamin Strong Papers. New York: Federal Reserve Bank of New York.

Tallman, Ellis W., and Jon R. Moen. 1990. "Lessons from the Panic of 1907." *Economic Review,* vol. 75 (May/June):2–13.

————. 1995. "Private Sector Responses to the Panic of 1907: A Comparison of New York and Chicago." *Economic Review* (March):1–9.

Wicker, Elmus. 2000. *Banking Panics of the Gilded Age.* Cambridge, UK: Cambridge University Press.

Wiebe, Robert H. 1967. *The Search for Order 1877–1920.* New York: Hill & Wang.

Tumbling Tower of Babel: Subprime Securitization and the Credit Crisis

Bruce I. Jacobs
Principal
Jacobs Levy Equity Management
Florham Park, New Jersey

Financial products that purport to reduce the risks of investing can end up actually magnifying those risks.[1] In the 1980s, portfolio insurance, which was intended to protect stock portfolios against loss, contributed to the crash of 19 October 1987 (see Jacobs 1998, 1999a). In the 1990s, supposedly low-risk globally diversified arbitrage strategies led to the 1998 meltdown of Long-Term Capital Management and the consequent market turbulence (see Jacobs 1999a, 1999b; Jacobs and Levy 2005). We are now seeing the destructive results of structured finance products that disguised the real risks of subprime mortgage loans as low-risk, high-return investment opportunities.

The current crisis has been characterized by a lack of due diligence on the part of mortgage brokers, lenders, and investors, a lack of oversight by banks and credit-rating agencies, and a lack of regulation and enforcement by government agencies. The low interest rates set by the Fed following the tech stock bubble of the late 1990s and the terrorist attack of 11 September 2001 prepared the foundation for hundreds of billions of dollars in untenable loans. The overbuilt edifice itself, however, was based on structured finance products that seemed to be reducing the risks of lending and investing while actually multiplying those risks and spreading them throughout the global financial system.

Risk-Shifting Building Blocks

Risk sharing is very different from risk shifting (Jacobs 2004). *Risk sharing* works by combining risk exposures in such a way that they offset one another to some degree; thus, the risk of the whole is less than the sum of the risks of the individual parts. *Risk shifting* works by moving risk from one party to another; for example, buying a stock index put option on a stock portfolio shifts the systematic risk of a market decline from the put option buyer to the put option seller.

---

[1] The current crisis reverberates with some of the concerns expressed in Jacobs (1983).

Editor's Note: This is an updated version of the article originally appearing in the *Financial Analysts Journal* (March/April 2009).

Mortgages are essentially risk shifting with regard to underlying housing prices. A mortgage loan provides the homebuyer with a put option that allows some of the risk of a decline in the value of the house to be shifted to the mortgage lender.[2] If the value of the house declines below the value of the mortgage, the homebuyer can default on the loan. Default, however, can entail costs for the homebuyer. In some jurisdictions, lenders may have recourse to the assets and income of a defaulting borrower in order to make good on any shortfall between the price at which the house is resold and the value of the mortgage loan. To the extent that such recourse is available and can be successfully implemented, it reduces the value of the homeowner's put. Recourse may not be pursued, however, because of the costs the lender would incur to recover and the low likelihood of recovery. In such cases, the homebuyer can essentially "put" the house back to the mortgage lender and walk away with a limited loss. This loss is the down payment on the house.[3]

Down payments relative to the value of the mortgaged house are generally smaller for subprime than for prime borrowers. For subprime mortgages issued in 2006, the average size of the loan as a percentage of the home's value (the loan-to-value, or LTV, ratio) was about 15 percentage points higher than the average LTV ratio for prime mortgages (Gorton 2008). Furthermore, for a substantial portion of subprime loans—particularly in the hottest geographic real estate markets—borrowers took out piggyback home equity loans or second mortgages to cover down payments. These borrowers are highly leveraged and, barring price appreciation, have little or no equity in their homes.

Subprime loan default rates are likely to be more sensitive than prime loan default rates to declines in underlying housing prices because the subprime borrower is more likely than the prime borrower to use the put option. Having made a smaller down payment than the prime borrower, the subprime borrower has less to lose by defaulting. Moreover, in the event of default and recourse, the subprime borrower has fewer assets and less income to attach than the prime borrower. If housing prices decline, subprime borrowers—with high LTV ratios—are more likely than prime borrowers to be "underwater," owing more on their mortgages than their homes are worth. Therefore, they are more likely than prime borrowers to default.

For mortgage lenders, lending to a large number of borrowers is a form of investment diversification that can reduce the lenders' exposure to default risk. This type of diversification is what a traditional insurance company does to protect itself against the monetary risk of a particular home burning down; it diversifies geographically among policyholders. The likelihood of all insured houses burning at

---

[2]Mortgage borrowers can also exercise a call: They can realize an increase in the value of the house on resale, or they can refinance to take advantage of lower interest rates. This call may be less valuable for subprime borrowers, however, because, unlike the vast majority of prime mortgages, subprime mortgages generally impose prepayment penalties.

[3]The loss would also include any principal payments made on the mortgage loan.

the same time is minuscule. Even if a few houses burn, the well-diversified insurance company can use the proceeds from other insurance premiums to pay off the losses. Risk is essentially *shared* among policyholders.

Diversification of mortgage loans can reduce a lender's exposure to default by a given homeowner when that default is the result of a specific, diversifiable event—say, the borrower's loss of a job. Risk of default resulting from housing-price declines, however, is unlikely to be that specific a risk. The value of one house rarely declines in isolation. Usually, a decline in the price of one house signals broader woes that affect the prices of surrounding houses. For instance, after the 1987 stock market crash, housing prices fell broadly throughout the New York metropolitan area (Jacobs 2004). The risk-reducing benefits of diversification are limited when the underlying risk is systematic, and the risk of a decline in housing prices is more systematic than the risk of a house fire.[4]

Mortgage lenders, however, do not have to retain this risk because much of it can be shifted to others. Mortgages can be pooled, repackaged, and sold to various types of investors. This process of securitization has been used since the 1970s to reduce risk and increase the funds available for prime mortgages. Since the late 1990s, it has been increasingly used in the subprime mortgage market as well as for other types of loans, including credit card debt. The relatively high interest rates on subprime mortgages have made them particularly appealing candidates for securitization and resale.

Residential Mortgage-Backed Securities. Mortgages are generally securitized and sold through special purpose vehicles (SPVs) established by mortgage originators or by banks that buy mortgages from the originators. SPVs pool hundreds or even thousands of residential mortgages to create residential mortgage-backed securities (RMBS). Moving mortgages to an SPV removes them—and their risk exposures—from the lender's balance sheet. With less risk on its balance sheet, the lender is generally subject to reduced capital requirements by regulators and internal risk management systems. Capital is thus freed up for making more loans.

The pooling of mortgages for an RMBS has diversification benefits. Rather than taking on the risk of default by one or a few borrowers in a given locality, a single RMBS diversifies risk exposures among numerous individual mortgages spread over a large area. The effects of default by one mortgage holder, or even defaults by several mortgage holders in a locally depressed area, are diluted within a pool of otherwise healthy mortgages. The primary risk-reducing mechanism of mortgage-backed securities (MBS), however, is not risk *sharing* but risk *shifting*.

---

[4]As indicated in Jacobs (2004), the systematic nature of this risk presents a problem for the insurance of home values, as proposed by Shiller (2008), and for the suggestion that financial institutions sell such insurance via options (Merton 2003).

RMBS rely on structured securitization, which takes the payments on the underlying mortgages and redirects them—and any associated losses on them—to three categories of securities, called tranches, each of which offers a different risk–return profile.[5]

At the top, the senior tranche offers the lowest interest rates and is the least risky because it is protected from loss by the tranches below it; it is the first to receive each cash flow from the underlying mortgage pool. Therefore, it is the last tranche to incur losses and the first to be paid down.

Cash flows not required to pay the promised interest on the senior tranche then flow to the next most senior tranche (the mezzanine tranche), and so on until all of the cash flows from the mortgage pool have been distributed. Any losses are absorbed first by the bottom, or equity, tranche (commonly called "toxic waste"); if losses totally erode that tranche, further losses are directed to the mezzanine tranche, and so on. The equity tranche is the riskiest, but if the underlying assets perform well, this tranche can offer very high returns.

With subprime RMBS, the protection afforded the senior tranche by the subordinate tranches is usually supplemented by overcollateralization and excess spread. *Overcollateralization* means that the security's assets exceed its liabilities; *excess spread* means that the interest payments on the underlying mortgages are expected to exceed the payments offered to the purchasers of RMBS tranches, as well as any anticipated expenses. Thus, subordination shifts risk within the RMBS structure and allows the transformation of subprime underlying mortgages into AAA rated senior tranches and (for instance) BBB rated mezzanine tranches, with a generally small, unrated equity tranche supposedly bearing the brunt of the risk.

These various risk–return trade-offs are designed to appeal to a range of potential investors, including commercial and investment banks, hedge funds, insurance companies, mutual funds, pension funds, foreign central banks, and individuals. The sale of RMBS tranches shifts the risks and the returns of the underlying mortgages from the lender to the investors. In particular, it shifts the risk of default—and the largely nondiversifiable, systematic risk of a decline in housing prices—to these investors (especially the investors in the equity and, to a lesser extent, mezzanine tranches). The sale of tranches also provides the lender with funds for the purchase of more mortgages for more RMBS issuances.

Asset-Backed Commercial Paper, Structured Investment Vehicles, and Collateralized Debt Obligations. Potential buyers of RMBS include asset-backed commercial paper (ABCP) conduits and structured

---

[5]For simplicity of exposition, this discussion refers to three general categories of tranches, but the actual number is usually greater because senior and mezzanine tranches may be subdivided into ever-finer specifications of risk and return. The basic formula calls for 6 tranches (the so-called six-pack), but one RMBS was alleged to have had 125 tranches.

investment vehicles (SIVs). SIVs issue short-term commercial paper and medium-term notes for purchase by money market funds and other risk-averse investors. The receipts of the commercial paper and note sales fund the purchase of the collateral, including structured finance products. The long-term nature of the underlying mortgages and other assets is thus transmuted into supposedly less risky, shorter-term instruments. In 2007, SIVs had a hefty exposure to residential and commercial MBS, including an 8.3 percent exposure to subprime mortgages (International Monetary Fund 2008).

SIVs also hold large amounts of collateralized debt obligations (CDOs) that are heavily invested in such asset-backed securities as RMBS (Gorton 2008). These asset-backed CDOs (hereafter, CDOs), like RMBS, represent a pool of underlying assets carved into tranches of differing risk–return profiles.[6] Hedge funds and banks, largely through SPVs, pool several hundred individual RMBS tranches to create one CDO. As with RMBS, the risk of a CDO is shifted from the upper to the lower tranches. And the sale of CDOs provides CDO issuers with funds to buy more RMBS or to underwrite more mortgages to be securitized.

Credit Default Swaps. RMBS, CDOs, and SIV commercial paper and notes can be protected by sellers or buyers through the purchase of credit default swaps (CDS). Monoline insurers such as Ambac Financial Group and MBIA sell CDS that "wrap" individual RMBS or CDO tranches or SIV issuances and thus confer on the products the insurer's own credit rating. CDS are also sold by other financial institutions—banks, insurance companies, and hedge funds. In exchange for a negotiated premium, the CDS seller agrees to "make whole" the buyer of the contract if the latter suffers because a default or other specified credit event (e.g., a credit-rating downgrade) causes a loss on a specified underlying asset. The underlying asset may be a particular debt issue, a tranche, or (since 2006) an index referencing one of a number of RMBS tranches.

The insurance provided by monolines is subject to capital requirements designed to ensure that the funds required to cover commitments are available. CDS not sold by monolines do not have to meet the same collateral requirements; they are largely unregulated derivatives, not regulated insurance.

Multiple CDS can be sold on a given underlying asset. (In contrast, an insurance company cannot market a life insurance policy that allows multiple buyers to speculate on the health of a particular individual.) Thus, a market for CDS exists, with prices that reflect the perceived financial health of the underlying asset. As surrogates for the underlying assets, CDS can be used to create "synthetic" CDOs,

---

[6]CDO tranches are also sliced and diced to produce other CDOs (known as "CDO²s"), and CDO² tranches are sometimes used to make CDO³s.

which serve in place of actual portfolios of RMBS tranches. The volume of subprime mortgage exposures in CDOs can thus exceed (and did come to exceed) the amount of subprime mortgages actually securitized.

CDS may seem to be the ultimate bearer of the risk of loss caused by defaults stemming from housing-price declines. One point that seems to have been forgotten in this long chain of structured products and structuring mechanisms, however, is that shifting risk does not eliminate or even reduce it. Diversification among mortgage loans may reduce exposures to specific geographic areas, and combining mortgage loans with securitizations of other types of debt may reduce the exposure to subprime loans alone. For the most part, however, the underlying systematic risk represented by housing-price declines is merely shifted from borrower to lender, from one tranche to another, from lender to investor, from investor to guarantor. Although hidden, the risk remains, and it eventually brought down the entire financial edifice.

What Goes Up . . .

In mid-2003, subprime mortgages started to gain ground quickly, with the pace of subprime originations rising from about $200 billion per year to more than $500 billion by mid-2004 (Federal Reserve Bank of San Francisco 2008). At their height (2005–2006), subprime originations totaled roughly $600 billion a year. During that period, they accounted for about 20 percent of all new residential mortgages, a significant increase from their historical 8 percent share (Gorton 2008; Krinsman 2007). All residential investment represented 6.3 percent of U.S. GDP by the end of 2005; thus, the portion underwritten by subprime mortgages made up a rather small part of the economy. Yet, that small part created huge problems for the whole.

In the middle of 2006, as housing prices began to decline, foreclosure rates on subprime mortgages started to increase significantly (Office of Federal Housing Enterprise Oversight 2008a). Subprime mortgage originations subsequently dropped off by more than half between mid-2006 and mid-2007 (Federal Reserve Bank of San Francisco 2008). Major subprime-related problems became apparent in a number of markets in mid-2007, but these troubles proved to be merely the preface to the autumn of 2008.

The construction of the great tower of RMBS, CDOs, SIVs, and CDS and its subsequent collapse are inextricably linked to the underlying subprime market and integral elements of the subprime crisis. Much like portfolio insurance's required sale of stocks in 1987 and the forced unwinding of arbitrage positions undertaken by Long-Term Capital Management in 1998, the structured finance instruments and mechanisms that manipulated the cash flows to and from mortgage loans formed a positive-feedback system that magnified underlying trends and their effects. The disconnect between the relatively high returns offered by subprime mortgage-based products and their perceived low risk fueled demand for the products, thereby increasing funding for mortgages, facilitating home purchases, and raising housing prices. The complexity and opacity of the instruments and mechanisms and the web of interrelationships they constructed between firms and between markets magnified the effects.

The Rise of Subprime. Subprime mortgages offered higher interest rates than did prime mortgages. Initial fixed rates on subprime mortgages were roughly 200 bps higher than rates on fixed prime mortgages (Federal Reserve Bank of San Francisco 2008).[7] The rate differential, especially meaningful in a low-interest-rate environment, allowed RMBS and CDO packagers to retain or improve their profit margins while offering competitive returns on both senior and mezzanine tranches of their securitizations. Subprime loans thus proved extremely attractive both as candidates for securitization and as investments.

Securitization became a major profit source for financial intermediaries and came to be viewed as an indispensable source of yield enhancement for most asset managers (Ashcraft and Schuermann 2008). Citigroup—with fees of 0.4–2.5 percent on securitizations of more than $20 billion in 2005 (up from $6.3 billion in 2003)—reportedly made hundreds of millions of dollars in securitization fees alone that year (Dash and Creswell 2008). UBS's postmortem of its 2007 write-downs on subprime investments noted that the consultant that was brought in to hone the firm's broad business plan had recommended

> that UBS selectively invest in developing certain areas of its business to close key product gaps, including in Credit, Rates, MBS Subprime and Adjustable Rate Mortgage products . . ., Commodities and Emerging Markets. ABS [asset-backed securities], MBS, and ARMs [adjustable-rate mortgages] . . . were specifically identified. (UBS 2008)

Securitization of subprime mortgages became an ever-larger portion of the ABS market. In 2001, subprime mortgages accounted for less than 9 percent of mortgages issued and about 6.5 percent of MBS; by 2005, subprime made up more than 22 percent of mortgages and almost 23 percent of MBS (Ashcraft and Schuermann 2008). Subprime mortgages proved to be particularly popular CDO ingredients. According to one credit-rating agency, as a share of the collateral pools of CDOs, subprime RMBS grew from 43.3 percent in 2003 to 71.3 percent in 2006 (Securities and Exchange Commission 2008).

The popularity of subprime products was epitomized by the mushrooming growth of new entrants into the mortgage origination field. Many of these entrants, including more than 50,000 independent brokers, were not subject to federal supervision (Gramlich 2007). Most were dependent for their financing on the capital markets (i.e., securitization or selling mortgages for securitization) rather

---

[7]Subprime rates were generally fixed for the first two or three years and were then floated at some spread (usually about 6 percentage points) over LIBOR.

than deposits (Gorton 2008). Commercial and investment banks bought up these new originators to secure their own supplies of subprime mortgages; in 2006, for example, Merrill Lynch purchased First Franklin, a domestic subprime lender, reportedly "to generate in-house mortgages that it could package into CDOs" (Morgenson 2008).

Between 2004 and 2006, the issuance of CDOs more than tripled globally, to nearly $552 billion; more than half of these CDOs incorporated structured finance securities, such as subprime RMBS (Gorton 2008). The mezzanine tranches of RMBS were particular favorites of CDO packagers because they offered relatively high returns and could be transformed via subordination into AAA rated products. The popularity of these instruments was so great that the demand outstripped the supply of raw material. CDO exposure to mezzanine RMBS issuance—65 percent in 2004—grew to 160 percent in 2005 and 193 percent in 2006 (Bank for International Settlements 2008a). The excess exposure was created synthetically by the use of CDS, which, as noted, can be surrogates for underlying CDO exposures.

Shiller (2008) has argued that the subprime crisis is a product of the housing bubble itself and that it was created from a faddish belief in never-ending housing-price appreciation. Price appreciation was a necessary foundation, and without it, the whole edifice did come tumbling down, but the bubble itself was prolonged and enlarged by the mortgage market's expansion into subprime lending. Much of this expansion was driven by the demand for product—particularly subprime RMBS—on the part of CDO packagers and others. One can cogently argue that the housing bubble was the product of an enabling set of financial instruments and practices.

The question is, Would lending to the subprime market have grown, and grown so substantially, had lenders *not* been able to off-load their risky loans via structured securitization? And would they have marketed those loans so aggressively if investors had not been so eager for the high-return, supposedly low-risk securitized products? Was not the expansion of the subprime market itself instigated largely by financial intermediaries' desire for the underlying high-yield products, which they could transform into even more profitable structured products?

This dynamic created a trend-reinforcing, positive-feedback loop. Just as portfolio insurance, with its trend-following purchases of stock as stock prices rose, buttressed the equity market's run-up before the 1987 crash (Jacobs 1999a), so did the interaction between structured finance products and subprime lending help inflate the housing-price bubble of recent years.

Low Risk for Sellers and Buyers. The relatively high yields on underlying subprime mortgages—and on structured finance products that included subprime mortgages—were accompanied by irresistibly low perceived risk, which widened the scope of subprime's popularity. For lenders and many financial intermediaries, this perception was built on their ability to shift some or all of the credit risk of the mortgages to RMBS and CDO buyers. For those buyers, risk perception was distorted by several factors.

Diversification offered some protection. Structured finance products were more diversified than their underlying mortgages. After all, RMBS might hold thousands of mortgages, and CDOs might hold hundreds of RMBS. The structured instruments seemed to offer smoother payouts because the effects of refinancings and defaults were more diversified (Gerardi, Lehnert, Sherlund, and Willen 2008). Furthermore, CDOs with subprime RMBS were often perceived as more diversified than the underlying RMBS because the CDO tranches were backed by more geographically diverse mortgage pools (Criado and Van Rixtel 2008). The pooling of the mortgages also afforded RMBS and CDO buyers some protection against adverse selection, whereby sellers with superior information could cherry-pick mortgages, securitizing the least attractive ones for sale and retaining the best.[8]

The structured securitization process offered another layer of protection. The extent of overcollateralization and excess spread and the relative sizes of the tranches were designed to allow for an anticipated level of losses on cash flows from borrowers. Losses exceeding this level were absorbed by sequential tranches from the bottom up. The AAA tranche (or, in some cases, a super senior AAA tranche above it) appeared to be very well protected from loss caused by default. Through the magic of subordination, underlying subprime loans were transformed into AAA rated RMBS tranches and underlying BBB rated RMBS tranches were transformed into AAA rated CDO tranches.

Credit-rating agencies played a crucial role in the success of subprime mortgage securitization, inasmuch as their ratings came to be viewed as virtual guarantees of investment quality. Many potential investors—including insurance companies, mutual funds, pension funds, and third-party banks—desired the highest ratings on their investments. Money market funds required AAA ratings on any ABCP and SIV paper they purchased.

The process by which ratings are assigned by third-party credit-rating agencies (e.g., Moody's Investors Service, Standard & Poor's, and Fitch) starts with the subordination schedules (including overcollateralization and excess spread) submitted by the structured product packagers. According to postcrisis reports from the U.S. Securities and Exchange Commission, or SEC, these agencies perform stress tests to determine default rates and apply predicted recovery rates in the event of default (Securities and Exchange Commission 2008). They look at the individual mortgages underlying an RMBS, including each loan's principal amount, its geographic location, the borrower's credit history, the loan amount in relation to the value of the property, and the type of loan. For CDOs, however, the agencies routinely analyze the underlying RMBS tranches but not the original mortgages.

---

[8]Keys, Mukherjee, Seru, and Vig (2008) modeled securitization of mortgage loans and found that investors were not well protected in this regard: Mortgages likely to be chosen for securitization defaulted at a rate 10–25 percent higher than did mortgages with similar characteristics but a lower probability of being securitized.

Unlike the agencies' analyses of corporate bonds, which rely heavily on fundamental factors and company histories, analyses of structured products are dependent on financial modeling (Bank for International Settlements 2008b). None of the credit-rating agencies examined by the Securities and Exchange Commission (2008) had specific written procedures for rating subprime instruments, as opposed to other MBS and CDOs.

Structured product providers used CDS to solidify or bolster credit ratings; structured product purchasers used CDS to hedge their investments. Monolines insured about $125 billion of super senior tranches of CDOs containing subprime RMBS (Bank for International Settlements 2008a). Monoline insurance of structured products carried AAA ratings, in line with the insurers' credit ratings. Collateral requirements for CDO insurance products, however, were set in line with the monolines' other basic product, municipal bond insurance, which meant that the value of the insurance could be up to 150 times the value of the underlying collateral (Crouhy, Jarrow, and Turnbull 2008).

A final fallback for structured products was the ability to sell them if worse came to worst. By the end of 2006, for example, many institutions purchasing subprime mortgages or mortgage pools were starting to recognize the increased risk of the underlying loans and requiring sellers to contract to buy back loans that defaulted within three months of purchase (Krinsman 2007). But most arrangements were much less formal. Securitization appeared to transform illiquid assets—individual loans—into more liquid, transferable assets—namely, MBS (Criado and Van Rixtel 2008)—and investors seemed to rely on their ability to tap this liquidity as needed. SIV commercial paper purchasers perceived their investments as very liquid, even though the underlying collateral had much longer maturities than the commercial paper.

The belief that one can get out before everyone else is what helps sustain bubbles, including the tech stock bubble (Jacobs 2000). Thus, investors may have thought themselves well positioned; by early 2007, thanks to such instruments as RMBS, CDOs, and CDS, markets for mortgages appeared to be more liquid than ever.

High Risk for the System. The RMBS, SIVs, CDOs, and CDS may have appeared to reduce risks for individual market participants—such as the lenders that made the mortgage loans, the banks that structured them into RMBS and SIVs, the investment banks that held CDOs, and the investors that purchased ABCP—but these instruments ended up increasing risk for the entire financial sector and the economy. They did so by facilitating an increase in leverage—underwritten by the expansion of balance sheets and perceived reduction in risk that structured finance instruments and vehicles enabled—and an extension of the funding sources beyond the leveraged financial sector and well beyond U.S. borders.

In 2007, about 40 percent of subprime mortgage exposure—50 percent if government-sponsored Fannie Mae (Federal National Mortgage Association) and Freddie Mac (Federal Home Loan Mortgage Association) mortgages are included—was held by U.S. leveraged financial institutions, mostly commercial and investment banks and hedge funds (Greenlaw, Hatzius, Kashyap, and Shin 2008). These institutions tend to increase their leverage levels as their measured risk levels fall (Adrian and Shin 2008). For banks, leverage and risk are limited by capital requirements set by such authorities as the Bank for International Settlements (BIS) and/or by such internal risk management systems as value at risk (VaR). In general, however, the lower the measured risk of an entity's assets, the higher the level of leverage it can support. Thus, low risk leads to high leverage (in the ratio of total assets to equity).

Securitization enabled financial institutions to free up capital for lending, to pass the riskier portions of their mortgage loans on to investors, to earn profits on the sales, and to retain low-risk products for their own portfolios. The imprimatur of agencies' credit ratings and the protection offered by monoline insurers and other CDS sellers enhanced the perception that subprime mortgage loans and structured finance products based on subprime mortgages were low risk. In fact, the spread between subprime and prime mortgage rates declined by almost 250 bps between 2001 and mid-2004; per unit of risk, the spread declined even more and for longer (into 2006) as the riskiness of subprime loans increased over the period (Demyanyk and Van Hemert 2008). Not surprisingly, Greenlaw et al. (2008) documented a sharply positive relationship between total asset growth and leverage growth for both commercial and investment banks over the 1998–2007 period.

Securitization also allowed the expansion of funding for subprime mortgages to move beyond the leveraged financial sector to such traditionally unleveraged investors as insurance companies, pension funds, and mutual funds. These incremental sources of credit increased the supply of funding for subprime loans. At the same time, an expansion in the loan supply was perceived as an increase in funding liquidity, which reduced the perception of risk and the probability of default. This situation, in turn, resulted in further expansion of the credit supply, more lending, lower perceived risk and default probabilities, and so on (Shin 2009). So, the positive feedback initiated by the demand for subprime mortgages and structured finance products was reinforced by the enlargement of funding.

Of course, the entire leveraged system rested on a shaky foundation: loans to high-risk borrowers. Furthermore, subprime loans had themselves become increasingly leveraged, with LTV ratios rising more than 6 percentage points between 2001 and 2006 (Demyanyk and Van Hemert 2008).

. . . Must Come Down

The S&P/Case–Shiller U.S. National Home Price Index shows that the average price of U.S. homes (seasonally adjusted) rose by 10.6 percent, 10.7 percent, 14.6 percent, and 14.7 percent in each year, respectively, from 2002 through 2005. In 2006, prices were essentially flat (–0.2 percent) for the year but actually began declining in the second quarter. The LTV ratio of the average subprime mortgage issued that year was nearly 86 percent (Demyanyk and Van Hemert 2008).

Delinquency rates on subprime loans, which had picked up in mid-2005, continued to build in 2006 (Federal Reserve Bank of San Francisco 2008). Mortgage lenders that had agreed to repurchase any loans that defaulted early found themselves increasingly called upon to make repurchases in the fourth quarter of 2006 (Krinsman 2007), just as investment banks started shutting down credit lines to independent mortgage lenders (Tavakoli 2008). Highly dependent on funding from securitization flows, these lenders started running out of capital to repurchase the bad mortgages.

For 2007, the S&P/Case–Shiller U.S. National Home Price Index shows that home prices ended the year off 8.7 percent. They dropped even more steeply in 2008, falling 18.2 percent, the largest annual decline in the history of the series.[9] Subprime mortgage originations declined with housing prices, falling from $93 billion in the first quarter of 2007 to $14 billion in the fourth quarter and all but disappearing in 2008 as delinquencies and foreclosures rose (Greenlaw et al. 2008).

Positive Feedback's Negative Consequences. Many of the positive-feedback dynamics that had buttressed the tower of structured finance products underlying the housing bubble now helped undermine its foundations. As default rates on subprime mortgages increased, credit ratings of subprime-based RMBS and CDOs were downgraded and VaR estimates increased. The feedback between risk and leverage that had helped inflate the subprime bubble when risk was low now acted to deflate it by shutting down the flow of funds. A given dollar contraction in the balance sheet of a typical firm in the U.S. leveraged financial sector can produce a cutback in lending of many times that size (see, e.g., Greenlaw et al. 2008).[10]

---

[9]The S&P/Case–Shiller Index shows stronger price rises and declines than the Home Price Index compiled by the Office of Federal Housing Enterprise Oversight (OFHEO), now the Federal Housing Finance Agency. OFHEO prices, for example, show a decline of only 7.9 percent between their April 2007 peak and the end of the third quarter of 2008 (see Office of Federal Housing Enterprise Oversight 2008a; Federal Housing Finance Agency 2008). One of the notable differences between the two series is the S&P/Case–Shiller Index's inclusion of more homes purchased with subprime lending. For an explanation of the differences, see Office of Federal Housing Enterprise Oversight (2008b).

[10]As many commentators have noted, the contraction of financial institutions' balance sheets was exacerbated by the need to mark mortgage-related assets to market. Like VaR, marking to market is procyclical in that it encourages lending when times improve and discourages lending when times deteriorate.

The rating agencies began issuing warnings about subprime RMBS and CDOs in the spring of 2007. In April, New Century Financial Corporation, the second largest subprime lender in 2006, succumbed to borrower defaults—one of many such lenders to disappear. In June, two Bear Stearns hedge funds failed, brought down by their investments in subprime CDOs (especially in the toxic waste tranches of the CDOs); one of the funds was leveraged by more than 21 to 1 (Kelly and Ng 2007). In July, the credit-rating agencies downgraded hundreds of subprime tranches. The German bank IKB took a substantial hit on U.S. subprime mortgage investments and required an emergency infusion of funds from shareholders and the German government. In August, the French bank BNP Paribas was forced to halt redemptions from three funds that could not be valued because their subprime holdings had become so illiquid.

As liquidity dried up in the summer of 2007, ABCP conduits began to have increasing difficulty locating buyers for their paper. Mortgages represented the single largest category of collateral, and buyers of short-term paper did not know how much of this exposure represented subprime mortgages (Criado and Van Rixtel 2008).

Hedge funds were major buyers of equity tranches of subprime structured products and were major players in CDO and CDS markets. They were also heavily leveraged. With so many subprime tranches receiving rating downgrades, some hedge funds faced large margin calls. To delever and reduce risks, they sold their most liquid assets, including common stocks (if they held any). On 9 August 2007, the stock market declined substantially, causing large losses for equity investors, particularly quantitative-oriented equity investors, which held many of the same names as the liquidating hedge funds.

After the tremors of August, problems continued in the form of heightened volatility in equity markets and contracting liquidity in credit markets. Subprime RMBS and CDOs started piling up on banks' balance sheets (Sender 2007). Citigroup, Bank of America, and JPMorgan Chase began to unwind sponsored SIVs and take the assets and liabilities onto their own balance sheets, with resultant balance sheet stress and further tightening of lending.

At year-end 2007, UBS announced a $10 billion write-down, largely the result of losses on subprime AAA rated tranches of CDOs held as investments or warehoused for future packaging. Many of these positions were unhedged or underhedged because UBS had planned to sell them, purchase guarantees on them, or sell credit indices short against them, but the firm discovered that the potential counterparties for these strategies disappeared after the market disruption in August 2007 (UBS 2008). (UBS had to be bailed out by the Swiss government in October 2008.)

In January 2008, Bank of America bought Countrywide Financial, the largest subprime lender, which faced mounting delinquencies and imminent bankruptcy. Monoline insurers were struggling to retain their AAA credit ratings in the face of losses on their subprime-related guarantees. As subprime troubles began to undermine the monolines' reputations, the yield spreads (relative to U.S. Treasury securities) on their primary insured securities—municipal bonds—rose to historic levels.

In March 2008, Bear Stearns—one of the major suppliers of subprime credit and still reeling from the demise of its two hedge funds almost a year earlier—was brought down by its $46 billion in mortgages, RMBS, and CDOs. The prices of CDS that paid off in case of a Bear Stearns credit event soared. As Bear Stearns hovered on the brink of bankruptcy, with its customers fleeing, JPMorgan Chase, aided by a $29 billion guarantee from the U.S. government, took over the firm for $10 a share (up from the $2 originally offered and accepted).

In the first of a series of unprecedented moves, the Fed opened its discount window to investment banks and offered to lend them up to $200 billion in Treasury securities, to be collateralized by MBS. Between August 2007 and the early spring of 2008, the U.S. government provided nearly $1 trillion in direct and indirect support to financial institutions. Nevertheless, the banks' ability and willingness to lend became more and more reduced. As spring ended, estimated write-downs and losses on subprime-related investments ranged from $400 billion to $1 trillion. (By year-end 2008, the estimate was more than double the upper bound of that range.)

By June 2008, the three major credit-rating agencies had downgraded the AAA ratings of monoline insurers MBIA and Ambac. This action meant downgrades on the municipal bonds they insured, which raised municipalities' borrowing costs, as well as increased collateral requirements for the monolines. In July, IndyMac Bank, once a major independent mortgage lender, was seized by the U.S. government after a run by depositors. Subprime troubles were becoming systemic.

The government-sponsored agencies Fannie Mae and Freddie Mac, the largest purchasers of U.S. mortgages, had to be taken fully under the wing of the federal government in early September. On 10 September 2008, declines in the values of Lehman Brothers' mortgage-related holdings led to a large loss at the firm, which faced huge margin calls from creditors and threats of a downgrade from credit-rating agencies. Wary of creating moral hazard and public outrage, the government declined to shore up the storied Wall Street firm. Lehman Brothers, filing for Chapter 11 bankruptcy on 15 September, became the largest bankruptcy in U.S. history. On the same day, Bank of America bought Merrill Lynch, another fabled investment bank, which had suffered many billions of dollars in write-downs on mortgage-related products.

Barclays, based in the United Kingdom, eventually bought most of Lehman's U.S. business, but Lehman's failure wiped out the investments of thousands of German and Asian holders of structured notes that Lehman itself had guaranteed. Most significantly, Lehman's collapse set off an implosion at American International Group (AIG), whose London-based subsidiary had sold CDS that "insured"

Lehman's debtholders. The prices of CDS written on AIG spiked, and its equity shares sold off sharply. On 16 September 2008, the U.S. government acquired most of AIG for $85 billion. (AIG eventually needed additional government funds.)

September 2008 ended with the government's seizure of Washington Mutual and the sale of its branches and assets to JPMorgan Chase. A $700 billion government rescue package for the U.S. financial sector was voted down by the U.S. House of Representatives, which caused the largest one-day percentage decline in the stock market since the crash of 1987. Despite the passage of the Troubled Asset Relief Program (TARP) on 3 October 2008, the stock market continued its slide, ending down 17 percent for the month of October—its worst monthly loss since October 1987.

By the end of 2008, central banks in Europe, the United States, Japan, and other countries had pumped several trillions of dollars into the global banking system. The U.S. government rescued Citigroup, once the country's largest financial institution, which faced up to $65 billion in losses—half of which was on mortgage-related assets. More money—up to $600 billion—was pledged in support of Fannie Mae and Freddie Mac debt, and TARP was expanded to absorb losses on small-business and consumer loans, as well as to bail out two of the Big Three automakers.

In the fourth quarter of 2008, the U.S. economy contracted at a sharp annual rate of 6.3 percent, corporate profits experienced their sharpest drop since 1953, and consumer spending continued to fall significantly. Moreover, the recession continued into 2009. The first quarter of the year was the worst quarter for developed countries since 1960; the GDP of the G–30 countries fell 2.1 percent from the previous quarter. In the United States, the unemployment rate in March hit its highest level since 1983, and Chrysler and General Motors had to seek bankruptcy protection. Home prices continued to decline; the S&P/Case–Shiller U.S. National Home Price Index showed a record fall of 19.1 percent for the 12 months ended March 2009, a 32.2 percent decline from the index peak in the second quarter of 2006. Increases in delinquencies and foreclosures spread to prime loans and commercial property (although remaining significantly below subprime levels).

In February 2009, U.S. President Barack Obama announced plans for spending up to $275 billion to aid homeowners in refinancing and modifying existing mortgages.[11] The Fed announced in March that it was buying $300 billion in long-term Treasury securities, with the aim of exerting downward pressure on mortgage rates, and would extend more funds to shore up Fannie Mae and Freddie Mac. Also in March, the U.S. Treasury launched a Public-Private Investment Program (first proposed in February) to use TARP funding, Federal Reserve financing, and FDIC

---

[11] In February 2009, Congress passed a fiscal stimulus bill with $787 billion in spending and tax cuts and the U.S. Treasury proposed a Consumer Business Lending Initiative for up to $1 trillion in new consumer and business loans.

guarantees in conjunction with private investment to purchase up to $1 trillion of illiquid real estate–related assets. (This proposal had not met with much success by midsummer 2009; potential sellers of the toxic waste were reluctant to take the substantial discounts that potential investors would require.)

Some tentative signs of easing of the crisis became visible in mid-2009. The S&P 500 Index, a leading indicator of economic direction, fell to a 12-year low in early March 2009, more than 57 percent below its October 2007 peak, but it rebounded quite strongly in the spring and summer. Equity volatility, which peaked at three to four times typical levels in November 2008, later declined considerably. International markets experienced similar price and volatility movements.

The U.S. unemployment rate continued to rise, hitting 9.5 percent in June 2009, but the rate of increase slowed. And although credit markets remained distressed, with high-yield bonds at very large spreads over Treasury securities, spreads were down substantially from their peaks of late 2008. Commodities, after some truly vertiginous descents, appeared to be recovering some ground. Oil prices fell from a record $145 a barrel in July 2008 to below $40 a barrel in late December 2008 and continued to experience a great deal of volatility.

Risk-shifting structured finance instruments seemed to be risk-reducing mechanisms in 2003, when the subprime run-up began, and CDS seemed to solve the problem of who would ultimately bear that shifted risk. But who becomes the risk bearer of last resort if the risk-bearers fail? As I wrote in 2004:

> It may be the taxpayer, if the government decides that the firms that offered these products are "too big to fail." Often, it's investors in general, who must bear the risk in the form of the substantial declines in price that are required to entice risk bearers back into the market. (Jacobs 2004, p. 28)[12]

Fault Lines. In hindsight, the risk of mortgage-backed securities was obviously underestimated. Some of the blame for this misperception may be laid at the feet of the credit-rating agencies. A BIS review of the performance of these agencies during the subprime cycle noted that they underestimated the severity of the decline in house prices largely because such a decline had not occurred on a nationwide scale since the 1930s (Bank for International Settlements 2008b). Although the agencies looked at diversification among borrowers within mortgage pools, they did not pay attention to diversification among mortgage originators and securitizers. The downgrades of subprime RMBS in July 2007 turned out to be concentrated in the hands of only four issuers: New Century, WMC Mortgage Corporation, Long Beach Savings, and Fremont General Corporation (Ashcraft and Schuermann 2008).

---

[12]The article containing this quotation, "Risk Avoidance and Market Fragility," and its findings were mentioned in the "Informer" column of *Forbes* (see Barrett 2004).

An SEC review of the three largest U.S. rating agencies found that they were unprepared to handle the huge volume of subprime business they were asked to rate in the years following 2003 (Securities and Exchange Commission 2008). According to an e-mail from one rating-agency analyst cited in the study, "It could be structured by cows and we would rate it" (Securities and Exchange Commission 2008, p. 12). Furthermore, although the agencies supposedly looked at data on individual loans, they were not required to verify any of the information given to them for rating purposes.

The 2008 SEC study mentioned the familiar conflict-of-interest problem that can arise with the "issuer pays" model, in which the entity seeking a rating pays for it. Some observers told the SEC that they believed the conflict was exacerbated by structured finance products because of the ability of the issuers to adjust the structures to obtain desired ratings. Those who structured RMBS and CDOs may also have had a large say in choosing the agency that rated the instruments. To date, no solid data have emerged indicating that conflicts of interest led to distorted ratings by rating agencies, but the agencies face subpoenas from several state attorneys general, as well as hundreds of civil lawsuits.

The actions of mortgage originators have also been called into question. In fact, legal actions have been taken against several figures prominent in the build-up to the crisis. The SEC has charged Anthony Mozilo, former CEO of Countrywide, with fraud in connection with the firm's representation to investors of the riskiness of its loan business. And Beazer Homes, one of the 10 largest home builders in the United States, has worked out an agreement to pay up to $50 million to homeowners in exchange for federal prosecutors dropping charges of criminal conspiracy with regard to the home builder's loan practices.

Securitization represents an "originate-to-distribute" model that has long been blamed for introducing baleful incentives into the lending process. The argument is that because securitization allows lenders to sell the loans and thereby rid themselves of the risks of the loans, lenders have little incentive to ensure the robustness of the loans. In fact, they have some disincentive because the more loans they make, the more fees they collect. With a short-term profit motive, they may lend as fast as they can and limit the time they spend on verifying borrowers' claims.[13]

---

[13]The propensity of lenders to take shortcuts with respect to borrower quality could, of course, be ameliorated if potential buyers of the securitizations performed adequate due diligence and demanded quality from issuers. These practices are unlikely to be the case if (1) the potential buyers can resell the products (e.g., turning RMBS into CDOs), (2) the products are complex enough that transparency is impaired (as is progressively the case with RMBS, CDOs, and CDO²s), (3) the buyers are less sophisticated than the sellers or have less information about the underlying assets, (4) the prevailing market environment is benign, which encourages complacency about risk, and/or (5) interest rates are low so that financial institutions are seeking yield.

One study (reported in Fitch Ratings 2007) found that some 70 percent of default losses were associated with fraudulent misrepresentations on loan applications. But many studies have concluded that foreclosures on subprime loans over the period are most strongly correlated with declines in housing prices—not with any measure of lending standards (see, e.g., Demyanyk and Van Hemert 2008; Bhardwaj and Sengupta 2008a, 2008b).

The LTV ratio of the underlying property also appears to be an important factor in subprime loan risk. The magnitude of the increase in LTV ratios as the subprime bubble grew was probably unknown to most investors in RMBS and CDOs, given the coincident rise in the percentage of loans with incomplete documentation (Gerardi et al. 2008). Whether or not adequate information was both available and disclosed, the investors in RMBS and CDOs seem to have relied largely on credit ratings rather than in-depth analyses. UBS (2008) admitted that its analyses did not "look through" the CDO structure to assess the risks of the underlying mortgage collateral. Instead, it relied on AAA ratings as the measure of safety. Furthermore, UBS's assessment of its risk control mechanisms found that its VaR and stress tests relied on only five years of data—much too short a period to capture the last large decline in U.S. housing prices. And the risk models that AIG applied to its CDS failed to take into account the effects of increased collateral needs following declines in the values of assets covered by the CDS; AIG was thus inadequately hedged and incurred large losses (Mollenkamp, Ng, Pleven, and Smith 2008).

Conclusion: Building from the Ruins

Structured finance products, including RMBS and CDOs, helped inflate the housing-price bubble by providing a ready market for subprime loans. That market was enlarged through securitization, leverage, and extension to unleveraged economic sectors. Moreover, expansion of the subprime market was probably assisted by a relaxation of lending standards, at least after 2005, on the part of mortgage originators (Zimmerman 2007).

The expansion of credit enabled by structured finance products—and the interconnectedness these products created between institutions and between markets—magnified the effects of the deterioration of the underlying subprime loans. As housing-price appreciation slowed and then reversed, delinquencies and defaults in the subprime sector increased beyond the expectations reflected in mortgage rates, RMBS yields, and CDS premiums. The real underlying risk of subprime mortgages, hidden for so long by the instruments used to shift that risk, became apparent.

At the same time, the extent of the problem remained opaque. The complexity of CDOs, in particular, made it difficult for market participants to discern which instruments and which entities were going to disintegrate next. The solvency of some critical institutions began to be questioned, counterparty risk came to the forefront of decision making, and liquidity dried up as banks hoarded their capital and declined to lend. The effects on both the U.S. and the international economies have been severe. What can be done in the coming years to reduce the possibility, or at least the malign effects, of the next "tumbling tower"?

The crisis itself has ameliorated some of the underlying problems. The independent subprime lenders that supplied the risk-shifting building blocks are greatly reduced in number.[14] Many of these lenders, such as New Century, are now defunct. Others have been taken over—for example, Countrywide by Bank of America and IndyMac by a group of private equity investors.

The big investment banks are also gone—bankrupt, bought out, or, in the cases of the Goldman Sachs Group and Morgan Stanley, transformed into bank holding companies. Investment banks had basically been allowed to set their own leverage levels since 2004 (Securities and Exchange Commission 2004). These new bank holding companies will have to abide by the constraints set by bank regulators. Of course, constraints and regulations can create their own problems. For example, BIS has been criticized for the capital requirements set by Basel II, which was just coming into use as the current crisis broke. In particular, Basel II allows the largest banks to use internal risk management procedures to determine capital adequacy—a choice that seems to have contributed to the current crisis—and fails to provide adequate protections for dealing with bouts of severe illiquidity.

In late June, the Obama administration sent to Congress a number of wide-ranging and controversial proposals designed to:

> build a new foundation for financial regulation and supervision that is simpler and more effectively enforced, that protects consumers and investors, that rewards innovation and that is able to adapt or evolve with changes in the financial market. (Department of the Treasury 2009, p. 2)

It is a tall order. The proposals include creation of a new oversight council to identify emerging systemic risk; new Fed authority to supervise all firms that could pose systemic risks; stronger capital and other standards for financial firms; SEC registration of hedge funds and private equity firms; comprehensive regulation of all OTC derivatives; a requirement that issuers of securitizations retain some financial interest in the underlying loans; a new agency to protect consumers of financial products; and improved international standards and cooperation.

The President's Working Group on Financial Markets (2008) and the Securities and Exchange Commission (2008) had encouraged credit-rating agencies to consider some method of differentiating between their ratings for ordinary corporate debt and for the much more complex structured finance products. The new proposals

---

[14]Terhune and Berner (2008) have reported that some former subprime lenders have reemerged as specialists in Ginnie Mae (Government National Mortgage Association) mortgages (fully guaranteed by the U.S. government) and are using some shady gimmicks to attract new subprime borrowers.

retain this recommendation. The proposals also recommend that the rating agencies disclose publicly and clearly the types of risk they measure and the methodologies they use so that market participants can make their own assessments and comparisons. Perhaps most importantly, the proposals suggest that regulators reduce their reliance on credit ratings and recognize the "concentrated systematic risk of senior tranches and re-securitizations" so that firms will no longer be able to use securitized products to reduce the levels of capital required of them when those products do not lower the firms' actual risks (Department of the Treasury 2009, p. 46).

Lack of transparency is another concern addressed in the new proposals. The securitized products involved in the crisis trade in an OTC market that is huge, highly leveraged, and virtually unregulated. Given the critical financial roles played by the counterparties in this market, credit failures have the potential to be highly disruptive not only to the credit market but also to other asset markets and the real economy. Under pressure from regulators, the dealers behind the Depository Trust & Clearing Corporation have begun releasing more information on CDS trading to assuage the fears of a public dumbfounded by the seemingly insane magnitude of the notional value of these swaps. Currently, several organizations—including CME Group, Intercontinental Exchange, Eurex, and the NYSE Euronext—are struggling to get CDS clearinghouses off the ground.

The new Obama proposals call for more-comprehensive regulation of derivatives, with all OTC derivatives coming under the jurisdiction of the SEC or the Commodity Futures Trading Commission. Standard OTC contracts would be traded via regulated clearinghouses, with robust margin requirements. Customized contracts would need to be reported to a regulated trade repository. Aggregate data on OTC trading would be made available to the public on a timely basis, and information on individual counterparty trades would be reported to regulators on a confidential basis. OTC dealers and others with large exposures to counterparties would be subject to more stringent capital requirements than is currently the case. These proposals would provide regulators and investors with more transparency about the extent of exposures to credit risk.

With regard to financial products in general, the Obama proposals emphasize simplification of products and protection of potential consumers. These measures need to be strong enough to protect against a recurrence of the dynamics that led to the subprime crisis. Securitizers motivated by large fees sold structured finance products to investors who were lured by the products' seemingly low risk and high yields. This process helped fuel mortgage lending to home buyers, who were happy to pay low rates and/or make small down payments. Increased demand for housing caused prices to rise, providing incentive for yet more home buying and more demand for mortgages. As the pool of possible homebuyers began to be exhausted at the elevated housing prices, however, prices eventually declined. The declines put many subprime borrowers, especially those with small down payments, underwater.

Some of these borrowers, exercising the put options in their mortgages, passed the downside risk of housing-price volatility back to lenders and, via structured finance vehicles, on to investors in CDOs and sellers of CDS.

Put exercise led to losses on mortgage-related products, and the solvency of some participating institutions became questionable. Lenders were reluctant to extend credit, and liquidity began to dry up. This chain of events led to further declines in housing prices, more defaults and foreclosures, and more losses for mortgage holders and investors in mortgage-related products. As with portfolio insurance in 1987, a mechanism that could reduce risk for some—equity investors in the case of portfolio insurance, homebuyers in the case of mortgage puts, and mortgage lenders in the case of structured finance products—ended up increasing risk for the system.

The effects of the expansion and decline in the residential housing market were magnified by the massive amounts of leverage that banks and, in particular, hedge funds used to underwrite mortgages and purchase mortgage-related products. And underlying all these leveraged positions were the highly leveraged home purchases by mortgage borrowers with very high LTV ratios.

Requiring meaningful down payments with all mortgages would reduce the leverage and the value of the put and, therefore, reduce borrowers' incentives to default when housing prices decline.[15] Although requiring substantial down payments would have social costs in the form of reduced rates of homeownership, there are economic costs to making uneconomic loans, as the current crisis has demonstrated. Establishing stricter criteria for borrower creditworthiness and reducing lenders' costs of pursuing recourse would further decrease the likelihood of default and/or ameliorate its deleterious effects.

The recent crisis has revealed that the U.S. patchwork of regulations is incapable of overseeing a world of increasingly large and integrated asset markets. Problems that arise in one market (the U.S. mortgage market) are all too readily transmitted well beyond that market to become systemic economic problems. A regulatory system that is consistent across markets and instruments is needed. Ideally, the system that eventually emerges from Congress will be capable of regulating financial products with a focus on their potential for destabilizing financial markets, taking into account the connections between markets and bringing previously unregulated instruments under the regulatory umbrella.

---

[15] Ellis (2008a, 2008b) found that U.S. homebuyers were much more sensitive than homebuyers in other developed countries to housing-price declines. This sensitivity reflects a rise in initial LTV ratios in the United States, the ready availability of interest-only and negative-amortization mortgage loans in the United States, and the relatively young age of most mortgages (a byproduct of the ease of refinancing in the United States and historically low mortgage rates in 2002 and 2003). All these factors made U.S. homebuyers more likely than those in other developed countries to find themselves with negative equity in their homes, given a decline in housing prices, and thus more likely to default.

Once again, as in previous crises, sophisticated, highly complex financial instruments and mechanisms were devised to shift risk from one part of the financial system to another. As in a shell game, the risk itself seemed to disappear in the shifting. But the underlying systematic risk remained and, magnified by huge amounts of leverage, blew up the very foundations of the financial system and, in turn, the economy.

REFERENCES

Adrian, Tobias, and Hyun Song Shin. 2008. "Liquidity and Financial Contagion." *Financial Stability Review*, no. 11 (February):1–7.

Ashcraft, Adam B., and Til Schuermann. 2008. "Understanding the Securitization of Subprime Mortgage Credit." Federal Reserve Bank of New York Staff Report No. 318 (March).

Bank for International Settlements. 2008a. "Credit Risk Transfer: Developments from 2005 to 2007." Bank for International Settlements consultative document (April).

————. 2008b. "Ratings in Structured Finance: What Went Wrong and What Can Be Done to Address Shortcomings?" Committee on the Global Financial System, Bank for International Settlements. CGFS Paper No. 32 (July).

Barrett, William P. 2004. "Weapons of Mass Panic." *Forbes* (15 March): www.forbes.com/forbes/2004/0315/044.html.

Bhardwaj, Geetesh, and Rajdeep Sengupta. 2008a. "Did Prepayments Sustain the Subprime Market?" Research Division, Federal Reserve Bank of St. Louis (October).

————. 2008b. "Where's the Smoking Gun? A Study of Underwriting Standards for US Subprime Mortgages." Research Division, Federal Reserve Bank of St. Louis (October).

Criado, Sarai, and Adrian van Rixtel. 2008. "Structured Finance and the Financial Turmoil of 2007–2008." Documentos Occasionales No. 0808, Banco de Espana (August).

Crouhy, Michel G., Robert A. Jarrow, and Stuart M. Turnbull. 2008. "The Subprime Credit Crisis of 07." Working paper (9 July): www.rmi.gsu.edu/bowles/Bowles2009/Turnbull_CreditCrisisof07.pdf.

Dash, Eric, and Julie Creswell. 2008. "Citigroup Pays for a Rush to Risk." *New York Times* (23 November).

Demyanyk, Yuliya, and Otto Van Hemert. 2008. "Understanding the Subprime Mortgage Crisis." Federal Reserve Bank of St. Louis (19 August).

Department of the Treasury. 2009. "Financial Regulatory Reform: A New Foundation: Rebuilding Financial Supervision and Regulation." U.S. Department of the Treasury.

Ellis, Luci. 2008a. "How Many in Negative Equity? The Role of Mortgage Contract Characteristics." *BIS Quarterly Review* (December).

————. 2008b. "The Housing Meltdown: Why Did It Happen in the United States?" BIS Working Paper No. 259 (September).

Federal Housing Finance Agency. 2008. "Statement of FHFA Director James B. Lockhart on Federal Reserve Action." Federal Housing Finance Agency news release (25 November): www.fhfa.gov/webfiles/186/FHFASTATEMENT112508.pdf.

Federal Reserve Bank of San Francisco. 2008. "The Subprime Mortgage Market: National and Twelfth District Developments." 2007 Annual Report.

Fitch Ratings. 2007. "The Impact of Poor Underwriting Practices and Fraud in Subprime RMBS Performance: U.S. Residential Mortgage Special Report." (28 November).

Gerardi, Kristopher, Andreas Lehnert, Shane Sherlund, and Paul Willen. 2008. "Making Sense of the Subprime Crisis." Brookings Papers on Economic Activity (Fall).

Gorton, Gary. 2008. "The Panic of 2007." Yale School of Management and NBER (4 August).

Gramlich, Edward M. 2007. *Subprime Mortgages.* Washington, DC: Urban Institute Press.

Greenlaw, David, Jan Hatzius, Anil K. Kashyap, and Hyun Song Shin. 2008. "Leveraged Losses: Lessons from the Mortgage Market Meltdown." U.S. Monetary Policy Forum.

International Monetary Fund. 2008. *Global Financial Stability Report: Containing Systemic Risks and Restoring Financial Soundness.* Washington, DC: International Monetary Fund.

Jacobs, Bruce I. 1983. "The Early Debate." Reprinted in *Capital Ideas and Market Realities: Option Replication, Investor Behavior, and Stock Market Crashes* (1999):301–304.

———. 1998. "Option Pricing Theory and Its Unintended Consequences." *Journal of Investing*, vol. 7, no. 1 (Spring):12–14.

———. 1999a. *Capital Ideas and Market Realities: Option Replication, Investor Behavior, and Stock Market Crashes.* Oxford, U.K.: Blackwell.

———. 1999b. "When Seemingly Infallible Arbitrage Strategies Fail." *Journal of Investing*, vol. 8, no. 1 (Spring):9–10.

———. 2000. "Momentum Trading: The New Alchemy." *Journal of Investing*, vol. 9, no. 3 (Winter):6–8.

———. 2004. "Risk Avoidance and Market Fragility." *Financial Analysts Journal*, vol. 60, no. 1 (January/February):26–30.

Jacobs, Bruce I., and Kenneth N. Levy. 2005. "A Tale of Two Hedge Funds." In *Market Neutral Strategies.* Hoboken, NJ: John Wiley.

Kelly, Kate, and Serena Ng. 2007. "Bear Stearns Bails Out Fund with Big Loan." *Wall Street Journal* (23 June).

Keys, Benjamin J., Tanmoy Mukherjee, Amit Seru, and Vikrant Vig. 2008. "Did Securitization Lead to Lax Screening? Evidence from Subprime Loans." University of Michigan (December).

Krinsman, Allan N. 2007. "Subprime Mortgage Meltdown: How Did It Happen and How Will It End?" *Journal of Structured Finance*, vol. 13, no. 2 (Summer):13–29.

Merton, Robert C. 2003. "Thoughts on the Future: Theory and Practice in Investment Management." *Financial Analysts Journal*, vol. 59, no. 1 (January/February):17–23.

Mollenkamp, Carrick, Serena Ng, Liam Pleven, and Randall Smith. 2008. "Behind AIG's Fall, Risk Models Failed to Pass Real-World Test." *Wall Street Journal* (3 November):A1.

Morgenson, Gretchen. 2008. "How the Thundering Herd Faltered and Fell: Merrill Lynch Couldn't Escape the Housing Crash." *New York Times* (9 November):BU1.

Office of Federal Housing Enterprise Oversight. 2008a. "Mortgage Markets and the Enterprises in 2007." U.S. Office of Federal Housing Enterprise Oversight (July).

———. 2008b. "Revisiting the Differences between the OFHEO and S&P/Case–Shiller House Price Indexes: New Explanations." U.S. Office of Federal Housing Enterprise Oversight (January).

President's Working Group on Financial Markets. 2008. *Policy Statement on Financial Market Developments.* Washington, DC: U.S. Department of the Treasury (March).

Securities and Exchange Commission. 2004. U.S. Securities and Exchange Commission Release Nos. 34-49830 and 34-49831 (8 June).

———. 2008. *Summary Report of Issues Identified in the Commission Staff's Examinations of Select Credit Rating Agencies.* Washington, DC: U.S. Securities and Exchange Commission.

Sender, Henny. 2007. "The Market Whisperer." *Wall Street Journal* (22 August).

Shiller, Robert J. 2008. *The Subprime Solution: How Today's Global Financial Crisis Happened, and What to Do about It.* Princeton, NJ: Princeton University Press.

Shin, Hyun Song. 2009. "Securitisation and Financial Stability." *Economic Journal*, vol. 119, no. 536 (March):309–332.

Tavakoli, Janet M. 2008. *Structured Finance and Collateralized Debt Obligations: New Developments in Cash and Synthetic Securitization.* Hoboken, NJ: John Wiley.

Terhune, Chad, and Robert Berner. 2008. "FHA-Backed Loans: The New Subprime." *BusinessWeek* (19 November): http://www.businessweek.com/magazine/content/08_48/b4110036448352.htm.

UBS. 2008. "Shareholder Report on UBS's Write-Downs." (www.ubs.com/1/ShowMedia/investors/shareholderreport?contentId=140333&name=080418ShareholderReport.pdf).

Zimmerman, Thomas. 2007. "The Great Subprime Meltdown of 2007." *Journal of Structured Finance* (Fall):7–20.

Volatility + Leverage = Dynamite

Howard Marks, CFA
Chairman
Oaktree Capital Management
Los Angeles

Nearly 15 years ago, in April 1994—at a time when absolutely no one was reading my memos—I published one called "Risk in Today's Markets Revisited." That is when I first proposed the formula Volatility + Leverage = Dynamite. I recycled it in "Genius Isn't Enough," on the subject of Long-Term Capital Management (October 1998).

The last few years have provided a great demonstration of how dangerous it can be to combine leverage with risky assets, and that is the subject of this memo. It will also pick up on some ideas from my last memo, "The Limits to Negativism" (15 October 2008).

My memo "Plan B" on the bailout proposal went out on 24 September 2008, and as I lay in bed later that night, I realized that I had not taken one part of it nearly far enough. In discussing a prime cause of the credit crisis, I wrote the following:

> I'll keep it simple. Suppose you have $1 million in equity capital. You borrow $29 million and buy $30 million of mortgage loans. Twenty percent (or $6 million) of the mortgages go into default, and the recovery on them turns out to be only two-thirds ($4 million). Thus you've lost $2 million . . . your equity capital twice over. Now you have equity capital of minus $1 million, with assets of $28 million and debt of $29 million. Everyone realizes that there'll be nothing left for the people who're last in line to withdraw their money, so there's a run on the bank. And you slide into bankruptcy.

That is true as far as it goes, but I am going to devote this memo to things that could have followed that paragraph.

The Problem at Financial Institutions

It is no coincidence that today's financial crisis was kicked off at highly leveraged banks and investment banks. The block quote above shows why that is true and why the problem is as big as it is. As I wrote in "Plan B":

> Because of the high regard in which financial institutions were held; because of the implied government backing of Fannie Mae and Freddie Mac; and because permissible leverage increased over time, financial institutions' equity capital was permitted to become highly inadequate given the riskiness of the assets they held. Or perhaps I should say institutions took on too many risky assets given the limitations of their equity capital. That, in a nutshell, is why institutions have disappeared.

Editor's Note: Reprinted here with permission from Oaktree Capital Management is a memo dated 17 December 2008 that Howard Marks, CFA, wrote to Oaktree clients.

So, what exactly did these institutions do wrong? Here are a few examples using Bank X, with $10 billion of capital, to illustrate:

- Bank X uses leverage to buy $100 billion of triple-A mortgage-related debt, under the assumption that it cannot lose more than 1 percent. Instead, home prices decline nationwide, causing it to write down its holdings by 10 percent, or $10 billion. Its capital is gone.

- Alternatively (but in fact probably simultaneously), Bank X sells Hedge Fund G $10 billion of credit default swaps on the bonds of Company A, and it buys $10 billion of the same credit protection from Investment Bank H. Company A goes bankrupt, and Bank X pays Hedge Fund G $10 billion. But Investment Bank H goes bankrupt, too, so Bank X cannot collect the $10 billion it is due. Its capital is gone.

- Bank X lends $50 billion to Hedge Fund P with equity of $10 billion, which then buys $60 billion of securities. The value of the fund's portfolio falls to $50 billion; the bank sends a margin call; no additional collateral can be posted; so the bank seizes and sells out the portfolio. But in the downward-spiraling market, the bank only realizes $40 billion. Its capital is gone.

- Hedge Fund Q also borrowed to buy securities. When Hedge Fund P got its margin call and its portfolio was sold out, that forced securities prices downward. So, Fund Q—which holds many of the same positions—also receives a margin call, perpetuating the downward spiral and bringing more losses to more institutions.

All of these scenarios, and many others, are connected by a common thread: the combination of leverage and illusory safety, which allowed institutions to take on too much risk for the amount of capital they had.

First, it should be clear from the above that the amount of borrowed money—leverage—that it is prudent to use is purely a function of the riskiness and volatility of the assets it is used to purchase. The more stable the assets, the more leverage it's safe to use. Riskier assets, less leverage. It is that simple.

One of the main reasons for the problem today at financial institutions is that they underestimated the risk inherent in such assets as home mortgages and, as a result, bought too much mortgage-backed paper with too much borrowed money.

Let us go back to the block quote on the first page. Here it is again:

> I'll keep it simple. Suppose you have $1 million in equity capital. You borrow $29 million and buy $30 million of mortgage loans. Twenty percent (or $6 million) of the mortgages go into default, and the recovery on them turns out to be only two-thirds ($4 million). Thus you've lost $2 million . . . your equity capital twice over. Now you have equity capital of minus $1 million, with assets of $28 million and debt of $29 million. Everyone realizes that there'll be nothing left for the people who're last in line to withdraw their money, so there's a run on the bank. And you slide into bankruptcy.

Suppose you set up your leveraged portfolio as described but only 2 percent of your mortgage holdings go bad, not 20 percent. Then, you only lose $200,000 (not $2 million) of your $1 million of equity, and you are still solvent. Or, suppose 20 percent of your mortgages default as in the original example, but you only levered up 10 times, not 30. You lose the same 6.7 percent of your assets, but based on $10 million, so it is just $670,000, or two-thirds of your equity. You are still alive. The problem lies entirely in the fact that the institutions combined highly risky assets with a large amount of leverage.

By now, everyone recognizes (a) how silly it was for the financial modelers to be so sure there could not be a nationwide drop in home prices (they felt that way because there never had been one—but did their data include the Great Depression?) and (b) the terrible job the agencies did of rating mortgage-related securities. So, the risk was underestimated, permitting the leverage to become excessive: end of story. Reason number one for today's problem, then, is the mismatch institutions turned out to have made between asset risk and leverage.

The second reason is that, given the degree by which mortgage defaults have exceeded expectations, no one feels like taking a chance on how bad things will get. Everyone agrees it will be bad, but no one can say how bad.

As I said in October 2008 in "The Limits to Negativism," when things are going well, no assumption is too optimistic to be accepted. But when things turn down, none seems too pessimistic. Today, with the ability to lose money on mortgages having been demonstrated so painfully, investors consider themselves unable to say where the losses will stop.

So, if a highly leveraged financial institution has significant mortgage holdings, few people are willing to risk money in the belief that the losses will be bearable. If a financial institution has book equity of $100 million and $500 million of mortgage assets, no one will grant that future losses will be less than $100 million—that is, that it will remain solvent. Maybe the write-downs will be $100 million. Or $300 million. Or $500 million. There is no assumption too negative. As a result, investors will just keep their money in their pockets.

A few sovereign wealth funds and others jumped in a year ago, and based on results so far, it looks like they acted too soon. In July, Goldman Sachs reported that 52 banks had raised capital and the providers of that capital were underwater at 50 of them, by an average of 45 percent. Certainly, things are much worse now.

Most people are behaving as if there were no such thing as investing safely in a financial institution. This widespread belief has the ability to greatly delay the restoration of faith, capital, and viability. Peter Bernstein put it succinctly in the *New York Times* of 28 September 2008. (Peter is one of the very wisest men around, in part because he is one of the few who can talk about the Depression from experience. I recommend this op-ed piece, "What's Free About Free Enterprise?")

> This time around, assets are evidently so rotten in so many places that no financial institution wants to risk doing business with any other financial institution without a government backstop.

That is the reason why no buyer could be found for Lehman Brothers over the weekend preceding its bankruptcy. No one could assess its assets and get comfortable regarding the status of its highly levered net worth, so everyone required a government backstop . . . which was not forthcoming.

The Right Level of Leverage

Although I communicate primarily in words, I tend to think a lot in pictures—certainly more than in numbers. My concept of appropriate leverage can easily be demonstrated through a few diagrams. I am going to overlook the differences between accounting value, market value, and economic value and confuse the terms. But I think you will get the idea.

The drawings below show the value of companies of different types. Due to the variability of their earnings, the values fluctuate differently over time (**Figure 1**).

Figure 1.

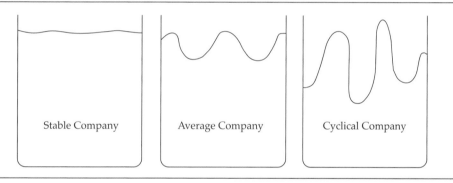

Here is a financial structure, except with the equity above the debt, not below as it would be on a balance sheet (**Figure 2**).

Figure 2.

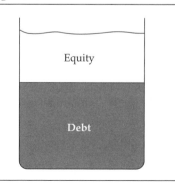

Now let us combine the two concepts. The bottom line is that in order for a company to avoid insolvency, its financial structure has to be such that its value will not fall through the equity and into the debt. In naive and far-from-technically correct terms, when the amount of debt exceeds the value of the company, it is insolvent (**Figure 3**).

Figure 3.

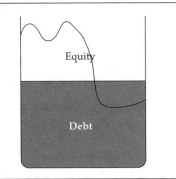

What the following doodles illustrate is that for every level of riskiness and volatility, there is an appropriate limit on leverage in the capital structure (**Figure 4**).

Figure 4.

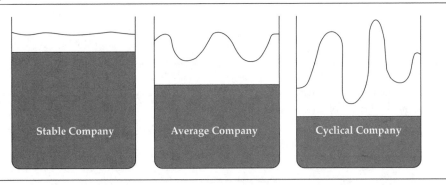

During the first leveraged buyout boom in the late 1970s and the 1980s, it was a watchword that they should be done only with stable companies. But in bullish times, rules like that are forgotten or ignored, and we get buyouts of companies in cyclical industries, like semiconductors or autos.

Extremely leveraged companies have existed for more than a century. They are called utilities. Because their profits are regulated by public commissions and fixed as a percentage of their stable asset bases, they have been extremely dependable. This shows that high leverage is not necessarily risky, just the wrong level of leverage given the company's stability.

It can be safe for life insurance companies to take risk on limited capital, because their operations are steady and their risks can be anticipated. They know everyone will die and roughly when (on average). But if a firm like MBIA was going to guarantee mortgage securities, it should have recognized their instability and unpredictability and limited its leverage. The insurance industry's way of saying that is that its capital should have been higher as a percentage of the risks assumed. MBIA insured $75 billion of residential and commercial mortgage paper on the basis of total capital—not capital devoted to its insuring mortgage securities, but total capital—of only $3 billion. Did anyone worry about the possibility that 5 percent of the mortgages would default?

Leverage is always seductive. If you have $1 million of capital and write $25 million of insurance at a 1 percent annual premium, you bring in $250,000 of premiums, for a 25 percent return on capital (before losses and expenses). But why not write $50 million of insurance and bring in $500,000? The answer is that policy losses might exceed 2 percent of the insurance written, in which case your losses would be greater than the capital you have to pay them with . . . and you might be insolvent. But in order to resist using maximum available leverage, you need discipline and an appreciation for the risks involved. In recent years, few firms had both.

Why Mortgages?

Why is it that residential mortgage-related paper set off the process endangering our institutions? Why not high-yield bonds or leveraged loans or even equities? One reason, of course, is the sheer size of the residential mortgage-related securities market: $11 trillion. But there are two others.

The first is the inability to value the underlying collateral. I feel comfortable when Oaktree's analysts value the debt or equity of a cash flow–producing company. To the extent an asset produces a stream of cash flows, and assuming they are somewhat predictable, the asset can reasonably be valued. But assets that do not produce cash flows cannot be valued as readily (this has been a regular theme of mine of late).

What's a barrel of oil worth: $33 in January 2004, $147 in mid-2008, or $42 earlier this month? Which price was "right?" All of them? Or none of them? We all know about the things that will influence the price of oil, such as finite supply, growing demand, and the unreliability of some of the producing nations. But what do those factors make it worth? No one can convert these intangibles into a fair price. That is why, a few months ago at $147, we were seeing predictions of $200 oil. And now, with the price down two-thirds, there is talk of $25.

The same is true of commodities, gold, currencies, art, and diamonds. And houses. What is a house worth? What it cost to build? What it would cost to replace today? What it last sold for? What the one next door sold for? The amount that was borrowed against it? (Certainly not.) Some multiple of what it could be rented for? What about when there are no renters? The answer is "none of these." On a given day, houses—and all of the things just listed—are worth only what someone will pay for them. Well, that is true in the short run for corporate securities, too, as we have seen in the last few months. But in the long run, you can expect security prices to gravitate toward the discounted present value of their future cash flows. There is no such lodestone for houses.

Think about one of the biggest jokes, the home appraisal. If a house doesn't have a "value," what do mortgage appraisers do? They research recent sales of similar houses nearby and apply those values on a per-square-foot basis. But such an appraisal obviously says nothing about what a house will bring after being repossessed a few years later.

Nevertheless, in recent years, a purchase price of $X, supported by an appraisal of $X, was used to justify lending 95 percent of $X—or maybe 100 percent or 105 percent—when a home was bought or refinanced. No wonder homes valued in the biggest boom in history have turned out to be unreliable collateral.

Second, these overrated mortgages were packaged into the most alchemical and fantastic leveraged structures. It is these, not mortgages themselves, that have jeopardized our institutions. There was a limited market for whole mortgage loans; they were considered a specialist market entailing risk and requiring expertise. But supposedly those worries would be obviated if one bought the debt of structured entities that invested in residential mortgage-backed securities (RMBS).

First question: Where did the risk go? We were told it disappeared thanks to the magic of structuring, tranching, and diversifying—permitting vast amounts of leverage to be applied safely. Second question: How reliable was the diversification? Answer: Again we were told, highly reliable; there had never been a national decline in home prices, so mortgages could be considered uncorrelated with each other. The performance of a mortgage on a house in Detroit would be unaffected by what went on in Florida or California. (Well, so much for what we were told.)

The institutions' write-downs generally are in collateralized debt obligations (CDOs), debt issued by special-purpose entities that borrowed huge amounts relative to their equity in order to purchase mortgage-related securities. As described earlier, underestimated risk led to the use of unwise amounts of leverage. But interestingly, the key losses are not in the riskier junior tranches of CDO debt, about which there was some leeriness. Rather, they are in the triple-A-rated tranches. It is to buy those tranches that our leading institutions took on too much leverage. Once again, greatly underestimated risk led to great leverage and thus great losses.

What did you need to steer clear of CDO debt? Computers, sophisticated programs, and exceptional analysis? Genius? No: skepticism and common sense. In RMBS, CDOs, and CDO-squareds (entities that borrowed to buy CDO debt), 90 percent or so of their capital structure was rated higher than the underlying collateral, all based on the linchpin assumption that mortgages were uncorrelated. That is all you had to know.

How good a piece of collateral is a subprime mortgage covering 100 percent of the purchase price of a house bought in a soaring market by an applicant who will pay a higher interest rate to be able to skip documenting income or employment? That is not a secured loan; it is an option on future appreciation. If the house goes up in price, the buyer makes the mortgage payments and continues to own it. If it goes down, the buyer walks away, in which case the lender gains ownership of a house worth less than the amount loaned against it. Thus, the viability of the mortgages was entirely dependent on continued home price appreciation.

Given the above, what was the credit quality of subprime mortgages? I'd say double-B at best. (I would much rather buy even the single-B "junk bonds" of profitable companies that we have held over the last 30 years than this inflated "home option" paper.) And yet, in a typical CDO, 80 percent of the debt was rated triple-A and 97 percent was rated investment grade (triple-B or better). Those high ratings made CDO debt very attractive to financial institutions that were able to borrow cheaply to buy high-rated assets, satisfying the strict rules regarding the "quality" of their portfolio holdings.

Financial engineers and investment bankers took unreliable collateral and packaged it into highly leveraged structures supporting debt that was rated high enough to attract financial institutions. What a superb example of the imprudent use of leverage. And what a simple explanation of how our highly leveraged institutions got into trouble.

How Bad Is Bad?

One of the prime lessons that must be learned from this experience is that in determining how much leverage to put on, you had better make generous assumptions about how risky your assets might turn out to be.

The example in the paragraph on the first page demonstrates the role of risk in the equation. The more your assets are prone to permanent loss, the less leverage you should employ. But it's also important to recognize the role of volatility. Even if losses are not permanent, a downward fluctuation can bring risk of ruin if a portfolio is highly leveraged and (a) the lenders can cut off credit, (b) investors can be frightened into withdrawing their equity, or (c) the violation of regulatory or contractual standards can trigger forced selling.

The problem is that extreme volatility and loss surface only infrequently. And as time passes without that happening, it appears more and more likely that it will never happen—that assumptions regarding risk were too conservative. Thus, it becomes tempting to relax rules and increase leverage. And often this is done just before the risk finally rears its head. As Nassim Nicholas Taleb wrote in *Fooled by Randomness* (2001):

> Reality is far more vicious than Russian roulette. First, it delivers the fatal bullet rather infrequently, like a revolver that would have hundreds, even thousands, of chambers instead of six. After a few dozen tries, one forgets about the existence of a bullet, under a numbing false sense of security . . . Second, unlike a well-defined precise game like Russian roulette, where the risks are visible to anyone capable of multiplying and dividing by six, one does not observe the barrel of reality. . . . *One is thus capable of unwittingly playing Russian roulette—and calling it by some alternative "low-risk" name.* (p. 28; italics added for emphasis)

The financial institutions played a high-risk game thinking it was a low-risk game, all because their assumptions on losses and volatility were too low. We would be watching an entirely different picture if only they had said, "This stuff is potentially risky. Since home prices have gone up so much and mortgages have been available so easily, there just might be widespread declines in home prices this time. So, we are only going to lever up half as much as past performance might suggest."

It is easy to say they should have made more conservative assumptions. But how conservative? You cannot run a business on the basis of worst-case assumptions. You would not be able to do anything. And anyway, a "worst-case assumption" is really a misnomer; there is no such thing, short of a total loss. Now we know the quants should not have assumed there could not be a nationwide decline in home prices. But once you grant that such a decline can happen—for the first time—what extent should you prepare for? Two percent? Ten? Fifty?

One of my favorite adages concerns the six-foot-tall man who drowned crossing the stream that was five feet deep on average. It is not enough to survive in the investment world on average; you have to survive every moment. The unusual turbulence of the last two years—and especially the last three months—made it possible for that six-foot-tall man to drown in a stream that was two feet deep on average. *Should the possibility of today's events have been anticipated? It is hard to say it should have been. And yet, it is incumbent upon investors to prepare for adversity. The juxtaposition of these sentences introduces an interesting conundrum.*

Consider these tales from the front lines:

- There had never been a national decline in home prices, but now the Case–Shiller index is down 26 percent from its peak in July 2006, according to the *Financial Times* of 29 November 2008.
- In my 29 previous years with high-yield bonds, including four when more than 10 percent of all outstanding bonds defaulted, the index's worst yearly decline was 7 percent. But in 2008, it is down 30 percent (even though the last 12 months' default rate is only about 3 percent).

- Performing bank loans never traded much below par in the past, and holders received very substantial recoveries on any that defaulted. Now, even though there have been few defaults, the price of the average loan is in the 60s.

The headlines are full of entities that have seen massive losses, and perhaps meltdowns, because they bought assets using leverage. Going back to Figures 1–4, these investors put on leverage that might have been appropriate with moderate-volatility assets and ran into the greatest volatility ever seen. It is easy to say they made a mistake. But is it reasonable to expect them to have girded for unique events?

If every portfolio was required to be able to withstand declines on the scale we have witnessed this year, it is possible no leverage would ever be used. Is that a reasonable reaction? (In fact, it is possible that no one would ever invest in these asset classes, even on an unlevered basis.)

In all aspects of our lives, we base our decisions on what we think probably will happen. And, in turn, we base that to a great extent on what usually happened in the past. We expect results to be close to the norm (A) most of the time, but we know it is not unusual to see outcomes that are better or worse (B). Although we should bear in mind that, once in a while, a result will be outside the usual range (C), we tend to forget about the potential for outliers. And importantly, as illustrated by recent events, we rarely consider outcomes that have happened only once a century . . . or never (D) (**Figure 5**).

Even if we realize that unusual, unlikely things can happen, in order to act, we make reasoned decisions and knowingly accept that risk when well paid to do so. Once in a while, a "black swan" will materialize. But if in the future we always said, "We can't do such-and-such because we could see a repeat of 2007–08," we would be frozen in inaction.

Figure 5.

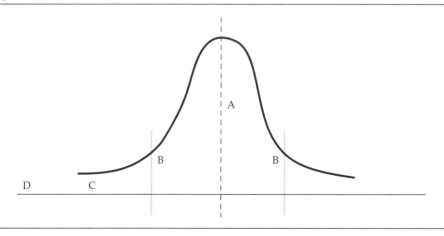

So, in most things, you cannot prepare for the worst case. It should suffice to be prepared for once-in-a-generation events. But a generation is not forever, and there will be times when that standard is exceeded. What do you do about that? I have mused in the past about how much one should devote to preparing for the unlikely disaster. Among other things, the events of 2007–2008 prove there is no easy answer.

Are You Tall Enough to Use Leverage?

Clearly, it is difficult to always use the right amount of leverage because it is difficult to be sure you are allowing sufficiently for risk. Leverage should only be used on the basis of demonstrably cautious assumptions. And it should be noted that if you are doing something novel, unproven, risky, volatile, or potentially life threatening, you should not seek to maximize returns. Instead, err on the side of caution. The key to survival lies in what Warren Buffett constantly harps on: margin of safety. Using 100 percent of the leverage one's assets might justify is often incompatible with assuring survival when adverse outcomes materialize.

Leverage is neither good nor bad in and of itself. In the right amount, applied to the right assets, it is good. When used to excess given the underlying assets, it is bad. It does not add value; it merely magnifies both good and bad outcomes. So, leverage should not be treated as a silver bullet or magic solution. It is a tool that can be used wisely or unwisely.

Our attitude at Oaktree is that it can be wise to use leverage to take advantage of high offered returns and excessive risk premiums, but it is unwise to use it to try to turn low offered returns into high ones, as was done often in 2003–2007.

Once leverage is combined with risky or volatile assets, it can lead to unbearable losses. Thus, leverage should be used in prudent amounts, to finance the right assets, and with a great deal of respect. And it is better used in the trough of the cycle than after a long run of appreciation. Bottom line: handle with care.

I never want to give the impression that doing the things I discuss is easy, or that Oaktree always gets it right. This memo calls on investors to gauge risk and use only appropriate leverage. At Oaktree, we assess fundamental riskiness and look to history for how markets might behave, and we heavily emphasize trying to build in sufficient room for error. But history is not a perfect guide. Although we have made no use of leverage in the vast majority of our investment activities, three of our evergreen funds did borrow to buy bank loans: the senior-most debt of companies, which in the past always has traded around par. Another used it to buy low-priced Japanese small-cap stocks. The companies generally are doing fine, but the prices of their loans and equities have collapsed under current market conditions, causing the funds to suffer. This shows how tough it is to prepare for all eventualities . . . in other words, to know in advance how bad is bad. So, I apologize if I ever come across as holier-than-thou. We have tried to use leverage only when it is wise, but no one is perfect. Certainly not us.

The financial markets have delivered a lifetime of lessons in just the last five years. Some of the most important ones center on the use and abuse of leverage.

- Leverage does not add value or make an investment better. Like everything else in the investment world other than pure skill, leverage is a two-edged sword—in fact, probably the ultimate two-edged sword. It helps when you are right and hurts when you are wrong.

- The riskier the underlying assets, the less leverage should be used to buy them. Conservative assumptions on this subject will keep you from maximizing gains but may possibly save your financial life in bad times.

- A levered entity can be caught in a downward spiral of asset price declines, market-value tests, margin calls, and forced selling. Thus, in addition to thinking about the right amount of leverage, it is important to note that there are two different kinds: permanent leverage, with its magnifying effect, and leverage that can be withdrawn, which can introduce collateral tests and the risk of ruin. Both should be considered independently. Leverage achieved with secure capital is not nearly as risky as situations where you are subject to margin calls or cannot bar the door against capital withdrawals.

Leverage was too easily accessed as recently as two years ago, and now it is virtually unavailable. And just as its use was often unwise a few years ago, this might be just the right time to employ some if you can get it . . . and if you can arrange things so you will not drown if the streambed dips ahead.

©Oaktree Capital Management

The Seven Lean Years

R. Jeremy Grantham
Co-Founder and Chief Strategist
GMO
Boston

Joseph, consigliere to the pharaoh, advised him that seven lean years were sure to follow the string of bountiful years that Egypt was then having. This shows an admirable belief in mean reversion, but unfortunately, the weather does not work that way. It, unlike markets, is almost completely random, so Joseph's forecast was like predicting that after hitting seven reds on a roulette wheel, you are likely to get a run of blacks. This is absolutely how *not* to make predictions unless, like Joseph, you have divine assistance, which, frankly, in the prediction business is considered cheating. Now, however, and definitely without divine help but with masses of help from our political leaders, we probably do face a period that will look and feel painfully like seven lean years, and they will indeed be following about seven overstimulated very fat ones.

Probably the single biggest drag on the economy over the next several years will be a massive write-down in perceived wealth. In the United States, the total market value of housing, commercial real estate, and stocks was about $50 trillion at the peak and fell below $30 trillion at the low. This loss of $20 trillion to $23 trillion of *perceived* wealth in the United States alone (although it is not a drop in real wealth, which consists of a stock of educated workers, factories, trucks, etc.) is still enough to deliver a life-changing shock for hundreds of millions of people. No longer as rich as we thought—undersaved, underpensioned, and realizing it—we will enter a less indulgent world, if a more realistic one, in which life is to be lived more frugally. Collectively, we will save more, spend less, and waste less. It may not even be a less pleasant world when we get used to it, but for several years, it will cause a lot of readjustment problems. Not the least of these will be downward pressure on profit margins that for 20 years had benefited from rising asset prices sneaking through into margins.

Closely related to the direct wealth effect is the stranded debt effect. The original $50 trillion of perceived wealth supported $25 trillion of debt. Now, with the reduced and more realistic perception of wealth at $30 trillion combined with more prudent banking, this debt should be cut in half. This unwinding of $10 trillion to $12 trillion of debt is not, in my opinion, as important to consumer behavior as the effect of the loss of perceived wealth, but it is certainly more

---

Editor's Note: This article is adapted, with permission, from "The Last Hurrah and Seven Lean Years" by Jeremy Grantham, *GMO Quarterly Letter* (May 2009).

important to the financial community. Critically, we will almost certainly need several years of economic growth, which will be used to pay down debt. In addition, we will need several years of moderately increased inflation to erode the value of debt, plus $4 trillion to $6 trillion of eventual debt write-offs in order to limp back to even a normal 50 percent ratio of debt to collateral. Seven years just might do it.

Another factor contending for worst long-term impact is the severe imbalance between overconsuming countries, largely the United States and the United Kingdom, and the overproducing countries, notably China, Germany, and Japan. The magnitudes of the imbalances and the degree to which they have become embedded over many years in their economies do not suggest an early or rapid cure. It will be hard enough to get Americans to save again; it will be harder still to convince the Chinese, and indeed the Germans and the Japanese too, that they really do not have to save as much. In China, in particular, they must first be convinced that there are some social safety nets.

A lesser factor will be digesting the much shrunken financial and housing sectors. Their growth had artificially and temporarily fattened profit margins as had the general growth in total debt of all kinds, which rose from 1.25× GDP to 3.1× in 25 years. The world we are now entering will, therefore, tend to have lower (more realistic) profit margins and lower GDP growth. I expect that, at least for the seven lean years and perhaps longer, the developed world will have to settle for about 2 percent real GDP growth (perhaps 2.25 percent) down from the 3.5 percent to which we used to aspire in the last 30 years. Together with all the readjustment problems and quite possibly with some accompanying higher inflation, this is likely to lead to an extended period of below-average P/Es. As I have often written, extended periods of above-average P/Es, particularly those ending in bubbles, are usually followed by extended periods of below-average P/Es. This is likely to be just such a period and as such historically quite normal. But normal or not, it makes it very unlikely with P/Es, profit margins, and GDP growth all lower than average that we will get back to the old highs in the stock market in real terms any time soon—at least not for the seven lean years, and perhaps considerably longer. To be honest, I believe that most of you readers are likely to be grandparents before you see a new inflation-adjusted high on the S&P 500 Index.

If we are looking for any further drawn-out negatives, I suspect we could add the more touchy-feely factor of confidence. We have all lost some confidence in the quality of our economic and financial leadership, the efficiency of our institutions, and perhaps even in the effectiveness of capitalism itself, and with plenty of reason. This lack of confidence will not make it easier for animal spirits to recover. This does not mean necessarily that we have not already seen the low, for, in my opinion, it is almost 50/50 that we have. It is more likely to mean a long, boring period when making fortunes is harder and investors value safety and steady gains more than razzle dazzle. (The flaky, speculative nature of the current rally thus bears none of the characteristics that I would expect from a longer-term market recovery.)

The VL Recovery

So, we are used to the idea of a preferred V recovery and the dreaded L-shaped recovery that we associate with Japan. We are also familiar with a U-shaped recovery, and even a double-dip like 1980 and 1982—the W recovery. Well, what I am proposing could be known as a VL recovery (or very long), in which the stimulus causes a fairly quick but superficial recovery, followed by a second decline, followed, in turn, by a long, drawn-out period of subnormal growth as the basic underlying economic and financial problems are corrected.

An Amateur's Assessment of the Stimulus Program

On the confidence topic, it would be a start if we could all believe in the effectiveness of our stimulus program, but it is not easy. The situation today is that an unprecedented amount of stimulus is being thrown at our problems, and it is being thrown on a global basis. Some hurlers, like the United States, are more prodigal than others, and some, like the Germans (whose only imaginative stimulus is a scrapping bonus, not surprisingly reserved for their beloved cars) are more frugal. But in total, the effort is unrivaled in history. The bad news comes in two bits: First, no one *really* knows if generous bailouts are a good idea in the long run; and second, no one really knows that even if they are indeed a good idea, whether this current stimulus is enough. What most people, including me, agree on is that the problems we face are unprecedented both in global reach and in the breadth of financial assets that are affected, which is to say everything.

My own personal and speculative take on this is that the stimulus program will have a positive effect on all countries, and in some cases, this will be enough to kick GDP growth back into positive territory quite soon for the most fortunate, in which group I include the United States.

It is ironic, by the way, that the United States would be less hurt than most given that Pied Piper Greenspan led all of us global rats into the river. And, yes, in this case the maestro (well named) had an orchestra pit filled with U.S. Treasury and Fed officials (especially the New York Fed) and such a large supporting cast of dancing CEOs of financial firms and their reckless board chums that even Cecil B. DeMille would have found them sufficient. So, we in the United States developed almost single-handedly the tech bubble of the late 1990s and then engineered a U.S. housing bubble and a flood of excess dollars that almost guaranteed that global assets would follow suit. Yet, unfairly or not, the United States has some considerable advantages in this mess we created. First, we have an unusually low percentage of our labor force in manufacturing and export-oriented companies, which will be the most immediately affected by the global downturn, unlike in Germany and China, to name two. Second, the dollar plays an important role that may cushion U.S. pain by allowing U.S. authorities the flexibility to make their own rules, whereas such other countries as Spain and Ireland have most decisions heavily constrained.

More profoundly, the United States is in a position where necessary sacrifices will simply be less painful. We affluent in the United States will have to buy two fewer teddy bears for our already spoiled four-year-olds. The third television set will be postponed as will the second or third car. We will have to settle for a slimmed down financial industry and fewer deal-oriented lawyers. Woe is us. China, in contrast, will close teddy bear factories and send its workers back to marginal or submarginal jobs in the countryside. That is the real world, and it delivers real pain. Even worse, in some ways, is that the Germans (and to a lesser extent the Japanese) make and sell the equipment that builds the teddy bear factories, no more of which will be needed for a long while. That, too, is real pain. To add to these advantages—at least in the short term—the United States is pouring on more stimulus than anyone else.

So, for the United States at least I have considerable confidence that GDP growth will kick back into positive territory (+0.8 percent) by late 2009 or early 2010. This, I concede, is a consensus view but one that comes with a significant caveat: I believe that there is a decent chance, say 20 percent, that we still badly underestimate the downward momentum of short-term economic forces. We know we are perfectly capable of doing this because as recently as November 2008 the "authorities" (such as the IMF) estimated a +0.5 percent GDP growth rate for the developed world in 2009, and it is now at −4 percent! Not bad . . . a 1 percent reduction per month where a 0.1 percent change per month for four months would normally be considered a landslide.

But to get back to the point. The stimulus program is not based on either persuasive economic theory or solid historical studies: There are simply too few examples and absolutely no controlled experiments, so we are reduced to guesswork. Almost everyone has had the thought that if overconsumption and excessive debt have caused our problems in the United States, then pushing rates so low that they practically beg us to borrow and consume some more seems an odd cure. We acknowledge that a stiff whiskey can get the drunk to stagger to his feet and make it a few blocks, but it does not seem like a successful long-term strategy to cure him of drunkenness. Yet we all override this thought by saying that because a great majority of dignified economists, although they all disagree on the details, seem to think stimulus is necessary, surely they must collectively have it right. However, we in the investment business are blessed by an example that allows us to keep an open mind. The widespread acceptance of rational expectations and the efficient market hypothesis has taught us never to underestimate the ability of the economics establishment to get an idea brutally and expensively wrong. They may have done so this time. It may indeed be a better long-term solution to accept a more punishing decline and let foolish overleveraged banks go under together with weak players in other industries. Surely assets would flow to stronger hands with beneficial long-term effects. Indeed, the quick 1922 recovery from the precipitous decline of 1919–1921 was so profound that the "roaring twenties" suppressed the memory of that earlier depression.

So, what do we really know about the merits of stimulus programs? We do know that National Socialist Germany claimed full employment by 1935 when we—Americans and Brits—still had 15 percent unemployment. They did this as far as one can tell by direct government expenditures: by building autobahns, "people's cars" (VWs), and the odd battleship. We also know that wartime preparations finally and absolutely cured the recalcitrant depression in the United States.

Germany and Japan sprang back from the ashes after World War II, but are we sure that this does not say more about remarkable economic resilience than it does about stimulus? On the one hand, the stimulus side certainly had the Marshall Plan, the very high point of enlightened and generous American foreign aid. On the other hand, surprisingly, the United Kingdom received more Marshall Aid than the Germans did, who had far more damage to their infrastructure. So, perhaps it is indeed more about resilience and work ethic than stimulus. We know that in 15 years, with a semi-flattened industrial sector, the Germans had flashed past the Brits and even the neutral Swedes for that matter. The U.S. economy was also back on its long-term growth trend in 1945 as if the depression and the war had never occurred. So, we know a lot about the powerful resilience of economies. *They are not such delicate flowers that we need to protect every foolish bank or be faced with wrack and ruin.* Current stimulus seems to be more about timing. We are unwilling to take a very sharp economic downturn even if such a downturn makes a quick, healthy recovery more likely. Rather, we seem to be making a desperate attempt to make the setback shallower, perhaps at the expense of a longer recovery period. What is likely to happen in the near term always has far more political influence than what may happen in the longer term. So, we have been more decisively selecting the Japanese route rather than the 1921 or the S&L (savings and loan) approach of a more rapid liquidation. Month by month we are voting for desperate life support systems—at the taxpayers' expense—for zombie banks and industrial companies that have been technically bankrupted by years of excess and almost criminally bad management.

I do think I know one thing, however. If a government invests directly, drawing employment from a large pool of the unemployed, and only invests in projects with a high societal return on investment—such as hiring workers with well-stocked tool belts to install insulation, or repair bridges and transmission lines, or lay track to accommodate a respectably fast train from Boston to Washington (yes!)—it seems nearly certain that such a government will not have to regret it. Keeping banks, bankers, or even extra auto workers in business seems, in comparison, far more questionable—so questionable in fact that it must be justified by politics, not economics. We should particularly not allow ourselves to be intimidated by the financial mafia into believing that all of the failing financial companies—or very nearly all—had to be defended at all costs. To take the equivalent dough that was spent on propping up, say, Goldman Sachs or related entities like AIG that were necessary to Goldman's well being, as well as the many other incompetent banks, and spending it instead on really useful, high-return infrastructure and energy conservation and oil and coal replacement projects would seem like a real bargain for society. Yes, we would certainly have had a very painful temporary economic hit from financial and other bankruptcies if we had decided to let them go, but given the proven resilience of economies, it would still have seemed a better long-term bet. But, as I said, this is all just speculative theory, and I do not have to deal with the U.S. Congress.

Let me end this essay by emphasizing once again the difference between real wealth and the real economy on the one hand and illusory wealth and debt on the other. If we had let all the reckless bankers go out of business, our houses and our factories would not have blown up, our machine tools would not have been carted off to Russia, and we would not have machine gunned any of our educated workforce, even our bankers! When the smoke had cleared, those with money would have bought up the bankrupt assets at cents on the dollar, and we would have had a sharp recovery in the economy. Moral hazard would have been crushed, lessons would have been learned for a generation or two, and assets would be in stronger, more efficient hands. *Debt is accounting, not reality.* Real economies are much more resilient than they are given credit for. We allow ourselves to be terrified by the "financial-industrial complex," as Eisenhower might have said, much to their advantage and to our cost.

Disclaimer

A Template for Understanding What Is Going On

Ray Dalio
Founder, President, and CIO
Bridgewater Associates
Westport, Connecticut

In this article, I will present a big-picture template for understanding economic and capital movements, which the current conditions reflect. I will then examine the deleveraging process more closely. This template consists of three big forces: (1) trendline productivity growth, (2) the long-term debt cycle, and (3) the business/market cycle. By understanding these forces and how they interact, one can go a long way toward putting what has happened and what is likely to happen into perspective. Although these forces apply to all countries' economies, I will use the U.S. economy over the past hundred years or so as an example and will follow it with in-depth examinations of other cases.

The Three Big Forces

Three main forces drive economic activity: (1) trendline productivity growth, (2) the long-term debt cycle, and (3) the business/market cycle. Because business/market cycles repeat frequently, they are fairly well understood, but the other two forces are less well understood, so I will explain all three. I will then show how, by overlaying the archetypal "business" cycle on top of the archetypal long-term debt cycle and overlaying them both on top of the productivity trendline, one can derive an excellent template for tracking most economic/market movements.

As shown in **Figure 1**, real *per capita* GDP increased at an average rate of a little less than 2 percent over the past 100 years and did not vary a lot from that level. Because knowledge increases over time, it, in turn, raises productivity and thus living standards. As shown in Figure 1, over the very long run, there has been relatively little variation from the trendline. Even the Great Depression in the 1930s looks rather small. As a result, one can be relatively confident that, with time, the economy will get back on track. Up close, however, these variations from the trend can be enormous. For example, typically in deleveragings, the peak-to-trough declines in real economic activity are about 20 percent, the destruction of financial wealth is typically more than 50 percent, and equity prices typically decline by around 80 percent. The losses of financial wealth by those who have it at the beginning of deleveragings are typically greater than these numbers suggest because there is also a tremendous shifting of who has wealth.

Figure 1. Real GDP per Capita, 1900–2010

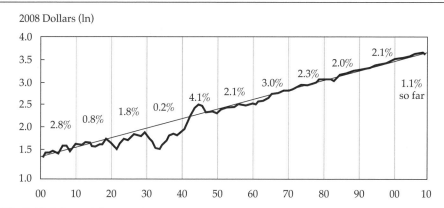

Swings around this trend are not primarily the result of expansions and contractions in knowledge. For example, the Great Depression did not occur because people forgot how to efficiently produce, and it was not set off by war or drought. All the elements that make an economy buzz were present, yet it stagnated. So, why didn't the idle factories simply hire the unemployed to use the abundant resources in order to produce prosperity? These cycles are not the result of events beyond our control, such as natural disasters. They are the result of human nature and the way the economic system works.

Most importantly, *major swings around the trend are caused by expansions and contractions in credit*: that is, credit cycles—most importantly, a long-term (typically 50–75 years) debt cycle (the "long-wave cycle") and a shorter-term (typically 5–8 years) debt cycle (the "business/market cycle").

About Cycles

I find that whenever I start talking about cycles, particularly the long-wave variety, I elicit reactions similar to those that one would expect if I were talking about astrology. This reaction is especially pronounced when those who have been trained in efficient market theory are in the audience. For this reason, before I begin explaining these two debt cycles, I will make a few comments about cycles in general.

A cycle is nothing more than a logical sequence of events leading to a repetitious pattern. In a capitalist economy, cycles of expansions and contractions in credit drive economic cycles, and they occur for perfectly logical reasons. Each sequence is not predestined to repeat in exactly the same way or to take exactly the same amount of time, although the patterns are similar, for logical reasons. For example, if you understand the game of Monopoly, you can pretty well understand credit and economic cycles. Early in the game of Monopoly, players have a lot of cash and few hotels, and it pays to convert cash into hotels: Those who have more hotels make more money. Seeing this result, players tend to convert as much cash as possible into property to profit from forcing other players to give them cash. But as the game progresses, more hotels are acquired, which creates more need for cash (to pay the rent for landing on someone else's property that has a hotel on it) just when many players have run down their cash to buy hotels. When players are caught needing cash, they are forced to sell their hotels at discounted prices; in other words, it pays to convert hotels to cash. So, early in the game, "property is king," and later in the game, "cash is king." Those who are best at playing the game understand how to hold the right mix of property and cash as this right mix changes.

Now let us imagine how this Monopoly game would work if we changed the role of the bank so that it could make loans and take deposits. Players would then be able to borrow money to buy hotels and, rather than holding their cash idly, deposit it at the bank to earn interest, which would provide the bank with more money to lend. If Monopoly were played this way, it would provide an almost perfect model for the way our economy operates. More hotels would be bought, and sooner than if there were no lending. The amount owed would quickly grow to multiples of the amount of money in existence, and the cash shortage for the debtors who hold hotels would become greater, so the cycles would become more pronounced. The bank and those who saved by depositing their money in it would also get into trouble when the inability to come up with needed cash caused withdrawals from the bank at the same time as debtors could not come up with cash to pay the bank. Basically, economic and credit cycles work the same way.

I will now look at how credit cycles—both the long-term debt cycle and the business cycle—drive economic cycles.

How the System Works

Prosperity exists when the economy is operating at a high level of capacity—in other words, when demand is pressing up against a pre-existing level of capacity. At such times, business profits are good and unemployment is low. The longer these conditions persist, the more capacity will be increased, typically financed by credit growth. Declining demand creates a condition of low capacity utilization. As a result, business profits are bad and unemployment is high. The longer these conditions exist, the more cost cutting (sometimes called "restructuring") will occur, typically including debt and equity write-downs. Therefore, prosperity equals high demand, and in our credit-based economy, strong demand equals strong real credit growth. Conversely, deleveraging equals low demand and, hence, lower and falling real credit growth. Contrary to now-popular supply-side thinking, recessions and deleveragings do not develop because of low productivity (i.e., an inability to produce efficiently); they develop from declines in demand.

Because changes in demand precede changes in capacity in determining the direction of the economy, one would think that prosperity would be easy to achieve simply by pursuing policies that would steadily increase demand. When the economy is plagued with conditions of low capacity utilization, depressed business profitability, and high unemployment, why doesn't the government simply give it a good shot of whatever it takes to stimulate demand to produce a far more pleasant environment of high capacity utilization, fat profits, and low unemployment? The answer has to do with what that shot consists of.

Money. Money is what you settle your payments with. Some people mistakenly believe that money is whatever will buy you goods and services, whether that is dollar bills or simply a promise to pay (for example, a credit card or an account at the local grocery). When a department store gives you merchandise in return for your signature on a credit card form, is that signature money? No, it is not because you did not settle the transaction. Rather, you promised to pay money. So, you created credit, which is a promise to pay money.

The U.S. Federal Reserve (Fed) has chosen to define "money" in terms of aggregates (i.e., currency plus various forms of credit—M1, M2, etc.), but this is misleading. Virtually all of what the Fed calls money is credit (i.e., promises to deliver money) rather than money. The total amount of debt in the United States is about $50 trillion, and the total amount of money (currency and reserves) in existence is about $2 trillion. So, if I use these numbers as a guide, the amount of promises to deliver money (i.e., debt) is roughly 25 times the amount of money in existence to deliver.[1] The main point is that most people buy things with credit and do not pay much attention to what they are promising to deliver and where they are going to get it from, so there is much less money than there are obligations to deliver it.

Credit. Credit is the promise to deliver money, and credit spends just like money. Although credit and money spend equally easily, when one pays with money, the transaction is settled, but when one pays with credit, the payment has yet to be made.

Demand can increase in two ways—with credit or without it. Of course, it is far easier to stimulate demand with credit than without it. For example, in an economy in which there is no credit, if I want to buy a good or service, I have to exchange it for a comparably valued good or service of my own. Therefore, the only way I can increase what I own and the only way the economy as a whole can grow is through increased production. As a result, in an economy without credit, the growth in demand is constrained by the growth in production. This constraint tends to reduce the occurrence of high prosperity and severe depression. In other words, it tends to produce swings around the productivity growth trendline of about 2 percent.

---

[1]Because a substantial amount of dollar-denominated debt exists outside the United States, the total amount of claims on dollars is greater than this characterization indicates, so it is provided solely for illustrative purposes.

By contrast, in an economy in which credit is readily available, I can acquire goods and services without giving up any of my own. A bank will lend money on my pledge to repay, secured by my existing assets and future earnings. In the short run, a monetary expansion supports a credit expansion because it makes it easier for me to pay off my loans (with money of less value) and makes the assets I acquired worth more through inflation. In turn, a monetary expansion improves my credit rating and increases my collateral, thereby making it that much easier to borrow and buy more. In such an economy, demand is constrained only by the willingness of creditors and debtors to extend and receive credit. When credit is easy and cheap, borrowing and spending will occur, and when it is scarce and expensive, borrowing and spending will be less. In the "business cycle," the availability and cost of credit are driven by central bankers, whereas in the "long-wave cycle," the availability and cost of credit are driven by factors that are largely beyond central banks' control. Both debt cycles cause swings around the long-term trendline growth shown in Figure 1 because there are limits to excess debt growth and all debts must be either paid off or defaulted on.

The most fundamental requirement for credit creation to exist is that both borrowers and lenders must believe that the deal is good for them. Because one man's debts are another man's assets, lenders have to believe that they will get paid back an amount of money that is greater than what they lent after adjustment for inflation (that is, more than they could get by storing their wealth in inflation hedge assets), net of taxes. And because debtors typically have to pledge their equity assets as collateral to convince lenders of their creditworthiness, they have to be confident in their ability to pay their debts to the extent that they value the equity assets that they pledged as collateral.

Another important consideration for investors is liquidity—the ability to sell one's investments for money and use that money to buy goods and services. For example, if I own a $100,000 Treasury bond, I have probably made the decision to do so based on the belief that I will be able to exchange it for $100,000 in cash and, in turn, exchange the cash for $100,000 worth of goods and services. But because the ratio of financial assets to money is so high, if a large number of people try to convert their financial assets into money and buy goods and services at the same time, the central bank will have to produce a lot more money (risking a monetary inflation) and/or allow a lot of defaults (causing deflationary deleveraging).

Monetary Systems. One of the greatest powers governments have is the creation of money and credit. They exert this power by determining their countries' monetary systems and by controlling the levers that increase and decrease the supply of money and credit. The monetary systems chosen have varied over time and by country. In the old days was barter (the exchange of items of equal intrinsic value). It was the original basis of money. When one paid with gold coins, the exchange was of items having equal intrinsic value. Then credit developed, where credit consisted of promises to deliver "money" having intrinsic value. With the emergence of fiat money (which has no intrinsic value or "value in use"), the next development was credit consisting of promises to deliver money that did not have intrinsic value.

Those who lend expect that they will get back an amount of money that can be converted into goods or services that are somewhat more valuable than the money they originally lent. In other words, they expect a positive (or at the very minimum, zero) real return on their loan. So, since credit began, creditors essentially have asked those who controlled the monetary systems, "How do we know that you won't just print a lot of money so that when we go to exchange it for goods and services in the future, it won't buy us much?" At different times, this question has been answered differently.

Basically, there are two types of monetary systems: *commodity-based systems*, those consisting of some commodity (usually gold), currency (which can be converted into the commodity at a fixed price), and credit (a claim on the currency), and *fiat systems*, those consisting of just currency and credit.

In the first of these systems, it is more difficult to create credit expansions because the public will negate the government's attempts to increase currency and credit by demanding that the government give them back the commodity that it is exchangeable for. As the supply of money increases, its value falls or, looked at the other way, the price of the commodity into which it is convertible rises. When the market price of the commodity rises above the fixed price, it is profitable for those holding credit (that is, claims on the currency) to sell their debt for currency to buy the commodity from the government at below the market price. The selling of the credit and the taking of currency out of circulation cause credit to tighten and the value of the money to rise. At the same time, the general price level of goods and services will fall. The result of this chain of events will be lower inflation and lower economic activity.

Because the value of money has fallen over time relative to the value of just about everything else, I could tie the currency to just about anything to show how this monetary system would work. For example, because a one-pound loaf of white bread in 1946 cost 10 cents, let us imagine we tied the dollar to bread. In other words, let us imagine a monetary system in which the government, in 1946, committed to buy and sell bread at 10 cents a pound and stuck to that system until now. Today, a one-pound loaf of white bread costs $2.75. If we had been on a "bread standard" since 1946, the price could not have gotten to $2.75 because we all would have bought our bread from the government at 10 cents instead of from the free market until the government ran out of bread. But to finish the illustration of how a commodity money works, let us say that the price of bread did actually reach $2.75. At that price, I would certainly be willing to take all of my money, buy bread from the government at 10 cents, and sell it in the market at $2.75; others would do the same. This process would cause the amount of money in circulation to be reduced, which would reduce the prices of all goods and services and increase the amount of bread in circulation (thus lowering its price more rapidly than other prices). In fact, if the supply of bread were not greatly increased, in this counterfactual example, because of its convertibility to currency, this tie—the use of a physical commodity as the basis of currency—would have dramatically slowed the last 50 years' rapid growth in currency and credit.

Obviously, what the currency is convertible into has an enormous impact on this process. For example, if instead of tying the dollar to bread I chose to tie it to eggs, currency and credit growth would have been less restricted because the price of eggs has risen much less than the price of bread: A dozen eggs cost 70 cents in 1947 and about $2.00 today.

Ideally, if one has a commodity-based currency system, one wants to tie the currency to something that is not subject to great swings in supply or demand. For example, if the currency were tied to bread, bakeries would, in effect, have the power to produce money, leading to increased inflation. Being difficult and expensive to find and extract from the ground, gold and, to a much lesser extent, silver have historically proven more stable than most other currency backings, although they are by no means perfect.

In the second type of monetary system—a fiat system in which the amount of money is not constrained by the ability to exchange it for a commodity—the growth of money and credit is very much subject to the influence of the central bank and the willingness of borrowers and lenders to create credit.

Governments typically prefer fiat systems because these systems give them more power to print money, expand credit, and redistribute wealth by changing the value of money. Human nature being what it is, those in government (and those not) tend to value immediate gratification over longer-term benefits, so government policies tend to increase demand by allowing liberal credit creation, which, in turn, leads to debt crises from time to time. Governments typically choose commodity-based systems only when the fiat money they have been issuing has lost almost all of its value. (This happens when the government "prints" a lot of fiat money to pay its own debts because the debts have grown so large that they cannot be paid out of tax revenues.) And governments abandon commodity-based monetary systems when the constraints to money creation become too onerous in debt crises. So, throughout history, governments have gone back and forth between commodity-based and fiat monetary systems in reaction to the painful consequences of each. Nevertheless, they do not make these changes often because monetary systems typically work well for many years, often decades, with central banks varying interest rates and the money supply to control credit growth well enough that these inflection points are rarely reached.

The Long-Term (i.e., Long-Wave) Cycle

Figure 2 shows U.S. debt to GDP going back to 1917 and illustrates the long-term debt cycle. (Here, "debt" means the sum of government, business, and private or individual debt.) These long-term debt cycles have existed for as long as credit has existed. Even the Old Testament described the need to wipe out debt once every 50 years; the year of debt cancellation was called the year of "Jubilee."

Figure 2. Total Debt as a Percentage of GDP, 1917–2009

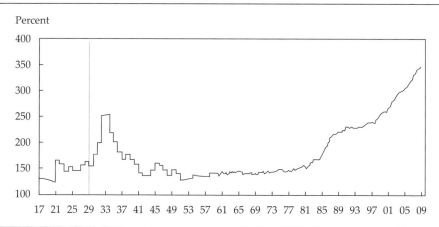

Upwaves. Upswings in the cycle occur, and are self-reinforcing, in a process by which money growth creates greater debt growth, which, in turn, finances spending growth and asset purchases. Spending growth and higher asset prices then allow even more debt growth. This last step occurs because lenders determine how much they can lend on the basis of the borrower's income, or cash flow, available to service the debt; the borrower's net worth and/or collateral; and their own capacity to lend. All of these factors tend to rise together in a self-reinforcing manner. For example, during the last upward cycle, incomes, housing prices, and stock prices all rose, so people's collateral increased in value, allowing them to borrow against it to increase their spending. This increased spending led to higher corporate earnings, which supported rising stock prices and other asset values, giving people more collateral to borrow more against, and so on.

In the upwave part of the cycle, promises to deliver money (that is, debts and debt service payments) rise relative to both (1) the supply of money and (2) the amount of money and credit that debtors have coming in (via incomes, borrowings, and sales of assets). This upwave in the cycle typically goes on for decades, with variations in it primarily caused by central banks tightening and easing credit (which makes business cycles). But the upwave cannot go on forever because it is impossible for obligations to deliver money (that is, debt) to rise *indefinitely* relative to the amount of money that is coming in. When promises to deliver money (debt) cannot grow any further relative to the money and credit that is coming in, the process works in reverse, and we have deleveragings.

Although Figure 2 shows the amount of debt relative to GDP—that is, the debt ratio—it is more precise to say that high debt service payments (principal and interest combined), rather than high debt levels themselves, cause debt squeezes that slow the economy because cash flows must clear: The portion of income available to service debt must at least equal the amount required by the creditor. For example, if interest rates fall enough, debts can increase without debt service payments rising enough to cause a squeeze. This dynamic is best conveyed in **Figure 3**. It shows interest payments, principal payments, and total debt service payments of U.S. households as a percentage of their disposable incomes going back to 1918. I am showing this debt service burden for the household sector because the household sector is the most important part of the economy; the concept, however, applies equally well to all sectors and all individuals. As shown, by 2007, the debt service burden of households had increased to the highest level since the Great Depression. Although it is obvious that this burden cannot continue to rise indefinitely, one must ask, what, specifically, triggers reversals?

The long-wave cycle top occurs when debt and debt service levels are high relative to incomes and monetary policy does not produce credit growth. Although tops can occur for many reasons (e.g., the excessive debts of Germany's Weimar Republic arose primarily because of war reparations), they occur most typically

Figure 3. Household Debt Service as a Percentage of Disposable Income, 1919–2009

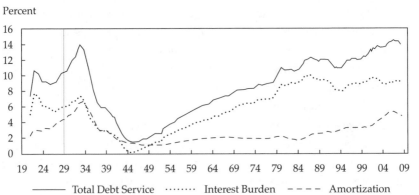

because assets are bought at high prices and on leverage[2] (i.e., because debt levels are set on the basis of overly optimistic assumptions about future cash flows) and because actual cash flows, when they come in, fall short of what are required for debtors to service their debts. And then monetary policy is ineffective in rectifying the imbalance. Ironically, quite often the cash flows fall short because of high interest rate monetary policies that are overdue attempts to curtail these bubble activities (as in 1928–1929 in the United States and 1989–1991 in Japan).

Downwaves. In deleveragings, debts fall rather than rise relative to money as they do in upwaves. Because the money coming in to debtors via incomes and borrowings is not enough to meet their obligations, assets must be sold and spending must be cut to raise cash. The ensuing drop in asset values reduces the value of collateral and, in turn, reduces incomes. Because of both lower collateral values and lower incomes, borrowers' creditworthiness is reduced, so they justifiably get less credit. This process continues in a self-reinforcing manner.

One can see this dynamic in Figures 2 and 3. The vertical line on these figures is at 1929. Figure 2 shows that the ratio of debt to GDP shot up from about 160 percent to about 250 percent between 1929 and 1933. Figure 3 shows the same picture: Debt service levels rose relative to income levels because income levels fell. In an economic and credit downturn, debt burdens increase at the same time that debts are being written down, so the debt liquidation process is reinforced. **Figure 4** shows the debt of the household sector, relative to its net worth, over time. This leverage ratio is shooting up from already high levels, as it did during the Great Depression, because of declines in net worth arising from falling housing and stock prices.

In a credit-based economy, as noted earlier, the ability to spend is an extension of the ability to borrow. For lending and borrowing to occur, lenders have to believe that they will earn a positive real rate of return and that they will be able to convert their debt into money. In deleveragings, lenders justifiably worry that these things will not happen.

Unlike in recessions, when cutting interest rates and creating more money can rectify this imbalance, in deleveragings, monetary policy is ineffective in creating credit. In other words, in recessions (when monetary policy is effective), the imbalance between the amount of money and the need for it to service debt can be rectified because interest rates can be cut enough to (1) stimulate economic activity by lowering monthly debt service payments relative to incomes and (2) produce a positive wealth effect. In deleveragings, however, this result cannot occur. In a

---

[2]This time around, residential and commercial real estate, private equity, lower-grade credits, and to a lesser extent, listed equities were the assets that were bought at high prices and on lots of leverage. In both the U.S. Great Depression and in the Japanese depression, stocks and real estate were also the assets of choice that were bought at high prices and on leverage.

Figure 4. Household Debt as a Percentage of Net Worth, 1917–2009

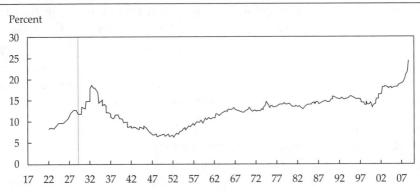

deleveraging, or deflationary depression, monetary policy is typically ineffective in creating credit. Interest rates hit zero, so they cannot be lowered. Consequently, other, less effective ways of increasing the money supply are followed. Credit growth is thus difficult to stimulate because borrowers remain overindebted, making sensible lending impossible. In an inflationary depression, monetary policy is ineffective in creating credit because increased money growth goes into hard-money currencies and real (inflation hedge) assets instead of domestic-currency-denominated assets that investors fear will depreciate in value.

All deleveragings start as a result of a shortage of money relative to the need for it (the "fundamental imbalance") as credit contracts. This situation leads to large numbers of businesses, households, and financial institutions defaulting on their debts and cutting costs, which, in turn, leads to higher unemployment and other problems. To try to alleviate this fundamental imbalance, governments inevitably create initiatives to encourage credit creation, ease the rules that require debtors to come up with money to service their debts (i.e., create forbearance), and increase the supply of money. Typically, these moves come in progressively larger dosages as the initial doses fail to rectify the imbalance and reverse the deleveraging process. These dosages, however, do typically cause temporary periods of relief that are manifest in bear market rallies in financial assets and increased economic activity. For example, during the Great Depression, there were six big rallies in the stock market (of between 21 percent and 48 percent) in a bear market that totaled 89 percent, with each of these rallies triggered by escalating government actions designed to reduce the fundamental imbalance. But these rallies did not foreshadow a true economic recovery because the fundamental imbalance was not eliminated.

Some people mistakenly think that the problem is just psychological—that scared investors move their money from riskier investments to safer ones (e.g., from stocks and high-yield lending to government cash)—and that problems can be rectified by coaxing investors to move their money back into riskier investments. This thinking is wrong for two reasons.

First, the deleveraging dynamic is not irrational but, instead, a reasoned response to the then-prevailing supply and demand conditions for credit, money, and goods and services. Second, it is not correct that the amount of money in existence remains the same and simply moves from riskier assets to less risky ones. Most of what people think is money is really credit, and it does disappear. For example, when you buy something in a store using a credit card, you do so essentially by saying "I promise to pay." The seller books that promise as an asset, so his net worth goes up. Together you created a credit asset and a credit liability. So, where did you take the money from? Nowhere. You created credit. It goes away in the same way.

A big part of the deleveraging process, then, is people's discovering that much of what they thought was their wealth is not really there.

When investors need cash, they try to sell their investments. In cases in which the investments prove illiquid, panic-induced "runs" and sell-offs of securities occur. Naturally, those who experience runs, especially banks (although this is true of most entities that rely on short-term funding), have problems raising money and credit to meet their needs, so they often fail. At such times, governments are forced to decide which institutions to save by providing them with money and whether to get this money through the central government (i.e., through the budget process) or through the central bank's ability to "print" more money. Governments inevitably do both, although in varying degrees. What determines whether a deleveraging is deflationary or inflationary is the extent to which central banks create money to negate the effects of contracting credit.

Governments with commodity-based monetary systems are more limited in their abilities to "print" and provide money, whereas those with fiat monetary systems are less constrained. In both cases, however, the central bank is eager to provide money and credit, so it always lowers the quality of the collateral it accepts and, in addition to providing money to some essential banks, it also typically provides money to some nonbank entities that it considers essential.

The central bank's easing of monetary policy, and the movement of investor money to safer investments, initially drives down short-term government interest rates, steepens the yield curve, and widens credit and liquidity premiums. Those who do not receive the money and/or credit needed to meet their debt service obligations and maintain their operations, which is typically a large segment of debtors, default and fail.

As credit collapses, workers lose jobs, and many of them, having inadequate savings, need financial support. So, in addition to needing money to provide financial support to the system, governments need money to help those in greatest financial need. Additionally, to the extent that they want to increase spending to make up for decreased private sector spending, they need more money. At the same time, their tax revenue falls because incomes fall. For these reasons, governments' budget deficits increase. Inevitably, the amount of money lent to governments at these times increases less than that of their needs (i.e., they have problems funding their deficits), despite the increased desire of investors to buy government securities to seek safety at these times. As a result, central banks are again forced to choose between "printing" more money to buy their governments' debts or allowing their governments and their private sector to compete for the limited supply of money, causing extremely tight money conditions.

Governments with commodity-based money systems are forced into having smaller budget deficits and tighter monetary policies than governments with fiat monetary systems, although they all eventually relent and print more money (i.e., those on commodity-based monetary systems either abandon these systems or "debase" the currency by reducing the amount of the commodity that they will exchange for a unit of money). This "printing" of money takes the form of central bank purchases of government securities and nongovernment assets, such as corporate securities and equities. In other words, the government creates new money ("prints" it) and uses it to negate some of the effects of contracting credit. If the money creation is large enough, it devalues the currency, lowers real interest rates, and drives investors from financial assets to inflation hedge assets.

Because governments need more money and because wealth and incomes are typically heavily concentrated in the hands of a small percentage of the population, governments raise taxes on the wealthy. These increased taxes typically take the form of greater income and consumption taxes because these forms of taxation are the most effective in raising revenues. Despite these greater taxes on the wealthy, increases in tax revenue are inadequate because incomes—both earned incomes and incomes from capital—are depressed and expenditures on consumption are reduced.

The wealthy experience a tremendous loss of "real" wealth in all forms (i.e., from their portfolios declining in value, from their earned incomes declining, and from higher rates of taxation, in inflation-adjusted terms). Quite often, they are motivated to move their money out of the country (which contributes to currency weakness), illegally dodge taxes, and seek safety in liquid, non-credit-dependent investments.

Workers who are losing jobs and governments that want to protect them become more protectionist and favor weaker currency policies. Protectionism slows economic activity, and currency weakness fosters capital flight. Debtor countries typically suffer most from capital flight.

When money leaves the country, central banks are once again put in the position of having to choose between "printing" more money, which lessens its value, and not printing money in order to maintain its value but allowing money to tighten. They inevitably choose to "print" more money, which is additionally bearish for the currency.

Debtor, current account deficit, countries are especially vulnerable to capital withdrawals and currency weakness because foreign investors also tend to flee as a result of both the currency weakness and the environment being inhospitable to good returns on capital. This is less true, however, for countries that have a great amount of debt denominated in their currencies (such as the United States now and during the Great Depression) because these debts create a demand for these currencies. Because debt is a promise to deliver money that one does not have, this environment essentially creates a short squeeze that ends when (1) the shorts are squeezed (i.e., the debts are defaulted on), (2) enough money is created to alleviate the squeeze, and/or (3) the debt service requirements are reduced in some other way (e.g., forbearance).

The risk at this stage of the process is that the currency weakness and the increased supply of money will lead to short-term credit (even government short-term credit) becoming undesirable, causing the buying of inflation hedge assets and capital flight rather than credit creation. For foreign investors, receiving an interest rate that is near zero and having the foreign currency that their deposits are denominated in decline produce a negative return, so this set of circumstances makes holding credit, even government short-term credit, undesirable. Similarly, for domestic investors, this set of circumstances makes foreign currency deposits more desirable. If and when this happens, investors accelerate their selling of financial assets, especially debt assets, to get cash in order to use this cash to buy other currencies or inflation hedge assets, such as gold. They also seek to borrow cash in that currency. Once again, such actions put the central bank in the position of having to choose between increasing the supply of money to accommodate this demand for it or allowing money and credit to tighten and real interest rates to rise. At such times, governments may seek to curtail this movement by establishing foreign exchange controls and/or prohibiting gold ownership. Also, price and wage controls may be put into place. Such moves typically create economic distortions rather than alleviate problems.

Although the deleveraging process seems horrible and certainly produces great hardships—in some cases, even wars—it is the free market's way of repairing itself. In other words, it gets the capital markets and the economy into a much healthier condition by rectifying the fundamental imbalance. Debts are reduced (through bankruptcies and other forms of debt restructuring), businesses' break-even levels are reduced through cost cutting, financial assets become cheap and attractive, and the supply of money needed to buy these assets and to service debts is increased by the central banks. So, capital formation becomes viable again.

The decline in economic and credit-creation activity is typically fast, lasting two to three years. The subsequent recovery in economic activity and capital formation, however, tends to be slow. It takes roughly a decade (hence the term "lost decade") for real economic activity to reach its former peak level. And it typically takes more than 20 years for real stock prices to reach their former highs.

As mentioned, these cycles are caused by human nature and the way the system works. Throughout this process, most everyone behaves pretty much as one would expect them to in pursuing their self-interests.

107

The Business Cycle

The business cycle is the shortest of the cycles described in this article and is overlaid on the longer trends and cycles. This description is brief and stylized, and I should caution that no business cycle evolves along precisely these lines. Consistent with my desire to provide a template, however, the generalities that follow are applicable more often than not.

The business cycle is primarily controlled by central banks' policies that (1) tighten when inflation is too high and/or rising uncomfortably because not much slack exists in the economy (as reflected in the output gap, capacity utilization, and the unemployment rate) and credit growth is strong and (2) ease when the reverse conditions exist. They can be described a bit differently by different people, but they are all about the same. The way I describe them is in six phases—four in the expansion and two in the recession.

***Expansion Phase* of the Cycle.** The *early cycle* (which typically lasts about five or six quarters) usually begins with the demand for interest rate–sensitive items (e.g., housing and cars) and with retail sales picking up because of low interest rates and lots of available credit. This increased demand pulls the average workweek and then employment up. Credit growth is fast, economic growth is strong (i.e., in excess of 4 percent), inflation is low, growth in consumption is strong, the rate of inventory accumulation is increasing, and the stock market is typically the best investment (because the economy is growing fast and interest rates are not rising because inflation is not rising). Inflation hedge assets and commodities are the worst performing assets.

The early cycle is typically followed by what is called the *mid-cycle* (which lasts an average of three or four quarters), in which real economic growth slows substantially (to roughly 2 percent), inflation remains low, growth in consumption slows, the rate of inventory accumulation declines, interest rates dip, the rate of increase in stock market prices tapers off, and the rate of decline in inflation hedge assets slows.

The mid-cycle, in turn, is followed by the *late cycle* (which typically begins about 2½ years into expansion, with variation depending on how much slack existed in the economy at the last recession's trough). At this point, economic growth picks up to a moderate pace (i.e., around 3.5–4.0 percent), capacity constraints emerge, but credit and demand growth are still strong. So, inflation begins to trend higher, consumption grows, inventories typically pick up, interest rates rise, the stock market stages its last advance, and inflation hedge assets become the best performing investments.

The late cycle is followed by the *tightening phase* of the expansion. In this phase, actual or anticipated acceleration of inflation prompts the Fed to turn restrictive, which shows up in reduced liquidity, interest rates rising, and the yield curve flattening or inverting. These changes, in turn, cause money supply and credit growth to fall and the stock market to decline before the economy turns down.

***Recession Phase* of the Cycle.** In the *early part of the recession*, the economy contracts; resources are underutilized (as measured by the output gap, capacity utilization, and the unemployment rate); stocks, commodities, and inflation hedge assets fall; and inflation declines because the Fed remains tight.

In the *late part of the recession*, the central bank eases monetary policy as inflation concerns subside and recession concerns grow. So, interest rates decline and the lower interest rates cause stock prices to rise (even though the economy has not yet turned up), while commodity prices and inflation hedge assets continue to be weak. The lower interest rates and higher stock prices set the stage for the expansion part of the cycle to begin.

Summary. Although I have referred to average time lags between each of these stages of the cycle, it is the sequence of events, not the specific timeline, that is important to keep an eye on. For example, given the previously described linkages, because inflation does not normally heat up until the slack in the economy is largely eliminated and the Fed does not normally turn restrictive until inflation rises, an expansion that starts off after a deep recession (i.e., one that produces lots of slack) is bound to last longer than an expansion that begins with less excess capacity. Similarly, as the cycle progresses through its various stages as a function of the sequences just described, the rate at which it progresses will be a function of the forcefulness of the influences that drive its progression. For example, an expansion that is accompanied by an aggressively stimulative central bank is likely to be stronger and evolve more quickly than one that is accompanied by a less stimulative monetary policy. Also, exogenous influences, such as China's entry into the world economy, wars, and natural disasters, can alter the progressions of these cycles.

Conclusion

Although the economy is more complicated than this template suggests, laying the business cycle on top of the "long-wave" cycle and laying them both on top of the trend per capita real GDP growth line gives a reasonably good road map for understanding the capitalist system and seeing both where we are now and where we are probably headed. One should always be careful about projecting any past cycle or pattern into the future because circumstances change each time and history never repeats itself exactly. A template is necessarily an incomplete description. The details of "what is different this time," as well as what is the same as it always has been, will be filled in as we observe history in the making.

©2009 Ray Dalio

The Limits of Convertible Bond Arbitrage: Evidence from the Recent Crash

Clifford S. Asness
Managing and Founding Principal
AQR Capital Management
New York City

Adam Berger, CFA
Head of Portfolio Solutions
AQR Capital Management
New York City

Christopher Palazzolo
Associate
AQR Capital Management
New York City

Like many investment strategies, convertible bond arbitrage suffered abysmal results in late 2008 following the collapse of Lehman Brothers. Because this strategy is closer to the theoretical concept of arbitrage than many others are, an examination of how convertible bond arbitrage fared during this volatile period offers a case study of how these strategies can break down in times of crisis and the opportunities they offer in the aftermath.

Background

Why do markets go to extremes? Why do they sometimes rise to shocking heights or plunge to extraordinary lows? These questions are a challenge for efficient market theory, in which asset prices cannot move far from fundamental values because any discrepancies between price and value are arbitraged away as they develop. Nevertheless, such opportunities (on both the up and down sides) seem to present themselves occasionally without being quickly arbitraged away. The markets of 1999–2000 and 2007–2009 are cases in point.

To maintain equilibrium—with markets efficient, prices fair, and extraordinary profit opportunities nonexistent—some amount of capital must be committed to arbitrage strategies. But at times, would-be arbitrageurs do not have access to the amount of capital needed to bring prices in line with fair values, particularly when the market price of a whole asset class is out of whack.[1] Thus, the no-arbitrage condition can sometimes be violated, markets can be inefficient, and investors can earn returns far in excess of what is predicted by general equilibrium theories, such as the capital asset pricing model. In this article, we focus on an example of the limits of arbitrage, namely, the convertible bond market in 2008 and 2009.[2]

Convertible Bonds and Convertible Bond Arbitrage

A convertible bond is a corporate bond that can, at the option of the holder, be converted into shares of the issuer's common stock. Convertible bonds are hybrid securities—essentially a corporate debt obligation that comes packaged with an equity call option. Each bond has a "conversion price," which is the stock price at which a convertible bondholder is indifferent between redeeming the bond (i.e., receiving par or face value in most cases) and receiving shares of common stock. For example, if a convertible bond has a face value of $1,000 to be paid at maturity and the conversion ratio is 50 shares per bond, the convertible bondholder will be indifferent between receiving the $1,000 face value and receiving 50 shares of common stock when the stock price is $20 ($1,000 par value = 50 shares × $20 stock price) at the time of maturity.

The value of a convertible bond is the sum of the value of the debt obligation component and the equity option component. Each component can be valued using market inputs. Combining these valuations results in a "fundamental value" for the bond.

At approximately $200 billion in the United States,[3] the size of the convertible bond market is meaningful, although much smaller than the markets for straight corporate debt or equity. Because of the limited market, convertible bonds tend to be relatively illiquid compared with these other securities (but much more liquid than, for instance, many types of private investments). Many bonds trade infrequently, and often only a few bond dealers are willing to make a market in any given bond. Transaction costs for trading convertible bonds tend to be high, especially outside the narrow universe of large, liquid issues. (Such is not the case, however, at the time of issuance, when companies are actively seeking bondholders and pay the costs associated with a bond underwriting.)

---

[1] This idea was developed in the classic article by Andrei Shleifer and Robert Vishny, "The Limits of Arbitrage," *Journal of Finance*, vol. 52, no. 1 (March 1997):35–55.

[2] Our colleagues Mark Mitchell, Lasse Heje Pedersen, and Todd Pulvino produced a similar analysis of the convertible bond market crisis of 2005 in their paper "Slow Moving Capital," *American Economic Review*, vol. 97, no. 2 (May 2007):215–220.

[3] Tatyana Hube and Yichao (Alan) Yu, *US Convertible Monthly*, Bank of America/Merrill Lynch (July 2009).

Convertible Bond "Cheapness." High-risk companies often choose to raise capital by issuing convertible securities. Doing so allows them to "monetize" the volatility of their equity because convertible bonds include an implicit call option on the issuer's stock. A long-term call option on a volatile stock can be valuable. To entice buyers to provide liquidity to issuing companies, convertible bonds are often issued at prices below their fundamental values (that is, below the values of the straight corporate debt and the embedded call option). Offering convertible bonds at a discount is attractive to issuers because they can access capital quickly (sometimes overnight) and avoid the lengthier process of a traditional equity or straight debt offering. Convertible bonds are attractive to investors because they can often hedge some or all of the underlying equity, credit, and interest rate exposure. After issuance, convertibles are less liquid than other bonds and thus often continue to trade at modest discounts to fundamental values. But when the bonds mature (or are called by the issuer or put by the bondholders), investors realize the current fundamental value of the bond. The disparity between fundamental value and price prior to maturity creates the possibility of arbitrage.

The attractiveness of the arbitrage (the potential return) can be measured by bond "cheapness," the ratio of current price to fundamental value. This measure is equivalent to the "discount" at which investors are buying the bonds. To determine fundamental value, the necessary inputs are the price and terms of the convertible bond, the issuer's stock price, the expected volatility of the issuer's stock, the credit spread associated with the convertible bond, and the term structure of interest rates. The assessment works for an individual bond and also for the market as a whole.

Using a proprietary dataset of U.S. convertible bonds of publicly traded issuers dating back to 1985, we measure the historical attractiveness of convertible bonds by determining cheapness on a bond-by-bond basis. To mitigate the impact of data errors in this large sample, we focus on the discount for the *median* bond in our universe, where the discount is the market price relative to the fundamental value.

Historically (prior to 2008), convertible bonds in the United States traded between 3 percent rich (i.e., at premium to fundamental value) and 3 percent cheap. Note that cheapness reflects only the discount at which convertible bonds trade relative to their fundamental values.[4] Such factors as credit rating, equity performance, and interest rates should play little direct role in the cheapness of a bond because these factors affect both the price and the fundamental value of a bond.

---

[4]Our definition of cheapness is conservative because it excludes the "call cushion." In theory, issuers should call their bonds as soon as the stock price exceeds the conversion price because doing so minimizes the value of the call option they have sold. In practice, however, issuers often do not call their bonds until their share price exceeds the conversion price by some margin. They do this to protect themselves from price volatility between the time the bonds are called and the time the purchases are settled. This extra window means the call option in a convertible bond is often worth more than the theoretical option value used to determine the fundamental overall value of the bond.

Liquidity, however, plays an important role in bond cheapness. Given the illiquidity of convertible bonds, their typical cheapness relative to fundamental value represents, at least in part, a liquidity premium. (In point of fact, some of the other factors listed have an indirect role because credit rating and equity performance tend to be correlated with liquidity.) Historical variations in the cheapness of convertible bonds simply reflect the willingness of investors to hold convertible bonds (versus their underlying components) at any point in time.[5] The historical cheapness of convertible bonds through 2007 is shown in **Figure 1**.

Convertible Bond Arbitrage. In constructing a portfolio, convertible arbitrageurs can seek to isolate the cheapness of convertible bonds while limiting their exposure to other unwanted risk factors that might affect the value of their convertible bond portfolios (for example, changes in stock prices, credit ratings, credit spreads, or interest rates).

Figure 1. Median Discount of Convertibles to Their Theoretical Values, 1995–2007

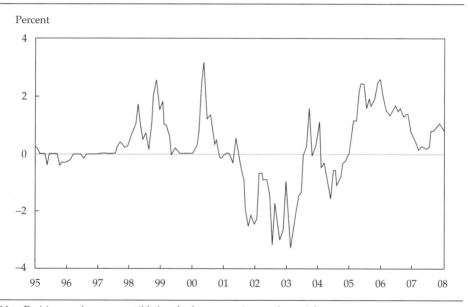

Note: Positive number = convertible bonds cheap; negative number = rich.

Source: Based on AQR/CNH proprietary models.

[5]The variations in cheapness over time may also reflect changing patterns in the typical offering terms of convertible bonds (e.g., takeover protection). Also, one might expect bonds in aggregate to get less cheap as investors are better able to hedge the idiosyncratic credit inherent in convertible bonds (e.g., through credit default swaps).

To minimize these risks, arbitrageurs generally go long a convertible bond and short the component parts of the bond (the straight debt and the equity option). Arbitrageurs can usually hedge the equity option component very easily by shorting stock and can dynamically readjust this hedge (delta hedge) as the stock price changes. The straight debt component may be harder to hedge—particularly because market prices for that debt may be scarce—but arbitrageurs can hedge some credit risk by selling short more equities and can also hedge with credit default swaps.

The fact that equity risk is easier to hedge directly than credit risk drives most convertible arbitrageurs to favor convertible bonds whose value comes more from the equity option and less from the straight debt component. The relative valuation of the equity and debt components of a bond depends on the price of the stock relative to the conversion price. Consider two examples, both based on a convertible bond with a face value of $1,000 that is convertible at the holder's option into 50 shares of stock, for a conversion price of $20.

On the one hand, if the stock price is $200, the fundamental value of the bond (if converted to stock) is $10,000 (50 shares worth $200 per share). If the bonds are not immediately convertible, the bond price may be lower than $10,000, but it will normally be close to $10,000. Most of the value of the bond will be linked to the equity option.

On the other hand, if the stock price is $1, then the conversion option is likely to be worthless because converting the $1,000 bond today realizes only $50 of stock. Holders of the bonds will simply wait to receive their $1,000 back at maturity. Most of the value of the bond will be linked to the straight debt.

Convertible bond arbitrageurs who seek to profit from the cheapness of a convertible bond will generally much prefer the first scenario—bonds that are equity sensitive. To measure the attractiveness of convertible bonds at any point in time, we focus on a universe of bonds whose "moneyness" or degree of being in the money (measured by the current stock price divided by the conversion price) is 0.65 or higher. This point tends to be the "sweet spot" for convertible arbitrage. By limiting our universe in this way, we also mitigate errors associated with inaccurate credit spread assumptions because credit spread assumptions are more important for bonds with deep out-of-the-money conversion options, which tend to trade more like distressed debt.

Returns to Convertible Arbitrage. Historically, convertible arbitrage strategies have delivered attractive returns for investors. From 1990 through 2007, the Hedge Fund Research (HFR) convertible arbitrage index delivered annualized returns of 10 percent, with annualized volatility (based on quarterly returns) of 5 percent. The Sharpe ratio of the strategy was 1.2. (By comparison, the S&P 500 Index had an annualized return of 11 percent, an annual volatility of 15 percent, and a Sharpe ratio of 0.4 for the same period.)

These returns benefit from the use of leverage. From 1995 through 2007, convertible bonds traded, on average, 0.8 percent cheap relative to fundamental value. Because properly implemented convertible arbitrage portfolios are immunized from most equity, credit, and interest rate risk, they tend to exhibit very low volatility. This ability to hedge the dominant risks of convertible bonds allowed financing counterparties to maintain low margin requirements, enabling arbitrageurs to substantially leverage their portfolios.

Imperfect Arbitrage. A "perfect arbitrage" is an investment that offers riskless profit. Convertible arbitrage, needless to say, is not perfect. Historically, convertible arbitrageurs generally have lost money in two ways—through default and unwinding.

When a convertible bond defaults, its fundamental value is dramatically reduced. In principle, an arbitrageur's short exposure (short both the equity option component and the straight debt component) should offset this loss. As noted earlier, however, the straight debt can be difficult to hedge in practice, and basis risk may arise between the straight debt component of the bond and the instrument used to short straight debt exposure. This basis risk can lead to portfolio losses, but the impact of any single bond defaulting can be significantly mitigated by holding a diversified portfolio of convertible bonds, each appropriately hedged. The ultimate loss from an individual convertible bond default depends significantly on the path of the default (a sudden shock versus a slow death) and the ultimate recovery rate realized by bondholders.

Arbitrageurs have also lost money by unwinding (sometimes without choice) their positions prior to realizing the fundamental value of the bonds they hold. In 1998 when the hedge fund Long-Term Capital Management (LTCM) experienced large losses, it was forced to liquidate investments across the entirety of its portfolio, including good investments. The liquidation of LTCM's convertible arbitrage portfolio caused the prices of bonds held by that fund to decline without corresponding declines in the values of the associated hedges. The losses forced other leveraged holders of convertible bonds to reduce their exposure by selling bonds. A similar situation occurred in 2005 when some investors in hedge funds that invested in convertible bond arbitrage withdrew their capital. To meet these redemption demands, hedge funds began to sell convertible bonds, causing bond prices to fall relative to fundamental values, which led to a subsequent wave of selling and price devaluation. In both cases, it took several months before bond prices returned to more normal levels and rough equilibrium was restored.

Convertible Bonds in the Credit Crisis

As the recent credit crisis unfolded, convertible bonds slowly, but inexorably, cheapened. Median bond cheapness rose from 0.9 percent at the end of 2007 to 1.4

percent at the end of February 2008. Despite the collapse of Bear Stearns in March 2008, the convertible bond market remained relatively healthy, with cheapness only growing to 1.7 percent by the end of March. As investors became more risk averse (and perhaps less willing to hold illiquid credit assets), bonds cheapened dramatically, ending the second quarter at 2.3 percent cheap. At that level, they were about as cheap as they had been during the LTCM crisis of 1998 and the convertible bond sell-off of 2005. By the end of August 2008, the bonds were even cheaper—trading 3.7 percent below fundamental value—representing a significant apparent "arbitrage," although in reality only foreshadowing the far more substantial events that were yet to come.

Considering the times, this performance is not especially surprising. Risk premiums for virtually all assets were rising over the period as investors became reluctant to hold risky assets and problems at financial institutions grew more serious.

The rising cheapness of bonds made convertible arbitrage an increasingly attractive strategy (because greater cheapness meant higher expected returns when prices ultimately converged to fundamental value). At the same time, the performance of convertible arbitrage managers suffered. The HFR convertible arbitrage index fell 9 percent in the first eight months of 2008.

After Lehman Brothers. The real disaster in convertible bond arbitrage came in September, after the collapse of Lehman Brothers. In the last four months of 2008, the HFR convertible arbitrage index fell 27 percent, to end 2008 down 34 percent. What happened, in essence, was that financing was withdrawn from the convertible bond market, causing problems for arbitrageurs who faced a mismatch between the relative illiquidity of their convertible bond portfolios and the short-term financing that supported those positions.

Going into late 2008, we estimate that 75 percent of convertible bonds outstanding in the United States were held by convertible bond arbitrageurs. Convertible bond arbitrage portfolios were typically run with 3–5× leverage, meaning for every $100 of capital invested, they owned between $300 and $500 of convertible bonds.

The financing for these positions typically was obtained from prime brokers, who resided within large investment or commercial banks. Prime brokers supplied financing to this market at attractive rates and with modest margin requirements because they knew that the relative ease with which convertible bond portfolios could be hedged limited the arbitrageurs' exposure to the direction of equity markets or interest rates.

The prime brokers, in turn, often raised the cash needed to fund these loans by rehypothecating those same convertible bonds to secure their own borrowings. For the prime brokers, these secured loans, often sourced through European banks, represented the lowest cost source of financing for their customers' convertible bond positions. An alternative was to fund them with internal sources of funds, perhaps funds available from the unsecured borrowings of the parent bank. But there is a meaningful difference in the cost of these forms of funding, and in late 2008, that gap become very wide—if unsecured funding was available at all to the prime broker (which it often was not).

When Lehman collapsed, the secured funding mechanisms for convertible bonds broke down. Lehman's secured lenders found that they had to liquidate the collateral Lehman had delivered to them to secure its loans, something they never expected to happen. Much of that collateral was easy for the lenders to liquidate, but some was not, in particular the convertible bond portfolios. Lenders with no expertise trading these assets were forced to sell difficult-to-price collateral in a chaotic environment. They quickly informed remaining bank borrowers that convertible bonds would no longer be accepted as collateral for secured loans. This policy change forced convertible bonds back onto prime broker balance sheets, where they could only be funded through expensive and now extremely scarce internal funds, a scarcity that persisted even past the extreme depths of the crisis as bank balance sheet pressure continued through year-end.

Against this backdrop, prime brokers were forced to push bonds back onto their leveraged customers' own balance sheets by removing financing (essentially raising margin requirements to as high as 100 percent). Because the community of convertible bond arbitrageurs was leveraged and many relied on short-term financing, managers were forced to liquidate their bonds or find new, but now very scarce, sources of funding.

Liquidity Recedes. With virtually no other financing available, most investors had to sell. The most vulnerable were managers of single-strategy convertible bond arbitrage funds. These managers had no other securities to offer as collateral and little other business with prime brokers that might have induced them to continue offering some financing.

Multistrategy managers had some insulation because they could potentially offer other securities (such as stocks) from their portfolios as collateral for loans. They also posed a greater business loss to prime brokers if they were able to take their business elsewhere in the wake of the crisis. Even these managers, however, faced pressure to reduce their leveraged convertible bond portfolios.

In the weeks following Lehman's collapse, we estimate that between selling and price deterioration, convertible arbitrage portfolios shrank by 50 percent or more in aggregate. Some of this selling was self-reinforcing. Prime brokerage financing is based on margin. Lenders limit financing by capping the ratio of the size of arbitrageurs' portfolios to the investment capital deployed. At times, this ratio could be 5× or higher, meaning arbitrageurs with $100 to invest could buy $500 of bonds. But in this example, if bond prices fall 5 percent (holding other factors constant), an investor holding $500 of bonds with $100 of capital is quickly in trouble. The $500 portfolio of bonds is now worth $475. This $25 loss depletes the investor's capital base, so the initial $100 is now only $75. At a ratio of 5:1, the investor is only permitted to hold $375 of bonds, so the investor must sell $100. This sale puts further pressure on prices, and the cycle intensifies.[6]

One counterweight to this cycle was the term financing arrangements used by some arbitrageurs and prime brokers. In these arrangements, prime brokers could not simply call back their financing (or change their terms) overnight. Typically, before these terms could change, either the prime broker had to give arbitrageurs advance notice (often 30–90 days) or the borrower or prime broker had to trip certain triggers. This arrangement gave some arbitrageurs time and flexibility, so in practice, all levered investors in convertible bonds did not have to sell in the exact same day or week.

Although the severely impaired financing market for convertible bonds was the dominant driver of price deterioration, other related factors contributed as well. There was a general flight away from illiquid investments (due in no small part to the difficulties in financing them). Competing asset types also had become very cheap, which limited the flow of new capital to convertible bonds. Finally, short-selling bans across a wide range of stocks also hurt the convertible bond market. The bans prevented potential new arbitrageurs (such as multistrategy hedge funds or opportunistic investors) from stepping in to purchase cheap convertible bonds whose equity was on the list of stocks that could not be shorted. Under the bans, arbitrageurs were prohibited from initiating new equity hedges on these bonds, even in cases where they were purchasing the positions from another arbitrageur who already had equity hedges in place. Without new arbitrage capital entering the market, bond prices had to fall far enough to attract interest from other market participants.

Crossover Buyers. Who was willing to buy the bonds that came up for sale? In a normal market, convertible bond arbitrageurs (either hedge funds or bank trading desks) typically step in to buy bonds when there is selling pressure in the market. They are the "buyer of last resort" for the bonds. In late 2008, these buyers became forced sellers. With no natural buyers available, bond prices went into a free fall, driving the cheapness of convertible bonds to new records. Whereas in earlier times cheapness of 2–3 percent was considered a significant dislocation in equity-sensitive convertible bonds, in 2008, the cheapness of these bonds sailed right through 4 percent and 6 percent and 8 percent to bottom out at close to 12 percent cheap, as shown in **Figure 2**.

---

[6]To get a sense of the magnitude of the selling pressure, consider the following anecdote. In the depths of the crisis (roughly late November 2008), investors in need of cash were offering bonds below their conversion value. In other words, a bond that could contractually (and at any time) be converted into, say, 20 shares of stock worth $60 per share might be selling below $1,200. The reason is that the conversion process can sometimes take more than a day or two before the shares are received and can be sold, and managers under pressure could not wait that long for the cash.

Figure 2. Median Discount of Convertibles to Their Theoretical Values, January 1995–August 2009

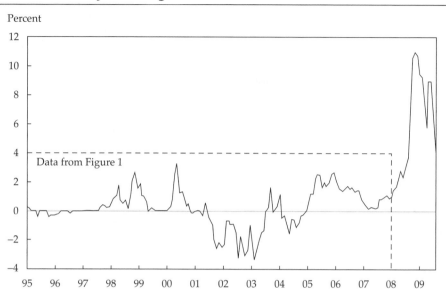

Note: Positive number = convertible bonds cheap; negative number = rich.

Source: Based on AQR/CNH proprietary models.

Bonds fell until they became cheap enough to attract new buyers, such as investors who usually held few or no convertible bonds but who were willing to commit capital when the expected returns became sufficiently high. Called "cross-over" buyers, they included value equity investors (some of whom sold stocks to buy convertible bonds when the risk–return trade-off of bonds became intriguing) and some multistrategy hedge funds that had not previously been big holders of bonds (and so had not been forced to delever).

Perhaps the most interesting crossover buyers were the issuers themselves. At one time, these issuers had gone to the market and been willing to sell bonds below fundamental value in order to raise capital. In late 2008, despite all the pressures on financing and balance sheets, certain convertible bond issuers stepped back into the market to repurchase their own bonds at a large discount to fundamental value. For issuers to make this move, they had to determine that their return on invested capital from buying back bonds would be greater than what they would receive from investing in new projects or business opportunities. It also meant that the return from repurchasing their debt was greater than their own cost of capital across the balance sheet, including equities, bank debt, other bonds issued, and equity capital—a significant hurdle in a liquidity-starved world, particularly with regard to convertible bonds where many issuers have weak credit ratings or no credit ratings at all.

Stabilization. In early 2009, the market began to recover and bonds became less cheap. Notably, this change happened during a period when equity prices were still falling and credit investments also fared poorly. But fundamental values of convertible bonds declined faster than convertible bond prices, so the bonds got "less cheap" and arbitrageurs whose hedges were short stock and credit made money.

A few drivers helped the market stabilize and recover. First, equilibrium began to be restored as prices fell far enough that the supply and demand of convertible bonds were back in better balance. Crossover buyers stepped in to provide new demand. The arbitrageurs that were forced to sell bonds completed their selling, removing the overhang of bonds for sale, and the convertible arbitrage market got smaller, requiring less overall financing from prime brokers. These changes halted the decline in bond prices but were not enough to lead to price appreciation.

For price appreciation to occur, a new wave of buyers had to come into the market. Some investors were willing to buy convertible bonds on the way down, recognizing that the cheapness relative to fundamental value could lead to extraordinary returns. Others were not willing to commit capital to a strategy in a free fall but became more tempted once the price declines abated, but bonds still remained cheap. Still others waited to see some initial signs of a rebound. With stabilization, new buyers emerged. With new buyers, recovery began.

These buyers were all able to buy bonds that, based on our data, were cheaper relative to fundamentals than at any time in recent decades (and perhaps ever). These new buyers, however, had different experiences depending on when they entered the market. When bonds were in a free fall, the supply in the market was enormous. In a market that was traditionally "illiquid," investors were able to purchase hundreds of millions, if not billions, of dollars of bonds in a single day. Once the market stabilized and began to recover, bonds were still for sale but in smaller quantities.

For the first quarter of 2009, the HFR convertible arbitrage index was up 11 percent.

The Return of Financing. The initial stabilization was somewhat precarious. Even as prices reached equilibrium, market participants recognized that some large players in the market might still be holding substantial positions that they had not yet been forced to unwind. The sell-off in convertible bonds was fast enough that arbitrageurs with term financing of 90 days (or even longer) were potentially able to hold their portfolios through the worst of the crisis. Some investors worried that these bonds represented an "overhang" that could depress prices further if their holders were ultimately forced to sell. Another possible overhang came from investors in hedge funds. The sell-off in bonds happened before many of these investors could redeem their capital. Many managers had raised gates or put into place other redemption restrictions. As these restrictions were relaxed, the possibility existed that investors would demand their capital back, spurring another round of convertible bond liquidation.

Given these concerns, the market's recovery was enhanced by the return of equilibrium in financing markets. The initial pullback by the ultimate lenders to prime brokers was—in hindsight—a panic driven by the fallout of Lehman's collapse. Eventually, lenders realized that they could still have a profitable business making loans to prime brokers with convertible bonds as collateral, provided they made appropriate adjustments ("haircuts") to reflect the difficulty and price pressures they might face in trying to sell convertible bond collateral. As prime brokers' own funding situation stabilized, they were again willing to lend against convertible bonds. Managers who had been told by their prime broker to sell bonds or move their business suddenly found themselves being offered new convertible bond financing.

The return of financing was gradual, but it also came in an environment where the demand for convertible bond financing had dropped sharply. It was not a return to the old days of convertible bond financing. Margin requirements were much stricter (forcing managers to use less leverage), and the borrowing costs charged by prime brokers were meaningfully higher. The panic and forced selling, however, receded.

By the end of April 2009, cheapness was down below 6 percent, almost half the levels at year-end 2008 (but still the cheapest on our record prior to the credit crisis). As the market strengthened through the second quarter of 2009, new convertible bond issuance resumed, which was an encouraging sign because it meant the environment was healthy enough that issuers were willing to pay market prices for financing. At the same time, it put a temporary halt to the decline in bond cheapness. New issues had to attract buyers, and they typically did so by coming to market at prices slightly cheaper than the bonds investors were already holding. Indeed, the universe of bonds actually became somewhat cheaper over the course of the second quarter, albeit under very different circumstances from those of the last quarter of 2008. Panic was largely gone from the market, and the return of financing and issuance suggested that the market had reached a new equilibrium—one that offered investors the prospect of much higher returns from convertible arbitrage than had ever existed before the credit crisis.

By the midpoint of 2009, with the financing situation more stabilized, the HFR convertible arbitrage index had gained 29 percent.

Implications

Convertible arbitrage is an excellent example of a relatively low-risk arbitrage. In theory, a perfect arbitrage is supposed to offer riskless profits. In practice, no perfect arbitrages exist. Still, arbitrage strategies of all stripes offer the *possibility* of profits, generally with low risk relative to the possible return and also with low correlation with the direction of the markets.

Convertible bond arbitrage fits neatly into this category. But the performance of convertible arbitrage during the credit crisis is a case study in the risks and limits of arbitrage. In theory, convertible arbitrage would have worked for investors who could have held their positions through the crisis. In theory, any investor would have been an aggressive buyer of hedged convertible bonds in late 2008. Unlike so many other "cheap" bets at the time, these were not even a bet on the economy recovering. In practice, however, virtually all arbitrageurs used leverage and faced an asset/liability mismatch between the term of their leverage (mostly 0–90 days) and the term of the convertible bond portfolios being financed. As a result, when the financing environment become extraordinarily tight, virtually all users of leverage were forced to sell, even as assets were becoming cheaper and arbitrage strategies were becoming more attractive.

This case study should be a warning to prospective investors in any type of arbitrage: Strategies based on some type of future "convergence" event are usually lower risk than strategies that depend on the direction of volatile markets, but these strategies are not riskless, particularly where leverage using short-term financing is involved. This does not make them bad investments, but it means investors must understand that their leverage, or the leverage used by other holders of the same assets, presents its own particular set of risks.

Although this crisis exposes a negative lesson, there is also a positive one. The dramatic returns enjoyed by convertible arbitrage investors in 2009 suggest that when arbitrage strategies go bad, opportunistic investors can step in and potentially earn outsize returns. An investor who saw the unprecedented cheapness in convertible bonds at the end of 2008 could have made spectacular profits in the first half of 2009. These profits were not riskless; at the time of investment in 2008, such an investor would still have faced a great deal of uncertainty about the future direction of the convertible bond market, the prospective availability of financing, and the possibility of near-term losses had the remaining leveraged investors been forced to continue selling. But for well-capitalized investors who used only modest leverage, these risks were readily manageable.

Opportunistic investors who balanced these risks against the unprecedented cheapness of the bonds, the expectation of convergence at maturity (typically two to four years out), and the dramatic sell-off that had already occurred would have been very successful.

In general, opportunistic investment strategies seek to provide liquidity to the markets in extreme periods by buying when the rest of the world wants to sell (and vice versa). Implementing these strategies is difficult. By definition, they always appear very risky at the time they emerge (because they tend to be going against the conventional wisdom). They are difficult to time because calling a bottom (or top) in almost any asset class or market is nearly impossible. But investors who can accept these difficulties are often well compensated. (Of course, they must face the possibility of not being compensated or else the opportunities would, by definition, be riskless and investors would pile in.)

Conclusion

The performance of convertible arbitrage during the credit meltdown is a textbook example of a liquidity crunch and the limits of arbitrage. The massive losses remind us that liquidity and financing are the lifeblood of many investment strategies and that such strategies face the risk of periodic panics if they evaporate. The behavior of prime brokers (and their ultimate lenders) reminds us that there can be enormous complexity in the financial system, even for investments that are far less "structured" than the collateralized debt obligations and mortgage securities that garnered so many headlines during the crisis. The substantial gains in 2009 remind us that opportunistic investing can yield impressive results for those with strong stomachs and strong balance sheets. Ultimately, the case of convertible bond arbitrage forces us to acknowledge the risks in financial markets and that with those risks come challenges and opportunities.

We would like to thank our colleagues Mike Mendelson, Mark Mitchell, Lars Nielsen, and Todd Pulvino for sharing their insights on the convertible bond market in 2008 and for their comments on earlier drafts of this article.

Disclosure

The Mark-to-Market Controversy and the Valuation of Financial Institutions

Edwin T. Burton
Professor of Economics
University of Virginia
Charlottesville, Virginia

The debate about what the rules should be that determine asset valuations on corporate balance sheets has come to be known as the "mark-to-market" controversy. Some argue that companies should be able to carry assets at whatever values they want so long as they can defend that valuation in some manner. Others argue that companies should be required as a matter of law to carry assets at valuations found in the marketplace. Because marketplace valuations of assets that are intended to be held as long-term investments often arise in a "fire sale" (distress sale), companies argue that they should not have to value their assets at these temporarily depressed levels. The companies argue that they may have no intention or need to sell these assets quickly, so why value the assets as if they did? Who is right, and does it matter? This article is an effort to shed some light on this controversy and to raise some surprising new issues that, so far, have not surfaced in this discussion and that have great importance for the valuation of financial institutions.

Background

A company with a negative net worth can survive and prosper in a modern economy. Indeed, most private companies have negligible or even negative net worth, mostly because of rationally responding to the income tax environment. So, if a company can thrive with negative net worth, why do accounting policies regarding asset valuations—where the object is to ascertain the net worth of the company—matter? The answer is that under normal circumstances, they do not matter all that much. Earnings and the prospects for the future growth of earnings matter more. But when concerns mount about the viability of a company's business model, then net worth does matter; and it may be all that matters. The financial crisis that surfaced in mid-2007 turned a spotlight on the accounting practices of financial services firms. In September 2007, markets eagerly awaited the third-quarter earnings releases of Lehman Brothers and Goldman Sachs to glean some understanding of the quality of the assets of those two investment banks. With the crash of the subprime lending market and the closing of the asset-backed securities market, investors wanted to know how much exposure the investment banks had to the plunging values of mortgage-related securities. Interestingly, both Lehman's and Goldman Sachs' earnings reports had asset write-downs and liability write-downs. Why liability write-downs?

Lehman and Goldman Sachs argued that the liability write-downs, taken in September 2007, reflected the fact that some of their liabilities were hedges against assets. As the assets were written down, the liabilities needed to be written down as well; otherwise, a hedged position would show a loss that really was not a loss. It was not obvious at the time, or even now, that these liability write-downs were appropriate because the assets that offset the liabilities may not have been "good" hedges. The details were not available to make this determination, but the very fact of the liability write-downs raised some important accounting and economic issues. When are liability write-downs appropriate? Obviously, if you no longer owe someone through some fortuitous event, then the write-down is appropriate. But can you write down one of your liabilities because your own financial situation has weakened and there is doubt in the marketplace about whether or not you will honor your liability?

Surprisingly, the answer to this question is not obvious. If you owe me money and I write down the debt on my balance sheet, do you still owe it? If I write my loan to you down by 50 percent, can you do the same on your balance sheet to the liability? What happens to the aggregate balance sheet of the economy (in this case, consisting of just you and me) if you do not? These considerations suggest that the issue of mark-to-market accounting may be more difficult than it seems at first glance.

Some might be thinking: Why does this matter? It turns out to matter a great deal if the answer to the question being asked determines the viability of the financial system as a whole. These are the four conclusions I have drawn:

1. Treating the same asset as having a different value depending on which side of the balance sheet it is placed on (asymmetric write-downs) can lead to a seriously incorrect estimate of the financial health of the financial system as a whole. This I would call the "Roubini effect," referring to New York University Professor Nouriel Roubini, who (as I will argue later) has erred by overestimating the damage done to the financial services sector by the crisis of 2007–2009.

2. Asymmetric write-downs can create a crisis of confidence in the short-term funding for a financial services company. It could be argued that asymmetric write-downs had much to do with the collapse of Bear Stearns and Lehman Brothers.

3. A correct solution is unlikely to involve more-liberal rules for writing down liabilities. It would be awkward, to say the least, if companies could generate earnings by announcing that they plan to be deadbeats in the future.

4. Whatever the correct solution may be, the principle of full and complete disclosure, although it creates serious problems for management of companies in crisis, should not be abandoned.

The Potential Mischief of Mark-to-Market Accounting

A simple thought experiment should clarify the issues here. Begin by considering the balance sheet for a greatly simplified financial services company, which I will call Company A, shown in **Exhibit 1**.

Exhibit 1.   Company A's Balance Sheet

Assets	Liabilities
$100 million (loan to Company B)	$100 million (owed to Company B)
$25 million (loan to business)	$10 million (commercial paper outstanding)
	Net Worth: $15 million

Note that Company A's balance sheet indicates that Companies A and B have offsetting $100 million loans to each other. If one assumes that the interest rate is identical on these two loans, the entire operating earnings of Company A will depend on the income generated by the $25 million loan to business less the interest expense of the $10 million in outstanding commercial paper. The actual reported earnings, as distinct from operating earnings, will be affected by how the $100 million loan to Company B and the $100 million loan from Company B are valued. At first glance, one might wonder how these two loans could have different values. But, in fact, these loans can, in principle, have different values on the balance sheet that will affect not only reported earnings (after write-downs or asset revaluations) but also reported net worth.

More ominously, there is a potential mismatch in the term structure of assets and liabilities in this simple example that is characteristic of a financial services firm. The $25 million in loan to business may be a three-, four-, or five-year loan, whereas the commercial paper outstanding may come due after 90 days. Normally, this mismatch is not that big of an issue, although if short-term commercial paper rates increase dramatically, both operating earnings and net worth can be affected negatively. One would expect Company A to be able to either weather this storm through the interest rate swap market if necessary or simply tough it out and absorb losses for a time period until a new loan to business can be put in place that reflect the higher rate environment.

But there is a scarier scenario for Company A as the world discovered in the financial crisis of 2008 with the saga of Bear Stearns, Lehman, Fannie Mae, Freddie Mac, AIG, and others.

Imagine that Company A's auditor has become nervous about the ability of Company B to make the interest payments on the loan that Company A has made to Company B. Perhaps a similar loan has traded somewhere at a price lower than full principal value (which in this case is $100 million). So, Company A's auditor insists that Company A write down the value of the loan from Company B.

Reducing the value of the loan from Company B to 90 from par (to $90 million from $100 million) will reduce net worth by $10 million, slashing net worth by two-thirds. The commercial paper market will notice this change. As the auditor continues to push Company A to reduce its balance sheet valuation of the loan from Company B, it will not be long before net worth is perilously close to zero or even negative. Reported earnings will be crushed and will turn negative, even though the loan from Company B continues to perform—interest payments continue to arrive on time. Thus, operating earnings are unimpaired, but reported earnings collapse and turn negative.

The nightmare scenario now arises when the commercial paper market closes for Company A. Imagine that buyers of commercial paper refuse to buy any more commercial paper when the current 90-day funding comes due. This situation creates a liquidity crisis for Company A and, absent a bailout, will lead to bankruptcy for Company A. This scenario is essentially a classic "run on the bank," triggered by a crisis in confidence that is induced by a deteriorating balance sheet. All of this happens even though operating earnings are unaffected. Had the auditor left well enough alone, perhaps Company A would have prospered and the commercial paper market would have provided funding without interruption.

Of course, the idea behind the markdown of assets, insisted upon by the auditor, is that sooner or later the deterioration in the value of the loan from Company B will translate into nonperformance. But in the real world, the nonperformance may never take place. So, ironically, the company's operating earnings could be doing fine, but reported earnings can collapse and bankruptcy could easily result if there is a funding mismatch.

Consider now the balance sheet of Company B, shown in **Exhibit 2**. Assume that Company B is simply a mirror image of Company A and that the entire financial sector is composed solely of Companies A and B.

Exhibit 2. Company B's Balance Sheet

Assets	Liabilities
$100 million (loan to Company A)	$100 million (owed to Company A)
$25 million (loan to business)	$10 million (commercial paper outstanding)
Net Worth: $15 million	

Imagine that the auditors for these companies, looking at the debt assets, insist that the companies "write down" the asset values from $100 million to $80 million because somewhere the price of 80 cents on the dollar has been revealed for debt assets of this type. So, each company then writes down the assets to $80 million, producing the balance sheets after revision shown in **Exhibit 3**.

Exhibit 3. Company A's and Company B's Balance Sheet

Assets	Liabilities
Company A	
$80 million (loan to Company B)	$100 million (owed to Company B)
$25 million (loan to business)	$10 million (commercial paper outstanding)
Net Worth: –$5 million	
Company B	
$80 million (loan to Company A)	$100 million (owed to Company A)
$25 million (loan to business)	$10 million (commercial paper outstanding)
Net Worth: –$5 million	

The aggregate value of the financial sector is –$10 million because each firm now has a net worth of –$5 million. Before the asset write-downs, the net worth of the financial sector was $30 million. The $40 million drop in the value of the financial sector is completely the result of the asset write-downs required by the auditors. Note that if Companies A and B merge (or merely agree to cancel their equal and offsetting obligations), the financial sector will have an immediate increase in value of $40 million, although nothing of substance really has taken place.

If this were the end of it, then the mark to market might still not matter much, but if the commercial paper market closes for both Company A and Company B, then the entire financial system will be bankrupt and both Company A and Company B will fail. This is a strange result but not that far removed in spirit from much of what took place in late 2008 as the financial crisis reached a climax. It is also worth noting that adjusting asset values asymmetrically may lead to problems for debt covenants and debt ratings, which can also snowball into financing problems for companies and lead to a crisis of confidence and a resultant cash crisis.

The financial sector as a whole cannot have a net value less than what would be ascribed to it if all debts internal to the financial sector were cancelled. Worth considering is the simple principle that a debt asset should have the same value to the debtor as it has to the creditor. This simple idea has important implications, and following it would have avoided the paradox of my example. (The paradox is that the disaggregation of the financial services industry into two essentially identical companies, A and B, creates the problem. When the companies are combined, the financial problem vanishes.)

When Roubini, the poster child prophet of doom for the 2007–08 financial crisis, argues that a $3.7 trillion "hole" exists in the financial sector, he is using an analysis very similar to the one just given: He is writing down debt assets but not the liabilities that correspond to those assets. Doing so will tend to create a misleading valuation of the financial services sector as a whole because a substantial portion of the balance sheet assets of the financial sector are debt assets whose liability side is held somewhere else in the financial system.

The argument can be made that the financial media's focus (and the ensuing widespread public attention) on the asset write-downs in the financial sector without a consideration of the offsetting decreasing liability values created an unrealistically pessimistic view of the underlying strength of the U.S. financial system. This same asymmetric view of debt assets permeated the analyses of other financial systems globally. Things were very likely never as bad as some thought, particularly those who focused only on the asset revaluations on the financial sector balance sheets. If this argument is valid and has empirical significance, something that cannot be decided here, then the heroic policy measures adopted in late 2008, with their attendant costs, may well have been unwarranted. The risk to the financial system, or "systemic" risk, may well have been substantially less than policymakers assumed at the time. That is not to say that bankruptcies would not have occurred in major financial institutions. They would have occurred. But the systemic impact of such bankruptcies would have been far less than most believed then or believe now.

Why Is a Financial Institution Different?

The balance sheet of a financial institution is very different from the balance sheet of a nonfinancial company. The assets of financial institutions are predominantly debt assets, and the liabilities are mostly, by definition, debt assets, actual or implied. It might be argued that *the dominance of debt assets on the balance sheet of financial institutions is one way of defining a financial institution.* For the purposes here, a debt asset is an obligation by one party to pay fixed payments at specific dates to another party. The party that receives payments, usually referred to as the creditor, owns the debt asset. The party that owes the payments is the debtor. Obviously, some assets do not meet this strict definition and yet routinely show up as assets and liabilities of financial institutions. But the bulk of debt assets will fit this definition, and I will use this definition in what follows.

So, what about debt assets? How are debt assets different from other assets, and why does it matter? When is an asset not a debt asset? Imagine you own an oil well. Your asset consists of reserves of oil waiting to be produced and sold. If that asset is suddenly destroyed and you have no insurance, then the asset is now worth zero and your net worth is reduced accordingly. Other than the drop in your assets and net worth, there are no other accounting entries required in the economy to reflect the loss of the oil well. But debt assets are different.

If you own a corporate bond and it is suddenly worthless, then your assets and net worth are suddenly lower by the amount of the loss in value of the corporate bond. But somewhere in the economy there is another accounting adjustment to be made. Someone had a monetary obligation evidenced by the existence of that corporate bond. That obligation was represented by a liability on the part of the issuer of the corporate bond. If the corporate bond is truly worth zero, then that liability is now worth zero. Or is it?

Transparency and Corporate Accounting

The guiding principle of U.S. securities regulation is the concept of "full disclosure," which translates into a demand for "transparency" by shareholder advocates. Transparency means, among other things, that accounting values should reflect current market values to the extent possible. After the passage of the Sarbanes–Oxley Act in 2002, the role of public company auditors shifted from service provider to regulator. Auditors began to exercise much more authority over the financial statements of their clients, and the Financial Accounting Standards Board (FASB) was crowned by the U.S. SEC as the rule maker for the auditing industry. The auditors could not defy FASB, and as a practical matter, public companies could not defy their auditors in this new regime.

The post-Sarbanes–Oxley demand for more transparency and the elevation of the role of auditors as the watchdog meant that there would eventually be a struggle over balance sheet asset valuations. Whenever an economic downturn arrived, an argument would be made, sure to be advanced by auditors, that balance sheet assets were not as strong as they had been earlier during more prosperous times.

On the one hand, companies would naturally resist this interpretation because of what happens when a company lowers the value of the assets on its balance sheet. This process of "writing down" assets on the balance sheet does not generally play well in the financial marketplace and can lead to higher borrowing rates or in the extreme, a collapse in available funding for the company. On the other hand, ignoring declining asset values could be seriously misleading to present and future shareholders and a violation of the spirit and letter of the disclosure requirements of securities laws.

If assets are impaired, meaning that earnings have been adversely affected, then it is pretty clear that asset write-downs are appropriate. A different set of considerations arises if there is an expectation, shrouded in uncertainty, that assets *may* become impaired in the future. Should these more "gray-area" valuation considerations lead to write-downs? Suppose an asset is still performing in the sense that current earnings from the asset are unchanged. Should that asset be written down because an apparently similar asset has traded at a price lower than that at which the asset is currently carried on the balance sheet? What if that lower price is a fire-sale price and not the price that a lengthy and serious sales process might produce? What if the apparently similar asset is not all that similar? None of these questions has an easy answer.

And what about the valuation of liabilities? If you have a corporate bond outstanding and it is trading at 50 cents on the dollar, should you be able to write that bond down to 50 and take income into the current quarter from that write-down? If that bond is owned by another company, the other company will be forced to take the write-down through mark to market. Why can't the debtor value the debt the same as the creditor? If a company repurchases outstanding corporate bonds for

50 cents on the dollar, it can, under current accounting rules, take that difference between 50 and par as income. Shouldn't it be able to take that same income without buying back the corporate bond, assuming 50 cents is the true market price? It is difficult to see why you have to actually buy the bond to show the income.

The problem, of course, is that if writing down liabilities creates current income, then companies may well use that expedient as a method of managing earnings in difficult times. Showing improved earnings because the company does not plan to meet future obligations is a bizarre form of transparency. It seems clear that liability write-downs of this type would tend to be more misleading than helpful to present and potential shareholders. So, expanding the use of liability write-downs is probably not the direction that disclosure rules should move in.

But there is still the problem of the Company A/Company B example. Cancelling the debt or merging the companies creates immediate, substantial value for no economic reason. That is not a very comforting result or a ringing endorsement of the current accounting rules.

What Is the Right Way to Mark Assets?

The right answer to this question may depend on the purpose of the inquiry. If a given company chooses to leave assets at values higher than those at which similar assets are currently valued in the marketplace, then, at the very least, the financial statements of the company should be footnoted to show where these assets are valued in the marketplace and the rationale for not reducing their values should be described. Full disclosure should not be a casualty of the mark-to-market controversy resolution.

But the principles that should apply to reporting balance sheet quantities for an individual company might not be appropriate when considering an aggregation of companies. For the analysis of systemic risk, it seems clear that a given asset should be treated as having the same value whether it is an asset or a liability. In practice, this means that such analysts as Roubini would be well advised to adjust the aggregate balance sheet exercises that they perform by decreasing system liabilities to the extent of the asset write-downs where it can be determined that identical debt assets may be involved. That would extend double-entry accounting principles to the problem of systemic risk and allow for more reasonable estimates of the system's fragilities.

This article has benefited from input from SNL Securities staffers as well as my own research assistants Meredith Winter, Jerome Meyinse, and Wilson Craig. I would also like to thank Larry Siegel and Rodney Sullivan, CFA, for their help and encouragement.

The History and Economics of Stock Market Crashes

Paul D. Kaplan, CFA
Vice President, Quantitative Research
Morningstar, Inc., Chicago

Thomas Idzorek, CFA
Chief Investment Officer
Ibbotson Associates, Chicago

Michele Gambera, CFA
Chief Economist
Ibbotson Associates, Chicago

Katsunari Yamaguchi
President
Ibbotson Associates Japan, Tokyo

James Xiong, CFA
Senior Research Consultant
Ibbotson Associates, Chicago

David M. Blanchett, CFA
MBA Candidate
University of Chicago Booth School of Business, Chicago

The phrase "irrational exuberance" is closely associated with Alan Greenspan, the former chairman of the U.S. Federal Reserve Board. As Shiller (2005) explains:

> [Greenspan] used [it] in a black-tie dinner speech entitled "The Challenge of Central Banking in a Democratic Society" before the American Enterprise Institute at the Washington Hilton Hotel [on] December 5, 1996. Fourteen pages into this long speech, which was televised live on C-SPAN, he posed a rhetorical question: "But how do we know when irrational exuberance has unduly escalated asset values, which then become subject to unexpected and prolonged contractions as they have in Japan over the past decade?" He added that, "We as central bankers need not be concerned if a collapsing financial asset bubble does not threaten to impair the real economy, its production, jobs, and price stability."
>
> Immediately after he said this, the Tokyo stock market, which was open as he gave this speech, fell sharply, closing down 3%. Hong Kong fell 3%. Then markets in Frankfurt and London fell 4%. The stock market in the US fell 2% at the open of trade.

Shiller goes on to explain:

> It appears that "irrational exuberance" are Greenspan's own words, and not a speech writer's. In his 2007 autobiography, *The Age of Turbulence: Adventures in a New World* Greenspan said "The concept of irrational exuberance came to me in the bathtub one morning as I was writing a speech." (p. 176)

Although it is unlikely that Greenspan's simple statement was intended to cause the reaction that it did, the term "irrational exuberance" has now become associated with any period when investors are in a heightened state of speculative fervor. Speculative fervors, or bubbles as they are more popularly known, may be easy to identify with the benefit of hindsight, but they are not nearly as easy to identify when they are occurring. Moreover, they are not by any means a new phenomenon. Even though the recent market crash beginning in 2007 is likely fresh on the mind of the reader, there have been many others, and far worse—for example, from August 1929 to May 1932, when the U.S. stock market fell 79 percent, and from December 1989 to March 2003, when the Japanese stock market fell nearly 72 percent. (These returns are *real total returns*; in other words, they include dividends and are adjusted for the effects of consumer price inflation or deflation.[1])

"Black Sunday," 14 September 2008

Much has been written about the 2008 crash, and certainly much more will be. At the time of this writing (mid-2009), the dust continues to settle. We will start with a brief version of what happened in the United States in 2008 and why.

Although markets had been in an orderly decline for the better part of a year, most observers agree that the catalyst that unleashed the full fury of 2008's global financial market meltdown occurred on Monday, 15 September 2008, when then-Secretary of the U.S. Treasury, Henry Paulson, announced that Lehman Brothers would be allowed to fail. Within minutes of this announcement, the various markets that were open tumbled and the credit markets began to freeze. The ensuing contagion resulted very quickly in a global financial crisis. **Figure 1** shows the intraday movement in various markets.

---

[1]We use real total returns, where possible, in this article because they represent the changes in purchasing power experienced by the investor. The use of nominal returns pretends that a dollar in 2009 is as valuable as a dollar in, say, 1900; it is not. The use of price-only returns (without dividends) omits one of the most important sources of return for investors, especially in past decades when dividend yields were higher than they are today.

Today's readers sometimes forget that the United States experienced a great deal of deflation during the Great Crash (1929–1932) period. Dividend yields were also high. Thus, the decline in real total return terms, just mentioned, was considerably less severe than the decline in the more familiar "nominal price-only" indices. Returns on nominal, price-only indices were as follows: The Dow Jones Industrial Average fell 89 percent on a top-day to bottom-day basis, and the S&P 90 (the precursor to the S&P 500 Index) fell 86 percent on a month-end (August 1929) to month-end (June 1932) basis.

Figure 1. Intraday Movement in Various Markets, 15 September–16 September 2008

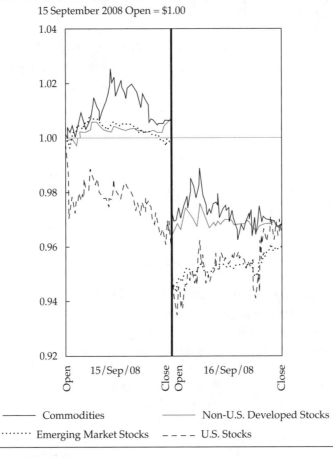

15 September 2008 Open = $1.00

——— Commodities ——— Non-U.S. Developed Stocks

········ Emerging Market Stocks – – – – U.S. Stocks

Vulnerabilities in the Financial System. What factors led to the bubble that burst in the fall of 2008? The first critical ingredient at the heart of all bubbles is human nature. Greed and misaligned incentives were present throughout the system, which created this leverage-driven real estate bubble. (And rest assured, more bubbles are in our future.) In addition to raw greed, several financial innovations that were designed to reduce or transfer risk were, ironically, the means by which risk was greatly magnified.

The continued development of asset-backed securities, and more specifically the securitization of mortgages, contributed significantly to the crash. Twenty years ago, most mortgage providers owned and serviced the mortgage loans they made. Under this business model, the mortgage provider had a strong incentive to conduct due diligence on the loan applicant prior to lending the money. After all, if the applicant was unable to pay the mortgage, it was the lender's problem. Additionally, when a borrower was in trouble, it was often possible for the borrower to make alternative arrangements with the lender. Over time, however, the mortgage business model changed. Mortgage providers began to sell off their mortgages to investment banks and other financial institutions that bundled the mortgages into mortgage-backed securities. This shift in the business model removed much of the incentive for mortgage providers to conduct due diligence on loan applicants and made it much more difficult for troubled borrowers to negotiate alternative arrangements.

The mortgage business model shift, in turn, fueled the development of a vast array of unconventional loans that would eventually be at the crux of the most "toxic" securities. (A toxic security, in current parlance, is one that has high risk or, especially, hidden risks.) The public was hungry for bigger and better homes that they could not truly afford; mortgage bankers and brokers craved the new business; investment bankers were eager to package and sell anything that the investing public would buy; and either the ratings agencies did not understand the true credit quality of these bundled mortgage-backed securities, or they were blinded by their conflicts of interest.

The second financial innovation that contributed to the recent bubble and crash was the development and widespread use of credit default swaps. Credit default swaps (CDS) are a form of "insurance" on bonds.[2] Should a bond default, the issuer (seller) of the CDS promises to make the purchaser whole. These risk-hedging devices had the unintended consequence of linking the financial stability of numerous financial firms together, creating a new kind of systemic risk capable of bringing down the financial system. As indicated later, the financial system very nearly succumbed to this risk.

CDS-issuing companies, such as AIG, dramatically underestimated the probability of widespread defaults and/or multiple defaults occurring in a short period of time. In addition, various financial institutions often held, as assets, large positions in bonds and other debt assets issued by other financial institutions; it was a widespread practice to hedge the default risk on these positions using CDS. This practice created a potential domino effect. The nearly simultaneous bankruptcy of several firms could immediately impair the CDS issuer(s), in turn, impairing additional financial institutions down the line and thus leading to a vicious cycle capable of destroying the financial system.

---

[2]The word "insurance" is in quotes because the buyer need not have an insurable interest. Thus, the notional amount of the insurance can be an unlimited multiple of the face value of the bonds. So, a CDS is essentially a naked short position, not an insurance policy, although the trigger feature of a CDS causes it to closely resemble insurance. This point is addressed in Peter Wallison's article in this book.

The environment prior to the crash could be described as one in which greed was rampant throughout the system; the lending system was out of control; ratings agencies completely failed at their job of giving accurate ratings to securities; and the risk-hedging system created a false sense of security, which inadvertently linked various players in the financial system together in an unhealthy way. We will resist the temptation to lambaste the market overseers that enabled these factors to exist in this form.

Deflation of the Real Estate Bubble and the Ensuing Financial Crisis. At the heart of the growing bubble was a leverage-driven residential real estate bubble that had started to deflate. **Figure 2** shows the S&P Case–Shiller Home Price Indices from January 1973 to June 2009, as well as several other house price metrics. As shown, house prices peaked around the beginning of 2006 and were clearly declining by the end of 2006. As real estate prices declined, the strain on the financial system increased, especially for firms with significant exposure to real estate–linked investments.

The first dramatic and highly visible sign of the pending meltdown began on 10 March 2008 as rumors of Bear Stearns' deteriorating financial health propagated through Wall Street. Bear Stearns had bet heavily on real estate, especially subprime mortgages. Falling real estate prices were quickly revealing the toxicity of many subprime mortgages. In addition to a large exposure to subprime mortgage-backed securities, Bear Stearns had sold billions of dollars of "insurance" on bonds in the form of CDS. The rumors became a self-fulfilling reality triggering a classic run on the bank. Within a week, Bear Stearns was on the brink of insolvency. After reviewing the web of interconnected CDS, Timothy Geithner, who was at the Federal Reserve Bank of New York at the time, and Ben Bernanke, the Federal Reserve chairman, deemed that allowing Bear Stearns to fail would cause multiple other financial institutions to fail. Bernanke arranged for JPMorgan Chase to acquire Bear Stearns at a bargain price and provided JPMorgan with a $30 billion guarantee to protect JPMorgan from further losses on Bear Stearns' toxic assets.

The Fed's move may have prevented the financial crisis from erupting in March 2008, but as time revealed, it had unintended consequences. Throughout mid-2008, house prices continued to fall, as Figure 2 shows. Falling house prices meant that ever larger numbers of homeowners owed more on their mortgages than their homes were now worth, removing a key incentive to pay their mortgages. The value of mortgage-related securities continued to drop. It was clear that the two largest home mortgage lenders—Fannie Mae and Freddie Mac—were in deep trouble. Fannie Mae and Freddie Mac were quintessential examples of financial institutions that had grown so large, and so interconnected with other institutions, that they were deemed too big to fail. Almost all Wall Street firms had significant exposure to debt issued by Fannie and Freddie. On 7 September 2008, the government ended months of speculation by nationalizing Fannie and Freddie.

Figure 2. U.S. House Price Measures, January 1973–June 2009

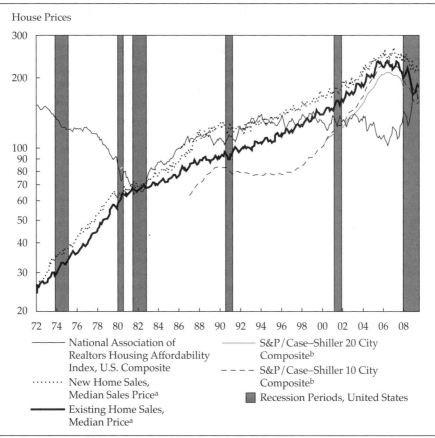

House Prices

Legend:
— National Association of Realtors Housing Affordability Index, U.S. Composite
········ New Home Sales, Median Sales Price[a]
━━ Existing Home Sales, Median Price[a]
— S&P/Case–Shiller 20 City Composite[b]
– – – – S&P/Case–Shiller 10 City Composite[b]
▓ Recession Periods, United States

[a]Thousands of U.S. dollars.
[b]2000: 1=100.

Source: Based on data from FactSet.

The Treasury and the Fed were in the midst of a firefight to prevent the financial crisis from worsening—a fight that they would eventually lose. A crisis of confidence had already begun. The ensuing two weeks would see multiple stunning and unprecedented events—the failure of Lehman Brothers, sending the global financial system into crisis; the freezing of the credit markets; the nationalization of AIG; a comprehensive congressional bailout bill; the purchase of Merrill Lynch by Bank of America; and the eventual disappearance of "Wall Street" (the community of independently owned and operated investment banks).

Like Bear Stearns was in March, Lehman Brothers was now the victim of a bank run. This time, however, the Treasury and the Fed were unable to arrange a shotgun marriage for Lehman Brothers, largely because of their unwillingness to offer a potential suitor the same toxic-asset guarantees provided to JPMorgan six months earlier. Paulson's 15 September announcement that Lehman Brothers would be allowed to fail immediately sent the financial system into crisis. Markets around the world were in a free fall, and the credit markets froze. The crisis of confidence reached the first of several peaks. If Lehman could fail, anyone could fail. Concern over counterparty risk brought lending to a halt.

The announcement of Lehman's bankruptcy immediately put AIG into trouble. The day following the Lehman announcement, the U.S. government announced it would nationalize AIG. Like Bear Stearns, but on a far larger scale, AIG had issued billions of dollars of CDS—or what we have described as "insurance" on bonds—that promised to make bondholders whole in what was hitherto perceived as the highly unlikely event of a bond default. Those unlikely bond defaults were under way. AIG did not have the reserves to cover its CDS, and with the credit markets freezing, it would be impossible to borrow the required money.

The next day, Wednesday, 17 September, Bernanke and Paulson abandoned their piecemeal approach to dealing with the crisis and developed a comprehensive plan to present to congressional leaders the following day. On Thursday, Paulson sent a three-page bill to Congress asking for a $700 billion bailout of the financial system. On Friday, Goldman Sachs and Morgan Stanley—the last two independent investment banks, following the earlier demise of Bear Stearns and Lehman Brothers—converted themselves into bank holding companies, thus submitting to the oversight of the Fed and obtaining access to the Fed's discount window.

On 29 September, the U.S. House of Representatives rejected the bill, sending the markets into another free fall. The Dow Jones Industrial Average experienced its single largest point loss, losing 777 points or 6.98 percent. The following day, Asian and European markets followed suit.

After witnessing the market sell-off following the rejection of the Paulson–Bernanke bailout plan, Congress pushed through a slightly revised bill a few days later. The key revision enabled the government not only to purchase toxic assets but also to make direct capital injections into troubled companies. On 12 October, Paulson and Bernanke called an emergency meeting of CEOs from nine of the nation's largest banks, in which they basically forced the banks to accept direct capital injections, or Troubled Asset Relief Program (TARP) money as it has become known.

The market crisis continued throughout the rest of 2008 and into early 2009. All of these events deepened the severity of the recession that officially began in December 2007 and that has not ended as of this writing (mid-2009).[3] The equity and credit markets have, however, rebounded strongly, suggesting that markets are expecting a much-improved economic situation in the future.

Bubbles and Crashes Globally

With hindsight gained from more than a century of capital market history, both in the United States and in other markets, one can see that stock market crashes are a regular occurrence globally. To place the market meltdown of 2008–2009 in historical perspective, we examine the long-term record of stock market total return indices[4] for the United States, the United Kingdom, and Japan.[5]

We also examine the record of the regional stock market indices (stated in U.S. dollars) for Asia ex-Japan, Europe, and Latin America from 1988 to the present and compare them with the indices for Japan and the United States over that same period to see which of the more-recent crashes were regional and which were global in nature.

Data. Because the data came from a variety of sources, we needed to make these data comparable both between markets and across time. Therefore, we adjusted each market index by its domestic consumer price index. As a result, we present *real total return* indices; these contrast with the nominal, price-only indices, such as the S&P 500 Index, that are most commonly used.

We gathered index returns and inflation rates for the various markets covered by this study from the sources shown in **Table 1**. Note that some of the data from the earlier periods are at an annual frequency, whereas the more recent data are at a monthly frequency. Hence, when discussing some of the early part of the historical record, we present important dates in terms of year-ends and switch to month-end dates when discussing the more recent periods.[6]

---

[3]The National Bureau of Economic Research, or NBER, is charged with the responsibility of "officially" defining recessions after the fact. It historically has used a rule that a recession consists of two consecutive quarters with negative real GDP growth, meaning that the current recession started in July 2008. But NBER has recently adopted a more complex definition of a recession, according to which the current recession started in late 2007.

[4]Total return indices include reinvestment of dividends.

[5]Given the emphasis on the United States that prevails in the other sections of this article and throughout this book, we dedicate more space here to the United Kingdom and Japan than we do to the United States.

[6]For the United States, we interpolated monthly nominal total returns for 1876–1925 using monthly price returns on the Dow Jones averages and annual price and total returns from Ibbotson, Goetzmann, and Peng (2000). See Appendix B for a description of the methodology.

Table 1.   Data Sources

Market/Data	Period	Frequency	Source
United States			
Nominal total return	1871–1925	Annual	Ibbotson, Goetzmann, and Peng (2000)
Nominal price return	1886–1925	Annual	Ibbotson, Goetzmann, and Peng (2000)
	Jan 1886–Dec 1925	Monthly*	Dow Jones (as reported in Pierce 1982)
Inflation rate	1871–1925	Monthly, Annual**	Shiller (2009)
Real total return	Jan 1926–Jun 2009	Monthly	Morningstar (2009)***
United Kingdom			
Real total return	1900–1969	Annual	Dimson, Marsh, and Staunton (2002)***
Nominal total return	Jan 1970–Jun 2009	Monthly	MSCI Gross Return U.K. Index***
Inflation rate	Jan 1970–Jun 2009	Monthly	International Monetary Fund***
USD total return	Jan 1988–Jun 2009	Monthly	MSCI U.K. Index in U.S. dollars***
Japan			
Real total return	Jan 1952–Jun 2009	Monthly	Inflation-Adjusted TOPIX***
Inflation rate	Jan 1970–Jun 2009	Monthly	International Monetary Fund***
USD total return	Jan 1988–Jun 2009	Monthly	TOPIX in U.S. dollars***
Asia ex-Japan, Europe, Latin America			
USD total return	Jan 1988–May 2009	Monthly	MSCI All Country (AC) Asia ex-Japan Index***
			MSCI All Country Europe Index***
			MSCI Emerging Markets Latin America Index***

*Converted from daily data.
**Converted from monthly data.
***As reported in Morningstar® EnCorr®.

Appendix A contains the methodology used to blend multiple data sources (with various frequencies) into the country-specific real total return indices used in the figures and the discussion.

U.S. Record. Figure 3 shows the real total return index and the peak values of the U.S. stock market over the period January 1871 through June 2009, a period of just more than 138 years. This plot shows that an investment in a hypothetical index fund of the U.S. stock market held over this period (with all dividends reinvested and no taxes, fees, or other costs) would have grown nearly 5,000-fold in real purchasing power. Nonetheless, a number of significant sharp and/or long declines occurred along the way. The periods where there are gaps between the peak and the index are the times—called "drawdowns"—when the market in question fell below its own immediate past peak and later recovered.

Figure 3. Real Total Return Index and Peak Values of the U.S. Stock Market, 1871–2009

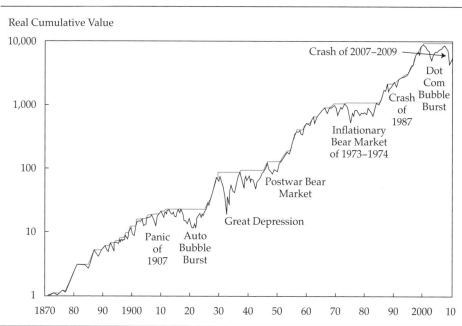

In **Table 2**, we list the major drawdown and recovery periods ("major" designating those periods with greater than 20 percent declines). We also identify some noteworthy events during the respective periods.

U.K. Record. The long-term equity returns for the United Kingdom bear a striking resemblance to those of the United States, highlighting how connected the two economies have been. The largest shock to the U.K. stock market over the past 109 years occurred shortly after the collapse of the Bretton Woods system and during the oil crisis that began 17 October 1973, when members of the Organization of Arab Petroleum Exporting Countries (OAPEC) proclaimed an oil embargo against select industrial governments of the world to pressure Israel during the fourth Arab–Israeli War.[7] The reduced supply of oil led to an increase in price, which, when combined with strikes by coal miners and railroad workers, led to an energy crisis during the winter of 1973–1974. Although the embargo was officially lifted in March 1974, the U.K. stock market did not regain the peak reached in April 1972 until January 1984, roughly 12 years later.

---

[7]The now better-known OPEC (Organization of Petroleum Exporting Countries) is a separate, overlapping organization.

Table 2. Largest Declines in U.S. Stock Market History, January 1871–June 2009 (real total return terms)

Peak	Trough	Decline	Recovery	Event(s)
Aug 1929	May 1932	79.00%	Nov 1936	Crash of 1929; first part of Great Depression
Aug 2000	Feb 2009	54.00	TBD	Dot-com bubble burst (2000–2002); crash of 2007–2009
Dec 1972	Sep 1974	51.86	Dec 1984	Inflationary bear market; Vietnam; Watergate
Jun 1911	Dec 1920	50.96	Dec 1924	World War I; postwar auto bubble burst
Feb 1937	Mar 1938	49.93	Feb 1945	Second part of Great Depression; World War II
May 1946	Feb 1948	37.18	Oct 1950	Postwar bear market
Nov 1968	Jun 1970	35.46	Nov 1972	Start of inflationary bear market
Jan 1906	Oct 1907	34.22	Aug 1908	Panic of 1907
Apr 1899	Jun 1900	30.41	Mar 1901	Cornering of Northern Pacific stock
Aug 1987	Nov 1987	30.16	Jul 1989	"Black Monday," 19 Oct 1987
Oct 1892	Jul 1893	27.32	Mar 1894	Silver agitation
Dec 1961	Jun 1962	22.80	Apr 1963	Height of the Cold War; Cuban Missile Crisis
Nov 1886	Mar 1888	22.04	May 1889	Depression; railroad strikes
Apr 1903	Sep 1903	21.67	Nov 1904	Rich man's panic
Aug 1897	Mar 1898	21.13	Aug 1898	Outbreak of Boer War
Sep 1909	Jul 1910	20.55	Feb 1911	Enforcement of the Sherman Antitrust Act
May 1890	Jul 1891	20.11	Feb 1892	Baring crisis

The 74 percent drawdown in the real total return index of U.K. stocks in the 1970s is much worse than that same market's decline in the Great Depression, despite the much more severe damage to the real economy in the earlier episode. Thus, markets do not always track real economic events exactly or even somewhat closely, as shown in **Figure 4** and **Table 3**.

Japanese Record. The Japanese economy experienced a strong recovery following World War II and had relatively consistent growth through the 1980s, with the stock market peaking in December 1989. The compound annual real total return of the Tokyo Stock Price Index (TOPIX) from January 1952 to December 1989 was 13.4 percent.[8] The market then declined for much of the subsequent two decades—with stock prices falling 71.9 percent from the 1989 peak, in real terms, by March 2009. **Figure 5** and **Table 4** include information on the major declines in the Japanese stock market during the past six decades.

It is important to distinguish between market declines caused by business cycles and those caused by sudden unexpected crashes in Japan as well as in other markets. For example, the decline that began in December 1972 was triggered by currency

---

[8]The Tokyo Stock Exchange (TSE) is divided into three markets: the first section, second section, and Mothers (venture capital market). The first section includes the largest, most successful companies. The TOPIX tracks all domestic companies of the TSE's first section (see www.tse.or.jp/english/faq/list/general/g_b.html).

instability and rising interest rates following the first oil crisis. The 1961–65 decline was caused, at first, by a tightening of monetary policy and deteriorating corporate earnings, culminating in a financial market crisis that led to a bailout of Yamaichi Securities in 1965. Those are bear markets—continuous declines caused by changes in fundamentals but without a big one-day or several-day "crash."

Figure 4. U.K. Stock Market History, 1900–2009

Real Cumulative Value

Table 3. Largest Declines in U.K. Stock Market History, 1900–2009
(real total return terms)

Peak	Trough	Decline	Recovery	Event(s)
Apr 1972	Nov 1974	73.81%	Jan 1984	Oil shock
1913	1920	45.85	1922	World War I
Dec 1999	Jan 2003	44.91	Apr 2007	Information technology bubble and collapse
1936	1940	43.71	1946	Second part of Great Depression; World War II
Oct 2007	Feb 2009	40.99	TBD	Crash of 2007–2009; global financial crisis
1968	May 1970	35.80	Apr 1972	Speculation in currencies; Bretton Woods
Sep 1987	Nov 1987	34.07	Nov 1992	"Black Monday," 19 Oct 1987
1928	1931	30.57	1933	First part of Great Depression
1946	1952	21.30	1954	Post–World War II correction

Figure 5. Japanese Stock Market History, 1952–2009

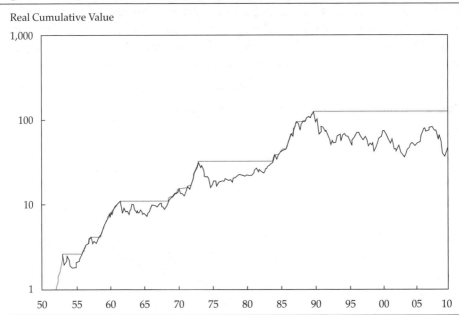

Real Cumulative Value

Table 4. Largest Post–World War II Declines in Japanese Stock Market History, January 1952–June 2009
(real total return terms)

Peak	Trough	Decline	Recovery	Event(s)
Dec 1989	Mar 2003	71.92%	TBD	Easy credit; real estate bubble
Dec 1972	Oct 1974	51.85	Dec 1983	Worldwide oil crisis
Jun 1961	Jun 1965	34.47	Aug 1968	Yamaichi Securities bailout
Jun 1953	May 1954	31.98	Dec 1955	Stalin shock
May 1970	Dec 1970	21.33	Jun 1972	Bretton Woods
Aug 1987	Dec 1987	19.79	Mar 1988	"Black Monday," 19 Oct 1987

When a large stock market crash occurs, market volatility (by definition) jumps up to an abnormal level. **Figure 6** shows the trailing 60-day volatility of the TOPIX over the past 60 years from December 1950 to March 2009.

Such abnormal spikes in daily volatility can usually be linked to specific events. The most recent crash after the Lehman shock in September 2008 led to a 4.3 percent daily standard deviation by the end of 2008, the highest average during these 60 years of Japan's history. The second highest level of trailing volatility occurred during the "Black Monday" episode in 1987. Until the 1980s, there was no significant jump in volatility except during the "Stalin shock" in 1953, when Joseph Stalin, prime minister of the Union of Soviet Socialist Republics and the general secretary of the Communist Party, died on 5 March of that year.

Figure 6. Daily Volatility of Japanese Stock Market, December 1950–March 2009

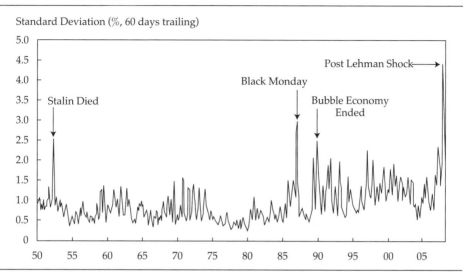

Although two of those crashes—"Black Monday" in 1987 and the Lehman shock in 2008—were global events, the long 1990–2009 downtrend in the Japanese stock market and the Stalin shock in 1953 were specific to Japan. These latter two events are described in more detail in the following sections.

■ *One big wave in five decades.* Over the past five decades, comprising essentially all of post–World War II Japanese history, there was basically one huge market event: a bull market or bubble that peaked around 1990 and the subsequent bear market or crash that extends through the present. A peculiar feature of this long wave is that land prices and stock prices increased together for the first 35 years and declined together in the following two decades. **Figure 7** shows a Japanese land price index and stock price index from 1955 to 2009.

Post–World War II industrial and commercial development in Japan were concentrated in a few large cities and their suburban areas—primarily the Tokyo metropolitan area, Nagoya, and Osaka. In the 1950s and 1960s, therefore, young workers began moving from rural areas to these urban areas for greater job opportunities and consequently began changing their careers from agriculture to manufacturing and commerce. Because of this massive demographic shift, the residential housing boom was sustained well into the 1970s. Because land is a scarce resource in Japan, land prices in urban areas continued to climb at a much faster pace than stock prices did in the 1960s and 1970s.

Although the abnormally high economic growth rate of the post–World War II period had already ended by the early 1970s, the Japanese economy continued to grow, powered by foreign demand for Japanese industrial goods primarily in the

Figure 7. Japanese Stock and Land Price Indices, 1955–2009

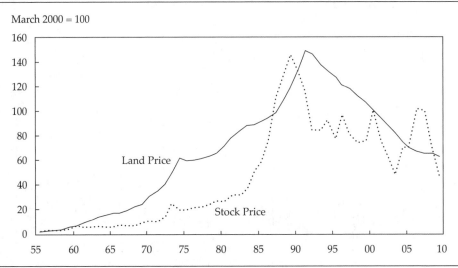

March 2000 = 100

Notes: Annual index value with March 2000 = 100. The stock price index is the TOPIX Price Return Index published by the Tokyo Stock Exchange. The land price index is the Urban Land Price Index (which includes land used for commercial, residential, and industrial purposes) published by the Japan Real Estate Institute. Both indices are in nominal terms and exclude income (dividend or rental) returns.

automobile and electronics industries. This export-driven growth, however, created trade conflicts with other countries, especially the United States. In September 1985, the Group of Five (G–5) finance ministers announced the Plaza Accord and intervened in currency markets to cause the Japanese yen, among other currencies, to appreciate against the U.S. dollar. The value of the yen more than doubled in dollar terms in three years, from ¥251 per dollar in December 1984 to ¥121 per dollar in December 1987.[9]

The sudden and substantial appreciation of the yen had an immediate depressing effect on exports, and the Japanese economy went into a recession. The Bank of Japan lowered the official discount rate four times in 1986, from 5 percent to 3 percent and then to 2.5 percent in early 1987. Along with monetary policy, fiscal policy encouraged domestic spending through a ¥5 trillion investment in public construction and through a ¥1 trillion tax cut in 1987. This ¥6 trillion stimulus represented 1.8 percent of GDP at that time.

---

[9]The yen is quoted "European style," that is, the number of non-U.S. currency units per U.S. dollar. Thus, for the 1984–87 period, the value of the dollar (quoted in Japanese yen) halved; the value of the yen (quoted in dollars) doubled. See DeRosa (2009, p. 61).

Monetary and fiscal easing, starting in 1986, fueled a speculative investment boom in real estate and stocks, not only in the domestic (Japanese) market but also overseas because of the strength of the yen. For example, Japanese banks and brokerage firms were massively buying U.S. government bonds. Most Japanese insurance companies set up investment vehicles in the Cayman Islands and other tax havens for foreign investment purposes. In October 1989, Mitsubishi Estate Co. purchased Rockefeller Center in New York City for ¥220 billion.

In domestic markets, speculative bubbles were growing in both real estate and stocks in the late 1980s, as shown in **Table 5**. Banks lent funds to industrial companies to invest in stocks and real estate, even though such investments were not the primary business of those companies. In urban areas, small houses and shops were bought by developers, often for the purpose of tearing them down and redeveloping them. Higher stock prices also made it attractive for companies to issue equity and convertible bonds, although the large amount of equity financing subsequently caused the return on equity of Japanese companies to deteriorate.

Table 5. Annual Returns of Japanese Stock and Land Price Indices, 1986–1991

Month-End	Stock Price Index	Land Price Index
Mar 1986	26.7%	2.8%
Mar 1987	47.8	5.4
Mar 1988	14.8	10.0
Mar 1989	15.0	7.6
Mar 1990	−9.8	14.1
Mar 1991	−11.5	10.4

Source: See note to Figure 7.

On the last day of December 1989, the Nikkei 225 Index hit its all-time high, to which it has yet to return: 38,915.87. The high prices of stocks reflected the fact that market participants believed in an ever brighter future for the Japanese economy. A survey of 50 economists and strategists in January 1990 showed that they were still bullish: The average of their forecasts for the December 1990 level of the Nikkei was 44,861, up 15 percent from the previous year-end. The actual result turned out to be a big drop. The Nikkei average declined by 39 percent in 1990, finishing the year at 23,848.71.

In the late 1980s, when the price-to-book ratio of the Japanese stock index was as high as 5:1 or 6:1, high land prices were used as a justification for the extraordinary valuation of stocks at that time. Why? Because many of the major industrial companies owned land they acquired many years earlier, sometimes before World

War II. Because land holdings were carried at their historical acquisition cost on many companies' balance sheets, these companies accumulated large "hidden" asset values when the land was valued at then-prevailing prices. Even though corporate earnings did not justify the high valuation, many investors believed that the value of land owned by them justified the high valuation. Some economists and analysts revived a valuation metric called the "*q* ratio" or "Tobin's *q*," proposed by the Nobel Prize–winning economist James Tobin and consisting of the market value of a corporation's stock plus debt divided by the replacement cost of the company's assets.[10] As long as land prices remained at high levels, the *q* ratio remained at a modest level, justifying "buy" recommendations—or at least justifying the continued holding of such stocks.

As the Bank of Japan became nervous about ever increasing asset prices, it started raising interest rates to stop the bubble from growing further. It had kept its official discount rate as low as 2.5 percent since February 1987, but it raised this interest rate three times starting in mid-1989, reaching 4.25 percent by year-end. It further raised the rate twice, getting up to 6 percent in 1990. Stock prices responded by tumbling quickly after their peak at the end of 1989.

Even after the stock market started its decline, the construction boom continued until land prices ultimately peaked two years later in 1991. Because the construction boom in the late 1980s was largely financed by bank lending, the declining value of real estate created a large debt overhang among the industrial corporations that owned the real estate, as well as bad loans held by Japanese banks. It took almost a decade to wipe out those bad loans and restore the balance sheets of industrial corporations and banks. By the end of the 1990s, the banking industry in Japan had gone through a massive restructuring. Many of the leading banks merged into the big three "megabank" groups: Mizuho Bank, Mitsubishi UFJ Financial Group, and Sumitomo Mitsui Banking Corporation. Other major banks and brokerage firms either went into bankruptcy or were bailed out by the government and foreign funds.

■ *Stalin crash in 1953.* After World War II ended in August 1945, the Japanese economy was struggling for recovery because of a lack of capital and excessive inflation. The Japanese economy was reported to be generating a GDP per capita of only $1,346 in "1990 dollars," two-thirds that of Mexico and only double that of impoverished India.[11] The Tokyo Stock Exchange (TSE) reopened on 16 May 1949, and the TOPIX ended up closing at 22.06, but because of the depressed economy, the index declined by more than 50 percent in one year to a low of 9.63 on 30 June 1950.

---

[10] See Tobin (1969).

[11] Maddison (2009). The units are "1990 International Geary–Khamis dollars," roughly equivalent to the value of a U.S. dollar in 1990.

The Korean War, which erupted on 25 June 1950, was the trigger event that turned around the economy and stock market. Suddenly, Japan became an important geopolitical nation for those nations fighting against the Communist bloc. Led by military demand, the first postwar economic boom started with strong momentum. By 1953, most economic indicators—such as industrial production, consumer spending, and GDP—had recovered to their pre–World War II levels. By 4 March 1953, the TOPIX had climbed to 35.42, almost quadrupling in less than three years.

On 4 March 1953, the Soviet Union announced that Stalin was seriously ill. He died the next day, 5 March, at the age of 74. Following his death, military- and defense-related stocks declined sharply, both in the United States and Tokyo, with the TOPIX declining 8.7 percent on 5 March alone. This was the biggest one-day decline for the TOPIX until "Black Monday" in October 1987.

As with many (but not all) crashes, the price level after the Stalin crash represented an extraordinary opportunity. Measured from their 1953 lows, Japanese stocks doubled (in real total return terms) by 1957 and doubled again by 1960. The postwar Japanese economic miracle had begun.

Global Perspectives on 1987 and 1929 Crashes and the Long Boom. Although the market crashes of 1987 and 1929 certainly originated in the United States, they were not confined to the United States. Their ripples were felt globally and were sometimes more severe in other markets.

▨ *Crash of 1987.* Prior to the most recent market drop, the largest collapse experienced by the vast majority of investors took place on 19 October 1987, an event commonly referred to as "Black Monday." Although some investors may believe the drop was limited largely to the United States, it was, in fact, a worldwide phenomenon. For the month of October, 19 of 23 country markets declined by more than 20 percent and all posted negative returns. The U.S. market had the 5th smallest decline in local currency units among the 23 countries but had the 11th smallest decline when the returns for each country are restated in U.S. dollars, as shown in **Table 6**.

The United States was also not the first market to decline sharply. The worst part of the collapse appeared to be in non-Japanese Asian markets on 19 October (their time), followed by European markets, then North American, and finally Japanese. Although markets were definitely connected in 1987, they had significantly lower correlations than they do today. In fact, from 1981 to 1987, October 1987 was the only month when all of the 23 markets moved in the same direction (down).

A variety of explanations have been proposed to understand the cause of the 1987 crash in the international stock market. In the United States, blame has been laid on the market's institutional structure and practices—such as computer-assisted trading, portfolio insurance, margin rules, and the absence of limitations of trading based on price movements (referred to as "circuit breakers"). Although these reasons

Table 6. October 1987 Stock Market Total Return

Rank	Country	Local Currency Units	Country	U.S. Dollar
1	Hong Kong	−45.8%	Hong Kong	−45.8%
2	Singapore	−42.2	Australia	−44.9
3	Australia	−41.8	Singapore	−41.6
4	Malaysia	−39.8	Malaysia	−39.3
5	Mexico	−35.0	Mexico	−37.6
6	Norway	−30.5	New Zealand	−36.0
7	New Zealand	−29.3	South Africa	−29.0
8	Ireland	−29.1	Norway	−28.2
9	Spain	−27.7	Ireland	−25.4
10	United Kingdom	−26.4	Spain	−23.1
11	Switzerland	−26.1	Canada	−22.9
12	South Africa	−23.9	United Kingdom	−22.1
13	Netherlands	−23.3	United States	−21.6
14	Belgium	−23.2	Switzerland	−20.8
15	France	−22.9	France	−19.5
16	Canada	−22.5	Belgium	−18.9
17	Germany	−22.3	Sweden	−18.6
18	Sweden	−21.8	Netherlands	−18.1
19	United States	−21.6	Germany	−17.1
20	Italy	−16.3	Italy	−12.9
21	Japan	−12.8	Japan	−7.7
22	Denmark	−12.5	Denmark	−7.3
23	Austria	−11.4	Austria	−5.8

Source: Based on data from Roll (1988).

may hold for the U.S. market, they cannot possibly explain the similarities across all markets given how much market structures differ between countries. A more plausible explanation is that the fundamental values of stocks in one country were influenced by stock market price declines in other countries. Still, it is hard to believe that the fundamental value of the world's corporate equities could be 20 percent lower one day than it was the day before.

■ *Crash of 1929.* Going further back in time reveals a historical period with stock market declines that resemble (and in fact exceed) those of 2007–2009: the stock market crash of 1929 and the ensuing Great Depression.

In contrast to "Black Monday" in 1987, which was not followed by any sort of depression, the crash of 1929 ushered in a Great Depression that had a tremendous ongoing impact, not only on U.S. markets but also on international markets. The depression in the real economy lasted well into the early 1940s for some nations and was the longest and most severe depression ever experienced by the industrialized Western world. **Figure 8** shows the cumulative price return of the stock markets of four countries—France, Japan, the United Kingdom, and the United States—in the periods before, during, and after the stock market crash.[12] Although the size of the market collapse varied considerably from country to country (Japan having by far the best performance in real total return terms), the returns across countries are highly correlated.

Figure 8. Real Stock Price Indices Excluding Dividends, 1929–1935

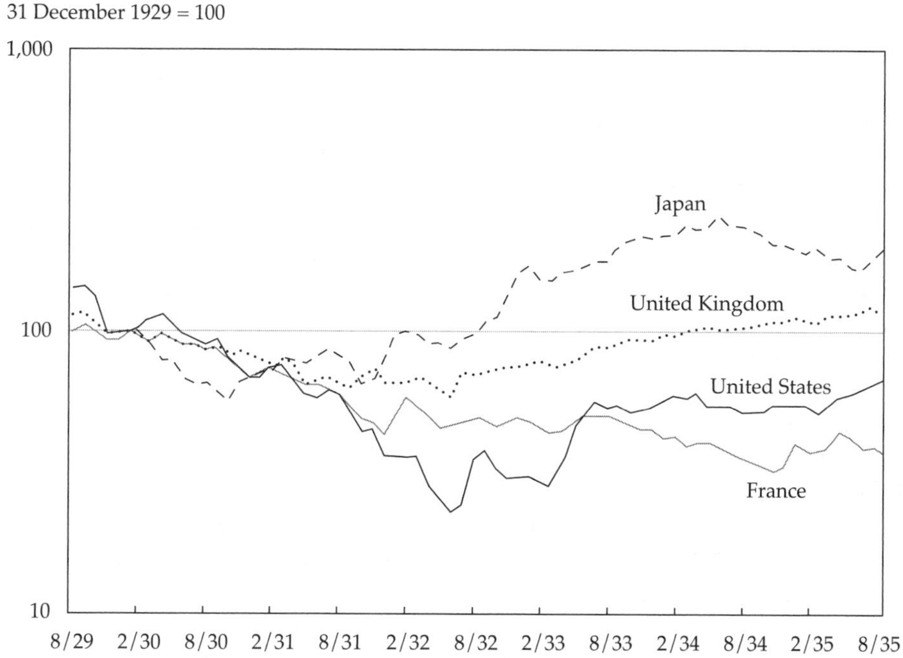

31 December 1929 = 100

Source: Based on data from Kindleberger (1973).

[12]Because the returns in Figure 8 are real returns (adjusted for the domestic inflation rate in each country shown), they portray the changes in purchasing power experienced by a domestic investor, holding domestic stocks, and consuming in the domestic goods and services markets in each country. It is not necessary to adjust further for changes in exchange rates to describe this experience.

However, an international investor (say, a U.S. investor diversifying his or her risk by holding U.K., French, and Japanese stocks) does care about exchange rates. The sharp devaluation of the yen (from ¥2.00 per U.S. dollar in 1929 to ¥4.91 per dollar in 1934) would have substantially reduced returns to a U.S. investor in Japanese stocks over that period. (In 1935, the yen was revalued to ¥3.40 per dollar.) The British pound fell from $4.85 in 1929 to $3.34 in early 1933, depressing returns to U.S. investors in British stocks, but then rose to $5 by 1934. The French franc did not vary much between 1929 and 1933 but then rose from Fr25.59 to the dollar in 1933 to Fr15.31 in 1935 before falling sharply later in the decade. The source of the exchange rate data is Bidwell (1970).

Before the crash, the U.S. market was consistently reaching new all-time highs, with the Dow Jones Industrial Average increasing from a low of 191 in early 1928 to a high of 300 in December 1928 and a peak of 381 on 3 September 1929, roughly doubling over the less-than-two-year period. The expansion of production outside Europe during World War I, as well as the complications and reparations of war, also likely played a key role in causing the Great Depression.

The United States emerged from World War I as a major creditor and financier for the rebuilding effort in postwar Europe. Even before the crash, U.S. banks had started calling back previous loans in Europe. Yet the European credit structure depended extensively on U.S. loans, and given the excessive international speculation—not only in the capital markets but also in foreign direct investment—once financing was withdrawn, the entire system began to unravel. The Great Depression had the greatest effect on the nations that were most indebted to the United States, such as Germany and the United Kingdom. By early 1932, unemployment had reached 6 million in Germany, roughly 25 percent of the workforce.

To counter reduced demand and in an effort to protect domestic production, the majority of countries increased tariffs or raised existing ones. These measures dramatically reduced the volume of international trade. The United States introduced the Smoot–Hawley Tariff Act (officially known as the United States Tariff Act of 1930), raising tariffs to record levels on more than 20,000 imported goods. The ensuing retaliatory tariffs by U.S. trading partners reduced U.S. exports and imports by more than half (U.S. imports decreased from $4.4 billion in 1929 to $1.5 billion in 1933, a 66 percent nominal decline) and greatly contributed to the severity of the Great Depression.

Countries dependent on exporting primary products, such as food, had already started feeling the effects of the Great Depression in the late 1920s. More-efficient farming methods and technological changes meant the supply of agricultural products was increasing faster than demand, causing prices to fall. This trend was good for consumers but bad for producers, so the net effect is unclear.

Liquidity also became a concern during the Great Depression. When the stock market crashed, U.S. banks, which had depended heavily on their stock investments, began calling some of their loans. Unfortunately for the banks, as the economy worsened, repayment became more difficult. By 1933, 11,000 of the 25,000 banks in the United States had failed, dramatically affecting consumer confidence and leading to a reduction in spending that aggravated the continuing downward spiral.

A very strong recovery in 1935–1936 propelled some markets to fresh highs. Interestingly, the 1937 peak of the U.S. real total return index (not shown in Figure 8 but visible on a small scale in Figure 3) was higher than the 1929 peak. However, a second depression followed; the two depressions (and interposed recovery) combined to form what is now usually regarded, in retrospect, as a single Great Depression.

■ *Drawdowns during the Long Boom (1982–2007).* Stock markets around the world have experienced a number of large drawdowns over the past 20 years. Although Japan's drawdown, beginning in December 1989 and covered earlier in this article, is perhaps the most well known, other markets experienced similar, although more temporary, drawdowns.

By definition, an economic expansion is the period between recessions—that is, a period of continued growth without a recession. Most of the period from January 1988 to June 2009 was just that for many countries and stock markets: a period of continued growth. This period, which began for many countries in the early 1980s, is often characterized as the "Long Boom," during which many world economies grew at a relatively fast clip, with their respective stock markets following suit. Drawdowns of more than 50 percent, however, have actually occurred relatively frequently, even during the Long Boom. Generally, they have occurred in emerging market nations.

Apart from the crash of 2007–2009, both the Asia ex-Japan and Latin American stock markets have experienced market declines (in some cases experienced as crashes) of more than 50 percent. **Figure 9** and **Table 7** include information on drawdowns around the world in various markets from January 1988 to June 2009. Unfortunately, we do not have data covering emerging markets in the first years of the Long Boom, 1982–1987.

Figure 9. Drawdowns around the World, January 1988–June 2009
(U.S. dollars)

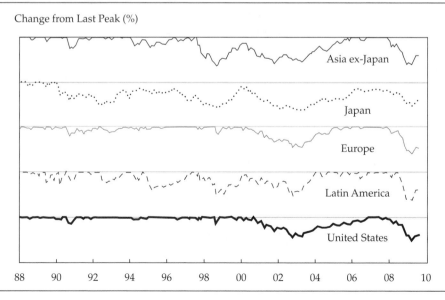

Table 7. Worst Drawdowns around the World,
January 1988–June 2009
(in U.S. dollars)

Peak	Trough	Decline	Recovery
Asia ex-Japan			
Dec 1993	Aug 1998	64.55%	Dec 2005
Oct 2007	Feb 2009	61.50	TBD
Jul 1990	Sep 1990	27.30	Dec 1991
Apr 1989	Jun 1989	11.25	Sep 1989
Jul 1988	Aug 1988	8.30	Dec 1988
Apr 2006	Jun 2006	7.78	Oct 2006
Oct 1992	Dec 1992	6.46	Feb 1993
Jun 1992	Aug 1992	5.77	Oct 1992
Mar 1990	Apr 1990	4.08	May 1990
May 1993	Jun 1993	2.61	Aug 1993
Japan			
Dec 1989	Mar 2003	62.81%	TBD
Feb 1989	Jun 1989	11.38	Sep 1989
Apr 1988	Aug 1988	11.00	Nov 1988
Sep 1989	Oct 1989	2.68	Nov 1989
Europe			
Oct 2007	Feb 2009	59.78%	TBD
Mar 2000	Sep 2002	45.73	Dec 2004
Jul 1990	Sep 1990	20.49	May 1992
Jul 1998	Sep 1998	16.50	Apr 1999
May 1992	Nov 1992	13.62	Aug 1993
Jan 1994	Jun 1994	7.41	Aug 1994
Dec 1999	Jan 2000	7.00	Mar 2000
Apr 1988	Aug 1988	6.91	Oct 1988
Sep 1989	Oct 1989	6.50	Dec 1989
Jul 1997	Aug 1997	5.62	Sep 1997
Latin America			
May 2008	Feb 2009	61.12%	TBD
Jul 1997	Aug 1998	51.34	Dec 2003
Sep 1994	Mar 1995	42.23	Apr 1997
Feb 1990	Mar 1990	30.80	Jul 1990
May 1989	Jun 1989	25.00	Feb 1990
May 1992	Sep 1992	24.85	Aug 1993
Jul 1990	Oct 1990	20.22	Feb 1991
Jan 1994	Jun 1994	17.12	Aug 1994
Apr 2006	May 2006	13.89	Oct 2006
Mar 2004	May 2004	11.08	Sep 2004

(continued)

Table 7. Worst Drawdowns around the World, January 1988–June 2009
(in U.S. dollars) (continued)

Peak	Trough	Decline	Recovery
United States			
Oct 2007	Feb 2009	50.95%	TBD
Aug 2000	Sep 2002	44.73	Oct 2006
Jun 1998	Aug 1998	15.37	Nov 1998
May 1990	Oct 1990	14.70	Feb 1991
Jan 1994	Mar 1994	6.93	Aug 1994
Dec 1999	Feb 2000	6.82	Mar 2000
Dec 1989	Jan 1990	6.71	May 1990
Jun 1999	Sep 1999	6.24	Nov 1999
Jul 1997	Aug 1997	5.56	Nov 1997
Mar 2000	May 2000	5.00	Aug 2000

Stock returns in individual emerging markets have been even more volatile than in these broad regional aggregations. For example, the Russian stock market declined by about 80 percent during that country's government debt default crisis in 1998. Several individual country markets in Asia declined by a similar amount around that time. Readers wanting more detail on emerging equity market returns, volatility, booms, and crashes should refer to Speidell (forthcoming).

Why Do Crashes Occur?

Financial crises and bank failures have occurred throughout history. As an example, Calomiris (2008) mentions a bank panic in ancient Rome in AD 33. But in economies where subsistence farming and barter were widespread, banking crises affected only a small part of the population. For instance, although the topic is a series of banking failures in Europe in the 1300s, Homer and Sylla (2005) suggest that the major drag on economic growth came from recurring plague epidemics and not from the defaults of the kings of England and France, which caused bank failures during the Hundred Years' War (1337–1453).

In today's world, banks and insurance companies affect a large part of the economy. As a result, the health of the financial sector is a key factor in the economic cycle. At the same time, economic theory has devoted increasing attention to the causes of financial crises.

Economic Thought and Financial Crises. Adam Smith stated that the existence of many small banks is a guarantee for the public because, among other things, it limits the systemic effect of the failure of any one bank (Smith 1776, Book II, Chapter II). The banks at the core of the recent crisis are very large ones; just a few small banks shut down. If Smith's observation is accurate, then something must be wrong with very large banks.

Apart from Smith's remarks, bank size was not at the heart of economic theory until recently. Marginalist economics, pioneered by the economists William Stanley Jevons (1835–1882) and Léon Walras (1834–1910), assumed that all markets were in continuous equilibrium. Actually, the Walrasian economic model of general equilibrium did not even involve a fiat currency. All contingent contracts could exist in terms of an arbitrary good chosen as the numeraire (adventurous readers may take a look at Debreu 1959), so cash was not necessary. Markets would be perfectly efficient, and by Say's law, anything produced would be sold. Therefore, there would be no crisis because of lack of aggregate demand.[13]

Schumpeter (1942) brought a new perspective. In his view, market disequilibrium was an effect of technical innovation. When an entrepreneur either found a new way to produce an existing good or invented a new good, that entrepreneur would be the monopolist of that special process or product. This situation would lead to excess profits, which contrasts with the results of a perfectly competitive equilibrium. Soon, imitators would enter the market and reduce those excess profits, gradually leading the market back to its competitive equilibrium with no excess profits. In other words, Schumpeter's view was that innovation brings short-term disequilibrium in markets and that such disequilibrium is a good thing because it fosters product variety and technical efficiency. Moreover, disequilibrium would be limited only to the markets where an innovation has recently occurred.

J.G. Knut Wicksell and Irving Fisher (see, for example, Fisher 1933) introduced a view of disequilibrium that centered on financial markets, particularly the difference between the market interest rate and the equilibrium interest rate. The Walrasian model shows that, in a competitive equilibrium, the interest rate should equal the marginal productivity of capital.[14] And it makes sense that the marginal product of capital (that is, the extra gain by adding an extra unit of capital goods) should equal the equilibrium interest rate (that is, the cost of hiring an extra unit of capital) because if capital did cost less, one could hire more of it and make money—which would violate the no-arbitrage condition. Some economists call this marginal cost of capital the "natural" interest rate.

---

[13](Jean-Baptiste) Say's law, "supply creates its own demand," sounds mysterious when so expressed. What Say meant was that the revenues generated in the production of a good are sufficient to buy it; thus, there can never be a general glut of goods.

[14]Financial practitioners may be a bit puzzled here because most economic theory relies on just one interest rate, with neither a yield curve (because models often focus on one or two periods) nor a credit spread (because there is no uncertainty). If that is your point of reference, please bear with us because there are useful insights for everyone in the finance viewpoint, which incorporates multiple time horizons and uncertainty.

Wicksell and Fisher pointed out that bankers may be overly optimistic about the future (that is, they estimate that the marginal productivity of capital will be very high in the future) because of some technological innovation, and they thus lend an excessive amount of money to entrepreneurs. This situation means that the market interest rate differs from the equilibrium interest rate.

When reality hits, however, entrepreneurs realize that they overinvested and are now plagued by excess capacity—as happened around the world with telecommunication infrastructures during the technology boom of the 1990s. As a result, capital investments come to a sudden stop, and aggregate demand plunges, leading to unemployment and an economic crisis. Only after some of the excess capital has become obsolete and must be replaced will entrepreneurs go back to investing. In the meantime, GDP growth suffers.

The theory presented by Wicksell and Fisher implies that excessive lending causes financial crises that can stop an entire economy because they cause first a bubble and then a crash in many markets at the same time. This situation was unconceivable for the marginalists, who did not think that disequilibrium conditions were possible.

Keynes (1936) set forth a theory that markedly differed from those of his predecessors. He argued, loosely speaking, that some special markets are almost never in equilibrium. The labor market is generally in disequilibrium, if nothing else because there always are some people who would like to work but are currently unemployed—for example, new college graduates who are looking for their first job or people who just quit their jobs and are about to start a new one. Moreover, nobody wants to get a salary cut if the economy slows down; therefore, companies agree not to cut salaries but to cut employees when demand decreases, thus creating cyclical unemployment. Financial markets, Keynes quipped, "can stay irrational longer than you can stay solvent." With this, he meant that financial markets are not perfectly efficient and that government policy, specifically fiscal "stimulus" (deficit spending to accelerate the demand for goods and services), may be a necessary remedy when a serious recession ensues. Not everybody knows that Keynes did not advocate large, persistent government budget deficits; he supported only focused actions against the most serious recessions.

Hayek (1932) had a different view on government policy. His view was that when governments and central banks try to expand credit to sustain the economy when a recession is feared, as they typically do, they end up causing a deeper recession. Therefore, Hayek criticized Keynes's intervention policy because he saw government intervention as the trigger of a Wicksell–Hayek crash, where the market interest rate diverges from the natural rate. Hayek trusted markets to be efficient enough to take care of themselves; prices and wages would change, and markets would go back to equilibrium right away. He thought that workers should accept lower wages when the marginal product of their labor decreased and that governments prevented wage falls for demagogic reasons, which in the end hurt workers.

Minsky (1986, 1992) studied why markets are, in Keynes's words, irrational, whereas modern portfolio theory relied heavily on market efficiency, which is the exact contrary. Minsky's insights fit nicely with the findings of behavioral finance. Briefly, Minsky argued that a lack of crises is the cause of future crises; that is, market stability is self-destructing. When market participants have been in a state of calm, they start believing that markets will remain calm for the foreseeable future and, therefore, start underestimating risk. As a result, they behave just like the overoptimistic bankers of Wicksell and Fisher. Minsky suggested some government intervention to prevent this kind of excess.

2007–09 Crash. How do the events of 2007–2009 fit into the aforementioned theories? It is now clear that many financial institutions had taken on too much debt and extended too much credit, thus accumulating an excessive amount of risk. In our opinion, this was a failure in several dimensions:

- Regulators allowed such accumulation of risk by allowing excessive leverage.
- Shareholders and boards of directors did not require sound risk management.
- Market participants underestimated risk.
- Academics believed too much in market efficiency and were reluctant to admit the possibility of market irrationality, even though some had spent the previous decade analyzing the technology bubble of the 1990s and the subsequent crash.
- Politicians were all too happy to see the economy grow at an excessive speed because that was good in the short run.
- Financial company CEOs were also quite happy to see short-term profits swell, hoping that the inevitable crash would occur after they had retired and cashed out of the company.

The events of the residential real estate markets in the United States, and in other countries such as Spain and Iceland, summarize the key points of the crisis. Home prices kept increasing, and people wanted to buy homes hoping not just to live in them but also to profit from their appreciation in value. Mortgage brokers, whose compensation depended on the number and size of mortgages they originated, gave mortgages to as many people as possible, regardless of whether these people could afford the mortgage. Banks, in a period of low spreads, were looking for fee income and looked for mortgages to be securitized and sold to investors. Investors, frustrated by otherwise low yields, were eager to purchase higher yielding mortgage-backed securities, without too much worry about the quality of the securities and, therefore, the sustainability of the yields. Bond-rating agencies, whose income (ironically) comes from bond issuers, made billions of dollars by trusting faulty risk models that gave AAA ratings to questionable mortgage-backed securities. Regulators did not recognize the risk of excessive leverage and allowed banks and other nondepository financial firms (e.g., investment banks) to use off-balance-sheet vehicles to hide the risks of securitization from their financial statements.

Therefore, this period saw market inefficiency, inadequate or inconsistent government vigilance, and a Wicksell–Fisher–Hayek–Minsky chain of events leading to excessive lending, a bubble, and a crash (see Cooper 2008). The crash causes a Keynesian aggregate demand drop with ineffective monetary policy because of already low policy interest rates. This is the so-called liquidity trap (see Keynes 1936), which can be represented in an IS/LM diagram by a horizontal line.[15] In such an environment, a monetary policy change has no effect on real output because any shifts to the right of the LM schedule do not change the intersection with the IS curve; therefore, income and interest rates remain the same. (For more about the liquidity trap in the current crisis, see Krugman 2008.)

Policy Conclusions

To prevent a repeat of the same type of crisis in the future, we believe that more-comprehensive regulation of the financial system is necessary. This does not mean that we advocate red tape but that supervisors must guarantee transparency and limit leverage. Moreover, this regulation should not be limited to banks but should also apply to insurance companies, investment banks, other nondepository financial institutions, and their holding companies (the so-called shadow banking system; see Paul McCulley's article in this book).

When market participants realized that a crash was imminent, they tried to sell all risky assets to take refuge in safe investments, such as short-term government bonds. The leading risk models used by most participants did not consider this possibility. As a result, we believe that risk models must consider scenarios of sudden flight to quality, and financial analysts should consider this kind of risk when building portfolios and developing their risk models (see Appendix B on risk models).

Moreover, we believe that some aspects of the financial infrastructure, such as the derivatives market, need reform. In particular, a reduction of over-the-counter derivatives transactions would lead to a more transparent and safe financial sector.

---

[15]The IS (investment = saving)/LM (liquidity demand = money supply) diagram illustrates the relationship between interest rates and GDP consistent with macroeconomic equilibrium in the real and monetary markets. John Hicks and Alvin Hansen, based on the work of Keynes, initially developed it. A summary of the model is available at http://homepage.newschool.edu/het/essays/keynes/hickshansen.htm.

Appendix A. Index and Drawdown Computation Methodology

Using the data from the sources identified in Table 1, we use the following methodology to create a series of inflation-adjusted indices.

Let

$R(s,t)$ = nominal total return on the index in local currency over the period s to t

$R\$(s,t)$ = nominal total return on the index in U.S. dollars over the period s to t

$\pi(s,t)$ = local currency inflation rate over the period s to t

$I(t)$ = real value of the index in local currency at time t

$I\$(t)$ = nominal value of the index in U.S. dollars at time t

An annual return is denoted if s and t are year-end dates, and a monthly return is denoted if s and t are month-end dates. Where price returns are used in place of total returns, because of limitations on data availability, this substitution is disclosed.

For the U.S., U.K., and Japanese markets, we calculate an inflation-adjusted (real) index that is 1.0 on the last day of 1870, 1899, and 1952, respectively.[16] Where the source is in nominal terms, we calculate the index levels from the total return and inflation data as follows:

$$I(t) = I(s) \frac{1 + R(s,t)}{1 + \pi(s,t)}.$$ (A.1)

For the United States, Japan, and the regions of Asia ex-Japan, Europe, and Latin America, we calculate U.S. dollar-denominated indices that start at $1 on the last day of 1987 as follows:[17]

$$I\$(t) = I\$(s)\left[1 + R\$(s,t)\right].$$ (A.2)

We define periods of drawdown and recovery. Drawdown is the simple (not annualized) percentage decline from the previously reached high point of an index to the subsequent low. To calculate drawdown, we first calculate, for each index, a corresponding time series of the peak values, P, of the index, which, like the index itself, starts at 1.0:

$$P(t + \Delta t) = \max\left[P(t), I(t + \Delta t)\right],$$ (A.3)

---

[16]The starting dates for the U.S. and U.K. indices were determined by the starting dates of what we consider to be reliable data. The returns reported by Dimson, Marsh, and Staunton (2002) show the Japanese stock market losing more than 97.5 percent of its real value over the 1943–47 period, clearly a result of World War II. Because data on the TOPIX starts just a few years later in 1952, for Japan, our analysis takes 31 December 1951 as the starting point.

[17]The last day of 1987 is the start date of the MSCI regional indices.

where Δt is the most granular time increment available in the data at time t.

Figures 3, 4, and 5 plot the indices and peaks for our historical real total return series for the United States, the United Kingdom, and Japan, respectively. The periods with gaps between the peak and the index are where the market in question fell below its own immediate past peak and later recovered. Where the gap is large, we refer to such periods as consisting of drawdown and recovery. To measure the extent of a crash or bear market and the length of the subsequent recovery period, we calculate a time series of drawdowns, D, as follows:

$$D(t) = \frac{I(t)}{P(t)} - 1. \tag{A.4}$$

When $D = 0$, the index is climbing to a new peak. When D falls below zero, a drawdown period has begun. When D returns to zero, the recovery (to the previous peak) period is over and the index is starting to move toward a new, higher peak.

Let t_0 and t_1 be the beginning and end of a drawdown–recovery period. In other words, $D(t_0) = D(t_1) = 0$ and

$$D(t) < 0 \text{ for } t_0 < t < t_1. \tag{A.5}$$

The maximum drawdown for the period is

$$D_{max}(t_0, t_1) = \min\left[D(t) \,|\, t_0 < t < t_1\right]. \tag{A.6}$$

The trough, t^*, is the time at which the maximum drawdown is realized:

$$D(t^*) = D_{max}(t_0, t_1). \tag{A.7}$$

In our summary of the history of market crashes, we focus on the time of the peak (t_0), the severity of the decline (D_{max}), and the time until recovery ($t_1 - t^*$).

To interpolate monthly total returns for the United States from 1886 through 1925, we relied on data in Pierce (1982).

Pierce reports daily closing values for the various Dow Jones averages from their inceptions. We use the month-end values for four averages as follows:[18]

Dow Jones Average	Period
12-stock average	Jan 1886–Sep 1889
20-stock average	Sep 1889–Dec 1896
Prewar DJIA	Jan 1897–Jan 1915
Modern DJIA	Jan 1915–Dec 1925

[18]We thank Kailin Liu for manually entering the data in Pierce (1982) into a spreadsheet file. To our knowledge, this is the first electronic record of this dataset.

The first Dow Jones average that we use is a 12-stock mixed (railroad and industrial) average and runs from January 1886 to April 1896. (We use the value of this average on the first trading day of January 1886 as if it occurred on the last day of December 1885 so that we can calculate a return for January.) A broader (20-stock mixed railroad and industrial) average was started in September 1889 and runs to December 1896. Because we use the broadest index whenever possible, we switch to the 20-stock average in September 1889.

The pre–World War I Dow Jones Industrial Average (DJIA) is a 12-stock industrial average that starts January 1897. Because the 20-stock average was discontinued after December 1896, we switch to the prewar DJIA in January 1897 with no overlap between the series.[19] During 1914, the market was closed for almost five months, so Pierce contains no month-end values for August through November. To maintain a continuous monthly series, we fill in the July value for these months, thus making their price returns zero.

When the market reopened, Dow Jones had decided to constitute a new, broader industrial average. Both the old and new DJIAs were calculated through September 1916. The ratio of the value of the two indices is highly variable throughout the common period because they contained different stocks. In 1987, Ibbotson Associates determined that the best month to switch series was January 1915. We do the same here.

To link together the four series, we calculate three divisors as follows:

1. $Div1$ links the 12-stock average and the 20-stock average. It is the September 1889 value of the 20-stock average divided by that of the 12-stock average.

2. $Div2$ links the 20-stock average and the prewar DJIA. Because there is no overlap between these two indices, we divide the value of the prewar DJIA on the first trading day of January 1897 (2 January 1897) by the month-end December 1896 value of the 20-stock average. In other words, we assume that the daily return on the 20-stock average on 2 January 1897 would have been zero had the index existed.

3. $Div3$ links the prewar DJIA and the modern DJIA. It is the January 1915 value of the modern DJIA divided by that of the prewar DJIA.

Our final series is calculated as follows:

Period	Calculation
Jan 1886–Aug 1889	12-stock avg × $Div1$ × $Div2$ × $Div3$
Sep 1889–Dec 1896	20-stock avg × $Div2$ × $Div3$
Jan 1897–Jan 1914	Prewar DJIA × $Div3$
Jan 1915–Dec 1925	Modern DJIA

---

[19] See the construction of the divisor $Div2$ later for details on how we linked these nonoverlapping series.

Price Returns. Ibbotson, Goetzmann, and Peng (2000), henceforth IGP, report annual price and total returns for the U.S. stock market for years prior to 1926. For a given year, let:

PR_{IGP} = the annual price return reported by IGP

$P_{DJ}(m)$ = the value of our linked Dow Jones index in month m

$P_{DJ}(0)$ = the value of our linked Dow Jones index for December of the prior year

$PR(m)$ = our interpolated price return for month m

For m = 1, 2,..., 12, we calculate

$$PR(m) = \left[\frac{1 + PR_{IGP}}{P_{DJ}(12)/P_{DJ}(0)}\right]^{\frac{1}{12}} \left[\frac{P_{DJ}(m)}{P_{DJ}(m-1)}\right] - 1. \tag{A.8}$$

In this way, the difference of the annual price growth rates of the IGP and our Dow Jones series is spread equally across the 12 months of the year.

Total Returns. For each year, we interpolate monthly total returns by assuming a constant level of monthly dividends, d. Let

TR_{IGP} = the annual total return reported by IGP

$TR(m,d)$ = our interpolated price return for month m if the dividend level is d

$CPR(m)$ = the cumulative price return for months 0 through m

We calculate

$$CPR(m) = \begin{cases} 0, & \text{if } m = 0 \\ \prod_{n=1}^{m}\left[1 + PR(n)\right] - 1, & \text{if } m > 0 \end{cases} \tag{A.9}$$

so that

$$TR(m) = PR(m) + \frac{d}{1 + CPR(m-1)}. \tag{A.10}$$

The 12 monthly total returns must link to TR_{IGP}. Hence, we find d by solving the equation

$$\prod_{m=1}^{12}\left[1 + TR(m,d)\right] = 1 + TR_{IGP}. \tag{A.11}$$

Appendix B. Mathematical Models of Market Crashes

Mathematical models of stock market crashes have been studied extensively, but no single model satisfies every researcher. In this appendix, we will discuss some of the more interesting models that are used to describe and explain the characteristics of market crashes. First, we will cover statistical distribution models that describe the distribution of stock market returns more realistically than the conventional normal distribution (Gaussian) or lognormal model does.[20] Returns have historically generated "fatter tails" than are implied by the normal or lognormal distribution. Next, we will cover extreme value theory, which focuses only on the tails of distributions, and how to estimate these from the data. Last, we will explore herd behavior and explain why it can give rise to fat tails.

Statistical Distribution Models. The most common model of asset returns is the normal or Gaussian distribution, which was first suggested by the French mathematician Louis Bachelier in his 1900 doctoral dissertation. This model is natural if one assumes that the return over a time interval is the result of many small independent shocks. The central limit theorem (CLT) implies that, under such conditions, returns follow a Gaussian distribution. The central limit theorem states that the sum of a sufficiently large number of independent random variables, each with finite mean and variance, will be approximately normally distributed. The model provides a first approximation of the behavior observed in empirical stock return data. Return distributions, however, are more leptokurtic (or "fat-tailed on the left-hand side") than implied by the Gaussian distribution model.

The normal distribution can be used to describe, at least approximately, any variable that tends to cluster around the mean. The probability of an asset return (or event) occurring that is three standard deviations below its mean (also known as a three-sigma event) is only ~0.13 percent (i.e., one would expect this to occur only 13 in every 10,000 times).

For example, from January 1926 to April 2009, the S&P 500 total return index had a monthly mean return of 0.91 percent and a monthly standard deviation of 5.55 percent. A negative three-sigma event would be a return of −15.74 percent. During this time period, there were 10 monthly returns worse than −15.74 percent, as shown in **Table B1**. These data imply that the probability of a three-sigma event is 1 percent rather than 0.13 percent, or eight times greater than one would expect under a normal distribution. Hence, a normal distribution fails to describe the "fat" or "heavy" tails of the stock market.

---

[20]The lognormal model differs from the classic Gaussian normal distribution model by assuming that the logarithms of return relatives, $\ln(1 + r)$, not the returns themselves (r), are distributed normally. This adjustment reflects the fact that stock returns cannot be less than −100 percent.

Table B1. Worst 10 Monthly Returns for the S&P 500, January 1926–April 2009

Period	S&P 500 (%)
Sep 1931	−29.73
Mar 1938	−24.87
May 1940	−22.89
May 1932	−21.96
Oct 1987	−21.52
Apr 1932	−19.97
Oct 1929	−19.73
Feb 1933	−17.72
Oct 2008	−16.79
Jun 1930	−16.25

Source: Based on data from Morningstar EnCorr.

By definition, market crashes are distributed in the far left tails, as shown in Table B1. Because the normal distribution model fails to describe the heavy tails, it will also fail to describe market crashes.

Many statistical models have been put forth to account for the heavy tails. Examples are Benoit Mandelbrot's stable Paretian hypothesis (Mandelbrot 1963), Student's *t*-distribution (Blattberg and Gonedes 1974), and the mixture of Gaussian distributions model (Clark 1973). The latter two models—Student's *t*-distribution and the mixture of Gaussian distributions model—both possess finite variance and fat tails, but they are not stable, which implies that their shapes are changing at different time horizons and that distributions at different time horizons do not obey scaling relations.

An alternative model is the Lévy (1925) stable distribution model, also known as the stable Paretian distribution or simply the stable distribution. In 1963, Mandelbrot, the mathematician best known as the father of fractal geometry, studied changes in cotton prices over time. He found that the changes did not follow a normal distribution but instead a stable distribution, where the distribution of returns had an infinite variance. Later, his student Eugene Fama applied the model to changes in stock prices in his doctoral dissertation (Fama 1965).

In the context of logarithm of asset return "relatives" (where the relative is the asset return plus 1), the corresponding models are the lognormal and log-stable models. Kaplan (2009) illustrates that the lognormal distribution fails to fit the left tails of the S&P 500 return distribution and that the log-stable distribution does a much better job. The stable distribution, however, suffers from an infinite variance as mentioned earlier, and thus, its tails are perhaps too fat. A simple solution is to truncate the tails of the stable distribution, which results in what is known as the Truncated Lévy Flight (TLF). The TLF distribution has finite variance and fat tails.

Previous studies (Mantegna and Stanley 1999) have demonstrated that the TLF model describes return distributions measured at high-frequency time horizons quite well. **Figure B1** compares the log-TLF model with the lognormal model in fitting the historical return distributions for the S&P 500 (Xiong 2009). One can see that the log-TLF model provides an excellent fit for the S&P 500 in all aspects: center, tails, minimum, and maximum.

Extreme Value Theory. Stock market crashes are extreme realizations of the underlying return distribution. The bulk of statistical methods is concerned about finding the probabilistic characteristics of the whole population of a dataset (i.e., its mean, variance, and distribution). In contrast, extreme value theory (EVT) focuses only on the tails of distributions and how to estimate them from data.

EVT requires extensive data because the most informative events are historical crises, which are relatively rare events by their very nature. It is critically important that the data used to estimate extreme events contain some information about extreme events.

Figure B1. The Semi-Log Historical Distributions of S&P 500 Monthly Returns Fitted by the Log-TLF and Lognormal Models, January 1926–April 2009

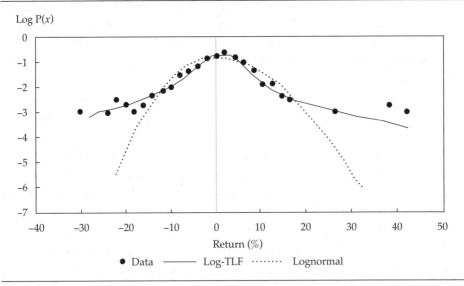

Source: Based on data from Xiong (2009).

EVT is a practical tool that allows risk managers to estimate tail risk. It can be used to compute the probabilities of extreme events. An interesting application is to determine whether emerging markets have fatter left tails than developed countries have. LeBaron and Samanta (2005) demonstrated that crashes appear to be more frequent in emerging than developed markets. The characteristics of emerging market crashes within the same region, such as Latin America or Asia, appear to be very similar, indicating the geographical nature of market crashes. This fact has important implications for international portfolio managers.

Herd Behavior and Stock Market Crashes. The statistical models discussed earlier consider the market to be a "black box" and are not based on any economic model. Economic models are needed to explain why market crashes occur and what to do about them.

Cooper (2008) reminds us of the important role of Minsky's financial instability hypothesis in understanding the origin of financial crises (Minsky 1986, 1992). Cooper noted that the existence of extreme events, such as bank runs, has been well understood in finance for hundreds of years; however, their presence is entirely ignored by mainstream financial theory. In contrast, Minsky's theory of self-reinforcing positive feedback processes can be used to understand these extreme events.

The positive feedback processes are closely related to herd behavior. Shiller (2000) provides massive evidence to support his argument that irrational exuberance produced the ups and downs of the stock and real estate markets. He demonstrates that psychological factors, such as herd behavior and epidemics, exert important effects on markets. For example, the influence of authority over the human mind can be enormous, and people are ready to believe authorities even when they plainly contradict matter-of-fact judgment; people tend to imitate other people's actions rather than choosing to exercise their own judgment about the market; most people purchase stocks based on direct interpersonal communication instead of independent research; and so on.

A mathematical model that connects herd behavior to fat tails was developed by Cont and Bouchaud (2000). The model assumes that agents group together in clusters. For example, a cluster can represent a group of security analysts who herd together. The Cont and Bouchaud model ultimately gives rise to heavy tails in the distribution of stock price variations, similar to distributions observed in empirical studies of high-frequency market data. The model provides a link between two well-known market phenomena: the heavy tails observed in the distribution of stock market returns, on the one hand, and herding behavior in financial markets, on the other hand.

REFERENCES

Bachelier, Louis. 1900. "Théorie de la spéculation." Doctoral dissertation, *Annales Scientifiques de l'École Normale Supérieure*, vol. 3, no. 17:21–86. Translated into English and published in Paul H. Cootner, ed. 1964. *The Random Character of Stock Market Prices.* Cambridge, MA: MIT Press.

Bidwell, R.L. 1970. *Currency Conversion Tables: A Hundred Years of Change.* London: Rex Collings.

Blattberg, Robert C., and Nicholas J. Gonedes. 1974. "A Comparison of the Stable and Student Distributions as Statistical Models for Stock Prices." *Journal of Business*, vol. 47, no. 2 (April):244–280.

Calomiris, Charles W. 2008. "Banking Crises." In *The New Palgrave Dictionary of Economics.* 2nd ed. Edited by Steven N. Durlauf and Lawrence E. Blume. Basingstoke, Hampshire, United Kingdom: Palgrave Macmillan.

Clark, Peter K. 1973. "A Subordinated Stochastic Process Model with Finite Variance for Speculative Prices." *Econometrica*, vol. 41, no. 1 (January):135–155.

Cont, R., and J.P. Bouchaud. 2000. "Herd Behavior and Aggregate Fluctuations in Financial Markets." *Macroeconomic Dynamics*, vol. 4, no. 2 (June):170–196.

Cooper, George. 2008. *The Origin of Financial Crises: Central Banks, Credit Bubbles and the Efficient Market Fallacy.* New York: Vintage Books.

Debreu, Gérard. 1959. *Theory of Value: An Axiomatic Analysis of Economic Equilibrium.* New Haven, CT: Yale University Press.

DeRosa, David F. 2009. *Central Banking and Monetary Policy in Emerging-Markets Nations.* Charlottesville, VA: The Research Foundation of CFA Institute.

Dimson, Elroy, Paul Marsh, and Mike Staunton. 2002. *Triumph of the Optimists: 101 Years of Global Investment Returns.* Princeton, NJ: Princeton University Press.

Fama, Eugene F. 1965. "The Behavior of Stock-Market Prices." *Journal of Business*, vol. 38, no. 1 (January):34–105.

Fisher, Irving. 1933. "The Debt-Deflation Theory of Great Depressions." *Econometrica*, vol. 1, no. 4 (October):337–357.

Greenspan, Alan. 2007. *The Age of Turbulence: Adventures in a New World.* New York: Penguin Press.

Hayek, Friedrich A. 1932. "Das Schicksal der Goldwährung" [The Fate of the Gold Standard]. *Der Deutsche Volkswirt*, vol. 6, no. 20.

Homer, Sidney, and Richard Sylla. 2005. *A History of Interest Rates.* 4th ed. Hoboken, NJ: Wiley Finance.

Ibbotson, Roger G., William N. Goetzmann, and Liang Peng. 2000. "A New Historical Database for the NYSE 1815 to 1925: Performance and Predictability." *Journal of Financial Markets*, vol. 4, no. 1 (January):1–32.

Kaplan, Paul D. 2009. "Déjà Vu All Over Again." *Morningstar Advisor* (February/March).

Keynes, John Maynard. 1936. *The General Theory of Employment, Interest, and Money.* New York: Harcourt Brace and Company.

Kindleberger, Charles P. 1973. *The World in Depression, 1929-1939.* Berkeley, CA: University of California Press.

Krugman, Paul. 2008. *The Return of Depression Economics and the Crisis of 2008.* New York: W.W. Norton.

LeBaron, Blake, and Ritirupa Samanta. 2005. "Extreme Value Theory and Fat Tails in Equity Markets." *Computing in Economics and Finance 2005*, No. 140, Society for Computational Economics.

Lévy, Paul P. 1925. *Calcul des probabilités.* Paris: Gauthier-Villars.

Maddison, Angus. 2009. "Statistics on World Population, GDP, and Per Capita GDP, 1-2006 AD," accessed at www.ggdc.net/maddison/Historical_Statistics/horizontal-file_03-2009.xls on 25 August 2009.

Mandelbrot, Benoit. 1963. "The Variation of Certain Speculative Prices." *Journal of Business*, vol. 36, no. 4 (October):394–417.

Mantegna, Rosario N., and H. Eugene Stanley. 1999. *An Introduction to Econophysics: Correlations and Complexity in Finance.* Cambridge, U.K.: Cambridge University Press.

Minsky, Hyman P. 1986. *Stabilizing an Unstable Economy.* New Haven, CT: Yale University Press.

———. 1992. "The Financial Instability Hypothesis." The Jerome Levy Economics Institute of Bard College, Working Paper No. 74 (May): www.levy.org/pubs/wp74.pdf.

Morningstar. 2009. *2009 Ibbotson Stocks, Bonds, Bills, and Inflation (SBBI) Classic Yearbook* (http://corporate.morningstar.com/ib/asp/subject.aspx?xmlfile=1414.xml).

Pierce, Phyllis S., ed. 1982. *The Dow Jones Averages, 1885–1980.* Homewood, IL: Dow Jones Irwin.

Roll, Richard. 1988. "The International Crash of October 1987." *Financial Analysts Journal*, vol. 44, no. 5 (September/October):19–35.

Schumpeter, Joseph A. 1942. *Capitalism, Socialism, and Democracy.* New York: Harper.

Shiller, Robert J. 2000. *Irrational Exuberance.* Princeton, NJ: Princeton University Press.

———. 2005. "Definition of Irrational Exuberance" (www.irrationalexuberance.com/definition.htm).

———. 2009. "Online Data Robert Shiller," accessed at www.econ.yale.edu/~shiller/data.htm on 10 September 2009.

Smith, Adam. 1776. *An Inquiry into the Nature and Causes of the Wealth of Nations.* London: Printed for W. Strahan and T. Cadell.

Speidell, Lawrence. Forthcoming. *Frontier Equity Market Investing.* Charlottesville, VA: The Research Foundation of CFA Institute.

Tobin, James. 1969. "A General Equilibrium Approach to Monetary Theory." *Journal of Money, Credit, and Banking*, vol. 1, no. 1 (February):15–29.

Xiong, James X. 2009. "Using Truncated Lévy Flight to Estimate Downside Risk." Working paper.

Regulating Systemic Risk

Robert E. Litan

Senior Fellow in Economic Studies
Brookings Institution
Washington, DC

Vice President for Research and Policy
Ewing Marion Kauffman Foundation
Kansas City, Kansas

The ongoing financial crisis that began in 2007 has revealed a fundamental weakness in our financial regulatory system: the absence of a regulator charged with overseeing and preventing "systemic risk," or the risks to the health of the entire financial system posed by the failure of one or more "systemically important financial institutions" (SIFIs).

Ideally, all federal financial regulatory activities should be consolidated in two agencies, a financial solvency regulator and a federal consumer protection regulator, with systemic risk responsibilities being assigned to the solvency regulator. As a second-best option, clear systemic risk oversight authority should be assigned to the U.S. Federal Reserve (Fed). Either of these options is superior to creating a new agency or regulating systemic risk through a "college" of existing financial regulators.

The systemic risk regulator (SRR) should supervise all SIFIs, although the nature and details of this supervision should take account of the differences in types of such institutions (banks, insurance companies, hedge funds, private equity funds, and financial conglomerates). The SRR should also regularly analyze and report to the U.S. Congress on the systemic risks confronting the financial system.

There are legitimate concerns about vesting any financial regulator with such large responsibilities. But as long as there are financial institutions whose failure could lead to calamitous financial and economic consequences, and thus invite all-but-certain federal rescue efforts if the threat of failure is real, then some arm of the federal government must oversee systemic risk and do the best it can to make that oversight work.

Although the United States should continue to cooperate with governments of other countries in reforming financial systems, notably through the G–20 process, policymakers here should not wait for international agreements to be in place before putting our own financial house in order.

Editor's Note: This article was originally published as part of the Initiative on Business and Public Policy at Brookings, Fixing Finance Series, 2009-03, 30 March 2009: www.brookings.edu/papers/2009/0330_systemic_risk_litan.aspx. It is reprinted here with permission from the Brookings Institution.

The initial draft of this article was prepared before the Obama administration offered its comprehensive plan in March 2009 for repairing the nation's financial regulatory system. Some of the ideas discussed in this article are found in that plan; others are not. In any event, in preparing the final version of the article, I have deliberately chosen not to substantially rewrite the initial draft and indicate at every relevant place where the thoughts expressed here agree or conflict with the administration's plan or with other reform proposals that have since been proposed by other political leaders and experts.

Introduction

There is a vigorous debate under way in the wake of the current economic and financial turmoil about whether the U.S. Congress should vest one or more financial regulatory agencies with the ability to monitor and attempt to reduce "systemic risk"—the risk that one or more failures of key financial institutions or markets could wreak havoc on the overall financial system. For example, the inability of a large financial institution to pay its many creditors could force these creditors into bankruptcy or cause them to significantly curtail their activities. Likewise, if the short-term uninsured creditors of one large financial institution are not paid, short-term creditors of other similar financial institutions may be unwilling to roll over their loans or extend new credits, bringing down these other institutions. The economy could be severely damaged through either of these channels.

It was the fear of systemic risk, after all, that motivated the various recent federal rescues: the forced sale of Bear Stearns to JPMorgan Chase, the Fed takeover of AIG, the conservatorships established for the government-sponsored mortgage enterprises Fannie Mae and Freddie Mac, the temporary expansion of deposit insurance for bank deposits, the extension of federal guarantees to money market funds, and the creation of the Troubled Asset Relief Program (TARP) to support the banking system. Likewise, the Fed has greatly expanded its balance sheet—lending in a variety of innovative ways and purchasing assets—in an effort to keep fear from paralyzing the nation's credit markets.

It is clear that we never again want to see the economy come as close to experiencing a systemic meltdown as we have during the past year. And yet, as Fed Chairman Ben Bernanke and Treasury Secretary Timothy Geithner, among others, have pointed out, our current financial regulatory structure is institution specific. That is, regulators are charged with overseeing the safety and soundness of individual financial institutions, but none is held responsible for monitoring and assuring *systemwide* stability.

Chairman Bernanke has urged Congress to fill this gap in our financial regulatory system by establishing a systemic risk regulator. He has not claimed that the Fed should be that regulator but that at the very least it can play a central role in any future monitoring and regulation of systemic risk. I agree.

In this article, I set out the case for having a systemic risk regulator; discuss four options regarding which agency or agencies might be assigned that role; describe some of the key functions that such a regulator could be expected to perform; and answer objections to authorizing a risk regulator. I conclude by discussing ways to reduce systemic risk other than by regulating SIFIs, the main object of a systemic risk regulator.

The Case for a Systemic Risk Regulator

The Fed is already de facto responsible for containing systemic risk through its regular monetary policy activities. After all, a principal reason Congress created the Fed was to act as a lender of last resort to provide liquidity to the economy when others would not.

The clear challenge raised by recent events (especially the extraordinary bailouts of creditors arranged by the Fed and the Treasury in 2008–2009) is to find better ways of preventing threats to systemwide financial stability in the first place. In particular, if the SIFIs whose creditors were rescued had not suffered the kind of credit losses that we have seen or if they had not been as leveraged as they were, the various financial rescues would not have been necessary. It is for this reason that stronger regulation of SIFIs is called for.

In theory, a different monetary policy—one aimed at containing asset price bubbles—might also have prevented what has happened. But monetary policy is a very blunt tool for preventing systemic risk, especially when that risk arises in a specific sector of the economy, such as mortgage origination and the insurance of mortgage-related securities—through bond insurance or derivatives such as credit default swaps (CDS). Thus, the Fed could have restrained the housing price bubble in the past decade by running a far less expansionary monetary policy than it did, but the Fed would have then done so at the cost of slower economic growth and higher unemployment throughout the period. A more targeted regulatory approach, one that would have imposed minimum down-payment and income verification requirements on mortgage borrowers, could have been equally effective but without the collateral impacts on overall economic activity.

Nonetheless, there are limits to what can be done by, and realistically expected of, any SRR. Systemic risk will exist as long as there are financial institutions sufficiently large and interconnected with the rest of the financial system and the economy such that their failure could lead to many other failures or significant financial disruption. It is unrealistic, therefore, to expect that systemic risk can be eliminated entirely.

Likewise, history has shown time and again that asset price bubbles are endemic to market economies. Often, bubbles are associated with some new technology, which many entrepreneurs and investors embrace in the hope of being one of the few winners after others are shaken out by competition. Well before the internet boom and bust, bubbles occurred with automobiles, telephone companies, and other breakthrough technologies. It would be a mistake for government to try to second guess the market each time one of these technological bubbles occurs and to try to snuff it out or contain it. In the process, government could snuff out the next Microsoft, Apple, Intel, or Google.

What has made this crisis different from previous technological bubbles, however, *is that it was preceded by an asset (housing) price bubble that was fueled by a combination of excesses in the financial sector*: imprudent mortgage lending, excessive leverage by financial institutions, and imprudent insurance or insurance-related activities (unsound bond insurance underwriting and inadequate collateral and capital backing CDS in the case of AIG). These are the kinds of activities to which an SRR can and should alert Congress, other regulatory agencies, and the public. More broadly, as I discuss later, the SRR should have special oversight responsibilities with respect to SIFIs to ensure that they have the financial resources—both capital and liquidity—to withstand reasonably severe adverse economic shocks, both to the economy generally and to their important counterparties.

Choosing the Systemic Risk Regulator: The Options

Which agency should be the SRR? I see four alternatives: a new consolidated financial solvency regulator, the Federal Reserve, a new systemic risk regulatory agency, or a college of existing financial regulators.

Option 1: A New Consolidated Financial Solvency Regulator.

Ideally, Congress would consolidate our current multiple financial regulatory agencies into just two: one for solvency, the other for consumer protection. The solvency regulator would oversee and supervise all banks (and thrifts, assuming their separate charter is retained, which I believe it should not be) and systemically important insurers.[1] The solvency regulator would also have a division specially charged with oversight of all SIFIs. The consumer protection regulator would combine the current activities of the U.S. Securities and Exchange Commission (SEC) and the Commodity Futures Trading Commission (CFTC), the current consumer protection activities of the federal banking agencies, and also the relevant financial consumer protection responsibilities of the Federal Trade Commission (FTC).

The Treasury Department under Secretary Henry Paulson outlined a similar plan for the Fed, except for designating the Fed as a separate SRR, with broad but ill-defined powers. Many have compared the Fed in this role with a "free safety" defensive back in football: It would have broad discretion to pick up the "uncovered man," or in this case the systemic financial issues that otherwise might fall through the cracks of other regulators.

---

[1]At the time of the final draft of this article, October 2009, Senator Dodd (chairman of the U.S. Senate Banking Committee) was backing a single prudential regulator.

The advantage of this first option is that it is clean and logical. It would eliminate current regulatory overlaps and jurisdictional fights, which are now supposed to be ironed out by the President's Working Group on Financial Markets.

Of course, under any systemic regulatory regime, the Fed may still have to act as a lender of last resort for specific institutions (as it did for AIG). For this reason, the Fed should have regular consultations and interactions with the solvency regulator, including the right to receive in a timely manner all information about SIFIs that it believes necessary. These interactions would inform the Fed's monetary policy activities and would ready the Fed for any rescues that might be required (although some of the planning for these events can and should be done beforehand, as will be discussed in the next section).

But as President Truman's famous "the buck stops here" sign makes amply clear, in any organization, the buck must stop somewhere. Otherwise, not only will regulators be prone to fight, but also regulated financial institutions can be confused and subjected to conflicting demands, especially at times of financial stress (according to recent press accounts, this appears to be a significant problem for Citigroup and possibly other banks that have received TARP funds).[2] Under this first ideal option, therefore, the buck-stops-here principle means that the solvency regulator, and not the Fed, would have the clear authority and responsibility for overseeing all federally regulated financial institutions, including SIFIs. The solvency regulator would also be responsible for producing regular reports to Congress about systemic risk (drawing on the expertise of the Fed and the President's Council of Economic Advisers).

Option 2: The Federal Reserve. If history is any guide, the financial regulatory agencies will not be as radically consolidated as I envisioned in the first option. Accordingly, a second-best solution is to assign systemic risk oversight to the Federal Reserve System. After all, the Fed is a lender of last resort to financially troubled SIFIs. Furthermore, the Fed's monetary policy goals can be frustrated or diverted by the failure of such institutions. As a result, the Fed is a logical choice for the SRR if a single prudential regulator is not established.

In my view, if the Fed is chosen as the SRR, it should not be as a "free safety" as envisioned by the Paulson Treasury. Giving the Fed broad but vague responsibilities is a recipe for agency infighting before the fact, and for finger pointing after the fact. Put simply, the free safety model violates the buck-stops-here principle. Instead, if the Fed is assigned systemic risk regulatory responsibilities, then it should have sole authority over solvency and associated reporting requirements relating to these institutions.

---

[2] See Monica Langley and David Enrich, "Citigroup Chafes under U.S. Overseers," *Wall Street Journal* (25 February 2009):A1.

Admittedly, assigning oversight of systemic risk, and specifically of the activities of SIFIs, to the Fed is not without significant risk, but in my view, most or all of these challenges can be met. One such risk, as some critics of this option have pointed out, is that making explicit the Fed's responsibility for preventing risk could compromise its mandate to pursue the best monetary policy. For example, as I noted earlier, the Fed could clamp down on asset bubbles but in the process generate higher unemployment. Conversely, in bailing out creditors of failed institutions or in an effort to provide liquidity to the market during a financial crisis, the Fed could lay the groundwork for future inflation.

But the reality is that the Fed already has *implicit* if not *explicit* authority for containing systemic risk; that is, after all, one of the main jobs of a lender of last resort. *Giving the Fed the appropriate regulatory tools to contain the risk posed by SIFIs would make its monetary policy job easier, not harder.* Thus, had the Fed tightened standards for subprime mortgage origination earlier in the decade, it would not necessarily have needed tighter monetary policy to restrain housing price inflation.

A related concern is that providing the Fed with explicit systemic risk responsibility could compromise its independence, which evidence has shown to be important for carrying out effective monetary policy, especially when the Fed tightens money in order to contain inflation. The argument here presumably is that Congress and/or the president would be emboldened to criticize and thus effectively constrain the Fed in its monetary policy activities if the Fed were to fall short in its regulatory duties. The response to this argument is that the markets clearly would frown upon political attacks on the Fed's independence. This is why presidents have learned to refrain from criticizing the Fed and why I believe Congress keeps its hands off as well.

There is more substance to the critique that Congress and/or the president could put pressure on the Fed in carrying out not its monetary duties but its *regulatory* activities. Specifically, in the future, it is quite possible, if not to be expected, that SIFIs under the regulation and supervision of the Fed could enlist some in Congress and or the administration to inappropriately lighten the Fed's regulatory stance when it may be ill-advised to do so or conversely to refrain from tightening its regulatory standards to keep a bubble from expanding. But this political risk already exists under the current regulatory structure, and it is hard to say how it would be worse if the Fed were explicitly assigned systemic risk oversight duties. Furthermore, the Fed or any SRR can insulate itself from political pressure by introducing a more automatic system of countercyclical capital standards than now exists, another topic discussed shortly.

Yet another fear that might be lodged against the Fed is that it might be excessively risk averse and regulate too heavily. Given what has just happened, any agency given systemic risk responsibility is likely to be risk averse (and to some degree, appropriately so). This objection goes more to regulation per se, not just by the Fed.

Still another challenge for the Fed, if given systemic responsibility, would be to build a staff appropriate to the task. Critics will argue that the Fed now has expertise to supervise only banks, not other financial institutions that might be deemed to be SIFIs (such as large insurers, hedge funds, and private equity funds), and that for this reason, it is not an appropriate SRR. But this same critique applies to any agency that would be given solvency regulatory duties with respect to any nonbanks not now regulated at the federal level.

In any event, the alleged staffing problem is a solvable one, especially in the current job market, which has seen layoffs of many qualified individuals in the financial sector. Some of these individuals would be grateful for secure, interesting employment at an SRR. To anticipate a potential objection to relying on private sector expertise, not everyone who once worked in finance is a crook or is responsible for our current mess. The Fed (or any SRR) should also be able to draw supervisory personnel overseeing large banks, in particular, from the Office of the Comptroller of the Currency (OCC), which already supervises these institutions. In addition, law and accounting firms, among others, would be fertile sources of potential new regulatory recruits.

Finally, some may fear that because the Fed's budget is effectively off-limits to the president and to Congress—the Fed pays its expenses out of the earnings from its balance sheet and returns the excess to the Treasury—giving the Fed more regulatory responsibility would permit it to exercise too much discretion and to spend too much money without effective political oversight. If Congress believes this to be a significant problem, it could always wall off and subject the purely regulatory (and related research) functions of the Fed (funding them through assessments for supervisory costs on the SIFIs) to the annual appropriations process while allowing the Fed to retain its current budgetary freedom with respect to its monetary policy functions.

Option 3: A New Systemic Risk Regulatory Agency. A third option is to create an entirely new systemic risk regulatory agency, whether or not the other financial regulatory agencies are consolidated in some manner. As with the first option, the Fed could have an advisory role in this new agency and should in any event be given the same timely access to the information collected by this agency as the agency itself has.

A principal objection to this approach is that it would add still another cook to the regulatory kitchen, one that is already too crowded, and thus aggravate current jurisdictional frictions. This concern would be mitigated by consolidating the financial regulatory agencies, as in the first option. But still, the activities of an SRR are fundamentally identical to the solvency regulatory functions now carried out by the banking agencies, including the Fed. Why go to the trouble of creating yet another agency with skills similar to those that already exist?

Option 4: A College of Existing Financial Regulators. A fourth option is to vest systemic risk regulatory functions in a group or "college" of existing regulators, perhaps by giving formal statutory powers to the President's Working Group on Financial Markets as well as additional regulatory authority for SIFIs that are not currently regulated by any federal financial regulatory agency (insurers, hedge funds, and private equity funds). This option may be the most politically feasible—because it does not disturb the authority of any individual financial regulatory agency while augmenting their collective authority—but it is also the least desirable in my view.

A college of regulators clearly violates the buck-stops-here principle and is a clear recipe for jurisdictional battles and after-the-fact finger pointing. It also keeps too many cooks in the regulatory kitchen and thus invites coordination difficulties. Admittedly, creating a college of regulators may reduce these problems, but it would not eliminate them.

As of October 2009, the supervisory college or council idea appears to have the most political traction, largely because of widespread concerns in Congress about concentrating too much authority in the Fed and also because of criticism that the Fed failed in its supervisory duties in the run-up to the crisis (an unfair critique, in my view, because all financial regulators, federal and state, bear their share of responsibility).

Functions of the SRR

It is one thing to identify the SRR; it is quite another to define precisely what it is supposed to do. Given the scope, importance, and complexity of the task, it would be best if Congress drafted any authorizing legislation in broad terms and permitted the designated agency to fill in most of the details by rulemaking or less formal guidance, subject to congressional oversight. Nonetheless, certain key issues—and tentative answers for each—can be anticipated now.

First, the SRR's mission must be clear: to minimize the sources of systemic risk or to reduce such risk to acceptable levels. For reasons already given, the goal should not be to *eliminate* all systemic risk; it is unrealistic to expect that result, and an effort to do so could severely constrain socially useful activity.

Second, there must be criteria for identifying SIFIs. The Group of Thirty has suggested that the size, leverage, and degree of interconnection with the rest of the financial system should be the deciding factors, and I agree.[3] The test should be whether the combination of these factors signifies that the failure of the institution poses a significant risk to the stability of the financial system. The application of this definition would cover not only large banks (for starters, the nine largest institutions that were required to accept TARP funds at the outset) but also large

---

[3]Group of Thirty, "Financial Reform: A Framework for Financial Stability" (January 2009).

insurers and depending on their leverage and counterparty exposures, hedge funds and private equity funds. It is also conceivable that one or more large finance companies (nondepository lenders, such as GE Capital, which are funded by commercial paper rather than deposits) could meet the test. And presumably the major stock exchanges and clearinghouses, as well as the contemplated clearing-house(s) for CDS, would qualify.

To be sure, no hedge fund or private equity fund in recent years has failed in a way that endangered the financial system—although the collapse of Long-Term Capital Management (LTCM) in 1998 provided a sufficient systemic scare that the Federal Reserve helped orchestrate a private sector rescue of that particular hedge fund. The problem now is what regulators *do not know* about the systemic risks posed by any one or more hedge or private equity funds because there is no comprehensive reporting by these funds currently in place. Accordingly, one job for the SRR would be to work with an appropriate federal financial regulator—presumably the SEC or its successor (a merged agency with the CFTC or a broad consumer protection regulator)—to establish reporting requirements that would enable the SRR to identify if any of these funds indeed poses a significant systemic risk. Had we had such a system in place well before LTCM grew to be so leveraged, it is possible, if not likely, that that fund would never have been allowed to put itself in a position where it could blow up. The problem now is that we really do not know if there is another LTCM in waiting.

As for the regulation of insurance, it is possible a number of our largest life and property/casualty insurers would satisfy the SIFI criteria and thus should be regulated by the SRR. *This would mean that some insurers would be regulated for solvency purposes at the federal level for the first time.* In my view, other insurers (excluding health insurers) should be given the option to be regulated at the federal level as well (although not by the SRR but by a new general financial solvency regulator, or failing the creation of such a body, then by a new office of insurance regulation analogous to the OCC for banks).

It is critical, however, that federal laws preempt the application of state laws and rules, such as rate regulation, to federally regulated insurers. Otherwise, states would be too easily tempted to force insurers to charge rates below actuarially appropriate levels, knowing that insurer solvency is no longer a state problem but a federal one. Where rate suppression exists, it can endanger the solvency of insurers and/or encourage them to cut back or drop their coverage, as a number of insurers already have done in Florida. Neither outcome is in consumers' interest. It is time to entrust the pricing of insurance, an industry with a low degree of concentration, to the marketplace, as is the case for other financial and nonfinancial products.[4]

---

[4]Robert E. Litan, "Regulating Insurance after the Crisis," Initiative on Business and Public Policy at Brookings, Fixing Finance Series, 2009-02 (4 March 2009): www.brookings.edu/papers/2009/0304_insurance_litan.aspx.

Third, the process for identifying SIFIs should be clear. Institutions so designated should have some right to challenge, as well as the right to petition for removal of that status, if the situation warrants. For example, a hedge fund that is initially highly leveraged should be able to have its SIFI designation removed if the fund substantially reduces its size, leverage, and counterparty risk.

Fourth, the nature of the regulatory regime for SIFIs must be specified. Here I principally have in mind standards for capital (leverage) and liquidity (on the asset and liability sides of the balance sheet) as well as reporting requirements both for the public and for the regulator (the latter should be able to receive more detailed and proprietary information than is appropriate for the public, such as the identity of counterparties and the size and nature of the exposure to specific counterparties). These requirements should take account of differences in the types of institutions and their activities. For example, what is an appropriate capital and liquidity standard for banks is likely to be different from what is appropriate for systemically important insurers, such as hedge funds, private equity funds, and clearinghouses and exchanges.

Broadly speaking, however, because of the systemic risks that SIFIs pose, the SRR should begin with the presumption that the capital and liquidity standards for SIFIs should be *tougher* than those that apply to financial institutions that are not SIFIs. Tougher requirements are also appropriate to meet the obvious objection that identifying SIFIs in advance leads to moral hazard. Appropriate regulation is required to offset this effect.

In this regard, the SRR should also consider reducing the pro-cyclicality of current capital requirements—which constrain lending in bad times and fail to curb it in booms—but only if minimum capital requirements (at least for SIFIs) are gradually increased in the process and if the criteria for moving the standards up or down are clearly announced and enforced. Otherwise, if regulators have too much discretion about when to adjust capital standards, they are likely to relax them in bad times but buckle under political pressure to lower them or at least not to raise them in good times. A clear set of standards for good times and bad would remove this discretion and also insulate the regulators from undue pressure to bend to political winds when they should not.

Fifth, the SRR will need to supervise the institutions under its watch not only to ensure compliance with applicable capital and liquidity standards but, as suggested by the Group of Thirty, also to ensure that the institutions are adhering to best practices for risk management, including daily, if not hourly, exposures to their largest counterparties.[5]

---

[5]In this regard, the SRR should draw on the excellent risk management practice suggestions offered by the private sector Counterparty Risk Management Policy Group (CRMPG) and the Institute of International Finance.

Sixth, as we have all witnessed, regulators are human beings, capable of mistakes. It is unrealistic to expect them to be clairvoyant, regardless of any new or more-intensive training they receive or new blood brought into their ranks as a result of this current crisis. For this reason, it is absolutely essential that regulators look to *stable sources of market discipline* to provide market-based signals of when institutions under their watch may be developing problems. By "stable," I mean capital that cannot easily run, like uninsured deposits in a bank, or commercial paper, or short-term repurchase agreements (repos) for other types of financial institutions. Common shareholders also cannot "run"—by demanding a return of their funds—but they do not have the ideal risk profile for discouraging imprudent risk taking by managers because they receive all of the upside while having limited downside risk.

Until federal authorities guaranteed the previously uninsured, unsecured long-term debt, or subordinated debt, issued by banks (and the housing government-sponsored enterprises Fannie Mae and Freddie Mac), this instrument had all the right characteristics. Such debt has no upside beyond the interest payments it promises, and thus its holders are likely to be more risk averse than common shareholders (or certainly more than insured depositors). Under current bank capital rules, however, banks are allowed but not required to issue such debt. If there were such a requirement, then the interest rates on this debt would provide important early market-based signals to regulators about the possible deterioration in the bank's health.

But now that the government has established the principle that subordinated debt of large banks will be protected in a crisis, regulators need to be creative in thinking of other ways of harnessing stable market discipline. In September 2009, the Shadow Financial Regulatory Committee (of which I am a member) proposed two interesting alternatives: (1) The Treasury could create a "prediction market" for future bailouts of institutions by selling a failure prediction contract (FPC) that pays out in the event a bank (or another type of financial institution) fails, is bailed out, or is taken over by regulators; and/or (2) regulators could require large financial institutions to issue a bond, analogous to catastrophe bonds that are now sold by insurers or reinsurers, that would not be repaid if the aforementioned events occur.[6] The prices of the proposed FPC or of the bond would provide market-based signals of financial danger that would not be distorted by the prospect of future government bailouts; to the contrary, the instruments would take such a possibility explicitly into account and price it.

Seventh, systemic risks associated with the CDS market must be addressed, as the failure of AIG so clearly demonstrates. A clearinghouse would permit offsetting CDS contracts to be netted out against each other while making the

---

[6]Shadow Financial Regulatory Committee, "Reducing Interference with Accounting Standards and Devising Securities to Price Moral Hazard," Statement No. 277 (14 September 2009): www.aei.org/paper/100048.

counterparties to the contract responsible to the clearinghouse rather than to each other. At this writing, several CDS clearinghouses are approved or nearly approved, which should somewhat mitigate the risk posed by the failure of one or more large CDS issuers in the future. But the clearinghouses themselves must be well capitalized and have sufficient liquidity to meet their obligations, which is why they should be regulated as SIFIs as well.

Yet even a well-capitalized and supervised central clearinghouse for CDS and possibly other derivatives will not reduce systemic risks posed by *customized derivatives* whose trades are not easily cleared by a central party (which cannot efficiently gather and process as much information about the risks of nonpayment as the principals themselves). The best solution to this problem is to require the SEC and CFTC, possibly in conjunction with the SRR, to set minimum capital and/or collateral rules for sellers of these contracts. At a minimum, more detailed reporting to the regulator by the participants in these customized markets should be on the table.

Finally, all SIFIs under the watch of the SRR should be required to file an "early closure and loss sharing plan"—in effect, a prepackaged bankruptcy plan without the extensive, costly, and time-consuming bankruptcy process itself—that would go into effect upon a regulatory determination that the institution is troubled but not yet insolvent. In effect, we have had such a prompt corrective action (PCA) system for banks since the passage of FDICIA (Federal Deposit Insurance Corporation Improvement Act) in 1991. As this crisis has illustrated, PCA has not worked perfectly for banks, but it did force the regulators to induce many banks at an early stage of the crisis to raise capital from the private markets (before they effectively shut down). This is a better outcome than what occurred in the 1980s when regulators exercised "regulatory forbearance" when confronted with the threatened failure of the nation's largest banks because of their troubled sovereign debt and other loans. The fact that PCA did not keep the largest banks from having to be rescued by the TARP is an argument for raising the threshold at which early corrective action is required, not for abandoning the concept of mandated early intervention.

Accordingly, high on the "to do" list of any future SRR is to extend PCA to all the SIFIs under its watch. This could be implemented by imposing minimum early intervention standards for all SIFIs, taking account of the differences in their businesses, or by accepting and then negotiating such early closure plans with the individual institutions. Whatever course is taken, the process must produce publicly announced statements by the SIFIs that make clear how losses of uninsured parties, including those among affiliates of the SIFI itself, are to be allocated in the event of regulatory intervention. The early intervention or closure plans should also envision a government-appointed conservator running the institution, with instructions to work with regulators to come to the least-cost resolution (by sale to other parties, by separation into a "good bank/bad bank" structure, or by other means).

The SRR need not, and arguably should not, be the institution that administers the resolution of failed institutions. This job could be handled by the existing FDIC (Federal Deposit Insurance Corporation), which has expertise in these matters, or by creating a new asset disposition agency of which the current FDIC would be a core part.

Complementary Approaches to Reducing Systemic Risk

Even if systemic risk is to be more systematically regulated, it would be a mistake to put all of our faith in any one regulator (or college of regulators) to do all the work. Like investment professionals who counsel not putting all one's financial eggs in one basket, policymakers should use other regulatory or policy "baskets" to supplement and reinforce the measures undertaken by the risk regulator.

Early Warning. For example, bank regulators, including the systemic risk regulator, should be required to issue regular (annual, perhaps more frequent or as the occasion arises) reports outlining the nature and severity of any systemic risks in the financial system. Presumably, such reports would put a spotlight on, among other things, rapidly growing areas of finance because rapid growth tends to be (but is not always) associated with future problems. Economists have recently been working hard on how to identify asset bubbles, and although the results are still not perfect, economists seem to be improving their capabilities. In my view, bubble forecasting is not much more prone to error than hurricane forecasting is. We engage in the latter, so we ought to start taking warnings of the former more seriously.

Establishing early warning systems does not necessarily mean that the Fed should alter its monetary policy to prick bubbles in formation. The virtue of regulation for dampening bubbles is that it can be more targeted and surgical than the blunt instruments of open market operations or changes in the discount rate.

A legitimate objection to an early warning-based regulatory system is that political pressures may be so great that policymakers will ignore them. In particular, the case can be made that if warnings about the housing market overheating had been issued by the Fed and/or other financial regulators during the past decade, few would have paid attention. Moreover, the political forces behind the growth of subprime mortgages—the banks, the once-independent investment banks, mortgage brokers, real estate developers and buyers, and everyone else who was making money off subprime originations and securitizations—could well have stopped any countermeasures dead in their tracks.

This recounting of history might or might not be right. But the exact manner in which the recent crisis unfolded should not matter. The world has changed with this crisis. For the foreseeable future, perhaps for several decades or as long as those who have lived and suffered through recent events are still alive and have an important voice in policymaking, the vivid memories of these events and their consequences will give a future systemic risk regulator much more authority with which to warn Congress and the public of future asset bubbles or sources of undue systemic risk.

The SRR and other financial regulators should explore ways to encourage the largest financial institutions in particular, and indeed all financial actors, to tie compensation more closely to long-term performance than to short-term gain. Clearly, had such compensation systems been in place earlier this decade, the volume of unsound subprime mortgages would have been far lower.

The challenge is to figure out how best to encourage long-term compensation. Exempting financial institutions from the antitrust laws so that they can agree on long-term compensation schemes is not a good idea and could open the floodgates to petitions for other exemptions. If we keep the current, complicated system of bank and insurer capital standards (which I criticize later), one could think of setting modestly lower capital requirements for institutions that tie pay to long-term performance. My preference, however, is for regulators to take this issue into account in their review of an institution's risk management controls. All other things being equal, institutions with long-term performance packages are more likely to prudently manage their risks.

I am less enthusiastic and indeed skeptical about two other ideas for constraining future bubbles. One such idea is to subject new financial products to safety and efficacy screening before permitting them to be used in the marketplace (similar to what the U.S. Food and Drug Administration does for products). This may sound nice in theory, but it is likely to be much more problematic in practice. For one thing, it is virtually impossible to predict in advance of the introduction of a new product how it will affect the economy, positively or negatively. Because regulators will be blamed for products that are later viewed to be unsound but will get little or no credit for socially productive innovations, the regulatory impulse under a prescreening system will always be to say "no." This would introduce an anti-innovation bias into U.S. finance, which however much it has been maligned because of this crisis is nonetheless a prime U.S. competitive asset that should not be quashed but steered in a more productive direction.

The better approach for addressing the risks of financial innovations, in my view, is to regulate them in a targeted fashion if they later prove to be dangerous, much as we regulate consumer products. Had we imposed a prescreening system on automobiles or airplanes, for example, objections certainly would have been raised that each technology could lead to unintended deaths and for that reason each could have been banned. And in fact, at the outset, each of these industry's products was unacceptably dangerous for most consumers; they quickly became much safer as the products were improved. The same is even true for the internet; one easily could have imagined early on that criminals and terrorists would take advantage of it, just as they use our highways, banks, and other accoutrements of daily life. Banning the internet, or more accurately its commercial use, would today seem unthinkable, but in a prescreening environment, it is impossible to know what would have happened.

Finally, it may be tempting to impose size limits on financial firms in addition to limits on leverage. Through the antitrust laws, we already have something of this kind but only if mergers result in an excessive degree of market concentration, or in the case of a monopoly only if the firm abuses its market dominance. There are well-established and defensible criteria for applying these rules. In contrast, I know of no nonarbitrary way to limit any financial institution's size.

In fact, further consolidation among financial institutions is one likely outcome of the current turmoil. Some might say that this will aggravate the systemic risk problem. It may, and it may not. Some of the institutions merging may already be so large as to be SIFIs. If the system results in mergers of SIFIs, we are likely to have fewer of them to watch over. Which is better: 10 banks, each of which may be considered to be an SIFI and thus in need of extra scrutiny, or just 5 of them but twice the size? Frankly, I do not know, and I know of no way of being sure which scenario poses the most systemic risk.

In the end, our world is complex, and we will inevitably have large financial institutions whose failure poses risks to the rest of the economy. The best we can do is harness our best regulatory resources and encourage stable market discipline in an effort to reduce the likelihood that any one of them could fail and to limit the concentrations of counterparty risk of these institutions. In addition, the financial resolution authority should be instructed to resolve troubled SIFIs in ways that minimize effects on financial concentration—breaking them up and selling the pieces if feasible and not unreasonably costly.

International Cooperation. The subprime mortgage crisis has triggered widespread economic damage in the rest of the world, demonstrating that, if there was any doubt about this before, the financial system today is highly globalized and interconnected across national boundaries. It is primarily for this reason that the Bush administration agreed to the G–20 meeting held in Washington, DC, in November 2008 and why the Obama administration has continued to engage the G–20 in constructive dialogue about improving the global financial regulatory system. In principle, there is great attractiveness to at least one of the premises of the G–20 effort, namely, that because finance is now global, the rules governing finance also should be global, or at the very least harmonized among the major countries. Some advocate a further step: overseeing the entire financial system, or at least the large international SIFIs, through a global regulator.

Both ideas are problematic. Our recent experience with the current bank capital standards developed by the Basel Committee—the so-called Basel II rules—demonstrates why.

The Basel II revisions took roughly a decade for the participating countries to debate and finalize, and by the time they were done, they were essentially irrelevant because the banking crisis had already begun. Beyond the excessive time that is inherent in any international rulemaking process is the inevitable complexity that such efforts are likely to entail. The Basel II rules eventually grew to more than 400 pages of complex rules and formulae, none of which is necessary. We would have been far better off over the past decade with a simple (but tougher) leverage requirement for our largest financial institutions coupled with a subordinated debt requirement that could not be overridden by government guarantees.

Meanwhile, the leading financial centers of the world—including the United States—are simply not ready to cede regulatory oversight to a new global body that does not even exist. If the politics that went into the development of the Basel standards are any guide—and they should be—a global regulator would be susceptible to the kind of bureaucratic and political intrigue that is out of place, and frankly dangerous, in today's fast-paced financial environment.

The United States and other countries nonetheless still have much to learn from each other in the way they regulate and supervise financial institutions and markets. Thus, I support a G–20 process that affords opportunities for cross-pollination of views. We also need coordination among central banks and finance ministries, of the sort that the Basel Committee already affords, especially during crises.

But when it comes to reform, the guiding principle should be one adopted recently by the Conference Board of Canada in issuing its recommendations for financial reform: "Think Globally, Act Locally."[7] It is true that failures in U.S. regulation and oversight were major causes of the current global financial crisis (although it has since come to light that there were failures elsewhere, too, that have amplified the effects of the crisis). We should not wait, and indeed cannot afford to wait, for international consensus to fix our system. We clearly do not need or want another decade-long Basel-like process to reach consensus on reform. We can and should do the fixing on our own.

Answers to Anticipated Objections

There will be plausible objections to implementing systemic risk regulation and putting one regulator or a group of them explicitly in charge. Nonetheless, I believe each can be answered.

---

[7]The Conference Board of Canada, "International Financial Policy Reform and Options for Canada: Think Globally, Act Locally" (February 2009): www.conferenceboard.ca/documents.aspx? DID=2938. The phrase originates with the environmental movement but applies likewise to financial risk management.

To begin, the most obvious objection is that identifying specific institutions will create moral hazard because it will effectively signal to everyone that if these institutions are threatened with failure, the federal government will come to the rescue of at least their short-term creditors and counterparties. These critics presumably argue that it is better to return to the policy of "constructive ambiguity" that reigned until this crisis hit: Better to keep market participants guessing about whether they will be protected in order to induce them to monitor the health of the institutions with which they do business and thereby discourage imprudent risk taking by the managers of the institutions.

Well, guess what? In light of the extraordinary bailouts over the past year, constructive ambiguity with respect to the government's protection of creditors of large financial institutions is dead. The only large troubled institution whose creditors took a hit during this period was Lehman Brothers, and I believe many policymakers, in private at least, will admit that was a mistake (although some also may continue to say that no federal entity had the legal authority to rescue Lehman's creditors).

In short, there is no turning back. We now know that at least the short-term creditors of large financial institutions will be bailed out if the institutions run into trouble. Given this condition, we should face the new set of facts and do our best to provide better capital and liquidity cushions under those institutions in advance. That is one answer to the moral hazard charge. A second answer, as outlined earlier, is that the SRR should consider imposing an extra dose of market discipline on SIFIs that is not required for smaller institutions.

A related, second objection to regulating SIFIs is that it will not work: Namely, why would the SRR do any better overseeing SIFIs than our current bank regulators who clearly failed to stop our largest banks from going over the edge? How can we expect regulators, who are paid less and have less financial sophistication than their private sector counterparts, ever to keep up with them? These are legitimate questions, and my best answer to them is to ask in reply: Can you show me a better alternative? The events of the last couple of years could not more clearly demonstrate that the failure to more vigorously oversee the large institutions whose creditors we have ended up protecting has led to the largest bailout in U.S. history and certainly the most calamitous economic circumstances since the Great Depression. Even a halfway effective SRR over the last decade would have given us a better outcome than we have now.

I believe we can meet or do better than even that minimal standard. For a good while, the market will not buy the kinds of nontransparent securities that our financial engineers cooked up during the subprime mortgage explosion. So, our regulators have some time to catch up. And, given the soft job market, the agencies should have an easier time attracting the right talent. Of course, as times get better, the agencies will need to raise salaries to keep their best personnel. Accordingly, the SRR should have more salary freedom to compete for the best and brightest in finance in the years ahead (and it would be able to pay for all this through the fees it charges SIFIs to supervise them).

A third objection is that once today's SIFIs are identified and regulated, what are we to do about tomorrow's new unregulated institutions that will surely take their place and potentially expose us to another round of financial damage? The answer is that if such institutions arise, the SRR regime will need to be expanded. Congress has a choice: Give the SRR broad regulatory power now to identify and regulate such entities, which I know many fear would be giving the agency a blank check, or wait until the new institutions arise and pose a recognized danger and then give the SRR expanded authority. The latter option, although perhaps more politically palatable, runs the risk of repeating a variation of what we have just witnessed: the rise of new institutions, namely state-chartered mortgage brokers, and new complex mortgage securities that in combination too freely originated and securitized subprime mortgages, landing us in the mess we are now in. I can easily imagine a new set of institutions in the future doing much the same thing, and with the political power to resist any preemptive regulation. So, if I had to err on any side, it would be at the outset to give the SRR the ability to expand its net to cover new kinds of SIFIs, subject to congressional limitation or override. As a growing body of economic evidence is suggesting, the "default" scenario matters a lot. Here, the default position for the scope of the SRR should be expansive rather than limited.

Furthermore, those who worry that the market will always invent its way around, or outsmart, our regulators should remember that the regulation of finance has always been a game of cat and mouse, with the private sector mice always one step ahead of the regulatory cats. The problem exposed by this crisis is that the mice now have grown huge and can wreak havoc on a scale previously unimagined. We need to respond by getting better regulatory cats, lions if you will. The fact that this game will continue to go on is not a reason to give up entirely and let the large mice eat their way through the entire economy.

The specter of a powerful SRR no doubt will lead to another objection: In the zeal to prevent a rerun of recent events, albeit surely in a different guise, regulators will clamp down excessively on financial institutions and risk taking and thus kill off or perhaps severely maim the entrepreneurial risk taking that is the lifeblood of our economy and that is key to our future economic growth. Despite this possibility, I draw some comfort from several observations. One is that a financial system that requires less-frequent bailouts of large financial institutions will have more room for risk capital and will be less susceptible to the kinds of episodes we are now experiencing that chill risk taking. A second consideration is that any system of regulating SIFIs should not touch venture capital, angel groups, or individual sources of wealth that are sources of start-up equity capital for new firms and that clearly are not SIFIs under any reasonable definition of the term.

Finally, some may reject the notion that government should behave as though some financial institutions are so systemically important that their short-term creditors must be bailed out in a pinch. Presumably, these critics would either retain the policy of constructive ambiguity or have the Fed and the Treasury make clear that henceforth, no more bailouts will be given. Under such a view, SIFIs do not exist, so there is no need for special regulation of them beyond what exists now.

The problem with this line of reasoning is that, as has been noted, events have passed it by. I cannot believe there is anyone in the markets or outside who would believe the government if it were now to announce such a nonbailout policy. Nor do I believe that this Fed chairman or future Fed chairmen would rule out rescues in order to save the financial system. In short, constructive ambiguity is dead.

Conclusion

There is widespread agreement on the need to strengthen our financial regulatory framework so that we are far less exposed to the kind of financial and economic crisis we are now experiencing without at the same time chilling the innovation and prudent risk taking that are essential for economic growth. It would be a major mistake to conclude that just because market discipline and sound regulation failed to prevent the current crisis, either one now should be jettisoned. Neither pillar alone can do the job. Market discipline requires rules, and these rules must be enforced.

Because the federal government and thus taxpayers are potentially always on the hook for massive financial system failures, then it is both logical and necessary that the federal government oversee the safety, in some manner, of the institutions that give rise to systemic risk.

Our current financial regulatory structure is institution specific in that regulators are charged with overseeing the safety and soundness of individual financial institutions, but none is held responsible for monitoring and assuring systemwide stability. Therefore, appropriate regulation is necessary to reduce the exposure of our financial and economic system to failures of SIFIs. An SRR should be created with special oversight responsibilities with respect to SIFIs to ensure that they have the financial resources—both capital and liquidity—to withstand reasonably large adverse economic shocks, both to the economy generally and to their important counterparties.

This article is based on the author's 4 March 2009 prepared testimony submitted to the Senate Committee on Homeland Security and Governmental Affairs; Martin Neil Baily, Robert E. Litan, and Matthew S. Johnson, "The Origins of the Financial Crisis," Initiative on Business and Public Policy at Brookings, Fixing Finance Series, 2008-03, November 2008; and Robert E. Litan and Martin Neil Baily, "Fixing Finance: A Roadmap for Reform," Initiative on Business and Public Policy at Brookings, Fixing Finance Series, 2009-01, 17 February 2009. All three documents are available at www.brookings.edu/projects/business.aspx.

Not a Failure of Capitalism—A Failure of Government

Peter J. Wallison
Arthur F. Burns Fellow in Financial Policy Studies
American Enterprise Institute for Public Policy Research
Washington, DC

Since the beginning of the turmoil in the financial markets that is now commonly referred to as the "financial crisis," many voices have asserted that this is a "crisis of capitalism." These are not merely the voices of socialist groups, who could be expected to see this event as a vindication of their views;[1] government officials also joined the chorus,[2] as did many commentators on financial matters. As Samuel Brittan observed early in the mortgage meltdown that ultimately became the financial crisis, "Any failures on the financial side are sure to bring the opponents of capitalism out of their burrows. Pundits who until recently conceded that 'capitalism is the only game in town' are now rejoicing at what they hope is the longed-for death agony of the system."[3] Billionaire investor George Soros, who had been arguing at least since 1997 that the capitalist system was "coming apart at the seams," finally found vindication, telling a group in New York in February 2009, according to a Bloomberg News summary, that "the current economic upheaval has its roots in the financial deregulation of the 1980s and signals the end of a free-market model that has since dominated capitalist countries."[4] In 2009, the debate over the responsibility of capitalism for the current crisis rose to such significance that the *Financial Times* ran a gloomy series on the future of capitalism.[5]

An examination of these contributions shows that, with the exception of the socialist view, the critics are not actually recommending the abandonment of a market system but only the imposition of stronger forms of government control over markets through greater regulation and supervision. Much of the rhetoric about

[1] Barry Grey, "The Wall Street Crisis and the Failure of American Capitalism," World Socialist Website (16 September 2008): www.wsws.org/articles/2008/sep2008/lehm-s16.shtml.

[2] Chris Giles and Jean Eaglesham, "Another Country?" *Financial Times* (20 April 2009), quoting President Nicolas Sarkozy of France after the G–20 meeting in April 2009 that the world had "turned the page" on the dominant model of Anglo-Saxon capitalism; see also "Global Crisis 'Failure of Extreme Capitalism': Australian PM," Breitbart.com (15 October 2008): www.breitbart.com/article.php?id=081015113127.9uzhf7lf&show_article=1.

[3] Samuel Brittan, "The Financial Crises of Capitalism," *Financial Times* (8 May 2008).

[4] Walid el-Gabry, "Soros Says Crisis Signals End of a Free-Market Model (Update 2)," Bloomberg.com (23 February 2009): www.bloomberg.com/apps/news?pid=newsarchive&sid=aI1pruXkjr0s.

[5] www.ft.com/indepth/capitalism-future.

crises or failures of capitalism either posits a straw man—an unfettered laissez-faire capitalism that does not exist in the United States, or for that matter anywhere else—or suggests that excessive deregulation has allowed banks to take excessive risks. It has certainly not been the policy of the U.S. government to allow financial markets to "regulate themselves," as some have claimed, although safety and soundness regulation—the supervision of the financial health of institutions—has been limited at the federal level to banks and to two government-sponsored enterprises (GSEs), Fannie Mae and Freddie Mac. Such regulation is logical because commercial banks are backed by the government through deposit insurance, a lender of last resort facility offered by the Federal Reserve, and a Federal Reserve payment system to which only banks have access. The GSEs, although not explicitly backed by the government, were seen in the markets as performing a government mission and, hence, as being government backed. Once any kind of financial institution is seen as being backed by the government, market discipline is severely impaired, and—to protect itself against losses—the government must impose some kind of safety and soundness regime.

Other major participants in financial markets—securities firms and insurance companies—are not backed by the government and are thus subject to a far less intrusive regulatory regime than banks are, but they nevertheless function within a complex web of regulation on business conduct and consumer protection. The condition of the banking industry today, far from offering evidence that regulation has been lacking, is actually a demonstration of the failure of regulation and its inability to prevent risk taking. Because this is not the first time that regulation has failed to prevent a major banking crisis, it makes more sense to question whether intrusive and extensive financial regulation and supervision is a sensible policy rather than to propose its extension to other areas of the financial sector.

What most critics of the current system do not seem to recognize is that the regulation of banks has been very stringent, particularly in the United States. As I will show, the commercial banks that have gotten themselves into trouble did so *despite* strong regulation. This is an uncomfortable fact—maybe what some would call an "inconvenient truth"—for those in the Obama administration and elsewhere who are advocating not only more regulation but also extending it to the rest of the financial system.

The critics seem to have been led into error by a faulty kind of inductive logic. It begins with the assumption that capitalism, if left unchecked by regulation, will produce instability. Thus, when instability appears—as it certainly has in the current financial crisis—it must be the result of a failure to adequately regulate financial markets. With this logical underpinning, critics almost uniformly make no effort to describe the "deregulation" that they are certain must have occurred. They may name a statute, such as the Gramm–Leach–Bliley Act of 1999, but they never explain how that law led to the current financial crisis, or any part of it. And because they assume their worldview is correct almost by definition, they also assume that the evidence is there to support it and that actual evidence does not need to be collected or critically examined. A more logical—and less ideological—approach would be to look for the causes of instability first and to propose an appropriate remedy after the causes have been established. As I will argue later, if that had been done by the critics in this case, their indictment would not have extended to capitalism, or even the lack of regulation, but to government intervention in the housing finance system in the United States.

Did Deregulation or Nonregulation Cause the Financial Crisis?

A good example of the faulty approach to the causes of the financial crisis is the recent book *A Failure of Capitalism* by Judge Richard Posner. Certainly the most surprising member of the group that sees deregulation as the cause of the crisis, Judge Posner is a highly respected and prolific writer of articles and books as well as legal opinions. Because of his reputation as a leader of the judiciary and an advocate of using economic analysis to address legal questions, his position has attracted a lot of attention from the media, with reviews and articles in the *New York Times*, *New York Review of Books*, and the *Atlantic Monthly*. But like so many other critics, Judge Posner merely asserts that deregulation is the cause of the financial crisis; he never cites the laws he is blaming. Where he describes deregulation without citing actual laws, he gets it wrong in material respects. Moreover, and perhaps more important, he never successfully connects the "deregulation" he identifies with the causes of the crisis in any way that makes sense either as economics or logic.

An example is what seems to be the central argument in the book—that "deregulation" permitted other financial firms, particularly money market mutual funds, to compete with banks, requiring banks to pay more for their money and, in turn, seek and obtain deregulatory action that allowed them to take greater risks in their lending. Here is the argument in his words:

> One thing that made banks safe was that they were forbidden to pay interest on demand deposits, traditionally their major source of capital... [M]oney market funds arose to provide people with checkable accounts, just like bank accounts (although uninsured)—except that they paid interest.... The deregulatory strategy of allowing nonbank financial intermediaries to provide services virtually indistinguishable from those of banks, such as interest-bearing checkable accounts offered by money market funds, led inexorably to a complementary deregulatory strategy of freeing banks from the restrictions that handicapped them in competing with unregulated (or very lightly regulated) financial intermediaries—nonbank banks, in effect.

As regulatory and customary restrictions on risky lending by banks eroded, banks became willing to make "subprime" mortgage loans—a euphemism for mortgage loans at high risk of defaulting.[6] (pp. 22–23)

There are many errors in this argument, and it is hard to know where to begin. First, money market funds were not the result of any kind of "deregulation." They were a product spawned by the mutual fund industry to take advantage of an ill-founded rate regulation on banks—the cap on bank interest rates that had been imposed by government regulation many years before. During the inflationary period of the late 1970s and early 1980s, interest rates in the money markets rose far above the 5 percent cap on bank interest allowed by a Fed-imposed limitation known as Regulation Q. As a result, funds flowed out of banks and into other instruments, such as Treasury bills and commercial paper. These instruments were sold in large principal amounts and were thus not suitable for retail investors.

Money market funds were an innovation that enabled retail investors and small businesses to participate directly in the safety and stability of investing in government securities and high-quality commercial paper by purchasing shares of a money market fund, which, in turn, bought and held these safe money market instruments. Prior to the advent of money market funds, bank deposits were the safest instruments for the retail investment because they were government insured. If bank interest rates had not been capped by government action, money market funds might never have developed. So, government *regulation* of bank deposit rates, not deregulation, was the initial cause of the competition banks encountered from money market funds.

Second, there is no evidence whatsoever that the higher costs of competing with money market funds caused banks to take greater risks in their lending, such as by purchasing subprime mortgages. For one thing, the threat from money market funds began in the late 1970s and accelerated in the 1980s until Regulation Q was abolished. Subprime lending did not begin in any size until more than 10 years later, in the mid-1990s, and did not become a major feature of the mortgage market until the early 2000s. The connection that Judge Posner draws between bank competition and bank risky lending on mortgages is simply wrong.

In addition, the idea that paying a market rate for funds might weaken banks, or require them to take more risks, harks back to the discredited idea—popular during the New Deal—that "excessive competition" is bad because it can be "ruinous" to competitors. The *benefit* of competition comes from the fact that it is ruinous to the less-effective competitors, forcing resources to flow to the more-effective ones. The focus on the health of individual firms, rather than on the benefits of competition itself for consumers and the health of the economy generally, is one of the mistakes most commonly made when discussing economics.

---

[6]Richard A. Posner, *A Failure of Capitalism: The Crisis of '08 and the Descent into Depression* (Cambridge, MA: Harvard University Press, 2009).

Glass–Steagall "Repeal." Another favorite target of the critics who are searching for deregulation in the U.S. financial system is the so-called repeal of the Glass–Steagall Act of 1933 by the Gramm–Leach–Bliley Act of 1999. For example, Kaufman writes:

> If you're looking for a major cause of the current banking meltdown, you need seek no farther than the 1999 repeal of the Glass–Steagall Act. . . . According to Wikipedia, many economists "have criticized the repeal of the Glass–Steagall Act as contributing to the 2007 subprime mortgage financial crisis. The repeal enabled commercial lenders such as Citigroup, the largest U.S. bank by assets, to underwrite and trade instruments such as mortgage-backed securities and collateralized debt obligations and establish so-called structured investment vehicles, or SIVs, that bought those securities."[7]

Wikipedia got it wrong. The portions of the 1933 Glass–Steagall Act relevant to this discussion consist of four small sections of text that did two things—prohibited commercial banks from (1) owning or dealing in securities or (2) being *affiliated* with firms that engage in underwriting or dealing in securities (i.e., investment banks). The Gramm–Leach–Bliley Act of 1999 (GLBA) repealed the affiliation restrictions of Glass–Steagall but left the restrictions on banks' securities activities intact. Thus, before the repeal, commercial banks could not underwrite or deal in securities, and the same rules applied to them after repeal. The only difference was that, after repeal, they were able to affiliate through subsidiaries and holding companies with firms engaged in underwriting and dealing in securities. In other words, the GLBA made no changes in what commercial banks themselves were permitted to do in the securities field. They remained forbidden to deal in or underwrite securities, including mortgage-backed securities or the other instruments mentioned in the Wikipedia entry.

But what about the affiliation repeal? Could it reasonably be argued that the affiliations now permitted between commercial banks and investment banks somehow caused commercial banks to take more risks or to behave less like banks? This is highly unlikely. Although all of the banks that got into trouble in the current financial crisis had securities affiliates, they got into financial difficulties because they made imprudent decisions as *banks*, not because of the activities of their securities affiliates. Citibank, Bank of America, Wachovia, IndyMac Federal Bank, Wells Fargo, and the rest weakened themselves by purchasing securities backed by mortgages and other assets that banks are allowed to hold as investments (but not to deal in or underwrite). Under banking rules, both before and after the repeal of the affiliation restrictions in Glass–Steagall, banks were permitted to hold asset-backed

---

[7]William Kaufman, "Shattering the Glass-Steagall Act," *Counterpunch* (19 September 2008): www.counterpunch.org/kaufman09192008.html. See also Nigel Lawson, "Capitalism Needs a Revived Glass-Steagall," *Financial Times* (15 March 2009).

securities if the underlying assets, such as mortgages and credit card receivables, were assets that banks were generally permitted to hold.[8] In other words, the claim that the GLBA, by repealing Glass–Steagall's affiliation provisions, enabled banks to invest differently from how they could before the GLBA is wrong.

Similarly, none of the investment banks got into trouble because of the affiliations with banks that were permitted after the GLBA. Although all of them had small banks or S&Ls (savings and loan associations) as subsidiaries, the parent companies—Bear Stearns, Lehman Brothers, Merrill Lynch, Morgan Stanley, and Goldman Sachs—were completely independent of control by banks or bank holding companies and also got into trouble by making the same imprudent investments they were allowed to make before the GLBA was passed. In other words, the repeal of Glass–Steagall's affiliation provisions had no effect on these investment banks and was not responsible for the losses they suffered by holding mortgage-backed and other risky securities as assets.

"Deregulation" of Credit Default Swaps. One final argument concerning deregulation is the claim that deregulation or a mania for free markets caused the Clinton administration and the U.S. Congress to deregulate credit default swaps (CDS). The episode is complicated, but it is not an example of deregulation because CDS had *never* been regulated. In 1999, the chair of the U.S. Commodity Futures Trading Commission (CFTC) asserted that CDS were subject to regulation by the CFTC. Because the assertion raised questions about the continued legality of trading in these derivatives, the Clinton administration (including Robert Rubin and Lawrence Summers at the U.S. Department of the Treasury and Arthur Levitt at the U.S. Securities and Exchange Commission) sought legislation that would permanently bar the CFTC from regulating these swap transactions, thus removing any doubt as to the legality of the unregulated CDS market.

The role of credit default swaps in the financial crisis has been as exaggerated as the role of the Glass–Steagall "repeal." Once again, the complexities of the matter have eluded the media, which have simply reported what they were told by people who were themselves speculating about the effect of CDS. There is no evidence that CDS caused any serious losses to any individual firm or the market as a whole after Lehman Brothers failed, and there is no evidence that American International Group (AIG) had to be bailed out because its CDS liabilities would have damaged the market or caused a systemic breakdown.

Many of the media stories about AIG have focused on AIG's Financial Products subsidiary and the obligations that this entity assumed through CDS. However, it is highly questionable whether there would have been a significant market reaction if AIG had been allowed to default on its CDS obligations in

---

[8] See Title 12, Code of Federal Regulations, Part 1, Sections 1.1–1.3.

September 2008. CDS are guarantee contracts that pay off when an issuer of a security defaults. If a CDS issuer fails, it is much the same as when a homeowner's insurance company goes out of business before there has been a fire or other loss to the home. In that case, the homeowner must go out and find another insurance company, but he has not lost anything except the premium he has paid. If AIG had been allowed to default, there would have been little if any near-term loss to the parties that had bought protection; they would simply have been required to go back into the CDS market and buy new protection. CDS contracts normally require a party like AIG that has sold protection (i.e., agreed to reimburse a counterparty's loss) to post collateral as assurance to its counterparties that it can meet its obligations when they come due. The premiums for the new protection might have been more expensive than what they were paying AIG, but even if that were true, many of AIG's counterparties had received collateral from AIG that could have been sold to defray the cost of the new protection.[9]

This analysis is consistent with the publicly known facts about AIG. In mid-March, the names of some of the counterparties that AIG had protected with CDS became public. The largest of these counterparties was Goldman Sachs. AIG's obligation to Goldman was reported as $12.9 billion; the others named were Merrill Lynch ($6.8 billion), Bank of America ($5.2 billion), Citigroup ($2.3 billion), and Wachovia ($1.5 billion). Recall that the loss of CDS coverage—the obligation in this case—is not an actual cash loss or anything like it; it is only the loss of a guarantee against a possible future default on a debt that is held by a protected party. For institutions of this size, with the exception of Goldman, the loss of AIG's CDS protection would not have been a problem, even if they had in fact already suffered losses on the underlying obligations that AIG was protecting. Moreover, when questioned about what it would have lost if AIG had defaulted, Goldman said its losses would have been "negligible." This claim is entirely plausible. Goldman's spokesman cited both the collateral it had received from AIG under the CDS contracts and the fact that it had hedged its AIG risk by buying protection from third parties against the possibility of AIG's default.[10] Also, as noted earlier, Goldman only suffered the loss of its CDS *coverage*, not a loss on the underlying debt the CDS was supposed to cover. If Goldman, the largest counterparty in AIG's list, would not have suffered substantial losses, then AIG's default on its CDS contracts would have had no serious consequences in the market.

---

[9] A full description of the operation of credit default swaps appears in Peter J. Wallison, "Everything You Wanted to Know about Credit Default Swaps—But Were Never Told," *Financial Services Outlook* (December 2008): www.aei.org/publication29158.

[10] Mary Williams Walsh, "A.I.G. Lists Banks It Paid with U.S. Bailout Funds," *New York Times* (16 March 2009).

Inadequate Regulatory Authority. Finally, after considering all the allegations about the relationship between deregulation and the financial crisis, it is necessary to consider whether the problem is one of insufficient regulatory authority, rather than deregulation. The problem might not be that regulatory authority was taken away from the regulators by deregulation but simply that it was never given to them at all. That argument, however, is not supported by the facts. Since 1991, the regulators of all insured banks have had plenty of authority to crack down on bank risk taking. Their authority was significantly *strengthened* immediately after the S&L debacle, when much of the S&L industry collapsed and almost 1,600 commercial banks were closed by the FDIC. At that point, Congress adopted the Federal Deposit Insurance Corporation Improvement Act of 1991 (FDICIA), a reform measure developed by the first Bush administration. FDICIA was a very tough regulatory law. Among other things, it provided for prompt corrective action (PCA) by supervisors when a bank's capital position began to erode. As that happened, PCA required regulators to take increasingly stringent actions to control the bank's activities and to close the bank entirely if they believed that it would become insolvent in the future. The law also provided for personal fines of up to $1 million a day on bank directors and officers who violated bank regulations. FDICIA was so tough that Alan Greenspan, then the chair of the Federal Reserve, complained that it was too tough on banks. He might have been on to something. Now, 18 years later, we are in the midst of the worst banking crisis since the Great Depression.

Thus, none of the explanations for the financial crisis that blame capitalism or deregulation, or Glass–Steagall, or any one of a number of other alleged deficiencies in the regulatory regime applicable to banks, has any validity. The banking system is in very bad shape today, as is the world's economy, but none of the explanations usually advanced by commentators, and reported in the media, can be plausibly shown to be a cause of the financial crisis.

If Deregulation or Nonregulation Did Not Cause the Financial Crisis, What Did?

Many analyses of the current crisis have pointed to the existence of a massive housing bubble that—according to the Case–Shiller Index—began to deflate in mid-2006. There is no question that the deflation of any large asset bubble will cause a downturn in the U.S. economy. Before the collapse of the housing bubble, a similar asset bubble in internet-related equities (known as the dot-com or tech bubble) caused a huge stock market decline and a recession when it deflated in 2001. Asset bubbles of various kinds are not unusual or unexpected, but they do not always cause worldwide financial crises. The key question is why the housing bubble that began to deflate in 2006 or 2007 had this effect.

It is a widely held, although by no means universally accepted, view that a principal cause of the Great Depression was government policy—particularly the actions of the Federal Reserve in tightening rather than loosening the money supply and credit as a major recession took hold. It is my view that U.S. government policy is again responsible for the current financial crisis. An explanation begins with some numbers that are not well known—even now. There are 25 million subprime and other nonprime mortgages currently outstanding in the United States, with an unpaid principal balance of more than $4 trillion. Subprime mortgages are loans made to people with blemished credit and low scores on the measures that are used to estimate credit quality. Other nonprime mortgages, which I will call Alt-A in this article, are considered poor quality because of the characteristics of the loans themselves and not the borrowers. Alt-A loans have adjustable rates, no or low down payments, and negative amortization or were made to people who did not have to state their income or to people whose income or jobs were not verified. Many of these borrowers were not intending to live in the homes they were buying but were investing or speculating in housing.

Twenty-five million subprime and Alt-A loans amount to almost 45 percent of all single-family mortgages in the United States. These poor quality mortgages are defaulting at unprecedented rates. As these mortgages decline in value, so does the capital and the financial condition of every bank and financial institution that is holding them. These include not only U.S. banks and financial institutions but also banks and other financial institutions around the world that invested in these mortgages, usually through mortgage-backed securities (MBS). More than any other cause, the sharp decline in the value of these mortgages accounts for the worldwide financial collapse we are now experiencing.

Financial institutions invested in these mortgages because they believed from historical evidence that Americans always pay their mortgages. This was certainly true when almost all mortgages were prime—made to people with jobs and substantial down payments and at fixed interest rates for 30 years. Even in the worst downturns, foreclosure rates rarely reached 4 percent. However, some projections of foreclosure rates for the subprime and Alt-A loans in the current downturn run as high as 30 percent—a completely unprecedented phenomenon, exceeding even the Great Depression.

The boom in subprime and Alt-A mortgages is something entirely new. These instruments always existed but were a small part of the total mortgage pool because of their high-risk characteristics. It was possible to have a profitable business as a subprime mortgage lender, but it was necessary to obtain a substantial risk premium to compensate for the high rate of foreclosure and loss. However, as outlined later, beginning in the early 1990s and continuing until 2007, government policy artificially inflated the value of subprime and Alt-A loans, reducing the necessary risk premium and leaving the holders of these mortgages with serious losses as they began to default.

The government policies that ultimately caused these developments have a long history. Since the beginning of the 20th century, the United States has had a policy of fostering homeownership. This policy caused regular economic downturns as the government attempted by various means to make it easier for Americans to buy homes. As reported by Steven Malanga, the first major campaign along these lines was initiated by Herbert Hoover, who was alarmed by a decline in homeownership revealed by the 1920 census.[11] Hoover began a campaign to increase homeownership, and Congress cooperated in 1927 by freeing banks to make more mortgage loans. Homeownership rates did indeed improve, rising from about 46 percent when Hoover began his program to almost 48 percent in 1930, but the number of defaults rose substantially during the ensuing depression. After World War II, there was another effort to increase homeownership, but Malanga observes:

> As homeownership grew, political pressure to allow riskier loans increased. . . . Under pressure to keep meeting housing demand, the government began loosening its mortgage-lending standards [on FHA and VA loans]—cutting the size of required down payments, approving loans with higher ratios of payments to income, and extending the terms of mortgages. (pp. 3–4)

The failure rate on these government-backed mortgages spiked, but Malanga notes, "the foreclosure rate of conventional mortgages barely increased, since many traditional lenders had maintained stricter underwriting standards, which had proved a good predictor of loan quality over the years" (p. 4).

The differences between government policy and private-lending policies began to change in 1977, with the adoption of the Community Reinvestment Act (CRA), which gave regulators the right to deny bank applications for expansion if an applicant had failed to lend sufficiently in minority neighborhoods. As Malanga reported, the most significant denial came in 1979, when the Greater New York Savings Bank was denied the opportunity to open a branch on the Upper East Side of Manhattan because it had not lent enough in its Brooklyn home market. In the early 1990s, the Clinton administration revised the regulations under CRA so that banks were required to make the loans, not just show good faith efforts to find borrowers in underserved communities. That was a turning point. Although the government had previously taken the risks of making weak loans, now—through CRA—the government was requiring private banks to take risks they had previously eschewed.

Many of the communities that CRA was intended to benefit contained borrowers who had blemished credit or no money for down payments or who did not have steady jobs or incomes. That did not excuse banks from making mortgage loans to these borrowers. They were directed to use "flexible underwriting

---

[11] Steven Malanga, "Obsessive Housing Disorder," *City Journal* (Spring 2009): www.city-journal.org/printable.php?id=4376.

standards." The bank regulators were supposed to enforce these rules. In effect, the regulators were required to suspend their normal attention to prudent lending. Loans they formerly would have criticized, they now had to consider good loans. In a letter sent to shareholders, the chairman of a local bank in Colorado described the difficulties of dealing with the regulators about CRA (the name of the bank has been withheld for obvious reasons):

> Under the umbrella of the Community Reinvestment Act (CRA), a tremendous amount of pressure was put on banks by the regulatory authorities to make loans, especially mortgage loans, to low income borrowers and neighborhoods. The regulators were very heavy handed regarding this issue. I will not dwell on it here but they required [our bank] to change its mortgage lending practices to meet certain CRA goals, even though we argued the changes were risky and imprudent.[12]

In the end, CRA did not produce enough weak loans to create a financial crisis, but it began the process of degrading the quality of mortgages to make them affordable for borrowers who had previously not been able to meet normal lending standards in the prime market. The flexible underwriting standards that the government wanted the banks to use really meant lowering down payments and not insisting on income, a steady job, or unblemished credit. The low-quality mortgages that were required by CRA—and approved by bank regulators—gradually spread to the rest of the mortgage market. By 2006, almost half of all mortgages made in the United States were subprime or Alt-A.

The vehicles for creating this astonishing growth of low-quality loans were two companies that were also subject—like regulated banks—to direct control by Congress: Fannie Mae and Freddie Mac. Being GSEs, Fannie and Freddie were—until they were taken over in September 2008 because they were insolvent—shareholder-owned entities that were chartered by Congress to perform a specific government mission. Initially, this mission was to maintain a liquid secondary market in residential mortgages, but their mission was expanded in 1992 to include promoting affordable housing. This obligation was backed up by regulatory authority that Congress granted to the U.S. Department of Housing and Urban Development (HUD). HUD's affordable housing regulations, implementing the new affordable housing mission of the two GSEs, were to be very important elements in the growth of subprime and other low-quality mortgages.

The importance of the GSEs sprang from their ability to access substantial and low-cost funding because of their perceived connection to the U.S. government. There were many reasons for this perception, but the fact that they were chartered by Congress to perform a government mission was probably the most important. Their government backing enabled them to raise funds cheaply—paying only a little more than the U.S. Treasury itself—and in virtually unlimited amounts. In addition,

---

[12]Letter, dated 20 January 2009, in possession of author.

their capital requirements were set by statute at a very low level, so they were able to operate at leverage of 60:1. These advantages enabled them to dominate the mortgage finance market; by 2003, they were buying about 57 percent of all mortgages made that year and 79 percent of all the loans that fell within their lending limits.

HUD's requirements that Fannie and Freddie promote affordable housing were gradually escalated over the years. Initially, in the early 1990s, 30 percent of the mortgages that Fannie and Freddie purchased from banks and other originators had to be loans made to low- and moderate-income (LMI) borrowers. By 2005, about 55 percent had to be LMI and 25 percent had to be to low- or very low-income borrowers. The real work in reducing the quality of mortgage loans was, therefore, done by Fannie and Freddie, operating under the lash of HUD's affordable housing regulations.

By the time they were taken over by the government in September 2008, Fannie and Freddie were responsible for the credit risk on approximately $5.3 trillion in mortgages that they either held in portfolio or had guaranteed through MBS. Thus, when Fannie and Freddie started to reduce the quality of the loans they would buy from banks and others, it had a real impact on what kinds of loans the market produced. Their initial steps were modest, and the subprime and Alt-A loans they bought were generally of high quality within that group. But by 1998, Fannie was offering a mortgage with a 3 percent down payment, and by 2001, a mortgage with no down payment at all. During the 2000–03 period, when unusually low interest rates drove huge numbers of refinancings, Fannie and Freddie bought about $1.3 trillion of subprime and Alt-A loans and securities, amounting to about 25 percent of their total purchases in those years. Many of these would be prepaid or refinanced in later years because they were made to buyers who could not, or had no intention to, pay the cost of these loans when interest rates rose. As long as housing prices were rising, it was possible for home buyers to prepay their mortgages by selling the home for more than the principal amount of the loan, or in cases where they received a low "teaser" rate, to refinance into another short-term loan at a low rate before the loan reset to a higher market-based rate.

But in 2004, both GSEs started on what can only be called a binge. Over the period from late 2004 to 2007, when interest rates had risen again and refinancings were not driving volume, they purchased about $1.7 trillion in subprime and Alt-A loans—about 50 percent of their total purchases during a period when originations and refinancings were substantially lower than in the earlier period. At the time they were taken over by the government, the remnants of their earlier purchases amounted to $1.6 trillion in mortgages and securities—about 10 million loans and 34 percent of their single-family portfolio.

As a result primarily of Fannie's and Freddie's purchases, homeownership rates rose. From the 1960s until about 1995, the rate in the United States had remained at about 64 percent, but after that year, it began to rise. By 2000, it had risen to 67.3 percent, and to a high point of 69.2 percent in 2004. So, the policy of increasing homeownership did work, but the unintended consequences were disastrous. Fannie's and Freddie's own losses will probably cost the taxpayers about $400 billion, perhaps more. But the other costs—the current financial crisis—are far worse.

Fannie's and Freddie's Role in the Financial Crisis

The connection between the GSEs' purchases and the current crisis is important to understand. Fannie's and Freddie's funding advantages allowed them to drive all private-sector competition to the edges of the housing finance market. This meant that Wall Street commercial and investment banks were relegated to buying and securitizing two kinds of mortgages—*jumbos*, which exceeded the size Fannie and Freddie were permitted by law to buy, and *junk*, which until the early 2000s, Fannie and Freddie would not buy in substantial amounts. For this reason, the subprime and Alt-A market was relatively small; the secondary market in these loans was carried on by commercial and investment banks, which would buy mortgages from the originators, package them into pools, and sell MBS backed by the payments of principal and interest on the mortgages in the pool. The pools were structured to create "tranches," or classes of securities with the same collateral but different levels of risk.[13] The lowest-risk tranche was typically rated AAA by the rating agencies; other tranches bore other ratings (sometimes also as high as AAA); and the highest-risk tranche was a small equity piece at the bottom of the structure.

This market was growing until 2003, when in the midst of a huge refinancing boom Fannie and Freddie started buying large amounts of the AAA tranches of the pools—known as "private label"—that Wall Street was creating. These purchases doubled in 2003 to $82 billion and doubled again in 2004 to $180 billion. In 2004, probably because they thought it was more efficient than paying Wall Street's fees for intermediation, they decided to buy large amounts of subprime and Alt-A loans directly from originators. Their chairmen—Franklin Raines of Fannie and Richard Syron of Freddie—went to meetings of mortgage bankers and other originators and asked for the mortgages of people with blemished credit. These loans were of substantial assistance to Fannie and Freddie in reaching HUD's increasingly ambitious affordable housing goals.

When someone with virtually unlimited funds asks for something as easy to deliver as subprime and Alt-A mortgages, the result is just as easy to predict: There was a huge frenzy at the originator level to produce the subprime and Alt-A loans that would then be sold to the GSEs or to the Wall Street investment banks and to commercial banks. In 2005, the GSEs began to buy large quantities of subprime and Alt-A loans directly from mortgage bankers and other firms, such as Countrywide

---

[13]A single pool of "collateral" (a group of mortgages) can be used to create tranches that differ in risk because they have different priority claims on the cash flows from the mortgages, much like senior and junior debt of a corporation, with an equity residual at the "bottom." Basically, all asset-backed (including mortgage-backed) securities' structures incorporate this design.

Financial, that specialized in originating subprime and Alt-A loans. Meanwhile, they continued to buy AAA rated tranches of mortgage-backed securities from Wall Street—more than $500 billion of them between 2005 and 2007.

The GSEs' purchases—driven by their need to meet HUD's increasingly tough affordable housing regulations—affected the market for subprime and Alt-A loans in three ways. First, by increasing competition for these loans, the GSEs' purchases drove down the risk premiums that subprime loans usually carried, putting more potential buyers with blemished credit in a position to qualify for mortgages. Second, the competition between the GSEs and Wall Street drove the numbers of subprime and Alt-A loans still higher. And finally, the quality of these loans increasingly declined; the competitors were scraping the bottom of the potential borrower barrel. During this period, conventional prime loans (including jumbo loans) declined from 69 percent of all mortgages in 2003 to 36 percent at the end of 2006, and subprime and Alt-A loans increased from 20 percent of all originations to 46 percent. In 2006, almost half of all mortgages made in the United States were subprime and Alt-A loans. The GSEs were responsible for buying 39 percent of 2006 originations of subprime and Alt-A loans. In the end, including the loans underlying the AAA rated tranches that they bought from Wall Street, Fannie and Freddie held or guaranteed 34 percent of all subprime mortgages and 60 percent of all the Alt-A loans that were outstanding on 30 June 2008.

Although many have argued that it was Wall Street that led the subprime boom, that claim is disproven by the total number of subprime and Alt-A mortgages that Fannie and Freddie ultimately became responsible for. As subprime and Alt-A loans became a larger and larger proportion of all mortgages in the United States, it was the purchases by Fannie and Freddie that drove this growth. The conventional wisdom—that they were trying to compete for market share with Wall Street—seems contradicted by the fact that Fannie and Freddie ultimately acquired nearly as many of these mortgages as the rest of the market combined. The more plausible way to look at the issue is that Fannie and Freddie were, by and large, the creators of the subprime and Alt-A boom and that they did this for political reasons (discussed later) and *not* for the economic reasons that would motivate a Wall Street firm. They first stimulated the development of the Wall Street acquisition and distribution system by purchasing huge amounts of AAA rated private label tranches. Then, in late 2004, they began to buy these junk loans in ever larger amounts themselves, competing for product with Wall Street.

The GSEs' binge on subprime and Alt-A loans was obviously a disastrous business policy; it eventually destroyed two companies that had solid gold franchises. But it was also responsible for turning what would have been a troubling housing-bubble deflation into a worldwide financial crisis. Although U.S. taxpayers will have to bear the losses that Fannie and Freddie will realize from their purchases of subprime and Alt-A loans, banks and other financial intermediaries in the United States and around the world will suffer equally large losses because of the

MBS—based in part on subprime and Alt-A loans—that they purchased from Wall Street banks and securities firms. Although these are not the direct responsibility of Fannie and Freddie, the GSEs bear indirect responsibility for stimulating the explosive growth in junk mortgage loans beginning in 2004.

Why It Happened

The pressures that drove Fannie and Freddie to buy junk mortgages are complex. Most commentators point to their desire to take market share from Wall Street, but as noted earlier, this is highly implausible. Fannie and Freddie had funding at such low cost that they had no serious competition for any assets they were allowed to buy. Once Fannie and Freddie began to enter the market for subprime and Alt-A loans, it was just a matter of time before the Wall Street banks and securities firms would lose substantial portions of their market. Only an *expansion* of the market—the growth in subprime and Alt-A loans—would enable them to maintain a profitable business. So, the real question for policymakers is why Fannie and Freddie entered this market with such force beginning in late 2004.

One answer, of course, is HUD's affordable housing regulations. It is clear that the regulations were influential in determining what securities Fannie and Freddie purchased; subprime and Alt-A loans were both "goal rich" in terms of complying with the increasingly tight requirements for promoting "affordable" housing. We do not know the nature of any conversations that might have been held between the GSEs and the officials at HUD who oversaw the development of these regulations. But we do know from internal e-mail messages at Freddie and memoranda that were prepared at Fannie that both companies were well aware of the risks they were taking. It is difficult to believe that if the sole reason for taking those risks was to meet HUD's regulatory requirements, these risks could not have been brought to HUD's attention. In addition, many in the subprime housing business argue that there were plenty of high-quality subprime loans available in the market, but the GSEs did not look for them.

The most likely answer is that Fannie and Freddie were trying to retain support in Congress that would prevent new and tougher regulation. In 2003 and 2004, both companies had accounting scandals; they were found to have been manipulating their financial reports—to smooth earnings in Freddie's case and to hide massive hedging losses in Fannie's. At the time, there was a Republican Congress and a hostile Republican administration, raising the possibility that Congress might adopt legislation authorizing tough new regulation. Indeed, legislation of this kind passed the Senate Banking Committee in 2005 but never received a vote on the Senate floor. Alan Greenspan—who was highly regarded on Capitol Hill—was warning in virtually every appearance before Congress that the GSEs could cause a financial meltdown if they were not curbed, and economists at the Fed had recently done a study that showed the GSEs were not even successful in reducing interest rates for middle-class home buyers—the central justification they always claimed for their existence.

Under these circumstances, it is likely that Fannie and Freddie hoped to curry favor with their supporters in Congress by showing that they could boost home-ownership rates, especially in low-income communities. If that was their strategy, it worked; there was no new legislation that curbed their activities until July 2008. But by then, it was too late.

Conclusion

Explanations for the current financial crisis range widely: Some see it as a crisis or failure of capitalism; others see it as a case of excessive deregulation or just not enough regulation. Still others cite the Fed's failure to raise interest rates quickly enough after the economy began to recover from the dot-com collapse. There is no question that a housing bubble grew in the first seven years of the 21st century and then abruptly collapsed. But housing and other asset bubbles have deflated rapidly before without such dire consequences. The reason that this housing-price deflation created what is essentially a worldwide financial crisis is that the mortgages produced in the United States, beginning early in the 2000s and accelerating until 2007, were of much lower quality than had ever been true in the past. Not only were borrowers of lower credit quality, but also the loans themselves were not backed by the down payments or other equity that encouraged borrowers to continue making mortgage payments after housing values fell below the principal amount of the mortgage. Thus, the most plausible explanation for the extraordinary losses associated with the collapse of this bubble is the unprecedented growth of subprime and Alt-A mortgages in the United States. At the height of the housing bubble, in 2006, almost half of all mortgages originated in the United States were subprime or Alt-A. When these mortgages began to default, it was at unprecedented rates, weakening the financial condition of banks and other financial intermediaries around the world.

The growth of the market in subprime and Alt-A loans can be directly attributed to the policies of the U.S. government. For much of the 20th century, the government attempted to foster homeownership in the United States. In most cases, the government took the risks associated with this policy. But beginning in the 1990s, Congress and the administration began to require that private enterprises—insured banks and the GSEs Fannie Mae and Freddie Mac—take on the risks of lending to potential home buyers who did not have the credit records or resources to meet their obligations. In this process, the usual mortgage standards that prevailed in the private housing finance market were eroded, and the housing bubble was gradually engorged with poor-quality mortgages. Without this factor—the element of government policy—the collapse of the great housing bubble of the early 21st century would not have been nearly as calamitous.

The author wishes to thank Edward Pinto for assistance in the preparation of this article.

Of Candor and Conflicts: What Were We Thinking?

Marianne M. Jennings
Professor of Legal and Ethical Studies
Arizona State University
Tempe, Arizona

I used to assume that I could count on a financial scandal cropping up every 10 years. For example, when I first started teaching, the scandal surrounding Ivan Boesky and Michael Milken and junk bonds occurred. So, we threw them in prison and called for more regulation and said that such a thing would never happen again. Then came the savings and loan (S&L) scandal. So, we threw more people in prison and called for more regulation and once again said, "Never again." Then came the dot-com bubble—along with Enron Corporation, WorldCom, and Tyco International—and we put still more people in prison, more than I had ever seen. Then we passed even more regulation and once again said, "This will never happen again."

Today, we are not even five years out from the last scandal, and we are already into another one; this one is even worse than before. I fear that we are not internalizing the lessons that we ought to be learning. Despite the behavior we have seen lately, fraud is not a natural market adjustment; it is preventable. As Tully (2007) wrote in *Fortune* when the magnitude of the financial meltdown was finally becoming apparent, "Two things stand out about the credit crisis cascading through Wall Street: It is both totally shocking and utterly predictable."

The best mathematical models, the best minds, the best of the best were all engaged in creating a financial disaster that was, indeed, utterly predictable. Nevertheless, two respected senior fund managers—the first to be indicted in the United States for their roles in the collapse of Bear Stearns Companies—found themselves sitting in a jail cell and asking one another how on earth they had gotten there. Yet, anyone who had asked the right questions or paid attention to human behavior within the organizations involved could have predicted the inevitable result.

My intention, therefore, is to discuss three factors that are typical precursors to the ethical failings that lead to such scandals:
- pressure and myths about success;
- conflicts, tone, and our resistance to both; and
- gray areas that are not really gray.

Editor's Note: This article is an updated version of the presentation printed in *CFA Institute Conference Proceedings Quarterly* (March 2009: www.cfapubs.org).

Pressure and Myths about Success

Any company that has had any type of ethical or legal issue and that is now grappling with the current financial collapse had within it people who were fully aware that problems were occurring. Yet, that knowledge did not reach the people it needed to reach in order for a change to occur because people made choices not to move the information forward.

The Choices Phenomenon. The choices that people make determine whether bad practices are brought to a halt or are allowed to snowball into something catastrophic. Because actual occurrences provide the best insights into this phenomenon, I will offer several examples of the choices people have made (or failed to make) when placed under pressure. The first is an example from the previous cycle of scandals of about five years ago. It is a quote taken from an e-mail from WilmerHale, one of the most respected securities law firms in the world, to the in-house counsel of Tyco. It reads as follows:

> We have found issues that will likely interest the SEC. . . . [C]reativeness is employed in hitting the forecasts. . . . There is also a bad letter from the Sigma people just before the acquisition confirming that they were asked to hold product shipment just before the closing.[1]

Certainly, the lawyers at WilmerHale saw something suspicious. Certainly, they were concerned. And such concerns are clear signs that people know instinctively that something is wrong. But neither the internal nor the external counsel of Tyco did anything to rectify the problems.

The next example comes from a Standard & Poor's analyst. She was anxious about the ratings she was giving collateralized debt obligations and other mortgage-backed securities, so she sent a text message to a colleague and expressed her concerns. She said that she was quite nervous because she was making evaluations without having all the necessary information. The client, she said, was not giving her all the data.

The colleague responded by reminding her that S&P relied on fees from its clients and that all the client wanted was a rating. Clearly disgusted, the analyst wrote back, "It could be structured by cows, and we would rate it."[2] As more internal documents emerged, so did even more stark evidence of concern. Another analyst wrote, "Rating agencies continue to create [an] even bigger monster—the CDO market. Let's hope we are all wealthy and retired by the time this house of cards falters."[3] Once again, intelligent people knew what was happening but chose not to do anything.

---

[1] Cohen and Maremont (2002).
[2] SEC (2008b).
[3] SEC (2008b).

Another example refers to the banking practices of Wachovia Corporation, which, we all know, had to be acquired to keep from failing. The company's operations should have been a signal that problems existed. Indeed, just the growth in the number of branches should have been a sign. But this particular example refers to Wachovia's practice of selling lists of its customers' names to marketing firms. There was nothing untoward about this practice; Wachovia had received its customers' permission to do so. But some of the companies Wachovia was dealing with were not at all reputable. They were withdrawing money from customers' accounts either without authorization at all or beyond the amounts that the customers had authorized.

A Wachovia vice president who was aware of the situation wrote the following to her superior:

YIKES!!!!

DOUBLE YIKES!!!!

There is more, but nothing more that I want to put into a note.[4]

She then met with her superior and warned him that in just a two-month period, the bank had received 4,500 complaints of fraud from customers who had been fleeced of $400 million by marketing firms that had paid the bank large fees for access to these customers. The superior did not make a decision at the meeting, so the vice president wrote him again and asked what she should do. He wrote back and said, "We are making a ton of money from them." He did not want to pull the plug, so the practices continued—until the U.S. government stepped in. Wachovia was required to pay a $144 million fine just a few months before it collapsed.[5] (This last coincidence—regulatory signals that foreshadow deeper troubles—is an instance of a phenomenon I will discuss later.)

Now consider American International Group (AIG). Anyone who did not see the problems with AIG after 2005 was just not paying attention. This firm was sending signals about as clearly as can be imagined. This particular example comes from a deal that AIG was arranging with General Re Corporation (Gen Re). As it turns out, AIG shareholders were complaining that AIG's reserves were insufficient (and hindsight shows the shareholders were onto something). They wanted to see more in reserves. So, AIG came up with a sham transaction with Gen Re for which Gen Re was paid about $5.2 million for what has been called "renting reserves."

---

[4]Duhigg (2008b).
[5]Duhigg (2008a).

A telephone exchange between Cologne Re and Gen Re (regarding AIG's practices) went like this:

"How much of this sort of stuff do they do? I mean, how much cooking goes on in there?"

— John Houldsworth, former CEO, Cologne Re Dublin

"They'll do whatever they need to [do to] make their numbers look right."

— Richard Napier, former Gen Re executive[6]

Note that both of these men entered pleas in court. In fact, five executives were tried, and after about seven days of deliberations, they were convicted on all counts.

Not only was it internally clear that things were not right at AIG, but it was also clear to those on the outside who were doing business with AIG. Robert Graham, another former executive at Gen Re (in fact, its former general counsel), said the following in another taped conversation:

[AIG's] organizational approach to compliance issues has always been pay the speeding ticket. I'm pretty comfortable that our own skirts are clean but that they have issues . . . ."[7]

Finally, about 18 months before the subprime problems started taking hold of the market, one of the fund managers who later ended up in a jail cell in Brooklyn for processing on felony charges sent the following through a private e-mail account. He did not want such opinions to be traced to his Bear Stearns account:

[T]he subprime market looks pretty damn ugly. . . . If we believe [our internal modeling] is ANYWHERE CLOSE to accurate I think we should close the funds now. The reason for this is that if [our internal modeling] is correct then the entire subprime market is toast. . . . If AAA bonds are systematically downgraded then there is simply no way for us to make money—ever.[8]

The indictment in the case describes a situation in which two men struggling with an issue ultimately succumbed to silence, even as they protected their own funds. The colleague that he had e-mailed then invited him to a meeting at his house on a Sunday evening. The two of them gathered with several other employees from Bear Stearns and went over the numbers. By the end of the meeting, the fund manager had been convinced that he could continue to sell Bear Stearns's products to his customers, which he did. He was not, however, convinced enough to continue keeping his own money in such products, and that is why he was indicted. He withdrew his own money from his accounts, but he continued to sell the products to other people. He and his colleagues understood that problems existed, and yet they made choices that they knew could only be detrimental. One reason that people make such choices is the pressure they feel to maintain the status quo.

---

[6] Bianco (2008).
[7] Bianco (2008).
[8] SEC (2008b).

Pressure of the Status Quo. The pressure of the status quo affects all of us, no matter what our profession. We understand a problem—either instinctively or rationally—but then we disregard the warning bells going off in our heads because we do not want to upset the status quo. We go along to get along. As the former general counsel for PeopleSoft, Anne Joran, is quoted as saying, "You tend to [go along] with how things are [already] being done."[9] She then left PeopleSoft before it was acquired by Oracle.

Pressure from the status quo creates dangerous ethical dilemmas, which are made only more dangerous when the market is involved. For-profit higher education offers several terrific examples. It was an excellent growth industry, but when double-digit growth continues year after year, thoughtful people ought to start asking questions. For instance, the Apollo Group, which owns the University of Phoenix, is a useful illustration. It used some terrible practices to recruit students. Its model for aggressive recruiting simply could not keep going, hence the returns it was earning could not go on in perpetuity. Credit solicitation had similar troubles and has been pulled back. But the one area that I worry about most—because I see so much unfolding—is the unhealthy relationship between pharmaceutical companies and doctors. By not keeping these two groups separated, we have gutted the trust in the pharmaceutical industry and perhaps even in doctors.

Now consider the fraudulent use of backdated stock options from just a few years ago. That practice has resulted in 200 companies coming under some level of scrutiny, either by the U.S. Department of Justice or the U.S. SEC. More than 250 companies have had to conduct internal probes. Seventeen company officers have been indicted. Eight officers have made guilty pleas. One CEO has been convicted, as has one vice president of human resources. Of charges made against general counsels of corporations, 3 of 10 individuals have been charged, and 42 executives or directors have resigned. The amount of overstatement of income because of stock options has come to $5.3 billion, so far.[10]

Pressure in the Ranks. Greg Reyes, former CEO of Brocade Communications Systems, was the first CEO in the United States convicted of backdating stock options. The first time he proposed doing so, he took the paperwork to his administrative assistant. She thought he was asking her to do something illegal, and she told him so. His response to her was, "It is only illegal if you get caught."

Because he was her boss and the CEO of the company, she went ahead and did as she was told. Such are the pressures that employees in the ranks can feel so powerfully. When the U.S. government began its investigation, the FBI (Federal Bureau of Investigation) questioned her, and she subsequently testified against Reyes. On cross-examination, defense lawyers established that she knew that what

---

[9]Jones (2006).
[10]See Bandler and Scannell (2006) and Jennings (2006).

she was doing was incorrect under accounting procedures that she handled. Reyes's conviction was a slam dunk, and the behavior of his administrative assistant is further proof of my long-standing belief that cheaters can never trust their fellow cheaters.

Another example of pressure in the ranks comes from a Merrill Lynch executive. When investigators were trying to figure out how operations could have gone so far astray, a Merrill Lynch executive said that there was so much pressure to meet the numbers and keep up with the high flyers, like Goldman Sachs, that "it got to the point where you didn't want to be in the office on Goldman earnings days."[11] Managers did not want to be put on the spot and asked why their numbers were not as good as those of Goldman Sachs. So, the pressure was on to do whatever was necessary to meet the numbers.

The next example demonstrates the pressure placed on auditors both by clients and by their own superiors. In this case, the client was New Century Financial Corporation and the auditor was KPMG. John Klinge, an audit specialist, was working on New Century Financial accounts and was concerned about New Century's accounting practices that did not accurately reflect loans that needed to be written down. Klinge e-mailed his senior audit partner and said that the assets needed to be written down. When he did not get a satisfactory response, he apparently pressed the issue, to which the senior partner responded: "I am very disappointed we are still discussing this. And as far as I am concerned we are done. The client thinks we are done." When pressed further, the senior audit partner responded again: "As far as I am concerned, we are done. The client thinks we are done. All we are going to do is piss everybody off."[12]

The pressure that was being placed on the junior audit specialist did not, of course, begin with the senior auditor. It also came from the client. As can be seen in the findings of the lawyer for New Century Financial's bankruptcy trustee, "I saw e-mails from the engaged partner," noted the lawyer, "saying we are at risk of being replaced. They acquiesced overly to the client, which in the post-Enron era seems mind-boggling."[13]

The pressure in the ranks, the pressure to keep those clients, is the same pressure that was witnessed in all the other scandals we have seen—the dot-coms, Enron, the S&Ls. It just keeps re-emerging. In fact, the pressure exists in government agencies, nonprofits, and any organization where those working there feel the pressure to achieve. The recent revelations about the two-track admission system at the University of Illinois, with one track for the children of donors and the politically connected, illustrates how pressure clouds judgment and produces a fog around what should be a clear ethical dilemma that requires drawing a definitive line between right and

---

[11] Smith (2007).
[12] Baja (2008).
[13] Baja (2008).

wrong. The dean of the College of Liberal Arts and Sciences asked for a special admission track for the child of a potentially generous donor, "Given his father's donor status I may be asking you to admit him. We are about to launch a huge campaign and we can't be alienating big donors by rejecting their kids."[14]

The reality, of course, is that everyone experiences pressure. We feel pressure from time and deadlines. The power of the clock can be used to apply pressure in all kinds of ways. We feel pressure from revenue goals, budget goals, personal goals—the pressure to achieve results, make margins, lower costs, pay the mortgage. Company executives feel the pressure to recoup sunk costs and maintain rankings and ratings. All of these pressures are reflected in a normal human fear of losing what we have—losing an investment, losing a job, losing a client. Such pressure clouds judgment at all levels of an organization when it is not placed in the context of strong values and lines that are not to be crossed to achieve those numbers.

The Regulatory Cycle. Regulation goes through cycles of laxness and strictness. When the phrase "everybody else does it" dominates ethical decision making, then I have a good idea where the regulatory cycle is—a phase in which a certain activity, generally something that takes advantage of a loophole in law and regulation, is widespread.

In 2002, Warren Buffett said some things about stock options and accounting that highlighted the flawed thinking in the corporate world at the time. He said, "If options aren't a form of compensation, what are they? If compensation isn't an expense, what is it? And, if expenses shouldn't go into calculations of earnings, where in the world should they go?"[15]

Yet, in 2002, critics were dismissed out of hand when they questioned the ways in which companies accounted for stock options. Options, and expensing them, turned out to be not only an ethical but also a legal issue, as noted earlier, for more than 200 companies; thus, the excuse that "everybody else does it" had to be set aside. As the regulatory cycle changes, business leaders need to realize that there is a strategic competitive advantage in developing and preserving trust. For example, one of the reasons people move from earnings or other accounting measures to dividends in assessing the value of a company is because they know they can rely on dividends. When investors can no longer understand or rely on the accounting numbers nor trust the people who generate those numbers, they know they can still rely on dividends. Creating and maintaining trust, therefore, is its own strategic reward.

But many companies live, and die, in that beginning stage of lax regulation. Some companies develop a new product or concept, such as subprime loans or stock options, that allows them to move into unregulated territory or at least to take

---

[14]University of Illinois Admission Review Commission Report (6 August 2009):21 (www.admissionsreview.illinois.gov).

[15]Hitt and Schlesinger (2002).

advantage of an accounting or regulatory loophole. Few people understand the concept entirely or the accounting methods being used for this new instrument, security, or product, and some people end up making a lot of money. But as people become more aware of the reality behind the hype, they find that the value is just not there. The public moves from the confusion of the unknown to the awareness that there are some issues and risks and then to a stage of activism that demands reform. When the exotic instruments, products, and securities collapse, the litigation begins, the government steps in, and the market is reined in by more regulation and the inevitable sell-off that a lack of trust brings.[16]

According to University of Chicago Professor Richard Leftwich, there is a truism in accounting that it takes the Financial Accounting Standards Board two years to develop a new rule and the finance guys two weeks to find a way around it.[17] We all must be aware of that. Not only do auditors, regulators, and the public need to understand the numbers; they also have to know what nuances in accounting might allow companies to move into unregulated areas in which they can do nothing apparently illegal and yet be able to structure their accounts in ways that are misleading and advantageous only to themselves.

I have a case study on Ford Motor Company from about 2005 that I use to help my students understand how misleading the numbers can be. Based on a superficial examination of Ford's accounting reports from the period, it appeared to be selling trucks as no one else had ever sold trucks before. Business was great. But as the students delve into the numbers, they find that probably 75 percent of the reported earnings were derived from clever and perfectly legal uses of rules concerning currency adjustments, one-time events, and other areas that had not yet been clarified under accounting rules.

Another truism to be learned from this case study is that the numbers are only as good as the people who calculate them. Sadly, the numbers are only as good as the rules that are meant to control them. Loopholes in those rules mean interpretation and the ability to seize the moment in that regulatory cycle before everyone else does and the cycle moves.

One of the realities that all companies learn eventually is that regulation catches up with manipulation, as happened in the case of stock options. As new regulations take over, the cost of compliance goes up and the opportunities for capitalizing on the situation go down. In short, the regulator pulls the rug out from under the manipulator. It happens every time. The regulators close a loophole; another loophole is found. Eventually, though, investors and customers assume that companies are trying to take advantage of them, and they flee to integrity. When

---

16James Frierson's (1985) work on public policy forecasting was the first to address the possibility of a regulatory cycle.

17Holtzman, Venuti, and Fonfeder (2003).

customers believe that they cannot trust the companies that they do business with, the whole system slows down. This effect is sometimes referred to as "the speed of trust." Without integrity, there is no trust; without trust, the system gums up and leaves us with a situation much like the one we are living through right now. We are now paying the costs of short-term thinking over long-term thinking.

Interestingly, many of the companies involved in recent scandals are relatively new companies, shown in **Table 1**, which may be an indicator that a business cannot behave unethically for long and expect to survive. Note that Adelphia Communications Corporation, although founded in 1952, did not go public until 2000.

Table 1. Companies Involved in Scandal and Year of Founding

Company	Year
Adelphia Communications Corporation	1952[a]
Tyco International	1962
HealthSouth Corporation	1984
Enron Corporation	1985
Finova Group	1994
WorldCom	1995
Global Crossing	1997
K-tel International	1998

[a]Adelphia went public in 2000.

Older firms have also collapsed. Bear Stearns and Lehman Brothers Holdings are two examples. But when I ask myself why they collapsed, the answer I come back to is that they lost sight of the long-term basics that they had originally built their businesses on. They went for the loopholes and forgot their principles. One such principle is that you never sell a customer anything that you cannot explain. In April 2008, Warren Buffett said, "Be fearful when others are greedy. Be greedy when others are fearful."[18] Those are sound long-term principles to keep in mind.

Analysts should not, therefore, rely only on the numbers. They must step back and ask themselves what they know about the companies, the loopholes, and the regulations. Those who allow themselves to be caught up in the herd mentality are likely to pay dearly. As a KPMG partner once noted about the firm's problems with tax shelters, "We came to the party late. We drank more, and we stayed longer."[19]

---

[18]Buffett (2008).

[19]Lynnley Browning, "How an Accounting Firm Went from Resistance to Resignation," *New York Times* (28 August 2005):A1.

Conflicts, Tone, and Our Resistance to Both

Almost all the troubles we are experiencing in the market today began with some sort of conflict of interest. Although I am moving away from financial markets for a moment, I will illustrate my point with a study done on the relationship between physicians and pharmaceutical companies, a topic I mentioned earlier.

A movement is under way in medical schools in the United States to teach medical students and practicing physicians how to recognize and avoid conflicts of interest. One source of conflict is the potential influence that pharmaceutical representatives can have on doctors. Complimentary pens and coffee cups and sample doses of new medications seem so innocuous that medical students assume they need not be taken seriously. As one medical student at Georgetown University said, "I'm too smart to be bought by a slice of pizza." Schools, therefore, have found that medical students are enormously resistant to ethics training. Yet, a recent study has shown that a doctor spending one minute with a pharmaceutical sales representative translates into that doctor prescribing 16 percent more of that representative's products than the doctor had been prescribing before. When a doctor spends four minutes with a representative, the increase in that representative's products being prescribed by the doctor is 52 percent.[20]

Student Financial Aid and Unacknowledged Conflicts. All conflicts matter, and they are around us all the time. Yet, most of the time we choose not to acknowledge them. For example, on the most basic level, we all want to say that there is no conflict between our duty to a client and our duty to our company, but opportunities for conflict are inherent in those two calls to duty.

For example, consider the conflicts that recently came to light in college and university financial aid departments. The director of student financial services at the University of Texas at Austin was fired when it was discovered that he owned 1,500 shares and 500 warrants in Education Lending Group and that he had accepted these warrants and stock options in exchange for recommending Education Lending Group as the university's preferred lender. When auditors uncovered the conflict and the administration confronted the director, he denied that a conflict existed and asserted that those stocks and warrants had not unduly influenced him.

"I did not do anything wrong," he said.

Another director of student financial aid, this time at Johns Hopkins University, was quoted as saying things like the following:
- We have ethics here.
- Appearance of impropriety is as important as impropriety itself.
- The new generation of administrators just do not have the same moral center.

---

[20] See Weintraub (2008).

Around the same time she was saying these things, she was found to have accepted $160,000 in consulting fees and tuition reimbursement from student lenders. She is now a former director of student financial aid.

As with the physicians and their relationships with pharmaceutical representatives, compromising conflicts do not necessarily begin with large sums of money changing hands. As a U.S. Senate report indicated about this former financial aid officer at the University of Texas at Austin, conflicts can start in the most innocuous ways: "Larry loves tequila and wine. Since becoming director at UT Austin, he has not had to buy any tequila or wine. Lenders provide this to him on a regular basis."[21] The conflict may have begun with tequila, but it ended with Larry accepting stock shares.

We ask ourselves how people can be so oblivious to their own behavior and situations, but it happens more often than we would like to think. There are only two ways, therefore, to manage conflicts. Either remove the opportunity altogether or disclose it. It is that simple.

Even the legendary and well-respected Peter Lynch of Fidelity Investments found himself sunk in controversy a few years ago. While investigating potential conflicts of interest of several Fidelity employees, SEC investigators learned that Lynch had asked for and received thousands of dollars worth of tickets to such things as U2 and Santana concerts, *The Nutcracker*, golf tournaments, and *The Lion King*. When these transgressions were exposed, Lynch said, "In asking the Fidelity equity trading desk for occasional help locating tickets, I never intended to do anything inappropriate, and I regret having made those requests." Doug Bailey, a spokesperson for Fidelity speaking in defense of Lynch, added, "He doesn't deserve to be lumped in with this other crowd. It was only tickets; it wasn't expensive cases of Bordeaux or trips on jets like these other cases."[22]

The disclosure of the "friends of Angelo" loan program at Countrywide was stunning in the range of beneficiaries—everyone from the household staff of Angelo Mozilo (former CEO of Countrywide) to Fannie Mae board members to senators—who enjoyed below-market interest loans for amounts that fit into the jumbo category, but all without the jumbo rates. No matter what position a person holds nor how trite the compromise appears to be, it is still a conflict of interest to accept gifts and gratuities from those who are supposed to be kept at arm's length.

Quid Pro Quo and Soft Dollars. Finally, consider the *quid-pro-quo* relationship between Jack Grubman, former lead telecom research analyst for Salomon Smith Barney, and Sandy Weill, former CEO of Citigroup. Grubman was trying to get his twins into a prestigious preschool in Manhattan. Weill had a co-CEO (Reed) who he wanted to oust, but to do so he needed the support of his

---

[21] www.c-spanarchives.org/congress/?q=node/77531&id=7628558.
[22] Scannell, Craig, and Levitz (2008).

board of directors. One of the board members was the CEO of AT&T. So, Weill contacted Grubman and said that if Grubman would upgrade AT&T, which would help Weill get the ouster votes he needed, Weill would help Grubman get his twins into preschool. In an e-mail to another analyst, Grubman explained how the transaction worked:

> I used Sandy to get my kids in 92nd Street Y pre-school (which is harder than Harvard) and Sandy needed Armstrong's vote on our board to nuke Reed in showdown. Once [the] coast was clear for both of us (i.e., Sandy clear victor and my kids confirmed) I went back to my normal negative self on [AT&T].[23]

Investors around the world relied on the honesty of Grubman's analysis and assumed, probably, that his information was based on sophisticated models, not favors. But the information that we all rely on is only as good as the people providing it.

Such *quid-pro-quo* situations demonstrate the difficult environment that soft dollars can create. They create a gray zone that is best dispelled by transparency and by potential participants remembering to think about the consequences of their actions.

Tone at the Top. I often hear executives say that it is the tone at the top that determines a company's ethical behavior and, ergo, how reliable its numbers are. But too often those very same executives seem to forget to set the right tone. Certainly, they seem to forget which things they should be doing to set that tone. Therefore, based on 30 years of experience investigating ethical dilemmas, following is my advice.

First, check a company's 10-K for perks. The more perks included in the 10-K, the more likely the culture of the company is experiencing some kind of issue; that is, something is afoot. It may be as simple as not recognizing the proper boundaries that should separate those things that belong to the shareholders and those that are suitable for employees. Furthermore, my experience indicates that the closer a company comes to an inevitable earnings restatement or even a collapse, the more perks are likely to increase.

Second, examine executives' judgment. Bad judgment is bad judgment. In most ethically compromised companies, the CEOs demonstrate some type of misconduct that is a precursor to the ultimate fall. It may be an ugly battle with another officer in the company. It may be sexual misconduct. But the bad judgment demonstrated in personal conduct often translates into bad judgment in business.

Third, find out how open the company's culture is to internal questioning and internal analysis of the numbers, because, as I have said before, the numbers are only as good as the people who generate them. Consider the behavior of employees

---

[23]Gasparino (2002).

at Tyco. Dennis Kozlowski, former CEO of Tyco, was not the only one who knew that company funds were being paid to his girlfriend. Yet, following is the judgment of the company's counsel when the news became public:

> There are payments to a woman whom the folks in finance describe as Dennis's girlfriend. I do not know Dennis's situation, but this is an embarrassing fact.[24]

Well, it is more than an embarrassing fact. It is embezzlement.

Unfortunately, I have often found that a company's ethical conduct is approaching shaky ground about the same time that company officers begin showing off their commitment to ethics and compliance. Too often the talk is simply a cover for actual behavior. From governors to senators to CEOs, bad judgment is bad judgment, and personal peccadilloes are often signals to examine professional indiscretions as well.

Therefore, as the SEC deputy director said after the investigation of Fidelity executives:

> The tone is set at the top. If higher-ups request tickets from a trading desk, it may send a message to the traders that such misconduct is tolerated and could contribute to the breakdown of the compliance culture on the desk.[25]

Source of Information. Fortunately, the best source of information about what is really going on in a company can be found right in the company. The best source is not outside auditors, not internal auditors, not government investigators, but employees. Employees are on the loading docks, in the mail room, at the filing cabinets. They see the spreadsheets and hear the gossip at the water coolers. A recent study substantiates this view and even recommends offering financial incentives, such as *qui tam* recovery (lawsuits that allow private parties to bring actions on behalf of the government, as when there is a reward for an employee who seeks to recover overbilling by an employer on federal contracts), to obtain more information from employees.[26]

Gaining access to employees' knowledge of company misconduct, however, is often obstructed by a phenomenon I call the "sandwich effect." Those at the top of the organization assume that employees will tell them when misconduct is occurring, and those at the bottom assume that top executives do not want to hear about such activities. The information, therefore, gets trapped between these two perceptions of what is expected.

A good example of the sandwich effect can be seen in the results of a recent investigation of Hallmark/Westland Meat Packing Company, once rated as a supplier of the year for school cafeterias in the United States. A rule of thumb in meat processing plants is that only "standers" can go into the meat supply. That is,

[24]Cohen and Maremont (2002).
[25]Scannell, Craig, and Levitz (2008).
[26]See Dyck, Morse, and Zingales (2007).

if a cow cannot stand up, it is probably diseased and should be euthanized, not processed. But because of an incentive program in the company, employees had developed a rather liberal definition of what constitutes a stander. In this case, it appears that employees had decided that if they could prop a cow up with a forklift or shock it into standing up, it was a stander.

For almost three weeks, an investigator for the Humane Society surreptitiously videotaped employee practices in the plant. When Hallmark/Westland executives were asked whether such lax practices occurred in their processing plant, they said absolutely not and apparently believed what they were saying because when they were shown the videotape, they displayed genuine shock and the general manager said: "The video just astounded us. Our jaws dropped. . . . We thought the place was sparkling perfect."[27] But therein lies the problem. Executives need to root out the information that is caught in the sandwich effect. They also need to anticipate the side effects of their incentive plans and structure them to avoid such pitfalls because employees do respond to incentive plans.

One way to gather honest information is for management to spend unscheduled time interacting with employees. Executives often say they meet with employees on a regular basis, such as quarterly or semiannually. But that is not the kind of interaction that is needed. Executives need to spend time in the ranks because research shows that employees use neither hotlines nor computer reporting systems. The fear of reprisal is tremendous. But if employees are actually shoulder to shoulder with someone, they are more likely to disclose the issues that concern them. Furthermore, that type of interaction flattens the organization and makes it more likely that the information that is needed will actually reach management.

I used to be a regulator in the utility industry, and I still spend time interacting with people in that industry, especially with utilities that have nuclear plants. When I am asked to go on a plant evaluation, one of the first things I do is go outside and stand with the smokers. Simply by standing around with employees involved in an unofficial activity, I find that I can glean a lot of information.

Another valuable tactic is to change executive offices. Companies that tend to be stable have executives who move their offices to different parts of the company. One benefit is that a CEO who moves offices is less likely to become attached to physical perks, such as expensive furniture and artwork. More important, though, is that such mobility puts executives into different pockets of the company where they can gain new perspectives. The goal, once again, is to create a flatter, more interactive organization. When I see an imperial CEO, I see a potential for misconduct.

---

[27] Kesmodel and Zhang (2008).

Effective Company Cultures. Based on my own observations, the companies that suffered the fewest losses because of the subprime market demonstrated the following characteristics and behaviors:

- Did not follow models blindly. (Successful companies were intuitive and relied more on human nature.)
- Considered qualitative factors, not just quantitative factors.
- Kept lines of communication open between risk management, CEOs, and chief financial officers.
- Encouraged open and realistic discussions of risk exposure.
- Probed and challenged risk measures.[28]

Early in my career I was given some excellent advice. When I was in charge of a meeting, I was told to be sure that I was the last, not the first, to speak. The companies that ran into trouble with subprime loans tended to be those with CEOs who went into meetings and said, "This is what I want." With such an attitude, employees left those meetings wondering only what they needed to do to meet the numbers. Those same CEOs should have been asking, "What are your views?" Such openness would have encouraged employees to give their honest appraisal of the numbers and may have allowed the companies to avoid much grief down the road.

Finally, on the topic of tone, almost all flawed companies presented some precursor before their financial collapse. Perhaps the SEC or some other regulatory body was beginning to investigate them. Perhaps a lawsuit had been filed by an employee or a shareholder. Even when lawsuits are dismissed or investigations end in a clean bill of health, people should not assume that nothing was wrong. The mere occurrence of the lawsuit or investigation should have sent up red flags. It could be that the legal case was simply not yet fully developed. Someone should have taken a few of those public affidavits and dug a little bit deeper. Certainly, the boards of directors of those companies should have taken a closer look, but they did not, and that was their mistake.

Federal National Mortgage Association (Fannie Mae), AIG, HealthSouth Corporation—all possessed this common factor, yet no one noticed the signal. Everyone assumed that the outcome was good news, and share prices rebounded. People should have seen the smoke and sold their stocks.

---

[28]The Senior Supervisors Group, an international group that consists of representatives from the U.S. Federal Reserve, the SEC, the U.S. Comptroller, and banks from France, Great Britain, and Switzerland, also concludes that these differences (and others beyond my area) were critical and made the difference between demise and survival. See www.newyorkfed.org/newsevents/news/banking/2008/SSG_Risk_Mgt_doc_final.pdf.

Gray Areas That Are Not Really Gray

All too often I hear people talk about ethical issues that fall into what they call a "gray area." I believe, however, that we create that gray area by using what I call "warm language" that obscures fraudulent behavior. For example, instead of using a direct phrase, such as cooking the books, which implies a clearly fraudulent intent, I hear people using such phrases as financial engineering, managing earnings, smoothing earnings, or getting results. Instead of saying that they changed the numbers, they say that they made a pro forma adjustment. Instead of saying that they were backdating options, they say that they deseasonalized the data or that they conducted "periodic look-backs," as counsel for Reyes called them.

Executives and managers should be constantly vigilant about their use of language because once they fall into the habit of warm language, they are in danger of creating a gray zone and giving themselves permission to behave fraudulently. Bill Schaff of Berger Information Technology Fund has said, "There's a big difference between being aggressive and being fraudulent."[29] We should never kid ourselves about the reality that we may not see the line as clearly as we should. Operating in gray areas causes us to lose definitive lines. Start with black and white rules, and define gray carefully, narrowly, and rarely.

Therefore, when executives and managers find themselves using warm language and telling themselves that their behavior is defensible because they are operating in a gray area, they should ask themselves the following questions:

- Why is it important to me that this be a gray area?
- Is it legally gray?
- Is it ethically gray?
- Is it a good-faith disagreement?
- What if it is not a gray area?
- Does everyone believe it is a gray area?
- Am I dealing with an interpretation, a loophole, or an actual nondisclosure of relevant information?

Consider an example from my home state of Arizona. A state rule requires that anyone who intends to subdivide property into more than six parcels go through a government process for approval. To avoid this rule, one of the major developers in the state bought a piece of property and divided it into six parcels and then, by prearrangement, sold each of those parcels to six other people who then divided their parcels by six. Using this arrangement with a chain of about 120 people, the developer was able to create an entire subdivision without any type of regulatory compliance. One could argue that he was merely taking advantage of a loophole, but his intent was fraudulent, and that was the issue.

---

[29] See http://news.cnet.com/After-Andersen,-accounting-worries-stick/2100-1017_3-936813.html.

If you ask me if any of the companies involved in the primary and secondary subprime mortgage markets violated any laws, my answer is, "absolutely not." Criminal sanctions will spring from their secondary actions, such as not disclosing the loss in values of the instruments and properties, but not from the instruments themselves. If, however, you ask me if what was done in these markets was ethical, my answer is also, "absolutely not." Fundamentally, those involved gave false impressions about the nature and quality of the mortgages and financial instruments. Just because these markets could be created and expanded as much as they were did not mean they should have been expanded as much as they were. And therein lies the role of ethics.

We have lived through this pattern before, that of legal and gray. Al Dunlap, who took over as the CEO of Sunbeam-Oster, which later went into bankruptcy, provides an example from another market debacle. At the time he took over, he was considered the wizard who could turn things around, and when he first started with Sunbeam, he produced phenomenal results. Just the fact that he had taken over caused the share price to go up. But then he entered his own gray area. The last quarter of one year, he realized that he would not make his numbers. To meet the projected numbers, he asked the manager of a warehouse where spare parts were stored to buy the parts for $11 million, which was the amount that the numbers were short of projections. The warehouseman said he would be happy to buy the parts except that they were worth only $2 million. Dunlap told the warehouseman not to worry about the discrepancy because Sunbeam would reverse the transaction after the first of the year. The transaction was intended for reporting purposes only.[30]

The audit partner was fully aware of the transaction, but he approved it because, as he said, it was quantitatively immaterial, which was true. But qualitatively, the transaction spoke volumes because it was simply a loophole intended to fix the appearance of meeting projected earnings. It was an unsustainable model, as Sunbeam's shareholders soon discovered, and Dunlap was fired and eventually sued for millions of dollars.

The worst part about this obsession with making the numbers is that it turns management away from the company's strategic operation, and the company is ultimately doomed.

We are now living through a market that has caused a deep undermining of trust. What is worse, we have had little time to recover from the previous cycle of scandals that also undermined trust. Therefore, it is time to begin refocusing on the value of ethical behavior and regaining trust. To do so, we need to rebuild a culture of ethics. Such a culture is built on three fundamental tiers:

- government and systems regulation,
- company regulations, and
- individual action.

---

[30]See Norris (2001).

The last item is key. Individual action determines the ethical tone of the organization, and the tone from the top, as I said before, provides individuals in the organization with the guidance they need to choose appropriate behavior. Ultimately, we are dependent on individuals to do more than write their e-mails and text messages of concern. We rely on them to voice those concerns in a forum where the concerns can be acted upon. We count on their organizations to listen, reflect, and where necessary, self-correct. That self-discipline and restraint is the stuff of ethics. And market trust springs from ethics.

Conclusion

Most executives understand that the tone of a company comes from the top. Unfortunately, executives can be seduced by the perks of their positions. Furthermore, the pressure to meet the numbers and achieve unsustainable levels of return encourages executives and other company employees to slip into short-term thinking and forget the long-term needs of the business and its shareholders.

In sum, conflicts of interest should be clearly identified and avoided, the use of "warm language" should be discouraged, honest communication should be encouraged, early missteps should be closely watched, and those who raise questions about decisions and actions should be rewarded for bringing ethics back into the discussions of market performance.

REFERENCES

Baja, Vikas. 2008. "Inquiry Assails Accounting Firm in Lender's Fall." *New York Times* (27 March): A1, A20.

Bandler, James, and Kara Scannell. 2006. "In Options Probes, Private Law Firms Play Crucial Role." *Wall Street Journal* (28 October):A1, A2.

Bianco, Anthony. 2008. "In Trial of Former General Re Executives, Taped Calls Play Crucial Role for Both Sides." *New York Times* (17 January):C3.

Buffett, Warren. 2008. "Buy American. I Am." *New York Times* (16 October):A16.

Cohen, Laurie P., and Mark Maremont. 2002. "E-Mails Show Tyco's Lawyers Had Concerns." *Wall Street Journal* (27 December):C1.

Duhigg, Charles. 2008a. "Papers Show Wachovia Knew of Thefts." *New York Times* (6 February): C1, C8.

———. 2008b. "Big Fine Set for Wachovia to Settle Suit." *New York Times* (26 April):B1.

Dyck, Alexander, Adair Morse, and Luigi Zingales. 2007. "Who Blows the Whistle on Corporate Fraud?" NBER Working Paper No. 12882 (February).

Frierson, James. 1985. "Public Policy Forecasting: A New Approach." *SAM Advanced Management Journal* (Spring):18–23.

Gasparino, Charles. 2002. "Ghosts of E-Mails Continue to Haunt Wall Street." *Wall Street Journal* (18 November):C1, C13. See www.pbs.org/wgbh/pages/frontline/shows/wallstreet/wcom/players.html.

Hitt, Gregg, and Jacob M. Schlesinger. 2002. "Stock Options Come under Fire in Wake of Enron's Collapse." *Wall Street Journal* (26 March):A1, A8.

Holtzman, Mark P., Elizabeth Venuti, and Robert Fonfeder. 2003. "Enron and the Raptors: SPEs That Flourish in Loopholes." *CPA Journal* (8 June):7.

Jennings, Marianne M. 2006. "Stock Options: What Happened Here?" *Corporate Finance Review*, vol. 11, no. 2:44–48.

Jones, Ashby. 2006. "Silicon Valley's Outsiders: In-House Lawyers." *Wall Street Journal* (2 October):B3.

Kesmodel, David, and Jane Zhang. 2008. "Meatpacker in Cow-Abuse Scandal May Shut as Congress Turns Up Heat." *Wall Street Journal* (25 February):A1, A10.

Norris, Floyd. 2001. "S.E.C. Accuses Former Sunbeam Official of Fraud." *New York Times* (16 May):A1, C2.

Scannell, Kara, Susanne Craig, and Jennifer Levitz. 2008. "'Gifts' Case Nabs a Star." *Wall Street Journal* (6 March):C1, C3.

SEC. 2008a. Litigation complaint (19 June): www.sec.gov/litigation/complaints/2008/comp20625.pdf.

———. 2008b. "Summary Report of Issues Identified in the Commission's Examination of Select Credit Rating Agencies" (8 July).

Smith, Randall. 2007. "O'Neal Out as Merrill Reels from Loss." *Wall Street Journal* (29 October): A1, A16.

Tully, Shawn. 2007. "Wall Street's Money Machine Breaks Down." *Fortune* (26 November):65.

Warren, Elizabeth. 2004. "The Over-Consumption Myth and Other Tales of Economics, Law and Morality." *Washington University Law Quarterly*, vol. 82:1485–1511.

Weintraub, Arlene. 2008. "Just Say No to Drug Reps." *BusinessWeek* (4 February):69.

Weiss, Elliott J. 2003. "Some Thoughts on an Agenda for the Public Company Accounting Oversight Board." *Duke Law Journal*, vol. 53:491–516.

Wilmarth, Arthur E. 2002. "The Transformation of the U.S. Financial Services Industry." *University of Illinois Law Review*, vol. 215.

How Psychological Pitfalls Generated the Global Financial Crisis

Hersh Shefrin

Mario L. Belotti Professor of Finance
Santa Clara University
Santa Clara, California

In this article, I present evidence that psychological pitfalls played a crucial role in generating the global financial crisis that began in September 2008. The evidence indicates that specific psychological phenomena—reference point–induced risk seeking, excessive optimism, overconfidence, and categorization—were at work. I am not saying that fundamental factors, such as shifts in housing demand, changes in global net savings rates, and rises in oil prices, were not relevant. They most certainly were relevant. I suggest that specific psychological reactions to these fundamentals, however, rather than the fundamentals themselves, took the global financial system to the brink of collapse.

To what extent did analysts see the crisis coming? In late 2007, four analysts (among others) forecasted that the financial sector would experience severe difficulties. They were Meredith Whitney, then at Oppenheimer; Dick Bove, then at Punk Ziegel & Company; Michael Mayo, then at Deutsche Bank; and Charles Peabody at Portales Partners (see Berman 2009). For example, in October 2007, Mayo issued a sell recommendation on Citigroup stock. Two weeks later, Whitney issued a research report on Citigroup stating that its survival would require it to raise $30 billion, either by cutting its dividend or by selling assets. More than any other analyst, Whitney raised concerns about the risks posed by the subprime mortgage market—and by the attendant threat to overall economic activity.

How timely were analysts in raising the alarm? As it happens, public markets had begun to signal concerns early in 2007. At that time, the VIX was fluctuating in the 9.5–20 range, having fallen from its 20–50 range for 2001–2002. On 27 February 2007, an 8.8 percent decline in the Chinese stock market set off a cascade in the global financial markets. In the United States, the S&P 500 Index declined by 3.5 percent, which was unusual during a period of relatively low volatility. Among the explanations that surfaced in the financial press for the decline in U.S. stocks was concern about weakness in the market for subprime mortgages.

In a book published in 2008, I argued that psychological pitfalls have three impacts that analysts should be aware of (Shefrin 2008a): First is the impact on the pricing of assets, particularly the securities of firms followed by analysts. Second is the impact on decisions by corporate managers that are germane to companies' operational risks. Third is the impact on the judgments of analysts themselves.

The financial crisis contains illustrations of all three impacts. I use five specific cases to explain how psychological pitfalls affected judgments and decisions at various points along the supply chain for financial products, particularly home mortgages, in the crisis. The cases involve (1) UBS, a bank; (2) Standard & Poor's (S&P), a rating firm; (3) American International Group (AIG), an insurance company; (4) the investment committee for the town of Narvik, Norway, an institutional investor; and (5) the U.S. SEC, a regulatory agency.

I use these cases to make two points. First, common threads link the psychological pitfalls that affected the judgments and decisions of the various participants along the supply chain. In this respect, a relatively small set of psychological pitfalls were especially germane to the creation of the crisis. The key mistakes made were not the product of random stupidity but of specific phenomena lying at the heart of behavioral finance.

Second, the major psychological lessons to be learned from the financial crisis pertain to *behavioral corporate finance* (Shefrin 2005). Many readers think of behavioral finance as focusing on mistakes made by *investors,* but issuers (corporations, governments, and so on) are people too and are just as prone to mistakes; behavioral corporate finance focuses on their side of the equation. Specifically, behavioral corporate finance focuses on how psychology affects the financial decisions of corporate managers, especially those in markets that feature mispricing. The key decisions that precipitated the crisis need to be understood in the context of behavioral corporate finance. Moreover, behavioral corporate finance offers guidelines about what to do differently in the future. For analysts, the general lesson to be learned is the importance of including a behavioral corporate perspective in their toolbox.

The five cases are intended to be representative. For example, UBS is hardly unique among investment banks, as the fates of Lehman Brothers, Merrill Lynch, and Bear Stearns illustrate. As discussed later in the article, Citigroup engaged in strategies similar to those pursued by the investment banks. Indeed, in April 2009, the *Washington Post* reported that banks relied on intuition instead of quantitative models to assess their exposure to a severe downturn in the economy. This statement was based on interviews with staff at the Federal Reserve Bank of New York and the U.S. Government Accountability Office.

The source material for the five cases is varied. For UBS, the main source is an internal document from the firm itself. For the SEC, the main source material is an audio transcript from an SEC meeting. For the other three cases, the main source material is press coverage. Material from press coverage features both strengths and weaknesses. One of the key strengths is that information comes from the level of the individual decision maker, as revealed in interviews with decision makers and their colleagues. From a behavioral perspective, this level of detail is invaluable. One of the key weaknesses is that press coverage is less than fully comprehensive and is prone to distortion. In this regard, I discuss an example illustrating a case of distorted coverage.

Fundamentals and Controversy

Mohamed El-Erian (2008) described a broad set of fundamentals related to the financial crisis. He identified the following three structural factors associated with changes in the global economy during the current decade: (1) a realignment of global power and influence from developed economies to developing economies, (2) the accumulation of wealth by countries that in the past were borrowers and that have now become lenders, and (3) the proliferation of new financial instruments, such as collateralized debt obligations (CDOs) and credit default swaps (CDS).[1]

El-Erian described how these structural factors worked in combination. Developing countries' external accounts, which had been in deficit before 2000, switched to being in surplus after 2000, with the current account surplus rising to more than $600 billion in 2007. In contrast, the United States ran an external deficit of almost $800 billion in 2007. El-Erian explained that these imbalances permitted U.S. consumers to sustain consumption in excess of their incomes. He pointed out that U.S. financial markets facilitated this pattern by providing a way for U.S. consumers to monetize their home equity. And, he added, emerging economies purchased U.S. Treasury instruments, mortgages, and corporate bonds as they converted their trade surpluses into long-term investment accounts.

El-Erian described how these structural elements have affected financial markets. For instance, in 2004, the U.S. Federal Reserve Board increased short-term interest rates with the expectation that long-term rates would also rise. Instead, long-term rates fell—to the point where, in November 2006, the yield curve inverted. This phenomenon puzzled many investors at the time. El-Erian suggested that the inversion might have been caused by emerging economies purchasing long-term T-bonds in an attempt to invest their growing trade surpluses at favorable (high) interest rates. Those purchases drove prices up and yields down. During the 2005–06 period, the yield spread of 10-year over 2-year T-bonds fell from +125 bps to more than −25 bps.

Typically, yield-curve inversions are precursors of recessions. The U.S. stock market was robust in 2005 and 2006, however, with the S&P 500 rising from 1,200 to 1,400, which hardly signaled recession. Moreover, perceptions of future volatility, as measured by the Chicago Board Options Exchange Volatility Index, were at very low levels. As a result, El-Erian concluded that the bond market, stock market, and options market were providing mixed signals during a period he characterized as exhibiting "large systemic uncertainty."

---

[1] For example, in an 18-month period beginning in January 2007, crude oil prices tripled—from $50 a barrel to $150 a barrel—and as the financial crisis unfolded in 2008, several sovereign wealth funds in Middle Eastern countries took positions in U.S. financial institutions that were in need of additional equity capital.

The biggest puzzle for El-Erian is what he called "the ability *and* willingness of the financial system to overconsume and overproduce risky products in the context of such large systemic uncertainty" (p. 20). He suggested that as risk premiums declined from 2004 on, investors used leverage in a determined effort "to squeeze out additional returns" (p. 21). This behavior created a feedback loop that further depressed risk premiums, which, in turn, induced additional leverage. He went on to say:

> Think of it: At a time when the world's economies seemed more difficult to understand . . . and multilateral financial regulation mechanisms were failing us, the marketplace ended up taking on greater risk exposures through the alchemy of new structured products, off-balance sheet conduits, and other vehicles that lie outside the purview of sophisticated oversight bodies . . . . More generally, the pressure to assume greater risk, especially through complex structured finance instruments and buyout loan commitments, combined with overconfidence in a "just in time" risk management paradigm led to the trio that would (and should) keep any trustee, shareholder, or policy maker awake at night: a set of institutions taking risk beyond what they can comfortably tolerate; another set of institutions taking risk beyond what they can understand and process; and a third set of institutions doing both! (pp. 51–53)

Is the institutional behavior that El-Erian described (1) rational risk taking in which the outcomes simply turned out to be unfavorable, (2) rational risk taking responding to problematic incentives, or (3) irrational risk taking? I argue that the phrases "beyond what they can comfortably tolerate" and "beyond what they can understand and process" suggest that the answer is irrational risk taking. In this regard, it seems to me that El-Erian laid out the market fundamentals that preceded the crisis and then described behavioral patterns that represent *irrational* responses to those fundamentals: Rather than responding to a riskier environment by cutting back on risk, institutions took more risk.

Akerlof and Shiller (2009) argued that irrational decisions associated with the subprime housing market were central to the financial crisis. In this respect, consider some history. From 1997 to 2006, U.S. home prices rose by about 85 percent, even after adjustment for inflation, making this period a time of the biggest national housing boom in U.S. history. The rate of increase was five times the historical rate of 1.4 percent a year. As a result, the authors suggested, the sentiment of many people at the time was that housing prices would continue to increase at well above their historical growth rates. This belief supported a dramatic increase in the volume of subprime mortgages, especially mortgages requiring no documentation and little or no down payment. Later in this article, I discuss the time-series properties of loan-to-value ratios (LTVs), limited documentation, and 100 percent financing in the mortgage market.

Housing prices peaked in December 2006, when the Federal Reserve was raising short-term interest rates, and then declined by 30 percent over the subsequent 26 months. During the decline, many new homeowners (and some old ones who had engaged in repeated cash-out refinancings) found that the values of their mortgages exceeded the values of their homes. Some in this situation chose to default on their mortgages. Some homeowners had taken out adjustable-rate mortgages with low initial rates that would reset after a period of time to rates that were much higher. These homeowners were planning on refinancing before rates reset. Once housing prices began to decline, however, they did not qualify for refinancing. Many were unable to afford the higher rates and had to default.[2]

The mortgage product supply chain began with mortgage initiation by financial institutions such as Indy Mac, Countrywide, and Washington Mutual. It continued with such firms as Fannie Mae and Freddie Mac, which purchased and "securitized" mortgages, thus creating mortgage-backed securities (MBS). Next in the chain were investment banks, such as Lehman Brothers, Merrill Lynch, Citigroup, and UBS, which created and sold CDOs backed by the MBS. The supply chain also included financial firms such as AIG, which insured against the risk of default by selling CDS. The risks of both the products and the financial firms were rated by rating agencies, such as Moody's Investors Service and S&P. At the end of the supply chain were the end investors, such as foreign banks, pension funds, and municipal governments, who ultimately held the claims to cash flows generated by the mortgages.[3] Along the way, the supply chain was subject to regulation by various bodies, such as the SEC, the Board of Governors of the Federal Reserve, the Federal Reserve Bank of New York, and the Office of Thrift Supervision.

Taken together, the viewpoints expressed by El-Erian and Akerlof–Shiller suggest that financial institutions exhibited behavior inconsistent with the predictions of the Akerlof adverse-selection, "lemons," model, in which all agents use the information at their disposal to make rational decisions. The lemons model predicts

---

[2]The proportion of all mortgage originations that were subprime increased from near zero in the early 1980s to 20.1 percent in 2006, although not monotonically. Chomsisengphet and Pennington-Cross (2006) described the history of subprime mortgage lending in the United States beginning in 1980 as follows: "Many factors have contributed to the growth of subprime lending. Most fundamentally, it became legal. The ability to charge high rates and fees to borrowers was not possible until the Depository Institutions Deregulation and Monetary Control Act . . . was adopted in 1980. It preempted state interest rate caps. The Alternative Mortgage Transaction Parity Act . . . in 1982 permitted the use of variable interest rates and balloon payments. These laws opened the door for the development of a subprime market, but subprime lending would not become a viable large-scale lending alternative until the Tax Reform Act of 1986 (TRA). The TRA increased the demand for mortgage debt because it prohibited the deduction of interest on consumer loans, yet allowed interest deductions on mortgages for a primary residence as well as one additional home" (p. 38).

[3]As an example of foreign banks in the supply chain, consider that the Industrial and Commercial Bank of China bought $1.23 billion in securities backed by mortgages.

the collapse of trade, resulting in, for example, a credit freeze when rational agents who perceive themselves to be at an information disadvantage assume the worst (e.g., all cars are lemons) when forming their expectations. In contrast to this model, despite the opaqueness of securitized asset pools, CDOs, and CDS—with their attendant information asymmetries—the subprime mortgage market did not collapse; it proceeded as if no cars could be lemons.

Whether financial institutions behaved irrationally and whether the associated market movements reflected market inefficiency are the subject of controversy. Posner (2009a) maintained that institutions behaved rationally in light of the incentives they faced. He wrote, "At no stage need irrationality be posited to explain" the collapse of financial markets in 2008 and the deep recession in 2009. In an interview, Eugene Fama contended that past market movements are consistent with the notion of market efficiency.[4]

In his critique of Akerlof and Shiller's 2009 book, Posner (2009b) stated, "But mistakes and ignorance are not symptoms of irrationality. They usually are the result of limited information." This line of reasoning leads him to conclude that the stock market increases of the late 1920s and late 1990s did not reflect mispricing and that in 2005 and 2006, people did not overpay for their houses in an *ex ante* sense.

Of Akerlof and Shiller's (2009) contention that irrational decisions in the subprime housing market were central to the financial crisis, Posner (2009b) wrote, "They think that mortgage fraud was a major cause of the present crisis. How all this relates to animal spirits is unclear, but in any event they are wrong about the causality."

Posner then provided his own list of what caused the crisis:

> The underlying causes were the deregulation of financial services; lax enforcement of the remaining regulations; unsound decisions on interest rates by the Federal Reserve; huge budget deficits; the globalization of the finance industry; the financial rewards of risky lending, and competitive pressures to engage in it, in the absence of effective regulation; the overconfidence of economists inside and outside government; and the government's erratic, confidence-destroying improvisational responses to the banking collapse. Some of these mistakes of commission and omission had emotional components. The overconfidence of economists might even be thought a manifestation of animal spirits. But the career and reward structures, and the ideological preconceptions, of macroeconomists are likelier explanations than emotion for the economics profession's failure to foresee or respond effectively to the crisis. (2009b)

Posner might well be correct in identifying problematic decisions in the regulatory process. Whether he is correct in his view that institutions acted rationally is another matter. One way of dealing with this issue is to examine decision making

---

[4]The interview with Fama titled "Fama on Market Efficiency in a Volatile Market" is at www.dimensional.com/famafrench/2009/08/fama-on-market-efficiency-in-a-volatile-market.html#more.

on a case-by-case basis, as I will do in this article, to identify the nature of the decision processes within financial institutions.[5]

This discussion needs to be based on a well-defined notion of rationality. In financial economics, rationality is typically understood in the neoclassical sense. Neoclassical rationality has two parts: rationality of judgments and rationality of choice. People make rational judgments when they make efficient use of the information at their disposal and form beliefs that are free from bias. People make rational choices when they have well-defined preferences that express the trade-offs they are willing to make and choose the best means to meet their objectives. In financial economics, rationality is typically said to prevail when decision makers act as Bayesian expected-utility maximizers who are averse to risk.

Behavioral Corporate Finance

Behavioral corporate finance highlights the psychological errors and biases associated with major corporate tasks—capital budgeting, capital structure, payout policy, valuation, mergers and acquisitions, risk management, and corporate governance. In my 2008 book, I suggested that suboptimal corporate financial decisions can largely be traced to the impact of psychological errors and biases on specific organizational processes (Shefrin 2008b). These processes involve planning, the setting of standards, the sharing of information, and incentives. Planning includes the development of strategy and the preparation of *pro forma* financial statements. Standards involve the establishment of goals and performance metrics. Information sharing results from the nature of organizational design. Incentives stem from the compensation system and are a major aspect of corporate governance. Sullivan (2009) emphasized the importance of governance failures in generating the crisis.

Among the main psychological pitfalls at the center of behavioral finance are the following:
- reference point–induced risk seeking,
- narrow framing,
- opaque framing,
- excessive optimism,
- overconfidence,
- extrapolation bias,
- confirmation bias,

---

[5]The five case studies are not intended to provide a comprehensive analysis of decision making in the financial crisis. Rather, the case studies are intended to provide examples of behavior that can be classified as rational or irrational. To deal with the issues raised by Posner (2009b), the focus is on financial institutions and government agencies, not on the behavior of individual homeowners. Nevertheless, many homeowners used subprime mortgages to purchase homes with the unfounded expectation that housing prices would continue to increase and that they would be able to refinance adjustable-rate mortgages in which the future interest rates would reset to a much higher rate.

- conservatism,
- the "affect heuristic,"
- "groupthink,"
- hindsight bias, and
- categorization bias.

I suggest that these pitfalls figured prominently in the decisions that precipitated the financial crisis. For this reason, I provide here a brief description of each.

Psychologically based theories of risk taking emphasize that people measure outcomes relative to reference points. A reference point might be a purchase price used to define gains and losses, as suggested by Shefrin and Statman (1985), building on Kahneman and Tversky (1979), or a level of aspiration, as suggested by Lopes (1987). *Reference point–induced risk seeking* is the tendency of people to behave in a risk-seeking fashion to avoid an outcome that lies below the reference point. As an illustration, consider El-Erian's comment that as risk premiums declined from 2004 on, investors used leverage in a determined effort "to squeeze out additional returns." This comment is consistent with the idea that investors had fixed aspirations and became more tolerant of risk as risk premiums declined.

Narrow framing is the practice of simplifying a multidimensional decision problem by decomposing it into several smaller subtasks and ignoring the interaction between these subtasks. The term "silo" is sometimes used to describe the impact of narrow framing because subtasks are assigned to silos.

Opaque framing versus transparent framing involves the level of clarity in the description of the decision task and associated consequences. For illustration, consider El-Erian's comment about institutions taking risk beyond what they can understand and process. This comment suggests opaque, or nontransparent, framing.

Excessive optimism leads people to look at the world through rose-colored glasses. *Overconfidence* leads people to be too sure of their opinions, a tendency that frequently results in their underestimating risk. Although excessive optimism and overconfidence sound related, they are really quite different psychological shortcomings in a decision maker. For example, somebody might be an overconfident pessimist—one who has too much conviction that the future will be gloomy.

Extrapolation bias leads people to forecast that recent changes will continue into the future. A pertinent example of extrapolation bias is the belief that housing prices will continue to grow at the same above-average rates that have prevailed in the recent past.

Confirmation bias leads people to overweight information that confirms their prior views and to underweight information that disconfirms those views.

Conservatism is the tendency to overweight base-rate information relative to new (or singular) information. This phenomenon is sometimes called "underreaction."

The *affect heuristic* refers to the making of judgments on the basis of positive or negative feelings rather than underlying fundamentals. Reliance on the affect heuristic is often described as using "gut feel" or intuition.

Groupthink leads people in groups to act as if they value conformity over quality when making decisions. Groupthink typically occurs because group members value cohesiveness and do not want to appear uncooperative, so they tend to support the positions advocated by group leaders rather than playing devil's advocate. Group members may also be afraid of looking foolish or poorly informed if they vocally disagree with a leader whom the majority of the group regards as wise.

Hindsight bias is the tendency to view outcomes in hindsight and judge that these outcomes were more likely to have occurred than they appeared in foresight. That is, *ex post*, the *ex ante* probability of the event that actually occurred is judged to be higher than the *ex ante* estimate of that *ex ante* probability. Consider Posner's (2009b) comment about equities being efficiently priced in the late 1990s or houses being efficiently priced in the first six years of this decade. In making this claim, he effectively charges Akerlof and Shiller (2009) with succumbing to hindsight bias in that he suggests that the subsequent price decline is nothing more than an unfavorable outcome that is being viewed as more likely in hindsight than it was in foresight.

Categorization bias is the act of partitioning objects into general categories and ignoring the differences among members of the same category. Categorization bias may produce unintended side effects if the members of the same category are different from each other in meaningful ways.

In the remainder of this article, I use the behavioral corporate finance framework to analyze each of the five cases. One way to think about this framework is in terms of the interaction of psychological biases with business processes, as illustrated in **Exhibit 1**. (Exhibit 1 is merely for illustration; only the first five pitfalls discussed in this section are displayed.) The intersections of the rows showing organizational processes with the columns depicting psychological pitfalls are shown as question marks to prompt questions for those using such a framework about whether a specific pitfall occurred as part of the business process. This perspective helps to show how psychological pitfalls affect the decisions made in connection with each process.

Exhibit 1. Interaction of Psychological Pitfalls and Business Processes

Process	Reference Point–Induced Risk Seeking	Narrow Framing	Opaque Framing	Excessive Optimism	Overconfidence
Planning	?	?	?	?	?
Standards	?	?	?	?	?
Information sharing	?	?	?	?	?
Incentives	?	?	?	?	?

UBS

At the end of 2007, UBS announced that it would write off $18 billion of failed investments involving the subprime housing market in the United States. In 2008, the write-offs increased to more than $50 billion. In October 2008, the Swiss central bank announced its intention to take $60 billion of toxic assets off UBS's balance sheet and to inject $6 billion of equity capital.

In April 2008, UBS published a report (2008) detailing the reasons for its losses. In this section, I quote extensively from the report to let UBS management speak for itself.

The report states, "UBS's retrospective review focused on root causes of these losses with the view toward improving UBS's processes" (p. 28). That is, the write-offs were the result of having ineffective processes in place, a statement that, I argue, failed to address psychological biases. In the following discussion, I view the UBS report through the prism of the four specific processes shown in Exhibit 1: planning, standards, information sharing, and incentives. As readers will see, biases permeated many of the decisions UBS made in connection with subprime mortgages and financial derivatives.

Planning at UBS. The report states, "[T]he 5 year strategic focus articulated for 2006–2010 was to aim for significant revenue increases whilst also allowing for more cost expansion. However the Group's risk profile in 2006 was not predicted to change substantially . . . ." (p. 8). In retrospect, the firm's risk profile did increase dramatically, which raises the question of whether UBS's management team displayed overconfidence.

UBS says that, in 2005, it engaged the services of an external consultant who compared UBS's past performance with that of its chief competitors.[6] Notably, UBS's performance trailed that of its competitors. To close the competitive gap, the consultant recommended the following:

> [S]trategic and tactical initiatives were required to address these gaps and recommended that UBS selectively invest in developing certain areas of its business to close key product gaps, including in Credit, Rates, MBS Subprime and Adjustable Rate Mortgage products ("ARMs"), Commodities and Emerging Markets. ABS (asset backed securities), MBS, and ARMs (in each case including underlying assets of Subprime nature) were specifically identified as significant revenue growth opportunities. The consultant's review did not consider the risk capacity (e.g. stress risk and market risk) associated with the recommended product expansion. (p. 11)

Notice that, although subprime was specifically identified as providing significant revenue growth opportunities, the consultant's review did not consider the implications for UBS's risk capacity. Given that risk and return lie at the heart of

---

[6]UBS relied on McKinsey & Company for consulting services. Peter Wuffli, who was UBS Investment Bank CEO at the time, had previously been a principal with McKinsey.

finance and that subprime mortgages feature more default risk than higher rated mortgages, the absence of an analysis of risk is striking.[7]

Standards for Risk at UBS. Standards for risk management include targets and goals that relate to accounting controls and include position limits and other risk-control mechanisms. The report tells how UBS reacted to the consulting firm's failure to address the implications of its recommendations for risk:

> There were not however any Operational Limits on the CDO Warehouse, nor was there an umbrella Operational Limit across the IB [the investment banking unit] (or the combination of IB and DRCM [the hedge fund subsidiary Dillon Read Capital Management]) that limited overall exposure to the Subprime sector (securities, derivatives and loans). (p. 20)

That is, UBS did not develop any operational limits that would restrict the firm's overall exposure to subprime loans, securities, and derivatives.

Was this behavior rational, or did UBS irrationally ignore risk for psychological reasons? One possibility is that by virtue of being behind the competition, UBS set a high reference point for itself and exhibited reference point–induced risk-seeking behavior. Perhaps this attitude is why it did not question the consulting firm's failure to address the risk implications of its recommendations and did not develop risk standards for itself. Its psychological profile led it to act as if it implicitly attached little or no value to avoiding risk.

UBS's internal report does indeed suggest that the reference point for the firm corresponded to the superior performance of its competitors. The report states:

> It was recognized in 2005 that, of all the businesses conducted by the IB, the biggest competitive gap was in Fixed Income, and that UBS's Fixed Income positioning had declined vis-à-vis leading competitors since 2002. In particular, the IB's Fixed Income, Rates & Currencies ("FIRC") revenues decreased since 2004, and accordingly, FIRC moved down in competitor league tables by revenue. According to an external consultant, the IB Fixed Income business grew its revenue at a slower rate than its peers. (p. 10)

CDOs are akin to families of mutual funds that hold bonds instead of stocks. Each member of the fund family, or tranche, holds bonds with a different degree of priority in the event of default from the priority of other tranches in the family. Investors pay lower prices for riskier tranches. Holders of the equity (riskiest) tranche absorb the first losses stemming from default. If at some point the holders of the equity tranche receive zero cash flows from the underlying assets, holders of

---

[7]The nature of the consultant's recommendation provides an interesting illustration of how a "follow the leader" approach results in herding. UBS followed a leader in its peer group, plausibly Lehman Brothers, although it does not say so explicitly. As I report later, a consultant advised Citigroup also to increase its risk exposure. Shefrin (2009) discussed how Merrill Lynch sought to emulate the subprime strategy of the industry leader (at the time, Lehman Brothers).

the next tranche begin to absorb losses. Holders of the senior tranche are the most protected, but the existence of a "super senior" tranche is also possible. If the CDO contains leverage, meaning that the issuer of the CDO borrowed money to purchase assets for the CDO, then some party must stand ready to absorb the losses once the holders of even the senior tranche receive no cash flows. Holders of the super senior tranche must play this role. Instead of paying to participate in the CDO, they receive payments that are analogous to insurance premiums.

UBS's investment banking unit did hold super senior positions, and that unit did consider the risk of those positions. Moody's and S&P both rated various CDO tranches. The report states:

> MRC [Market Risk Control] VaR [value-at-risk] methodologies relied on the AAA rating of the Super Senior positions. The AAA rating determined the relevant product-type time series to be used in calculating VaR. In turn, the product-type time series determined the volatility sensitivities to be applied to Super Senior positions. Until Q3 [third quarter] 2007, the 5-year time series had demonstrated very low levels of volatility sensitivities. As a consequence, even unhedged Super Senior positions contributed little to VaR utilisation. (p. 20)

Piskorski, Seru, and Vig (2009) found, conditional on a loan becoming seriously delinquent, a significantly lower foreclosure rate for loans held by banks than for similar loans that were securitized. Indeed, Eggert (2009) takes the position that securitization *caused* the subprime meltdown. In this regard, UBS's behavior provides examples of key psychological pitfalls related to securitization. For instance, in relying solely on risk ratings, UBS's risk management group did no independent analysis. The report states:

> In analyzing the retained positions, MRC generally did not "look through" the CDO structure to analyse the risks of the underlying collateral. In addition, the CDO desk does not appear to have conducted such "look through" analysis and the static data maintained in the front-office systems did not capture several important dimensions of the underlying collateral types. For example, the static data did not capture FICO [credit] scores, 1st/2nd lien status, collateral vintage (which term relates to the year in which the assets backing the securities had been sourced), and did not distinguish a CDO from an ABS. MRC did not examine or analyze such information on a regular or systematic basis. (p. 20)

> In a similar vein, it appears that no attempt was made to develop an RFL [risk factor loss] structure that captured more meaningful attributes related to the U.S. housing market generally, such as defaults, loan to value ratios, or other similar attributes to statistically shock the existing portfolio. (p. 38)

Was it rational for UBS to ignore the underlying fundamentals of the U.S. mortgage market? Was it rational for UBS to make no attempt to investigate key statistics related to the U.S. housing market, such as LTVs, percentage of loans that featured 100 percent financing, limited-documentation loans, and default rates?

Between 2001 and 2006, the following occurred: The LTVs of newly originated mortgages rose from 80 percent to 90 percent; the percentage of loans that were 100 percent financed climbed from 3 percent to 33 percent; and limited-documentation loans almost doubled—rising from 27 percent to 46 percent. In terms of increasing risk, these trends are akin to powder kegs waiting for a match.[8]

As for defaults, the insufficient focus on fundamentals, in combination with an overattention to historical default rates—a strong illustration of conservatism bias (i.e., the tendency to overweight base-rate information)—gave rise to the "risk-free illusion." UBS's CDO desk considered a super senior position to be fully hedged if 2–4 percent of the position was protected. They referred to such super seniors as AMPS (amplified mortgage protected trades). In this regard, UBS erroneously judged that it had hedged its AMPS positions sufficiently and that the associated VaR was effectively zero.

Was this judgment rational? Not in my opinion, because UBS assumed that historical default rates would continue to apply, despite the changed fundamentals in the U.S. housing market. The UBS report indicates in respect to AMPS that

> Amplified Mortgage Portfolio: . . . at the end of 2007, losses on these trades contributed approximately 63% of total Super Senior losses.
>
> Unhedged Super Senior positions: Positions retained by UBS in anticipation of executing AMPS trades which did not materialise. . . . at the end of 2007, losses on these trades contributed approximately 27% of total Super Senior losses. (p. 14)

Information Sharing at UBS. Narrow framing and opaque framing are two of the psychological pitfalls described previously. UBS's report criticizes its risk managers for *opaquely* presenting information about risks to be managed and decisions to be taken. The report states:

> Complex and incomplete risk reporting: . . . Risks were siloed within the risk functions, without presenting a holistic picture of the risk situation of a particular business.
>
> Lack of substantive assessment: MRC did not routinely put numbers into the broader economic context or the fundamentals of the market when presenting to Senior Management. (p. 39)

---

[8] In this regard, the President's Working Group on Financial Markets (2008) concluded, "The turmoil in financial markets was triggered by *a dramatic weakening of underwriting standards for U.S. subprime mortgages, beginning in late 2004, and extending into early 2007.*" In contrast, studies by Bhardwaj and Sengupta (2008a, 2008b) from the Federal Reserve Bank of St. Louis suggest that subprime mortgage quality did not deteriorate after 2004 because FICO scores improved at the same time that the other indicators of credit quality worsened. The authors also pointed out that adjustable-rate subprime mortgages are designed as bridge loans, with the view that they be prepaid when interest rates reset as homeowners refinance. They attributed the subprime meltdown to the decline in housing prices that began at the end of 2006 rather than to a lowering of lending standards.

When risk managers eventually recognized the deteriorating values of their subprime positions, they mistakenly assumed that the problem was restricted to subprime and would not affect the values of their other ABS positions.

As a general matter, risk managers did not properly share information with those who needed the information at UBS, and the information they did share was overly complex and often out of date. Examples of what went wrong are that risk managers often netted long and short positions, which obscured the manner in which positions were structured, and they did not make the inventory of super senior positions clear.

Information sharing takes place as part of the deliberations about which decisions to take. UBS managers exhibited groupthink in these deliberations by not challenging each other about the ways their various businesses were developing. The report states:

> Members of the IB Senior Management apparently did not sufficiently challenge each other in relation to the development of their various businesses. The Fixed Income strategy does not appear to have been subject to critical challenge, for instance in view of the substantial investments in systems, people and financial resources that the growth plans entailed. (p. 36)

UBS's risk managers also appeared vulnerable to confirmation bias. As the firm began to experience losses on its inventories of MBS in the first and second quarters of 2007, the risk management team did not implement additional risk methodologies. Then, matters got worse. In a subsection titled "Absence of risk management," the report states:

> In Q2 2007, the CDO desk was giving a relatively pessimistic outlook in relation to certain aspects of the Subprime market generally in response to questions from Group and IB Senior Management about UBS's Subprime exposures. Notwithstanding this assessment, the MBS CDO business acquired further substantial Mezz RMBS [mezzanine residential MBS] holdings and the CDO desk prepared a paper to support the significant limit increase requests. The increase was ultimately not pursued. (p. 29)

Incentives and Governance at UBS. In theory, compensation provides managers with incentives to maximize the value of their firms. Incentive compensation frameworks (beyond the base salary) often rely on a combination of (1) a bonus plan that relates to the short term and (2) equity-based compensation that relates to the long term.

In practice, UBS's compensation system was plagued by at least three serious flaws. The first flaw was that UBS's incentive structure did not take risk properly into account. The report states, "The compensation structure generally made little recognition of risk issues or adjustment for risk/other qualitative indicators" (p. 42).

Did this amount to rational governance? Keep in mind that fundamental value is based on discounted cash flow, where the discount rate reflects risk as well as the time value of money. Higher risk leads to a higher discount rate and, therefore, to lower discounted cash flows. UBS's compensation structure barely took risk issues into consideration and made little to no adjustment for risk. Therefore, employees had no direct incentive to focus on risk when making decisions, including decisions about positions involving subprime mortgages and their associated derivatives.

The second flaw concerned undue emphasis on short-term profit and loss (P&L) in overall employee compensation—specifically, bonuses—and insufficient attention to the implications of decisions about positions for long-term value. The report states, "Day1 P&L treatment of many of the transactions meant that employee remuneration (including bonuses) was not directly affected by the longer term development of positions created" (p. 42). To be sure, the compensation structure featured an equity component, which could have provided UBS employees with an indirect incentive to avoid risks that were detrimental to long-term value. The bonus focus, however, dominated. Bonus payments for successful and senior fixed-income traders, including those in businesses holding subprime positions, were significant. Particularly noteworthy is that UBS based bonuses on gross revenue after personnel costs but did not take formal account of the quality or sustainability of earnings.

The third flaw was that UBS's incentives did not differentiate between skill-based returns and returns attributable to cost advantages. The report states:

> [E]mployee incentivisation arrangements did not differentiate between return generated by skill in creating additional returns versus returns made from exploiting UBS's comparatively low cost of funding in what were essentially carry trades. There are no findings that special arrangements were made for employees in the businesses holding Subprime positions. (p. 42)

Are these reward systems, policies, and practices consistent with rational governance? The authors of the UBS report suggest not, and I concur.

Standard & Poor's

One of the major elements of the financial crisis was the fact that rating agencies assigned AAA ratings to mortgage-related securities that were very risky. As a result, many investors purchased these securities under the impression that they were safe, and they found out otherwise only when housing prices declined and default rates rose. Financial intermediaries such as UBS also paid a steep price when the securities they held in inventory declined in value and became illiquid.

In this section, I discuss the psychological issues that affected the judgments and decisions made by rating agencies. The processes of planning, standards, and information sharing were the most germane processes; also important were agency issues.

Planning and Standards at S&P. Consider some background. In August 2004, Moody's unveiled a new credit-rating model that enabled securities firms to increase their sales of top-rated subprime mortgage-backed bonds. The new model eliminated a nondiversification penalty that was present in the prior model, a penalty that applied to concentrated mortgage risk. According to Douglas Lucas, head of CDO research at UBS Securities in New York City, Moody's was pressured to make the change. He was quoted by Smith (2008) as having stated, "I know people lobbied Moody's to accommodate more concentrated residential mortgage risk in CDOs, and Moody's obliged."[9]

Notably, Moody's competitor, S&P, revised its own methods one week after Moody's did. In important ways, S&P shared traits with UBS at this time. Both firms found themselves behind their respective industry leaders and were thus susceptible to reference point–induced risk-seeking behavior.

The *Wall Street Journal* reported that in August 2004, S&P commercial mortgage analyst Gale Scott sent the following message to colleagues: "We are meeting with your group this week to discuss adjusting criteria for rating CDOs of real-estate assets . . . because of the ongoing threat of losing deals" (see Lucchetti 2008b). Richard Gugliada, a former S&P executive who oversaw CDOs from the late 1990s until 2005, replied to the e-mail, "OK with me to revise criteria" (see Smith 2008). The criteria for rating commercial mortgages were changed after several meetings. According to an S&P report that Scott co-wrote in May 2008, the change in criteria directly preceded "aggressive underwriting and lower credit support" in the market for commercial MBS from 2005 to 2007. The report went on to say that this change led to growing delinquencies, defaults, and losses.

Consider S&P against the backdrop of its parent organization, McGraw-Hill Companies. According to reports that appeared in the *Wall Street Journal*, CEO and Chairman Harold McGraw established unrealistic profit goals for his organization (Lucchetti 2008a). I suggest that these goals induced risk-seeking behavior in the rating of mortgage-related products. The *Wall Street Journal* reported that because McGraw-Hill had been suffering financially in other areas, it exerted pressure on S&P to expand 15–20 percent a year. McGraw-Hill's financial services unit, which includes S&P, generated 75 percent of McGraw-Hill's total operating profit in 2007, up from 42 percent in 2000. In 2007, the ratings business generated a third of McGraw-Hill's revenue.

Goal setting is the basis for establishing standards and planning, through which goals are folded into strategy. S&P's efforts to achieve its goals focused on increasing its revenues from rating mortgage-related products while keeping its costs down. In regard to the latter, Gugliada told *Bloomberg* that he was given tough budget targets (see Smith 2008).

---

[9]Interestingly, Lucas had been an analyst at Moody's and claims to have invented the diversity score in the late 1980s.

According to Lucchetti (2008a), the combination of high revenue goals and low cost goals led understaffed analytical teams to underestimate the default risk associated with mortgage-related products. Before the collapse in housing prices, S&P and Moody's earned approximately three times more from grading CDOs than from grading corporate bonds.

Consider how the ratings on mortgage-related securities came to be lowered over time. Once housing prices began to decline and homeowners began to default, raters eventually downgraded most of the AAA rated CDO bonds that had been issued in the prior three years. On 10 July 2008, Moody's reduced its ratings on $5.2 billion in subprime-backed CDOs. The same day, S&P said it was considering reductions on $12 billion of residential MBS. By August 2007, Moody's had downgraded 90 percent of all asset-backed CDO investments issued in 2006 and 2007, including 85 percent of the debt originally rated Aaa. S&P reduced 84 percent of the CDO tranches it had rated, including 76 percent of all those rated AAA.[10]

Information Sharing at S&P. Former employees at S&P have provided insights into the ways that information used for rating CDOs was shared. Kai Gilkes is a former S&P quantitative analyst in London. The following comments in Smith (2008) recreate the tenor of the discussion about the sharing of information and points of view:

> "Look, I know you're not comfortable with such and such [an] assumption, but apparently Moody's are even lower, and, if that's the only thing that is standing between rating this deal and not rating this deal, are we really hung up on that assumption?" You don't have infinite data. Nothing is perfect. So the line in the sand shifts and shifts, and can shift quite a bit.

Gilkes' remark about shifting lines needs to be understood in the context of group processes. The behavioral decision literature emphasizes that working in a group tends to reduce the biases of the group's members when the tasks feature clearly correct solutions, which everyone can confirm once the solution has been presented. For judgmental tasks that have no clearly correct solution, however, working in groups actually exacerbates the biases of the group members. Gilkes' remark about "shifting lines" effectively points to the judgmental character of the ratings decision.

Additional insight about the sharing of information and exchange of viewpoints has come from Gugliada, who told *Bloomberg* that when a proposal to tighten S&P's criteria was considered, the codirector of CDO ratings, David Tesher, responded: "Don't kill the golden goose."

---

[10]Still, in the last week of August 2007, Moody's assigned Aaa grades for at least $12.7 billion of new CDOs, which would be downgraded within six months.

Was groupthink an issue here, or were managers behaving rationally? The answer might depend on their personal ethics. In retrospect, Gugliada stated, competition with Moody's amounted to a "market-share war where criteria were relaxed. . . . I knew it was wrong at the time. It was either that or skip the business. That wasn't my mandate. My mandate was to find a way" (see Smith 2008).

To be sure, analysts at S&P were not oblivious to the possibility of a housing bubble. In 2005, S&P staff observed that the housing market was in a bubble, the bursting of which might lead housing prices to decline by 30 percent at some stage. The vague "at some stage" could have meant, however, next month or 10 years hence. The timing of the bursting of a bubble is highly uncertain. The report, including its implications for ratings, was discussed internally, but the discussion did not alter the rating methodology.

S&P had been telling investors that its ratings were but one piece of information about securities and that ratings were not a perfect substitute for being diligent about acquiring additional information to assess security risk. S&P's protocol was to accept the documentation as presented and to issue a rating conditional on that information. The firm's practice was not to verify the documentation. If S&P rated a security on the basis of limited-documentation mortgages, it did not seek to verify whether or not the information was correct. Just as UBS did, however, the investment bank treated AAA ratings on mortgage-related securities as unconditional ratings. Moreover, the same was true for many other investors, especially end investors, who were much less sophisticated than investment bankers.

As it happens, some of the analysts engaged in rating CDOs were highly skeptical of their assignments, and they shared this skepticism with colleagues. Lucchetti (2008b) reports that one S&P analytical staffer e-mailed another saying that a mortgage or structured-finance deal was "ridiculous" and that "we should not be rating it." The recipient of the e-mail famously responded, "We rate every deal," and added that, "it could be structured by cows and we would rate it." An analytical manager in the CDO group at S&P told a senior analytical manager in a separate e-mail that "rating agencies continue to create" an "even bigger monster—the CDO market. Let's hope we are all wealthy and retired by the time this house of cards falters" (Lucchetti 2008b).

AIG

AIG is an insurance company with a financial products division (AIGFP).[11] Because of AIGFP's involvement in the market for subprime mortgages, AIG required a $182 billion bailout from the U.S. government. In September 2008, the decision to bail out AIG was a defining moment in the unfolding of the global financial crisis. To understand the decisions that led to this event, consider some background.

---

[11]The source material for AIG is Lewis (2009).

AIGFP was created in 1987; it generated income by assuming various parties' counterparty risks in such transactions as interest rate swaps. It was able to do so because its parent, AIG, had a AAA rating and a large balance sheet. AIGFP was highly profitable during its first 15 years and, by 2001, was generating 15 percent of AIG's profit.

AIGFP's main role in the global financial crisis involved its trades in the market for CDS associated with subprime mortgages. Effectively, AIG provided insurance against defaults by homeowners who had taken out subprime mortgages.

AIGFP entered the market for CDS in 1998 by insuring against the default risk of corporate bonds issued by investment-grade public corporations. The default risk associated with these bonds as a group was relatively low. Although insuring corporate debt remained AIGFP's key business, over time the company also began to insure risks associated with credit card debt, student loans, auto loans, pools of prime mortgages, and eventually, pools of subprime mortgages.

Planning and Risk Standards at AIGFP. The need for a bailout of AIG stemmed from AIGFP having underestimated its risk exposure to subprime mortgages. The psychological pitfalls underlying the underestimation were categorization, overconfidence, and groupthink.

When the Federal Reserve began to increase short-term interest rates in June 2004, the volume of prime mortgage lending fell by 50 percent. At the same time, however, the volume of subprime mortgage lending increased dramatically.[12] Lewis (2009) related that, as a result, the composition of mortgage pools that AIGFP was insuring shifted over the next 18 months; the proportion of mortgages that were subprime increased from 2 percent to 95 percent of the total over that period. Yet, AIGFP's decisions were invariant to the change. The decision makers succumbed to categorization; that is, they treated a pool with 2 percent subprime mortgages as equivalent to a pool with 95 percent subprime mortgages.

Recall the failure of the rational lemons paradigm. A major reason the subprime market thrived instead of collapsed is that during 2004 and 2005, AIGFP assumed the default risk of subprime mortgages apparently unknowingly. AIGFP failed to assume the worst, as rational behavior in the lemons framework requires.

In addition to categorization, overconfidence and groupthink played key roles. AIGFP was headed by Joseph Cassano. His predecessor at the helm of AIGFP was Tom Savage, a trained mathematician who understood the models used by AIGFP traders to price the risks they were assuming. Savage encouraged debates about the models AIGFP was using and the trades being made. According to Lewis (2009), in contrast to Savage, Cassano stifled debate and intimidated those who expressed

---

[12]In 2003, the volume of subprime mortgages was less than $100 billion. Between June 2004 and June 2007, the volume of subprime loans increased to $1.6 trillion and Alt-A loans (limited-documentation loans) increased to $1.2 trillion.

views he did not share. Cassano was not a trained mathematician. His academic background was in political science, and he spent most of his career in the back office doing operations. Lewis reports that his reputation at AIGFP was that of someone who had a crude feel for financial risk and a strong tendency to bully people who challenged him. One of his colleagues said of him, "The way you dealt with Joe was to start everything by saying, 'You're right, Joe'" (Lewis 2009). When the issue of a shift toward taking more subprime mortgage risk eventually made its way onto a formal agenda, Cassano, pointing to the AAA ratings from Moody's and S&P, dismissed any concerns as overblown.

Eventually, Cassano did change his mind. It happened when he was persuaded to meet with a series of AIGFP's Wall Street trading partners to discuss the premises underlying the rating of CDO tranches based on subprime mortgages. Cassano learned that the main premise was that the historical default rate for the U.S. housing market would continue to apply in the future, a judgment consistent with conservatism bias. To his credit, Cassano did not accept the premise, and at the end of 2005, AIGFP ceased its CDS trades.

AIGFP's decision to stop insuring mortgage defaults did not stop Wall Street firms from continuing to create CDOs based on subprime mortgages. It did force Wall Street firms to bear some of the default risk, however, that AIGFP had previously borne. That outcome is a major reason Merrill Lynch, Morgan Stanley, Lehman Brothers, and Bear Stearns took the losses they did.

In August 2007, in a conference call to investors, Cassano made the following statement: "It is hard for us, without being flippant, to even see a scenario within any kind of realm of reason that would see us losing $1 on any of those transactions" (Lewis 2009). Major surprises are the hallmark of overconfidence. Cassano apparently based his statement on the fact that the subprime mortgages that were beginning to default had originated in 2006 and 2007, which were riskier years for mortgage issuance than 2004 and 2005, the years in which AIGFP had taken its CDS positions. The CDS contracts on which Cassano had signed off stipulated, however, that AIG would post collateral if its credit rating were downgraded. As it happens, AIG's credit rating did come to be downgraded, in September 2008 from AA to A, thereby triggering calls for collateral that AIG was unable to meet.

Incentives and Governance at AIGFP. Poor incentives were not the problem at AIGFP, which balanced long-term against short-term results. To its credit, AIGFP required that employees leave 50 percent of their bonuses in the firm, a policy that skewed their incentive toward the long run.[13] As for Cassano, in 2007, he was paid $38 million in total, but he left almost all of that amount ($36.75

---

[13]When AIG collapsed, employees lost more than $500 million of their own money.

million) in the firm. Clearly, he had a strong financial incentive to maximize the long-term value of AIG. His decisions destroyed value at AIG, however, and nearly brought down the firm.

Why did Cassano behave in ways that seem highly irrational? The reason is that when it comes to behaving rationally, psychological pitfalls can trump incentives. Good governance involves more than structuring good incentives.

A host of additional governance questions can be raised about AIG. Why did AIGFP's board of directors agree to appoint someone with Cassano's temperament to head the division? How thoroughly did the executives at the parent firm monitor Cassano's actions? To what extent did the resignation of AIG CEO Hank Greenberg in March 2005 make a difference to the risks assumed by the firm as a whole?

Most of these questions are difficult to answer. We do know that Greenberg, who had run AIG since 1968, was known for being a diligent monitor. His successor, Edward Liddy, lacked Greenberg's deep understanding of the firm. For the six-month period preceding the bailout, the firm had neither a full-time chief financial officer nor a chief risk assessment officer and was engaged in a search for both. As a result, in the period leading up to the bailout, the executives of the 18th-largest firm in the world had no clear sense of their firm's exposure to subprime mortgage risk.

Narvik

At the end of the supply chain for the financial products in this story are the investors who purchased and held the complex securities at the heart of the tale. Narvik, Norway, population 17,000 and located above the Arctic Circle, is just such an investor. It was featured in a February 2009 CNBC documentary titled "House of Cards," which explored issues surrounding the financial crisis.[14] Narvik had been losing population and its tax base. To address the issue, its local council invested $200 million in a series of complex securities that included CDOs. The purchase of the CDOs was part of a larger strategy in which the town took out a loan, using as collateral future revenues from its hydroelectric plant, and invested the proceeds in complex securities with the intent of capturing the spread. Narvik ended up losing $35 million, roughly a quarter of its annual budget.

Two main psychological features tie the situation in Narvik to the discussion in previous sections. First, given the decline in population and tax revenues, the council members in Narvik quite plausibly exhibited reference point–induced risk-seeking behavior. They were fiduciary managers of cash flows derived from their hydroelectric plant, but because money and population were higher in the past, they swapped those monies for what they hoped would be higher cash flows from U.S. mortgages and municipal bond payments.

---

[14] A video of the program is available at www.cnbc.com/id/28892719.

Second, the mayor of Narvik at the time, Karen Kuvaas, insists that the council members were not naive, but in this respect, she might have been overconfident; she also admits that she did not read the prospectus before signing off on the deal and was not aware that if some of the securities declined in value, Narvik would have to post payments. In defense of the council, Kuvaas indicated that the securities they purchased were represented to them as AAA rated and, therefore, as very safe.

The lesson here is that fiduciaries or other agents who may be knowledgeable enough in one set of circumstances may be way over their heads in another. One should always be on the lookout to see if one is falling prey to overconfidence.

The SEC

The SEC came under intense criticism for its lax oversight of investment banking practices and for failing to detect a large hedge fund Ponzi scheme run by Bernard Madoff.

A focal point of the criticism of investment bank oversight involved a meeting that took place at the SEC on 28 April 2004, when the commission was chaired by William Donaldson. That meeting established the Consolidated Supervised Entities (CSE) program, a voluntary regulatory program that allowed the SEC to review the capital structure and risk management procedures of participating financial institutions. Five investment banks joined the CSE program, as did two bank holding companies. The investment banks were Bear Stearns, Goldman Sachs, Lehman Brothers, Merrill Lynch, and Morgan Stanley, and the bank holding companies were Citigroup and JPMorgan Chase.

As part of the CSE program, the SEC agreed to a change in elements of the net capital rule, which limited the leverage of broker/dealer subsidiaries. Some analysts have suggested that this change led the CSE participants to increase their leverage—from approximately 12:1 to ratios exceeding 30:1—thereby greatly magnifying the losses these institutions later incurred on their subprime mortgage positions (Labaton 2008; Coffee 2008).

Prior to 2004, the SEC had limited authority to oversee investment banks. In 2004, the European Union passed a rule permitting the SEC's European counterpart to oversee the risk of both broker/dealers and their parent holding companies. This change could have meant that the European divisions of U.S. financial institutions would be regulated by European agencies, but the European Union agreed to waive regulatory oversight by its own agencies if equivalent oversight was provided by the host countries' agencies. This policy is what led the SEC to institute the CSE program, although the SEC required that the entities be large firms, firms with capital of at least $5 billion. Indeed, U.S investment banks, anxious to avoid European oversight, lobbied the SEC for the change.

The change to the net capital rule made it consistent with the Basel II standards. The key feature of the change was an alteration in the way net capital is measured. Prior to the change, net capital was measured by financial statement variables and was subject to formulaic discounts ("haircuts") to adjust for risk. The main change to the rule replaced the formulaic approach with discounts derived from the risk management models in use at the financial institutions.

Controversy surrounds the impact associated with the change to the net capital rule. The *New York Times* first reported the change to the rule (Labaton 2008), and this report was subsequently echoed by academics (e.g., Coffee 2008). The coverage by the *New York Times* might have been misleading, however, in that it suggested that this change allowed the leverage levels at parent holding companies to grow from 15 to above 30, thereby exacerbating faulty decisions about subprime mortgages. The SEC maintains that the change in provisions of the net capital rule applied to broker/dealer subsidiaries and had no discernible impact on the degree of leverage of the parent holding companies. Sirri (2009) argued that the change in the net capital rule left the same leverage limits in place and changed only the manner in which net capital is measured.[15]

Perhaps the most important feature of the CSE program was the SEC's failure to provide effective oversight of the risk profiles at the financial institutions in question. Consider the following remarks by Coffee (2008):

> Basel II contemplated close monitoring and supervision by regulators. Thus, the Federal Reserve assigns members of its staff to maintain an office within a regulated bank holding company in order to provide constant oversight. In the case of the SEC, a team of only three SEC staffers were [sic] assigned to each CSE firm (and a total of only 13 individuals comprised the SEC's Office of Prudential Supervision and Risk Analysis that oversaw and conducted this monitoring effort). From the start, it was a mismatch: three SEC staffers to oversee an investment bank the size of Merrill Lynch, which could easily afford to hire scores of highly quantitative economists and financial analysts, implied that the SEC was simply outgunned.

Planning at the SEC. Did the SEC display overconfidence in its planning process for the CSE program? Perhaps. Evidence suggesting overconfidence can be observed in the following two excerpts from the transcript of the 28 April

---

[15]The purpose of the net capital rule is not to limit overall leverage at financial institutions, so the rule did not impose leverage restrictions on parent holding companies. The rule's purpose is to provide protection of such assets as consumer receivables in case of liquidation by a broker/dealer. Indeed, leverage ratios for the major investment banks during the late 1990s averaged 27, well above the maximum ratio associated with the net capital rule.

2004 meeting. In the excerpt, Harvey Goldschmid, who was an SEC commissioner at the time, directs a question to an SEC staffer:[16]

> Harvey Goldschmid: We've talked a lot about this. This is going to be much more complicated—compliance, inspection, understanding of risk—than we've ever had to do. Mike, I trust you no end. But I take it you think we can do this?
>
> Group: [Laughter.]
>
> Mike: Well we've hired Matt Eichler and other folks as well who are skilled in quantitative analysis. They're both PhDs right now. And we've hired other people as well who are quantitatively skilled. So we're going to continue to develop that staff. And then we have a good accounting staff as well. And then our auditors in New York, as well as in Washington will be useful in this process.
>
> I mean, so we're going to have to depend on the firms, obviously. They're frontline. They're going to have to develop their entire risk framework. We'll be reading that first. And they'll have to explain that to us in a way that makes sense. And then we'll do the examinations of that process. In addition to approving their models and their risk control systems.
>
> It's a large undertaking. I'm not going to try to do it alone.
>
> Group: [Laughter.]

The two instances of group laughter in the above excerpt mark points at which "Mike" might have exhibited overconfidence about his ability to oversee risk management at seven major financial institutions with combined assets of about $4 trillion with the help of only two PhDs, some additional quantitatively oriented personnel, and agency accountants and auditors.[17]

Consider a second excerpt involving Goldschmid and Annette Nazareth, who at the time was the SEC director of the Division of Market Regulation. Their interchange is particularly interesting in light of the later collapse of Bear Stearns, Lehman Brothers, and Merrill Lynch:

> Goldschmid: We've said these are the big guys but that means if anything goes wrong, it's going to be an awfully big mess.
>
> Group: [Laughter.]

---

[16]An audio file of the relevant portion of the SEC meeting is available at www.nytimes.com/2008/10/03/business/03sec.html. Transcripts of open meetings of the SEC can be accessed at www.sec.gov/news/openmeetings.shtml.

[17]The audio contains information (especially about what the laughter signifies) that does not come across in the written transcript. In the first instance, the laughter comes as a response to the contrast between Goldschmid's remark about trusting staff and his question, including tone of voice, about the staff being capable of performing the task. The second instance of laughter comes in response to Mike's humorous statement that he will not be doing the task alone. Notably, he is serious when he describes the resources he envisages being allocated to the task. In my view, the group laughter in the second instance does not reflect doubt that the SEC staff was capable of performing the task or doubt that the resources described were woefully inadequate.

Annette Nazareth: Again, we have very broad discretionary.... As we mentioned, we're going to be meeting with these firms on a monthly basis. And hopefully from month to month you don't see wild swings. Among other things, we can require firms to put in additional capital, to keep additional capital against the risks. We can actually—the commission has the authority to limit their ability to engage in certain businesses, just as any prudent regulator would. We have hopefully a lot of early warnings and the ability to constrict activity that we think is problematic.

Goldschmid: I think you've been very good at thinking this through carefully and working this through with skill ....

The deliberations to establish the CSE program lasted less than an hour. The vote by the SEC was unanimous. Little probing for weaknesses in such a far-reaching proposal occurred. I suggest that overconfidence and confirmation bias were high. This kind of setting is where groupthink thrives.

Goldschmid left the commission in 2005. In an October 2008 interview with the *New York Times*, he reflected: "In retrospect, the tragedy is that the 2004 rule making gave us the ability to get information that would have been critical to sensible monitoring, and yet the SEC didn't oversee well enough" (Labaton 2008). I suggest that this recollection indicates that Goldschmid was overconfident in 2004.

Although Goldschmid was apparently overconfident at that time, other forces that led to weak oversight were also at work. In April 2004, when Goldschmid was serving as one of the commissioners, the SEC was chaired by Donaldson, but in 2005, Christopher Cox replaced Donaldson. Cox was generally regarded as favoring weaker regulations, which might explain why so few resources were allocated to the CSE program. In February 2009, Linda Thomsen, the director of enforcement at the SEC, resigned under pressure. It was on her watch that Wall Street investment banks made disastrous risk management decisions and the Ponzi scheme conducted by Madoff went undetected. In describing her resignation, the press noted that she should not have to bear the entire blame for these failures because Cox set the tone, including public criticism of SEC staff, for weak regulatory oversight.

Madoff and Behavioral Pitfalls at the SEC. According to an internal report by the SEC (2009), between 1992 and 2008, the agency received six distinct complaints about Madoff's operations, one of which involved three versions. Several of the complaints suggested that Madoff was running a Ponzi scheme. The report reveals that the SEC conducted investigations and examinations related to Madoff's investment advisory business but failed to uncover the fraud.

I suggest that confirmation bias lay at the heart of the SEC's failure to detect Madoff's Ponzi scheme. An excerpt from the SEC's internal report follows.[18] As

---

[18]The SEC's internal report rejects the possibility that political influence played a part in the SEC's failure to detect the Madoff fraud. Rather, it focuses the blame squarely on the judgment calls of agency investigators and staff.

you read through the excerpt, keep in mind that a person exhibits confirmation bias when he or she overweights information that confirms a view or hypothesis and underweights information that disconfirms the view or hypothesis. The report states:

> The OIG investigation found the SEC conducted two investigations and three examinations related to Madoff's investment advisory business based upon the detailed and credible complaints that raised the possibility that Madoff was misrepresenting his trading and could have been operating a Ponzi scheme. Yet, at no time did the SEC ever verify Madoff's trading through an independent third-party, and in fact, never actually conducted a Ponzi scheme examination or investigation of Madoff.

> In the examination of Madoff, the SEC did not seek Depository Trust Company (DTC) (an independent third-party) records, but sought copies of such records from Madoff himself. Had they sought records from DTC, there is an excellent chance that they would have uncovered Madoff's Ponzi scheme in 1992.

> The teams assembled were relatively inexperienced, and there was insufficient planning for the examinations. The scopes of the examination were in both cases too narrowly focused on the possibility of front-running, with no significant attempts made to analyze the numerous red flags about Madoff's trading and returns . . . .

> The investigation that arose from the most detailed complaint provided to the SEC, which explicitly stated it was "highly likely" that "Madoff was operating a Ponzi scheme," never really investigated the possibility of a Ponzi scheme. The relatively inexperienced Enforcement staff failed to appreciate the significance of the analysis in the complaint, and almost immediately expressed skepticism and disbelief. Most of their investigation was directed at determining whether Madoff should register as an investment adviser or whether Madoff's hedge fund investors' disclosures were adequate.

> As with the examinations, the Enforcement staff almost immediately caught Madoff in lies and misrepresentations, but failed to follow up on inconsistencies. They rebuffed offers of additional evidence from the complainant, and were confused about certain critical and fundamental aspects of Madoff's operations. When Madoff provided evasive or contradictory answers to important questions in testimony, they simply accepted as plausible his explanations.

> Although the Enforcement staff made attempts to seek information from independent third-parties, they failed to follow up on these requests. They reached out to the NASD [now, FINRA, the Financial Industry Regulatory Authority] and asked for information on whether Madoff had options positions on a certain date, but when they received a report that there were in fact no options positions on that date, they did not take any further steps. An Enforcement staff attorney made several attempts to obtain documentation from European counterparties (another independent third-party), and although a letter was drafted, the Enforcement staff decided not to send it. Had any of these efforts been fully executed, they would have led to Madoff's Ponzi scheme being uncovered. (pp. 23–25)

People who succumb to confirmation bias test hypotheses by searching for information that confirms the hypothesis they are testing. The antidote to confirmation bias is to search for information that *disconfirms* the hypothesis, to ask whether the hypothesis is untrue, a lie. What the SEC report strongly indicates is that its staff members actively avoided seeking disconfirming information to their view that Madoff was innocent of running a Ponzi scheme.

Confirmation bias was not the only psychological pitfall afflicting the SEC in connection with its investigations of Madoff. An incentive issue was also involved in respect to the way the SEC rewarded investigators. Nocera (2009) pointed out that the SEC bases its success on quantitative measures, such as the number of actions it brings and the number of cases it settles. He suggests that through its choice of standards and incentives, the SEC tends to pursue small cases, cases in which those being investigated will prefer to settle and pay a fine even if they are innocent. Madoff was not a small case.

Reference point–induced risk seeking was also a factor. Nocera indicated that the SEC finds it difficult to shut cases down once they have been initiated. Such behavior is throwing good money after bad, a phenomenon technically known as "escalation of commitment." Nocera stated:

> Even if the facts start to look shaky, the internal dynamics of the agency push its lawyers to either settle or go to trial, but never to abandon it. [quoting] "The staff has a real problem persuading the commission to cut off a case once it has begun."[19]

Given the SEC's limited resources, the costs of escalation of commitment can be very high.

In addition to confirmation bias and escalation of commitment, the SEC also exhibited poor information sharing. In this regard, the SEC report relates that the agency was unaware that it was running separate examinations out of two offices. The report states:

> Astoundingly, both examinations were open at the same time in different offices without either knowing the other one was conducting an identical examination. In fact, it was Madoff himself who informed one of the examination teams that the other examination team had already received the information they were seeking from him. (SEC 2009, p. 24)

Discussion and Conclusion

Opinions about the root cause of the financial crisis differ. Some argue that the root lies with a weak regulatory structure, within which private-sector decisions were largely rational. Others argue that the root lies with irrational decisions associated with the occurrence of a housing market bubble, a surge in subprime mortgage

---

[19]The person Nocera quoted is John A. Sten, a former SEC lawyer who represented a former Morgan Stanley broker whom the SEC prosecuted unsuccessfully for almost a decade.

lending, and the breakdown of the rational lemons paradigm. Still others blame poor corporate governance, explicit corruption, and unwise governmental mandates and guarantees. Differentiating among these various views requires a search for the devil in the details.

The details considered here involve five cases, all of which highlight (to a greater or lesser degree) irrational decision making at key points in the financial product supply chain. Consider decisions made at AIG. AIG facilitated the explosive growth in subprime mortgage lending in 2004 and 2005 by selling CDS that insured against default. AIG's financial product division irrationally failed to track the proportion of subprime mortgages in the pools being insured, thereby misgauging the risk of those assets and causing the associated CDS to be mispriced. Interestingly, this failure occurred despite incentives that balanced long-term performance against short-term performance. Moreover, conversations that AIG had with its trading partners indicate the presence of a widespread conservatism bias regarding the assumption that historical mortgage default rates would continue to apply.

Similarly, the UBS investment banking division admitted to misgauging subprime mortgage risk by not "looking through" the CDO structures and by assuming that historical default rates would continue to apply. UBS's underperformance relative to competitors led it to exhibit reference point–induced risk seeking. This behavior was compounded by poor incentive structures at UBS that emphasized short-term performance over long-term performance.

Recall that UBS placed no operational limits on the size of its CDO warehouse. It was not alone. Investment banks are typically intermediaries, not end investors planning to hold large positions in subprime mortgages. Some hold the equity tranches of CDOs as a signal to the buyers of the less risky tranches. What created many of the losses for investment banks, however, was inventory risk—risk stemming from warehousing the subprime positions that underlay CDOs. As the housing market fell into decline, many investment banks found that they could not find buyers for the CDOs and, as a result, inadvertently became end investors.

The rating agencies and investors' reliance on them played a huge role in the financial crisis. Both (supposedly) sophisticated investors, such as the investment bankers at UBS, and naive end investors, such as the Narvik town council, relied on the risk assessments of rating agencies. The rating agencies, however, explicitly indicated that their ratings were premised on accepting the information they received as accurate, even if the mortgages featured limited documentation. For this reason, the agencies suggested that their ratings be treated as only one piece of information when assessing risk. By this argument, users who accepted their ratings at face value behaved irrationally.

Did the rating agencies exhibit irrational behavior by weakening their risk assessment criteria to cultivate more business? This question is different from asking whether the ratings agencies behaved ethically. The major problem with the behavior of rating agencies might arise more from a conflict of interests (the principal–agent conflict) than irrationality, in the sense that the issuers of securities, not the end investors in the securities, pay for ratings. Still, the evidence suggests that reference point–induced risk seeking and groupthink were issues at S&P.

In addition to the five entities highlighted here, many others participated in the financial product supply chain. For example, press coverage suggests that the value-destructive dynamics at UBS were also at work at other financial institutions active in initiating subprime mortgages and in creating CDOs that included subprime mortgages (see Shefrin 2009).

In 2004 and 2005, the activities of these financial institutions might have been rational because they were able to shift default risk to AIG by purchasing CDS. Lewis (2009) quoted AIG employees as stating that their firm's willingness to sell CDS allowed the CDO market to grow at a rapid rate. After AIG stopped selling CDS, however, many financial firms took on the risk themselves, apparently under the illusion that housing prices would continue to rise and that default rates would not be affected by the increased ratio of subprime to prime mortgages. At one point, Merrill Lynch used CDS to create synthetic CDOs because the number of subprime mortgages available to create traditional CDOs was insufficient relative to the firm's aspirations.

The financial crisis also raises issues involving being "too big to fail" and moral hazard. Some might argue that the root of the financial crisis was a rational response by executives of large financial institutions to the perception that they could take on excessive risk because the U.S. government would intervene should those risks prove disastrous. To be sure, the executives must have been aware of such a possibility. The management failures at these institutions bore the telltale signs, however, of psychological pitfalls. In addition, a sign that intervention was not guaranteed came with the government's choice to let Lehman Brothers fail.

Not only was the SEC subject to confirmation bias, but also I believe overconfidence might have pervaded the entire regulatory landscape. Consider the comments of Alan Greenspan, who chaired the Federal Reserve during the key years in which the seeds of the crisis were sown. In June 2005, Greenspan testified before Congress that some local housing markets exhibited "froth." He pointed to the use of risky financing by some homeowners and suggested that the price increases in those local markets were unsustainable. He concluded, however, that there was no national housing bubble and that the economy was not at risk.[20] In the same vein, Greenspan's successor at the Fed, Ben Bernanke, gave a speech on

---

[20]Under Greenspan, in the recession that followed the bursting of the dot-com bubble, the Federal Reserve cut interest rates to 1 percent. Some have criticized the Fed for keeping interest rates too low for too long, thereby encouraging the dramatic increase in mortgage volume. See www.federalreserve.gov/BOARDDOCS/TESTIMONY/2005/200506092/default.htm.

17 May 2007 in which he stated, "[W]e do not expect significant spillovers from the subprime market to the rest of the economy or to the financial system."[21]

In 2008, Greenspan testified before the House of Representatives Committee on Oversight and Government Reform as follows:

[T]his crisis, however, has turned out to be much broader than anything I could have imagined . . . . Those of us who have looked to the self-interest of lending institutions to protect shareholders' equity—myself especially—are in a state of shocked disbelief. (Felsenthal 2008)

Consider the behavioral issues raised by Greenspan's comment about self-interest. Lending institutions are not masochists. The behavioral point is that psychological pitfalls created a gap between perceived self-interest and objective self-interest, thereby inducing irrational decisions.

Most parties involved in the financial crisis are asking what they can learn from the experience. Under the leadership of the SEC's new enforcement chief, Robert Khuzami, the SEC is instituting a series of new procedures, such as providing senior enforcement officers the power to issue subpoenas without requesting permission from commissioners. UBS has created a presentation titled "Risk Management and Controls at UBS." The presentation emphasizes that managers must pay explicit attention to a series of behavioral issues, such as irrational exuberance in asset pricing.

These steps are in the right direction. A body of academic literature describes how organizations can take steps to avoid behavioral pitfalls (see Heath, Larrick, and Klayman 1998), but dealing with psychological pitfalls is not easy. The application of behavioral corporate finance and behavioral asset-pricing theory is not yet widespread. Moreover, little evidence indicates that organizations have developed systematic procedures along these lines.

The most useful behavioral lessons we can learn from the crisis are how to restructure processes to incorporate the explicit elements of behavioral corporate finance that this article has discussed. I have suggested that to avoid the kinds of process weaknesses exemplified by the five cases described here, systematic procedures within organizations should focus on the four key organizational processes listed in Exhibit 1: planning, standards, information sharing, and incentives (Shefrin 2008b).[22] Checklists are no panacea, but they do make the issue of vulnerability an explicit agenda item.

Still, the removal of psychological biases is not easy. Psychological pitfalls are likely to persist and to continue to affect decisions. For this reason, managers, analysts, investors, and regulators would be well advised to keep three main points

---

[21]The speech was given at the Federal Reserve Bank of Chicago's 43rd Annual Conference on Bank Structure and Competition held in Chicago. See www.federalreserve.gov/newsevents/speech/bernanke20070517a.htm.

[22]Only a thumbnail sketch of the approach can be provided here; for the detailed approach, see Shefrin (2008b).

in mind. First, sentiment can affect asset pricing, particularly pricing of the securities of companies followed by analysts. Second, corporate managers are vulnerable to psychological biases (as we all are); therefore, these pitfalls are germane to companies' operational risks. Third, analysts themselves are vulnerable to psychological pitfalls and need to be mindful of how these pitfalls affect their own processes and decisions.

For example, consider what analysts might have missed about Citigroup before October 2007. Were Citigroup and AIG connected? In this regard, consider the CDS deals that AIGFP did in 2004 and 2005. Lewis (2009) quoted an AIGFP trader as saying, "We were doing every single deal with every single Wall Street firm, except Citigroup. Citigroup decided it liked the risk and kept it on their books. We took all the rest" (p. 1).

This remark should hold a lesson for analysts about applying tools from behavioral corporate finance. For example, analysts might use the framework encapsulated by Exhibit 1 to focus on the combination of process and psychological pitfalls in a situation. In the case of Citigroup, analysts could have focused on Citigroup's planning process in late 2004 and early 2005, when it was dealing with flagging profit growth. In that situation, Citigroup would have been especially vulnerable to reference point–based risk seeking. Indeed, Citigroup's board did decide to increase the firm's risk exposure after a presentation from a consultant, thereby taking a path similar to that of UBS.

Although analysts have no direct access to boardroom discussions, keeping the quality of governance in mind can be worthwhile. Consider whether Citigroup's board exhibited groupthink. In a *Wall Street Journal* article about Citigroup board member Robert Rubin, Brown and Enrich (2008) stated, "Colleagues deferred to him, as the only board member with experience as a trader or risk manager. 'I knew what a CDO was,' Mr. Rubin said" (p. 1).

As the cases discussed in this article attest, assuming that financial institutions will make intelligent, bias-free risk–reward decisions is a mistake. Looking back after the crisis unfolded, Brown and Enrich (2008) quoted Rubin as saying about Citigroup's decision to take on more risk, "It gave room to do more, assuming you're doing intelligent risk–reward decisions" (p. 1). Learning that decision makers have psychological biases is an important lesson, not just for analysts but for everyone. Moreover, the lesson applies at all times, a point to keep in mind even as economic conditions improve and the financial crisis that erupted in 2007–2008 fades into memory.

I thank Mark Lawrence for his insightful comments about UBS; Marc Heerkens from UBS; participants at seminars I gave at the University of Lugano and at the University of California, Los Angeles; and participants in the Executive Master of Science in Risk Management program at the Amsterdam Institute of Finance, a program cosponsored with New York University. I also express my appreciation to Rodney Sullivan, CFA, and Larry Siegel for their comments on previous drafts.

REFERENCES

Akerlof, George, and Robert Shiller. 2009. *Animal Spirits: How Human Psychology Drives the Economy, and Why It Matters for Global Capitalism.* Princeton, NJ: Princeton University Press.

Berman, David. 2009. "In Defence of a 'Sell' Analyst." *Globe and Mail* (10 April): http://pulse.alacra.com/analyst-comments/Portales_Partners-F594.

Bhardwaj, Geetesh, and Rajdeep Sengupta. 2008a. "Where's the Smoking Gun? A Study of Underwriting Standards for US Subprime Mortgages." Federal Reserve Bank of St. Louis, Working Paper 2008-036B.

———. 2008b. "Did Prepayments Sustain the Subprime Market?" Federal Reserve Bank of St. Louis, Working Paper 2008-039B.

Brown, Ken, and David Enrich. 2008. "Rubin, under Fire, Defends His Role at Citi—'Nobody Was Prepared' for Crisis of '08." *Wall Street Journal* (29 November): http://online.wsj.com/article/SB122791795940965645.html.

Chomsisengphet, Souphala, and Anthony Pennington-Cross. 2006. "The Evolution of the Subprime Mortgage Market." *Federal Reserve Bank of St. Louis Review*, vol. 88, no. 1 (January/February):31–56.

Coffee, John C., Jr. 2008. "Analyzing the Credit Crisis: Was the SEC Missing in Action?" *New York Law Journal* (5 December): www.law.com/jsp/ihc/PubArticleIHC.jsp?id=1202426495544.

Eggert, Kurt. 2009. "The Great Collapse: How Securitization Caused the Subprime Meltdown." *Connecticut Law Review*, vol. 41, no. 4 (May):1257–1312.

El-Erian, Mohamed. 2008. *When Markets Collide: Investment Strategies for the Age of Global Economic Change.* New York: McGraw-Hill.

Felsenthal, Mark. 2008. "Moment of Crisis Could Test Fed's Independence." Reuters (23 October): www.reuters.com/article/companyNewsAndPR/idUSN2338704220081023.

Heath, Chip, Richard P. Larrick, and Joshua Klayman. 1998. "Cognitive Repairs: How Organizational Practices Can Compensate for Individual Shortcomings." *Research in Organizational Behavior*, vol. 20:1–37.

Kahneman, Daniel, and Amos Tversky. 1979. "Prospect Theory: An Analysis of Decision Making under Risk." *Econometrica*, vol. 47, no. 2 (March):263–291.

Labaton, Stephen. 2008. "The Reckoning: Agency's '04 Rule Let Banks Pile Up New Debt." *New York Times* (2 October): www.nytimes.com/2008/10/03/business/03sec.html.

Lewis, Michael. 2009. "The Man Who Crashed the World." *Vanity Fair* (August):98–103.

Lopes, Lola. 1987. "Between Hope and Fear: The Psychology of Risk." *Advances in Experimental Social Psychology*, vol. 20:255–295.

Lucchetti, Aaron. 2008a, "McGraw Scion Grapples With S&P's Woes—Chairman Helped Set Tone in Profit Push as Ratings Firms Feasted on New Products." *Wall Street Journal* (2 August).

———. 2008b. "S&P Email: 'We Should Not Be Rating It'." *Wall Street Journal* (2 August):B1.

Nocera, Joe. 2009. "Chasing Small Fry, S.E.C. Let Madoff Get Away." *New York Times* (26 June): www.nytimes.com/2009/06/27/business/27nocera.html.

Piskorski, Tomasz, Amit Seru, and Vikrant Vig. 2009. "Securitization and Distressed Loan Renegotiation: Evidence from the Subprime Mortgage Crisis." Working paper, Columbia University.

Posner, Richard A. 2009a. *A Failure of Capitalism: The Crisis of '08 and the Descent into Depression.* Cambridge, MA: Harvard University Press.

———. 2009b. "Shorting Reason." *New Republic,* vol. 240, no. 6 (15 April):30–33.

President's Working Group on Financial Markets. 2008. (March): www.ustreas.gov/press/releases/reports/pwgpolicystatemktturmoil_03122008.pdf.

SEC. 2009. Office of Investigations. "Investigation of Failure of the SEC to Uncover Bernard Madoff's Ponzi Scheme: Public Version," Report No. OIG-509, Securities and Exchange Commission (31 August).

Shefrin, Hersh. 2005. *Behavioral Corporate Finance.* Burr Ridge, IL: McGraw-Hill/Irwin.

———. 2008a. *A Behavioral Approach to Asset Pricing:* Boston: Elsevier.

———. 2008b. *Ending the Management Illusion.* New York: McGraw-Hill.

———. 2009. "Ending the Management Illusion: Preventing Another Financial Crisis." *Ivey Business Journal,* vol. 73, no. 1 (January/February).

Shefrin, Hersh, and Meir Statman. 1985. "The Disposition to Sell Winners Too Early and Ride Losers Too Long: Theory and Evidence." *Journal of Finance,* vol. 40, no. 3 (July):777–790.

Sirri, Erik. 2009. "Securities Markets and Regulatory Reform." Speech given at the National Economists Club, Washington, DC (9 April).

Smith, Elliot Blair. 2008. "'Race to Bottom' at Moody's, S&P Secured Subprime's Boom, Bust." *Bloomberg* (25 September): www.bloomberg.com/apps/news?pid=20601109&sid=ax3vfya_Vtdo.

Sullivan, Rodney. 2009. "Governance: Travel and Destinations." *Financial Analysts Journal,* vol. 65, no. 4 (July/August):6–10.

UBS. 2008. "Shareholder Report on UBS Writedowns." Accessed at www.ubs.com/1/ShowMedia/investors/agm?contentId=140333&name=080418ShareholderReport.pdf on 16 July 2008.

The Shadow Banking System and Hyman Minsky's Economic Journey

Paul McCulley

Managing Director
Pacific Investment Management Company LLC
Newport Beach, California

As we look for answers to the current financial crisis, it is clear that creative financing played a massive role in propelling the global financial system to hazy new heights—before it led the way into the depths of a systemic crisis. But how did financing get so creative? It did not happen within the confines of a regulated banking system, which submits to strict regulatory requirements in exchange for the safety of government backstopping. Instead, financing got so creative through the rise of a "shadow banking system," which operated legally yet almost completely outside the realm of bank regulation. The rise of this system drove one of the biggest lending booms in history, and its collapse resulted in one of the most crushing financial crises we have ever seen.

Perhaps the most lucid framework for understanding this progression comes from the work of Hyman Minsky, the mid-20th-century U.S. economist whose theory on the nature of financial instability proved unnervingly prescient in explaining the rise and fall of shadow banking—and the dizzying journey of the global financial system over the past several years.

Nature and Origin of the Shadow Banking System

I coined the term "shadow banking system" in August 2007 at the U.S. Federal Reserve's (Fed's) annual symposium in Jackson Hole, Wyoming. Unlike conventional regulated banks, unregulated shadow banks fund themselves with uninsured short-term funding, which may or may not be backstopped by liquidity lines from real banks. Because they fly below the radar of traditional bank regulation, these levered-up intermediaries operate in the shadows without backstopping from the Fed's discount lending window or access to FDIC (Federal Deposit Insurance Corporation) deposit insurance.

The allure of shadow banking over the last decade or so is unambiguous: There is no better way for bankers to maximally leverage the inherent banking model (of borrowing cheap and lending rich) than by becoming nonbank bankers, or shadow bankers. And they did this in droves, running leveraged lending and investment institutions known as investment banks, conduits, structured investment vehicles, and hedge funds.[1] They did so by raising funding in the nondeposit markets, notably unsecured debt—such as interbank borrowing and commercial paper—and secured borrowing—such as reverse repurchase agreements (repo) and asset-backed commercial paper. And usually, but not always, such shadow banks maintained a reliance on conventional banks (those with access to the Fed's window) by securing lines of credit with these latter banks.

Shadow Banking's Relationship with Regulators and Rating Agencies

Because shadow banks do not have access to the same governmental safety nets that real banks do, they do not have to operate under meaningful regulatory constraints, notably regarding the amount of leverage they can use, the size of their liquidity buffers, and the types of lending and investing they can do. To be sure, shadow banking needed some seal of approval so that providers of short-dated funding could convince themselves that their claims were de facto "just as good" as deposits at banks with access to the government's liquidity safety nets. Conveniently, the friendly faces at the credit rating agencies, paid by the shadow bankers, stood at the ready to provide such seals of approval. Moody's and S&P would put an A-1/P-1 rating on the commercial paper, which, in turn, would be bought by money market funds. Of course, it is inherently an unstable structure. The rating agencies have a legitimate problem of putting ratings on innovative securities: The agencies have not had a chance to observe a historical track record on these securities—to see their performance over a full cycle.

The bottom line is that the shadow banking system created explosive growth in leverage and liquidity risk outside the purview of the Fed. And it was all grand while ever-larger application of leverage put upward pressure on asset prices. There is nothing like a bull market to make geniuses out of levered dunces.

Shadow Banking vs. Conventional Banking

Despite the extraordinary Keynesian public life-support system under way that was born out of the necessity to keep banks (and capitalism as a going concern) alive, capitalist economies usually want their banking systems owned by the private sector. As private companies, banks make loans and investments on commercial terms in the pursuit of profit, but also in the context of prudential regulation to minimize the downside to taxpayers of the moral hazard inherent in the two safety nets (FDIC deposit insurance and the Fed's discount window). But, as is the wont of capitalists, they love leveraging the sovereign's safety nets with minimal prudential regulation. This does not make them immoral, merely astute interpreters of the circumstances they face.

---

[1]This list is representative, not exhaustive.

Over the last three decades or so, the growth of "banking" outside formal, sovereign-regulated banking has exploded, and it was a great gig as long as the public bought the notion that such funding instruments were "just as good" as bank deposits.

Keynes provides the essential—and existential—answer to why the shadow banking system became so large, the unraveling of which lies at the root of the current global financial system crisis. It was a belief in what appeared to be a historical truth, undergirded by the length of time that the supposed truth held: Shadow bank liabilities were viewed as "just as good" as conventional bank deposits because they had, in fact, been just as good over any historical period that a prospective investor could observe. (That such a liability *could* default, and very well might under foreseeable future circumstances, was not in the historical track record, although it could have been discerned from analysis of the prospects for the items on the shadow bank's balance sheet.)

And the power of this conventional thinking was aided and abetted by both the sovereign and the sovereign-blessed rating agencies—until, of course, convention was turned on its head starting with a run on the asset-backed commercial paper (ABCP) market in August 2007, the near death of Bear Stearns in March 2008, the de facto nationalization of Fannie Mae and Freddie Mac in July 2008, and the actual death of Lehman Brothers in September 2008. Maybe, just maybe, there was and is something special about a real bank, as opposed to a shadow bank! And indeed that is unambiguously the case, as evidenced by the ongoing partial re-intermediation of the shadow banking system back into the sovereign-supported conventional banking system, as well as by the mad scramble by remaining shadow banks to convert themselves into conventional banks so as to eat at the same sovereign-subsidized capital and liquidity cafeteria as their former stodgy brethren.

Minsky and the Shadow Banking System

The shadow banking system, from its explosive growth to its calamitous collapse, followed a path that might have looked quite familiar to the economist Hyman Minsky. He passed away in 1996, but his teachings and writings echo today. Building from the work of many economists before him, most notably Keynes, Minsky articulated a theory on financial instability that describes in almost lurid detail what recently happened in the shadow banking system, the housing market, and the broader economy that brought us to the depths of financial crisis—and he published this theory in 1986. So, the first thing we do when we discuss Minsky is show reverence. He studied at Harvard and taught at Brown, Berkeley, and Washington University in St. Louis. After his retirement in 1990, he continued writing and lecturing with the Levy Institute, which now hosts an annual symposium in his honor.

Minsky may well have considered himself a Keynesian economist (he published his analysis and interpretation of Keynes in 1975), but Minsky's own theories headed off in a new direction. Keynes is arguably a solid place to start any adventure in economic theory. Remember that Keynes effectively invented the field of macroeconomics, which is founded on the proposition that what holds for the individual does not necessarily hold for a collection of individuals operating as an economic system. This principle is sometimes called the "fallacy of composition" and sometimes called the "paradox of aggregation." But we need not resort to fancy labels to define the common sense of macroeconomics. Anybody who has ever been a spectator at a crowded ball game has witnessed the difference between microeconomics and macroeconomics: From a micro perspective, it is rational for each individual to stand up to get a better view; but from a macro perspective, each individual acting rationally will produce the irrational outcome of everybody standing up but nobody having a better view.

The Financial Instability Hypothesis

Minsky took Keynes to the next level, and his huge contribution to macroeconomics comes under the label of the "financial instability hypothesis." Minsky openly declared that his hypothesis was "an interpretation of the substance of Keynes's *General Theory*." Minsky's key addendum to Keynes' work was really quite simple: provide a framework for distinguishing between stabilizing and destabilizing capitalist debt structures. Minsky summarized the hypothesis beautifully in 1992:

> Three distinct income-debt relations for economic units, which are labeled as hedge, speculative, and Ponzi finance, can be identified.
>
> Hedge financing units are those which can fulfill all of their contractual payment obligations by their cash flows: the greater the weight of equity financing in the liability structure, the greater the likelihood that the unit is a hedge financing unit.
>
> Speculative finance units are units that can meet their payment commitments on "income account" on their liabilities, even as they cannot repay the principal out of income cash flows. Such units need to "roll over" their liabilities (e.g., issue new debt to meet commitments on maturing debt)....
>
> For Ponzi units, the cash flows from operations are not sufficient to fulfill either the repayment of principal or the interest due on outstanding debts by their cash flows from operations. Such units can sell assets or borrow. Borrowing to pay interest or selling assets to pay interest (and even dividends) on common stock lowers the equity of a unit, even as it increases liabilities and the prior commitment of future incomes....
>
> It can be shown that if hedge financing dominates, then the economy may well be an equilibrium-seeking and -containing system. In contrast, the greater the weight of speculative and Ponzi finance, the greater the likelihood that the economy is a deviation-amplifying system. The first theorem of the financial instability hypothesis is that the economy has financing regimes under which it is stable, and financing regimes in which it is unstable. The second theorem of the financial instability hypothesis is that over periods of prolonged prosperity, the economy transits from financial relations that make for a stable system to financial relations that make for an unstable system.

In particular, over a protracted period of good times, capitalist economies tend to move from a financial structure dominated by hedge finance units to a structure in which there is large weight to units engaged in speculative and Ponzi finance. Furthermore, if an economy with a sizeable body of speculative financial units is in an inflationary state, and the authorities attempt to exorcise inflation by monetary constraint, then speculative units will become Ponzi units and the net worth of previously Ponzi units will quickly evaporate. Consequently, units with cash flow shortfalls will be forced to try to make position by selling out position. This is likely to lead to a collapse of asset values. (Minsky 1992, pp. 6–8)

Those three categories of debt units—hedge (note: no relation to hedge funds), speculative, and Ponzi—are the straws that stir the drink in Minsky's financial instability hypothesis. The essence of the hypothesis is that stability is destabilizing because capitalists, observing stability in the present, have a herding tendency to extrapolate the expectation of stability out into the indefinite future, putting in place ever-more risky debt structures, up to and including Ponzi units, that cause stability to be undermined.

The longer people make money by taking risk, the more imprudent they become in risk taking. While they are doing that, the expectation of a reward to risk taking is self-fulfilling on the way up. If everybody is simultaneously becoming more risk seeking, risk premiums shrink, the value of collateral goes up, the ability to lever increases, and the game keeps going. Human nature is inherently procyclical, and that is essentially what the Minsky thesis is all about. He says:

From time to time, capitalist economies exhibit inflations and debt deflations which seem to have the potential to spin out of control. In such processes the economic system's reactions to a movement of the economy amplify the movement—inflation feeds upon inflation and debt-deflation feeds upon debt-deflation. (Minsky 1992, p. 1)

This procyclical tendency applies to central banks and policymakers as well; I believe that having too much success in stabilizing goods and services inflation, while conducting an asymmetric reaction function to asset price inflation and deflation, can be dangerous. Yes, it can work for a time. But precisely because it can work for a time, it sows the seeds of its own demise. Or, as Minsky declared, stability is ultimately destabilizing because of the asset price and credit excesses that stability begets. Put differently, stability can never be a destination, only a journey to instability.

Minsky's hypothesis richly explains the endemic boom–bust cycles of capitalism, including the bursting of the bubbles in property prices, mortgage finance, and shadow banking that characterize the current bust. You may ask, why all these endemic boom–bust cycles? Is capitalism not driven by Adam Smith's invisible hand, where markets are efficient and always find just the right prices for things through what people like me call a "discovery process?" Well, much of the time that is right—but not all the time. Indeed, the most interesting, and profitable, times to be involved in investment management are when Smith's invisible hand is visibly broken. What Minsky's hypothesis did was to provide a framework for how and when Smith's hand would break.

Minsky's Economic Journey: Forward and Reverse

In Minsky's theory, economic cycles can be described by a progression—I like to call it a journey, in forward or reverse—through those three debt units: "hedge" financing units, in which the buyer's cash flows cover interest and principal payments; "speculative" finance units, in which cash flows cover only interest payments; and "Ponzi" units, in which cash flows cover neither and depend on rising asset prices to keep the buyer afloat.

The forward Minsky journey, this time anyway, was the progression of risk taking in the financial markets represented by the excess of subprime loans, structured investment vehicles (SIVs), and other shady characters inhabiting the shadow banking system. Their apparent stability begat ever-riskier debt arrangements, which begat asset price bubbles. And then the bubbles burst, in something I dubbed (years ago, in fact, when looking back on the Asian credit crisis) a "Minsky moment." We can quibble about the precise month of the moment in our present Minsky journey. I pick August 2007 but would not argue strenuously about three months on either side of that date.

Whatever moment you pick for the moment, since then, we have been traveling the reverse Minsky journey—moving backward through the three-part progression, with asset prices falling, risk premiums moving higher, leverage getting scaled back, and economic growth turning into economic contraction. Minsky's "Ponzi" debt units are only viable as long as the levered assets appreciate in price. But when the prices of the assets decline, as we have seen in the U.S. housing market, Minsky tells us we must go through the process of increasing risk taking in reverse—with all its consequences.

The recent Minsky moment encompassed three bubbles bursting: in property valuation in the United States; in mortgage creation, again, principally in the United States; and in the shadow banking system, not just in the United States but around the world. The blowing up of these three bubbles demanded a systemic repricing of all risk, which was deflationary for all risk asset prices. These developments are, as Minsky declared, a prescription for an unstable system—to wit, a system in which the purging of capitalist excesses is not a self-correcting therapeutic process but a self-feeding contagion: debt deflation.

The U.S. Housing Market's Minsky Journey

The bubble in the U.S. housing market provides a plain illustration of the forward Minsky journey in action: People bet that prices would stably rise forever and financed that bet with excessive debt. Indeed, the mortgage debt market followed

Minsky's three-step path almost precisely. The first type of debt, the hedge unit, is actually quite stable; the borrower's cash flow is sufficient to both fully service and amortize the debt. In the mortgage arena, this is known as an old-fashioned loan, like my parents had, as well as the one I used to have. Every month, you write a check that pays the interest plus nibbles away at the principal, and voila, when the last payment is made many years down the road, usually 30, the mortgage simply goes away and you own the house free and clear. You may even throw a little party and ritually burn the mortgage note.

The next, more risky, unit of debt (the speculative unit) comes about when people are so confident in stably rising house prices that they find the hedge unit to be, let us say, boring. Technically, Minsky defined the speculative unit as a loan where the borrower's cash flow is sufficient to fully service the debt but not amortize the principal. Thus, when the loan matures, it must be refinanced. In the mortgage arena, this type of loan is called an interest only, or IO, with a balloon payment at maturity equal to the original principal amount. Thus, these types of borrowers are speculating on at least three things at the time of refinancing: the interest rate has not risen; terms and conditions, notably the down payment, have not tightened; and, perhaps most importantly, the value of the house has not declined.

Minsky taught that when credit is evolving from hedge units to speculative units, there is no fear; the journey increases demand for the underlying assets that are being levered and drives up their prices. Think about it this way: Most people do not mentally take out a mortgage for X dollars, even though they literally do, but rather take out a mortgage that requires Y dollars for a monthly payment. In the mortgage arena, that means that a speculative borrower can take on a larger mortgage than a hedge borrower can because the monthly payment is lower for the speculative borrower—who is paying only interest, not that extra amount every month to pay off the principal over time. Thus, the speculative borrower can pay a higher price for a house than a hedge borrower with the same income. Accordingly, as the marginal mortgage is taken out by a speculative borrower, it drives up home prices, lessening the risk that the value of the house will fall before the balloon payment comes due.

Of course, speculative financing makes sense only so long as there is an infinite pool of speculative borrowers driving up the price, de facto collectively validating the speculative risk they took. Sounds like a recipe for a bubble, no? Demographics assure us that the pool of homebuyers is finite. In this case, expectations of stably rising home prices ultimately run into the reality of affordability—but that does not in and of itself stop the game.

There is a final leg to a forward Minsky journey, thanks to the reality that humans are not inherently value investors but momentum investors. Human beings are not wired to buy low and sell high; rather, they are wired to buy that which is going up in price. This seems to make no sense, particularly when there is a known limit to size and affordability constraints: Why would rational people buy a house for a higher price than other folks in the same financial circumstances could afford to pay? But we are not talking about rationality here but human nature; they are not the same. Humans are not only momentum investors, rather than value investors, but also inherently greedy and suffering from hubris about their own smarts. It is sometimes called a "bigger fool" game, with each individual fool thinking he is slightly less foolish than all the other fools. And yes, a bigger fool game is also sometimes called a Ponzi scheme.

Fittingly, the last debt unit on the forward Minsky journey is called a Ponzi unit, defined as a borrower who has insufficient cash flow to even pay the full interest on a loan, much less pay down the principal over time. How (and why) would such a borrower ever find a lender to make her a loan? Simple: As long as home prices are universally expected to continue rising indefinitely, lenders come out of the woodwork offering loans with what is called "negative amortization," meaning that if you cannot pay the full interest charge, that is okay; they will just tack the unpaid amount onto your principal. At the maturity of the loan, of course, the balloon payment will be bigger than the original loan.

As long as lenders made loans available on virtually nonexistent terms, the price did not matter all that much to borrowers; housing prices were going up so fast that a point or two either way on the mortgage rate did not really matter. The availability of credit trumped the price of credit. Such is always the case in manias. It is also the case that once a speculative bubble bursts, reduced availability of credit will dominate the price of credit, even if markets and policymakers cut the price. (Under such conditions, even good loans will not get made.) The supply side of Ponzi credit is what matters, not the interest elasticity of demand.

Clearly, the exotic mortgages (subprime; interest only; pay-option, with negative amortization, etc.) that have exploded into existence in recent years have been textbook examples of Minsky's speculative and Ponzi units. But they seem okay as long as expectations of stably rising home prices are realized. Except, of course, they cannot forever be realized. At some point, valuation does matter! How could lenders ignore this obvious truth? Because while it was going on, they were making tons of money. Tons of money do serious damage to the eyesight, and our industry's moral equivalent of optometrists, the regulators and the rating agencies, are humans too. As long as the forward Minsky journey was unfolding, rising house prices covered all shameful underwriting sins. Essentially, the mortgage arena began lending against only asset value, rather than asset value *plus* the borrowers' income. The mortgage originators, who were operating on the originate-to-distribute model, had no stake in the game—no incentive to make only loans they could collect—because they simply originated the loans and then repackaged them.

But who they distributed these packages to, interestingly enough, were the shadow banks. So, we had an originate-to-distribute model and no stake in the game for the originator, and the guy in the middle was being asked to create product for the shadow banking system. The system was demanding product. Well, if you have got to feed the beast that wants product, how do you do it? You have a systematic degradation in underwriting standards so that you can originate more. But as you originate more, you bid up the price of property and, therefore, you say, "These junk borrowers really are not junk borrowers. They are not defaulting." So, you drop your standards once again and you take prices up. And you still do not get a high default rate. The reason this system worked is that you, as the guy in the middle, had somebody bless it: the credit rating agencies. A key part of keeping the three bubbles (property valuation, mortgage finance, and the shadow banking system) going was that the rating agencies thought the default rates would be low because they *had been* low. But they had been low because the degradation of underwriting standards was driving up asset prices.

Both regulators and rating agencies were beguiled into believing that the very low default rates during the period of soaring home prices were the normalized default rates for low-quality borrowers, particularly ones with no down payment stake in the game. The rating agencies' blind-man act was particularly egregious because the lofty ratings they put on securities backed by these dud loans were the fuel for explosive growth in the shadow banking system, which issued tons of similarly highly rated commercial paper to fund purchases of the securities.[2]

It all went swimmingly, dampening volatility in a self-reinforcing way, until the bubbles created by financial alchemy hit the fundamental wall of housing affordability. Ultimately, fundamentals do matter. We have a day of reckoning—the day the balloon comes due, the margin call, the Minsky moment. If the value of the house has not gone up, then Ponzi units, particularly those with negatively amortizing loans, are toast. And if the price of the house has fallen, speculative units are toast still in the toaster. Ponzi borrowers are forced to "make position by selling out position," as Minsky phrased it (see earlier), frequently by stopping (or not even beginning) monthly mortgage payments, the prelude to eventual default or jingle mail.[3] Ponzi lenders dramatically tighten underwriting standards, at least back to Minsky's speculative units—loans that may not be self-amortizing but at least are underwritten on evidence that borrowers can pay the required interest, not just the teaser rate but the fully indexed rate on ARMs (adjustable-rate mortgages).

---

[2]To describe the full circularity of this process would require an endlessly circular sentence. Let me start: The issuance of this additional commercial paper created yet more demand for the services of the ratings agencies, which, remember, are paid by the issuer....

[3]Jingle mail (because of the sound made by house keys) is the return of collateral to the lender.

From a microeconomic point of view, such a tightening of underwriting standards is a good thing, albeit belated. But from a macroeconomic point of view, it is a deflationary turn of events, as serial refinancers, riding the back of presumed perpetual home price appreciation, are trapped long and wrong. And in this cycle, it is not just the first-time homebuyer—God bless him and her—who is trapped but also the speculative Ponzi long: borrowers who were not covering a natural short—remember, you are born short a roof over your head and must cover, either by renting or buying—but rather betting on a bigger fool to take them out ("make book" in Minsky's words). The property bubble stops bubbling, and when it does, both the property market and the shadow banking system go bust.

When the conventional basis of valuation for the originate-to-distribute (to the shadow banking system) business model for subprime mortgages was undermined, the asset class imploded "violently." And the implosion was not, as both Wall Street and Washington, DC, beltway mavens predicted, contained. Rather, it became contagious, first on Wall Street with all "risk assets" repricing to higher risk premiums, frequently in violent fashion, and next on Main Street with debt-deflation accelerating in the wake of a mushrooming mortgage credit crunch, notably in the subprime sector but also up the quality ladder.

Yes, we are now experiencing a reverse Minsky journey, where instability will, in the fullness of time, restore stability as Ponzi debt units evaporate, speculative debt units morph after the fact into Ponzi units and are severely disciplined if not destroyed, and even hedge units take a beating. The shadow banking system contracts implosively as a run on its assets forces it to delever, driving down asset prices, eroding equity, and forcing it to delever again. The shadow banking system is particularly vulnerable to runs—commercial paper investors refusing to re-up when their paper matures, leaving the shadow banks with a liquidity crisis. A shadow bank then needs to tap its back-up lines of credit with real banks or to liquidate assets at fire-sale prices. Real banks are in a risk-averse state of mind when it comes to lending to shadow banks. They lend when required by back-up lines but do not seek to proactively increase their exposure to the shadow banking system but, if anything, reduce it. Thus, there is a mighty gulf between the Fed's liquidity cup and the shadow banking system's parched liquidity lips.

The entire progression self-feeds on the way down, just like it self-feeds on the way up. It is incredibly procyclical. The regulatory response is also incredibly procyclical. You have a rush to laxity on the way up, and you have a rush to stringency on the way back down. And essentially, on the way down, you have the equivalent of Keynes's paradox of thrift—the paradox of delevering. It can make sense for each individual institution, for a shadow bank or even a real bank, to delever, but collectively, they cannot all delever at the same time.

Policy Reactions to the Reverse Minsky Journey

Along the way, policymakers have slowly recognized the Minsky moment followed by the unfolding reverse Minsky journey. But I want to emphasize "slowly" because policymakers, collectively, tend to suffer from more than a small amount of denial. Part of the reason is human nature: To acknowledge a reverse Minsky journey, it is first necessary to acknowledge a preceding forward Minsky journey—such as the bubble in asset and debt prices—as the marginal unit of debt creation morphed from hedge to speculative to Ponzi. That is difficult for policymakers to do, especially ones who claim an inability to recognize bubbles while they are forming and, therefore, do not believe that prophylactic action against them is appropriate. But framing policies to mitigate the damage of a reverse Minsky journey requires that policymakers openly acknowledge that we are where we are because they let the invisible, if not crooked, hand of financial capitalism go precisely where Minsky said it would go unless checked by the visible fist of countercyclical, rather than procyclical, regulatory policy.

That is not to say that Minsky had confidence that regulators could stay out in front of short-term profit-driven innovation in financial arrangements. Indeed, he believed precisely the opposite:

> In a world of businessmen and financial intermediaries who aggressively seek profit, innovators will always outpace regulators; the authorities cannot prevent changes in the structure of portfolios from occurring. What they can do is keep the asset-equity ratio of banks within bounds by setting equity-absorption ratios for various types of assets. If the authorities constrain banks and are aware of the activities of fringe banks and other financial institutions, they are in a better position to attenuate the disruptive expansionary tendencies of our economy. (Minsky 2008, p. 281)

Minsky originally wrote those words in 1986—more than 20 years ago! Today, we can only bemoan the fact that his sensible counsel was ignored and that the economy experienced the explosive growth of the shadow banking system, or what Minsky cleverly called "fringe banks and other financial institutions."

Minsky's insight that financial capitalism is inherently and endogenously given to bubbles and busts is not just right but spectacularly right. We have much to learn and relearn from the great man as we collectively restore prudential common sense to bank regulation—both for conventional banks and shadow banks.

In the meantime, we have a problem: We are on a reverse Minsky journey. The private sector wants to shrink and de-risk its balance sheet, so someone has to take the other side of the trade to avoid a depression—the sovereign. We pretend that the Fed's balance sheet and the U.S. government's balance sheet are in entirely separate orbits because of the whole notion of the political independence of the central bank in making monetary policy. But when you think about it, not from the standpoint of making monetary policy but of providing balance sheet support to buffer a reverse Minsky journey, there is no difference between the government's balance sheet and the Fed's balance sheet. Economically speaking, they are one and the same.

I think we are pretty well advanced along this reverse Minsky journey, and it is a lot quicker than the forward journey for a very simple reason. The forward journey is essentially momentum driven; there is a systematic relaxation of underwriting standards and all that sort of thing, but it does not create any pain for anybody. The reverse journey, however, does create pain, otherwise known as one giant margin call. The reverse journey comes to an end when the full faith and credit of the sovereign's balance sheet is brought into play to effectively take the other side of the trade. No, I am not a socialist; I am just a practical person. You have got to have somebody on the other side of the trade. The government not only steps up to the risk taking and spending that the private sector is shirking but goes further, stepping up with even more vigor, providing a meaningful reflationary thrust to both private sector risk assets and aggregate demand for goods and services.

Thus, policymakers have a tricky balancing act: Let the deflationary pain unfold, because it is the only way to find the bottom of undervalued asset prices from presently overvalued asset prices, while providing sufficient monetary and fiscal policy safety nets to keep the deflationary process from spinning out of control. Debt deflation is a burden that capitalism cannot bear alone. It is not rich enough; it is not tough enough. Capitalism's prosperity is hostage to the hope that policymakers are not simply too blind to see.

As long as we have reasonably deregulated markets and a complex and innovative financial system, we will have Minsky journeys, forward and reverse, punctuated by Minsky moments. That is reality. You cannot eliminate them. It is a matter of having the good sense to have in place a countercyclical regulatory policy to help modulate human nature.

REFERENCES

Minsky, Hyman P. 1992. "The Financial Instability Hypothesis." The Levy Economics Institute of Bard College, Working Paper No. 74 (May): www.levy.org/pubs/wp74.pdf.

———. 2008. *Stabilizing an Unstable Economy.* New York: McGraw-Hill. Originally published in 1986: New Haven, CT: Yale University Press.

What Went Wrong?

John Train
Chairman
Montrose Advisors
New York City

I doubt if the way out of the present imbroglio lies in programs, regulations, or bailouts. It is simpler and deeper than that. It is not an event; it is a syndrome.

We have forgotten prudence.

Prudence is the first Christian cardinal virtue (followed by fortitude and justice), and it is incidentally the central duty of investment managers. The Prudent Man Rule, which since 1830 has told trustees what they must do, has recently been replaced in all 50 states by the Prudent Investor Rule, which every trustee must obey and which, indeed, should be understood by anyone who looks after the investments of others. But either way, the key word is *prudent*.

The old rule instructed the trustee to look around, observe how men of prudence and discretion looked after their affairs, and be guided accordingly. Alas, that has become exceedingly hard. When I was young, and even today to some extent in England, if a citizen had a financial question, he would visit his "bank manager" to seek seasoned counsel. Or he might consult a college friend who had become a stockbroker, perhaps in a family-controlled firm, and who understood life. He had to be able to count on his adviser to be objective, to put the client's interest first.

Not anymore. Objective advice scarcely exists in banks and brokerage firms, which are in business to sell "products," some of which, such as all commodity and currency speculation, are intrinsically imprudent, designed to make money for the house at the expense of the customer.

The old Wall Street rule is "If the ducks quack, feed 'em." That is, when the cry is, let's all buy houses (or emerging markets, or hedge funds, or whatever), which "can only go up," then push them, hard! But such people are hustlers, not professionals.

The effect of all this on the fortunes of imprudent investors can easily be shown. The most obvious measure is the stock market itself. Depending on the period you choose, the very long-term total return of stocks, in general, is around 9 percent before inflation. For funds, you subtract costs. But the long-term return for individual investors is only half of that. Why? Because the average investor is imprudent. Convinced that she can outsmart the other average investors, she buys equities when the excitement is high, toward the top of the market, and then, discouraged by falling prices, sells again toward the bottom, running up costs both ways. The market itself is thus a Ponzi scheme—and not only the whole market but also the hot segments as they come and go. To coin a phrase: Nothing *ex*ceeds like success.

And take note that the end of every great bull market is that time's version of a margin account, enough different from the last one that most people do not recognize it for what it is. Obviously, leveraged buyout booms and hedge fund explosions are margin accounts because they are done with borrowed money, and so are houses bought for higher prices than one can afford with mortgages one cannot pay.

The way out of this misery is well known: prudence. Buy and hold quality issues for long periods. It should always have been obvious that the crowd cannot outtrade the crowd. Thus, the correct solution is to trade as little as possible; above all, resist tips and inspirations.

Then, consider imprudence at the governmental level. The housing bust was, in part, caused by the government pushing a good idea, encouraging home owner-ship via Fannie Mae and the like, beyond where it should go. In essence, it used political objectives to warp the logic of economics.

There could not be more obvious folly—or worse—than luring financially weak homebuyers in over their heads, when they ought to be renting, and letting them pay with wormy paper whose quality is then falsely certified by ratings agencies,[1] which are compensated by the sellers. And to further compound the problem, this wormy paper is then flogged off to trusting foreign buyers.

Or how about using the inflated value of our houses as a credit card? Or, nationally, how about buying goods we cannot afford from the Chinese in return for IOUs they may not find useful?

So, how do we learn prudence? Nobody is born prudent. The infant is a bundle of impatient desires. The Greeks had a maxim: *pathe mathos*—learn through suffering. Our Great Depression and the German hyperinflation after World War I—which prepared the ground for Hitler—burned their messages into people's consciousness with a branding iron. World War II taught Italy and Japan a dreadful lesson about militarism. In mountain climbing, when the guide, having learned his craft through the loss of men he knew, says, "Don't go," then nobody goes. He's unbudgeable. But we have almost no unbudgeable leaders today.

So, besides experiencing the punishments life reserves for folly, how, then, are we to learn?

One way is through teaching, both from our parents and in school. This is a far more agreeable way to form character than is the inferno of financial ruin. The problem, though, is that at times the elders may themselves be lacking in wisdom.

Consider, for example, the following, adapted from Plato's *Republic*, Book VIII:

> The father starts to behave like a child, and stands in awe of his sons; and a son behaves like a father, and no longer respects his parents...

---

[1] Warren Buffett, the principal owner through Berkshire Hathaway of Moody's Investors Service, a prime culprit, has not commented on its role.

The schoolmaster fears and flatters his pupils… the young copy their elders, and compete with them both in talking and acting; older men are jocular, like the young, so as not to seem morose or domineering.

Sound familiar? Isn't this where we are today?

Plato continues by explaining that democracy is destroyed by the object it defines as supremely good, freedom. He says that in a democratized city, you will be told that it has, in freedom, the most beautiful of possessions and that such a city is the only fit abode for a free man.

Plato goes on to say that in due course, the citizens of an overripe democracy resent even the slightest infringement on their liberty of action, with the result that such a state ceases to be self-governing. In *Maxims, Opinions and Characters, Moral, Political, and Economical, Volume 1*, Edmond Burke makes the same point in different language: "It is ordained in the eternal constitution of things, that men of intemperate minds cannot be free. Their passions forge their fetters."

I doubt if many of our young are taught these ideas.

The Chinese know quite a lot about life. They are our partners in a curious pact: We will buy your cheap goods, and you will accept our disappearing paper. Now we are printing a torrent of greenbacks, and the Chinese have fired a shot across our bow: Hold on, they are saying. If you want to pay us in funny money, we may move to another playground. The Chinese are in essence requiring that for the game to go on, we must save more, cut our trade and federal deficits, and plan realistically. We will need to work harder, spend less, and postpone our hopes.

But these conditions are no more than any long-term investor should ask. In my lifetime, a shoeshine in New York City has gone from 10 cents to $4, and the 10 cent subway fare to $2. It has been disastrous to save. Confidence in prudent control of our currency has itself become a highly imprudent bet. This is a symptom of social decomposition. The Chinese are quite right to hesitate.

So, what will it take for us to change our ways? The decay in our practices and our education will not be taught by parents or schools or the media unless we insist on it. And that will not happen until we have learned by suffering—*pathe mathos*. Let us hope it does not take too long.

What Can We Really Know about Economics?

Frank J. Fabozzi, CFA
Professor in the Practice of Finance
Yale School of Management
New Haven, Connecticut

Sergio M. Focardi
Professor of Finance
EDHEC Business School
Nice, France

Albert Einstein is considered to have had one of the most innovative minds of all time. His discoveries changed the world. Still, he believed that even the most profound breakthroughs are firmly rooted in the foundations of our cultural heritage. *Ideas and Opinions*, a collection of Einstein's essays published in 1954, a year before his death, includes his famous passage on what he called the "modernist's snobbishness":

> Somebody who reads only newspapers and at best books of contemporary authors looks to me like an extremely near-sighted person who scorns eyeglasses. He is completely dependent upon the prejudices and fashions of his times, since he never gets to see or hear anything else. And what a person thinks on his own without being stimulated by the thoughts and experiences of other people is even in the best case rather paltry and monotonous. There are only a few enlightened people with a lucid mind and style and with good taste within a century. What has been preserved of their work belongs among the most precious possessions of mankind. We owe it to a few writers of antiquity that the people of the Middle Ages could slowly extricate themselves from the superstitions and ignorance that had darkened life for more than half a millennium. Nothing is more needed to overcome the modernist's snobbishness. (Einstein 1994, p. 70)

The question is much debated whether human affairs, history, and (what interests us most in this discussion) economics can be understood in rational terms. So, it is not surprising that, given the current economic crisis, a renewed debate is going on as to whether economics and finance lend themselves to mathematical and computer modeling—one of the current flavors of rationality. Taking Einstein's advice, let us take a look backward at what our predecessors thought about our ability to understand the economy from the perspective of rationality.

A Look at the Classics

To review the history of economics in the context of rational thought, we will start with the ancient world and move to the modern world.

The Ancient World. The ancient Greek world had a fundamentally integrated view of human knowledge and learning. In the Greek world, a learned man was fluent in the seven arts: grammar, rhetoric, logic, arithmetic, geometry, astronomy, and music. Philosophy (back then a word meaning no more and no less than "the love of knowledge") came to embrace all branches of learning, including literature, science, technology, metaphysics, and even sports. The Greek games were an important component of the culture, and gymnastics was an integral part of a learned man's education. According to Dicaearchus of Messana, the great fifth century B.C. philosopher Plato was also a famous wrestler; he participated in matches at the Isthmian Games. The Greeks were not only great thinkers on abstract subjects; they were also interested in understanding physical phenomena, leading them to develop many innovative technologies to solve practical problems. In today's parlance, they were problem solvers. Take, for example, Archimedes, who invented the cochlea (Archimedes' screw) to pump water from a ship's hold (the lower part of the center of a ship's hull). The ancient Greeks even engineered and built the Diolkos, a primitive but effective railway that allowed ships to transit inland across the Isthmus of Corinth.

The ancient Greeks had a notion of physical causation and of philosophical necessity. They believed that the world was governed by causation and necessity and that human affairs were understandable. This belief is particularly evident in the writing of the "father of history," Herodotus of Halicarnassus.[1] Herodotus believed in a fundamental rationality in human affairs and, with the objective lucidity of a physical scientist, sought to explain events as seemingly inexplicable as the Trojan War.

Still, the ancient Greeks thought that humans were subject to the whims of capricious gods and to unknown fate (personified by three goddesses), to which even the gods had to bow. Ancient Greek tragedy is a literary representation of their beliefs as regards human affairs. Their heroes typically have some character fault, often excessive pride, that morally justifies their fall. Behind the plot of the tragedy is fate, the overarching scheme that ultimately governs human affairs. Fate is not irrational, but it is mysterious. In the Greek mind, there are two levels of rationality: (1) the rationality of physical causation and of necessity and (2) the mysterious rationality of fate, often cryptically revealed by oracles. Note that the Greeks were sailors, and although the sea is governed by physical principles, it is still unpredictable; a storm could sink a ship.

---

[1] Halicarnassus (presently known as Bodrum) was a Greek city on the southwest coast of present-day Turkey. It was famous in antiquity for its Mausoleum, considered one of the Seven Wonders of the Ancient World.

As we move on to the ancient Roman world, we see a slight change in attitude, perhaps because of the fact that Romans were people of the land, not of the sea. For Romans, the objective in life was to be *compos sui*—that is, to be *master of yourself*. This notion reflects a positive attitude regarding our ability to shape our own future. The Romans created a formidable organization capable of constructing buildings, roads, bridges, aqueducts, and defensive walls on an unprecedented scale. No wonder they had some faith in the ability of humans to shape their own destiny. Although fate, the unpredictable element, still played a role in Roman thinking, it was identified more closely with the gods than with an overarching mysterious rationality.

In summary, both cultures, the ancient Greek and the ancient Roman, considered human affairs as basically rational processes interspersed with exogenous unpredictable influences.

The Renaissance and Beyond. Following the cultural collapse of the Middle Ages, the Renaissance rediscovered the ancient texts, thereby paving the way for the development of modern science. The beginning of modern science, as we conceive it, can be dated to the publication of Newton's *Principia* in 1687—although Galileo and others can be identified as precursors. With Newton's work, physics became a mathematical science in the sense that all physical phenomena could be described with differential equations. The mathematics of differential equations gave determinism a new flavor. In fact, Newton's differential equations imply that if one knows initial and boundary conditions, the future can be mathematically determined. In 18th century physics, determinism meant that the future is perfectly predictable, conditional on knowledge of the initial state.

Pierre-Simon, marquis de Laplace, one of the greatest mathematicians of all time, expressed his faith in determinism in *A Philosophical Essay on Probabilities* (1814), in which he stated that a supernatural being with infinite computational power and knowledge of all the initial data could correctly compute the future evolution of the entire universe.

The transformation of physics into a mathematical science marked the separation between scientific culture and literary and philosophical culture. From the 18th century onward, the unity of learning that characterized the ancient Greco-Roman world was lost, replaced by a sharp separation between scientific and humanistic knowledge.

It is probably fair to say that, in the 18th and 19th centuries, the global perception of the evolution of historical events was not deeply influenced by the physical sciences. The Enlightenment had a rational view of history deeply influenced by the idea of progress. *The Decline and Fall of the Roman Empire*—with Volume I published in 1776 and the final volume (VI) published in 1788—by Edward Gibbon, the major historian of the Enlightenment, is perhaps the most lucid expression of the rationalistic historical perceptions of that period.[2] The Romantic Movement had a more dramatic and less rational view of history, centered on the heroic struggles of people to defend their identity. Romantic historiography is centered on the role of great individuals. Later, Georg Wilhelm Friedrich Hegel introduced the idea of historical determinism based on dialectical processes. Despite its obscurity, Hegel's view—which asserted that historical events could only be explained by unstoppable social forces, not by the actions of individuals—proved to be very influential: It provided the philosophical basis of Marxism.

Economics—A Quantitative Science?

The ancient Greek world was an explosion of intellectual prowess and enthusiasm. It has been said that in the fifth century B.C., Athens was a city of 20,000 free citizens who spent most of their time passionately discussing and arguing about ideas. Still, despite their achievements, the ancient Greeks did not like arrogance. *Hubris*—a legal term that indicated the humiliation of the adversary and disrespect of the sacred—was considered to be a capital offense.

In Greek myths and tragedy, *hubris* results in the final fall of the hero. Milo of Kroton, the "most illustrious of athletes" according to the ancient geographer Strabo, was a legendary wrestler who won six Olympic Games and successfully participated in all other major games. He enjoyed demonstrating his strength, for example, by holding a pomegranate in one hand and challenging people to take it from him. Despite the struggle during which no one was able to wrench the fruit from his clutch, the pomegranate was never smashed. But one day, later in life when walking in the woods, he saw a trunk split by a wedge. To prove he was still strong, Milo attempted to split the trunk with his bare hands. He succeeded, and the wedge was freed. But his hands were imprisoned by the trunk, and Milo was devoured by wild beasts.

Modern Hubris. A modern form of intellectual hubris is the belief that anything that escapes the formalized mathematical reasoning of the physical sciences must somehow be mysterious. We have come to regard mathematics and the use of computers as the ultimate solution to every scientific problem—so that if a phenomenon cannot be explained with current mathematics, it must be impossible to understand. This "modernist's snobbishness" has now permeated some strains of economics and finance theory, as well as other domains of knowledge.

The science of economics is in an uncomfortable position, somewhere between the physical sciences and the human sciences. Economics is naturally a quantitative science because most observable economic quantities are quantitative. For example, prices, industrial output, and savings are all quantitative. The rules that link these

---

[2]Gibbon's rationalistic views did not reflect his personal experience. His grandfather had lost most of the family's considerable fortune in the 1720 collapse of the South Sea Bubble.

quantities, however, are ultimately related to human behavior. In other words, in economics, our quantitative observables are driven by unobservables that are not naturally quantitative.[3]

Throughout the 19th century, economics developed along lines that were not quantitative in the sense that the physical sciences are quantitative. Although the work of such economists as David Ricardo had quantitative elements, there was no notion that all economic behavior and outcomes could be, or indeed needed to be, expressed mathematically.

Things began to change in the second half of the 20th century, with the invention of high-speed computers. Ever faster computers allowed economists to handle ever larger amounts of data and thus to explore statistical regularities. The process of transforming economics into an empirical and mathematical science has required, and will continue to require, conceptual innovation, often creating an original synthesis of ideas coming from different disciplines. One should be aware of the objective limits of introducing mathematics in economics and be ready to use setbacks as springboards for innovation.

One strain of economic thinking argues that economics cannot be understood mathematically because it is driven by unpredictable events. Nassim Nicholas Taleb's metaphor of the "black swan" (*The Black Swan: The Impact of the Highly Improbable*, 2007) is perhaps the best-known example of this conceptual attitude. Taleb argues that economics, and history in general, cannot be explained because human affairs are driven by black swans—single unpredictable events that have a large impact. In *Fooled by Randomness: The Hidden Role of Chance in Life and in the Markets* (2001), Taleb suggests that we instinctively try to impose an artificial order on phenomena that are purely random. We are, as the title of the book says, fooled by randomness because those events that are really important in economics are events that cannot be forecast by studying the past. Contrast this point of view with that of Herodotus, who started the study of history 25 centuries earlier under the opposite assumption—that we can, and indeed should, learn from the past.

Taleb's reasoning runs against the scientific spirit and the quest for knowledge that have driven the scientific endeavor for the last 25 centuries. Do we really believe that it was so easy for the ancient Greeks to resist the temptation to see black swans everywhere? They came out with daring hypotheses based on fundamental intuitions. Most of these hypotheses have since been proven wrong, but some of them proved to be very profound. For example, it took 24 centuries to finally vindicate Democritus' atomistic conjecture. And it took 21 centuries to understand the idea of mathematical continuum and to develop calculus, finally resolving Zeno's Paradox of the Tortoise and Achilles.

---

[3]Consider that in the human sciences we have observables that are not quantitative, at least not naturally. For example, a facial expression is highly meaningful for another human, but it is difficult to give facial expressions a quantitative value.

In 1960, Eugene Wigner, recipient of the 1963 Nobel Prize in Physics, discussed the "unreasonable effectiveness of mathematics in the natural sciences" in a paper of that very title. The marvel, for Wigner, is that there *is* a natural order that can be mathematically described. But there is no a priori reason why mathematics should be able to describe nature. The very fact that we can use mathematics as the language of science deserves explanation in itself.

The use of mathematics requires profound conceptual thinking. The major achievement of science in the 20th century was not the discovery of new equations but the introduction of new conceptual paradigms. In physics, Einstein's relativity theory violated all previous notions of physical reality by mixing time and space. Quantum mechanics went further, replacing the concept of matter with that of states that can overlap. The notion of determinism progressively gave way to notions of fundamental uncertainty—first with statistical mechanics, then with quantum mechanics, and lastly with chaos theory. If we look at other sciences, we find that attempts to introduce mathematics and computation required fundamental conceptual innovation, typically accompanied by many setbacks.

Success of Mathematics in Economics. We have no a priori reason to assume that mathematics will be "unreasonably successful" in the domain of economics and finance—at least not the type of mathematics that is used in physics and not if the test of success is that mathematics accurately forecast which way the markets or individual stocks will move. For the moment, as argued in Focardi and Fabozzi (forthcoming 2010) in their article "The Reasonable Effectiveness of Mathematics in Economics," mathematics is only *reasonably* successful in explaining financial phenomena, and this success arises by using mathematics that is different from that of physics. It cannot be otherwise: Our economic systems are designed to be uncertain to allow for profit opportunities.

Economic systems, and especially financial systems, are characterized by a high level of uncertainty. Highly uncertain systems cannot be successfully described with the tools of mathematical physics. These tools were designed to describe highly stable systems. Physical reality is very stable, so stable that it allows one to formulate the initial assumption of perfect determinism. Only at the end of the 19th century was the mathematics of uncertainty introduced in physics.

The description of financial systems, however, has followed a different path. The initial hypothesis in the 1960s was that of pure randomness; that is, prices were believed to evolve as random walks. It was later understood that there must be some residual forecastability, otherwise there could be no profit motive for analyzing securities: The entire speculative exercise would be pointless. But it was also realized that the amount of forecastability must be very small, otherwise the system would explode under the pressure of an inordinate amount of profits. One can say: In physics, we have lots of information corrupted by a little noise; in economics, we have lots of noise corrupted by a little information.

No wonder the mathematics of economics and finance is different from that of physics. Physics is formulated through all-encompassing theories, whereas economics and finance theory are formulated through a process of learning and model selection. In practice, both economics and finance theory make recourse to learning methods. Learning methods do not require a priori theoretical knowledge; rather, it is the model that learns patterns by adapting to the data. Learning, therefore, requires models that adapt to new data.

But given the noisy data (i.e., data that include some information but also meaningless noise) that we have in economics and finance, if the models are too flexible, they will try to adapt to noise. A model that adapts to noise will perform well on the sample data but poorly when applied to new out-of-sample data. Learning methods, therefore, include rules that constrain the adaptability of models so that they learn only information, not noise. A simple example is a filter used in wireless communications to extract the meaningful signal from noise by constraining the frequency band of the radio signal.

The only major all-encompassing theory in economics and finance theory is the concept of general equilibrium, which is formulated in a language similar to that of mathematical physics. But when we try to apply general equilibrium to actual economic processes, we run into difficulties because we are unable to specify some of the crucial terms of the theory. To make a physical parallel, general equilibrium theories are the Newtonian dynamics without the specification of force fields. There is no way that we can make predictions with such theories.

Understanding the evolution of economic systems over time and making predictions about them, however, is only one aspect of economic science. The analysis of economic structure (i.e., the understanding of the links and correlations between economic phenomena) is also an important object of study. This is a difficult endeavor that makes use of the mathematics of complexity. A number of important results have been obtained by modeling the economy as consisting of multiple heterogeneous interacting agents. For example, the paradigm of multiple interacting agents can explain the emergence of fat tails in economic and financial variables through processes of aggregation. This type of theory offers explanations as well as estimation methods for some of the extreme events that we find in economic phenomena.

The mathematical representation of human cognitive and creative abilities has proved to be a very difficult task; it will probably require some breakthrough innovation. Since the introduction of computers, we have witnessed a vast scientific endeavor to understand human cognitive capabilities in terms of computations. The fields of artificial intelligence and cognition theory have proposed a number of models of human cognitive capabilities that regard cognition as a computational process. In his Pulitzer Prize–winning 1979 book *Gödel, Escher, Bach: An Eternal*

Golden Braid, Douglas Hofstadter (the son of Robert Hofstadter, recipient of the 1961 Nobel Prize in Physics) gives an explanation of consciousness based on the self-referential capabilities of computational structures.

The ultimate goal is to understand how societies self-organize, in particular, why economies take specific structures. Presently, we can only analyze economic systems with a given structure. For example, Hyman Minsky showed how business conditions could be expected to alternate between boom and bust given some assumptions about the flow of money and credit. We know reasonably well how to perform this type of analysis, but we do not know how to analyze the decision-making process that will lead to economic structures more or less prone to boom-and-bust cycles.

Conclusion

Can economics be rationally understood as a mathematical science based on empirical data (if one assumes that we have gathered the data), or is the evolution of our economy irrational, driven by unpredictable black swans? The answer is threefold. First, we have powerful mathematical and computational tools to use for understanding our economic systems. Second, these tools are ultimately different from those of the physical sciences because economic systems are inherently uncertain; the tools of mathematical physics are not well suited for handling situations where noise prevails over information. Third, we do not yet have the conceptual and mathematical tools for understanding how economies and human societies at large self-organize. Developing this level of understanding will require conceptual breakthroughs. But the challenges involved in the development of human knowledge over the past 25 centuries have been no less daunting, and thinkers will eventually rise to this challenge as well.

References

Einstein, Albert. 1994. *Ideas and Opinions*. New York: Random House Publishing Group, Modern Library Series. Originally published in 1954 by Crown Publishers.

Focardi, Sergio, and Frank J. Fabozzi. Forthcoming 2010. "The Reasonable Effectiveness of Mathematics in Econonics." *American Economist*.